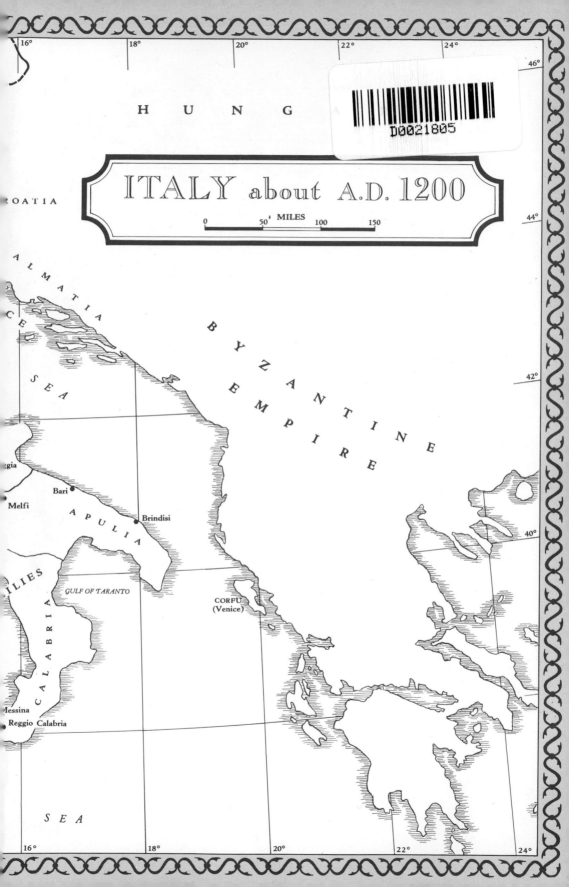

16° 18° 20° 22° 24° 46°

H U N G

ROATIA

ITALY about A.D. 1200

MILES
0   50   100   150

44°

ALMATIA

CE

SEA

B Y Z A N T I N E

E M P I R E

42°

gia

Bari

Melfi

A P U L I A

Brindisi

40°

ILIES

GULF OF TARANTO

CORFU
(Venice)

CALABRIA

Messina

Reggio Calabria

S E A

16° 18° 20° 22° 24°

LORDS OF ITALY

BY ORVILLE PRESCOTT

Lords of Italy: Portraits from the Middle Ages

History as Literature

Princes of the Renaissance

A Father Reads to His Children: An Anthology
of Prose and Poetry

The Undying Past

Midcentury: An Anthology of Distinguished
Contemporary Short Stories

The Five-Dollar Gold Piece: The Development
of a Point of View

In My Opinion: An Inquiry into the
Contemporary Novel

LORDS OF ITALY
Portraits from the Middle Ages

ORVILLE PRESCOTT

HARPER & ROW, PUBLISHERS
New York, Evanston, San Francisco, London

LORDS OF ITALY: PORTRAITS FROM THE MIDDLE AGES. Copyright © 1972 by Orville Prescott. All rights reserved. Printed in the United States of America. No part of this book may be used or reproduced in any manner whatsoever without written permission except in the case of brief quotations embodied in critical articles and reviews. For information address Harper & Row, Publishers, Inc., 10 East 53rd Street, New York, N.Y. 10022. Published simultaneously in Canada by Fitzhenry & Whiteside Limited, Toronto.

FIRST EDITION

STANDARD BOOK NUMBER: 06–013412–7

LIBRARY OF CONGRESS CATALOG CARD NUMBER: 72–79688

To the Lady Lilias

Contents

Illustrations

Introduction

No major period of European history seems more remote today than the Middle Ages. Ancient Rome in the time of Augustus seems to many of us easier to understand than medieval Rome in the time of Barbarossa. The kings and emperors, popes and bishops, saints and villains of the Middle Ages are wonderfully picturesque and they played their roles in a wonderfully gaudy and violent melodrama. They lived by such different unformulated assumptions, fervently believed in such a wide variety of supernatural phenomena and were regularly overcome by such violent emotions that it is difficult for citizens of the twentieth century to understand them. We know some of the things they believed and did. But a sympathetic, imaginative effort is necessary before we can know, only partially, what it was like to believe such odd things and to act in such a peculiar manner.

Nevertheless, the Middle Ages hold an enduring fascination. Romanticists dream about castles and captive princesses and legends of chivalry. Scholars labor to find out about rent rolls, taxes, guilds and agricultural techniques. And because the Middle Ages are so rich in colorful characters, many of them seemingly more than life-sized, many people have a slight acquaintance with a variety of medieval personages.

Plays, motion pictures, historical novels, biographies and works of history have introduced them to William the Conqueror, Richard Coeur de Lion, Henry II and Thomas à Becket, Héloise and Abélard, and Joan of Arc.

But medieval Italy is less familiar to most readers than either medieval England or France. It is the lords of medieval Italy—emperors, kings, conquerors, tyrants and popes—who are the principal characters (if not exactly the heroes) of this book. They rank among the most interesting and the most flamboyantly theatrical people who ever played stellar parts upon the stage of history. Their lives were complicated by the presence in Italy of two powerful institutions not represented in force in England and France—the Papacy as a temporal power and the Holy Roman Empire.

This book, like its predecessor, *Princes of the Renaissance*, is a popular narrative about the lives, personalities and public careers of extraordinary people. It is not a history of the Middle Ages in Italy, only an introduction to them. It is a series of biographical portraits selected in order to provide a nearly continuous narrative about the most representative, powerful and interesting men who ruled in Italy during the Middle Ages. Philip Guedalla in the preface to his *The Hundred Years* described his book in words which I quote because they seem to me to describe *Lords of Italy* equally well:

"A mosaic is no less a picture because it is made up of separate pieces. The selection is, of course, my own; but, though personal, it is by no means arbitrary, since I have tried to throw upon the screen those pictures which appear to be the most significant."

Biographies of some of the characters in this book are available. But much of the information presented here is only to be found in learned and obscure works, some of which have never been translated into English. Little of it will be new to medieval scholars. Much of it was new to me when I acquired it scattered through some 160 different sources; or as I traveled in Italy examining most of the works of art, churches, castles and sites associated with the lords of medieval Italy.

It is a pleasure to thank several people who made valuable suggestions or who helped find elusive material: Professor Gilbert Highet, author of *The Classical Tradition* and many other distinguished works; Robert W.

Carubba, Professor of Classics at The Pennsylvania State University; Mrs. Raphael Akuyz; Lilias Prescott, my wife; and Peter S. Prescott, my son.

I also wish to thank the kind people who courteously provided me with books from the following libraries: The New York Public Library, The Society Library of New York, The Pierpont Morgan Library, The Free Public Library of New Haven, Case Memorial Library of Hartford, The Bridgeport Public Library and The New Canaan Public Library.

O.P.

ITALY about A.D. 1200

0   50 MILES 100   150

8° 10° 12° 14° 16° 18°

48° 48°

46° 46°

I

LOMBARDY

Trento

Brescia   Treviso
Milan   Vicenza
Pavia   Verona   Padua
Lodi   Mantua   Venice
Asti   Cremona   ISTRIA
Alessandria   Parma   Ferrara
Genoa   ROMAGNA
Bologna

CROATIA

REPUBLIC OF VENICE

DALMATIA

44° 44°

TUSCANY

Florence
Pisa   PENTAPOLIS
Siena
Arezzo
Perugia   Assisi
Orvieto   SPOLETO   Spoleto
ELBA   Viterbo

PAPAL STATES

ADRIATIC SEA

42° 42°
CORSICA
(Pisa)

Rome   Palestrina
Anagni

PATRIMONY OF
SAINT PETER

Lucera   Foggia
BENEVENTO
CAPUA   Bari
Benevento
Naples   Melfi   APULIA   Brindisi
Salerno
Amalfi   SALERNO

SARDINIA
(Genoa)

KINGDOM OF THE TWO SICILIES

40°

TYRRHENIAN
SEA

CALABRIA

38° 38°

Palermo
Trapani   Cefalu   Messina   Reggio Calabria

MEDITERRANEAN

SICILY

36° 36°
AFRICA

10° 12° 14°   MALTA   16° 18°

I

The Saint and the Brigands

On the morning of June 18, 1053, thirteen years before the Battle of Hastings, a handsome and vigorous man dressed in a white robe stood on the ramparts of the small Italian city of Civitate some thirteen miles west of the present city of Foggia and watched on the plain below the total destruction of the army he had raised and personally led to war. Leo IX, the first but not the last pope to lead soldiers into battle, had for many years been widely considered a saint. An Alsatian nobleman and second cousin of the Emperor Henry III, the former Bishop of Toul was a sincere idealist, a reformer who energetically tried to elevate the moral standing and to expand the influence of the Papacy. He was said to weep continuously while at his prayers. By the primitive standards of the eleventh century he was a man of considerable culture. He had composed music in honor of the saints.

Although numerous commentators, from Saint Peter Damian, his contemporary, to Edward Gibbon, have denounced Leo for going to war against fellow Christians, there was much to be said for his cause. He intended to drive out of southern Italy the independent Norman adventurers who had reduced that unhappy region to a state of violent anarchy. Ever since the summer of 1017 Norman knights had been drifting down to Italy, singly and in small groups, serving as mercenary soldiers for the remnants of the Byzantine empire and for the local Lombard duchies. When opportunity offered they set up states of their own. And always they looted and plundered, stole livestock and destroyed crops in the immemorial way of robbers and robber barons.

Writing of Rainulf of Aversa, one of the first and most successful of the Norman brigands, the French historian Ferdinand Chalandon said: "Devoid of scruple, guided only by interested motives, in no way hampered by feelings of gratitude, he possessed all the requisite qualities for arriving at high political office." This cynical statement applies equally well to dozens of Rainulf's compatriots and particularly to the leaders of the small force which assembled to oppose Pope Leo's army.

Unlike their relatives who conquered England a few years later, the Normans in Italy were not the representatives of a powerful state and they were not a unified force commanded by a titled ruler. Younger sons, adventurers, refugees from the ill will of their Duke, they were poor and usually owned no more than their arms and horses. But they were the best fighters in Europe, wonderfully brave, expert horsemen, capable of disciplined cooperation. Dressed in linked chain mail, wearing conical helmets with a projecting bar to protect their noses, they carried kite-shaped shields and wielded enormous swords. These were two-edged but rounded at the tip—an oddity, for surely a point would have been useful.

No more unscrupulous, ruthless and greedy men ever lived; and yet they were pious Christians who revered the pope while they violated daily many of the commandments of the religion they professed. Four years before the Battle of Civitate, John, Abbot of Fécamp, wrote to Pope Leo describing the conditions he had observed during a pilgrimage: "Italian hatred of the Normans has now become so great that it is near impossible for a Norman, even if he be a pilgrim, to travel through the cities of Italy without being set upon, abducted, stripped of all he has, beaten and tied with chains—all this if he does not give up the ghost in a fetid prison."

In 1050 Pope Leo had written to the Byzantine Emperor Constantine IX that the Normans "with an impiety which exceeds that of pagans, rise up against the Church of God, causing Christians to perish by new, hideous tortures, sparing neither women, children, nor the aged, making no distinction between what is sacred and what is profane, despoiling churches, burning them and razing them to the ground." Obviously, such enthusiastic disturbers of the peace deserved to be chastised.

To do so Pope Leo spent several years trying to assemble an army, asking the German emperor in vain for a contingent of troops. Finally Leo obtained a force of 700 Suabian mercenaries, huge men of barbaric courage and appearance and of vast arrogance. They knew little about fighting on horseback and much preferred to fight on foot with their two-handed swords. These were the Pope's only reliable soldiers, but for his self-proclaimed holy war he enlisted in addition a considerable but unknown number of Lombard and Italian mercenaries.

Gibbon, who regarded most aspects of the Middle Ages with smug scorn, called Leo's troops "a vile and promiscuous multitude of Italians." With imaginative license he wrote: "The priest and the robber slept in the same tent; the pikes and crosses were intermingled in the front; and the natural saint repeated the lessons of his youth in the order of march, of encampment and of combat." They were "multitudes, who fought without discipline and fled without shame."

Before leading his army forth from the papal city of Benevento, Pope Leo blessed his troops from the walls of the town, absolved them from their sins and proclaimed that those who fell in battle would be martyrs certain of a welcome in heaven. The army then marched through the Apennines to Civitate. At the same time a Byzantine force was expected to march up from the south. Between them the two armies would crush the Normans.

For twelve years before the Battle of Civitate the Normans had ruled a considerable area in Apulia from their base in the fortified city of Melfi. Some 300 of them, under the leadership of twelve so-called counts, had seized the town, improved its fortifications and launched a permanent program of conquest and cheerful brigandage. A monk of nearby Monte Cassino wrote of their forays: "They went away rejoicing by the fields and gardens to Venosa, near Melfi. They were gay and joyful on their horses and caracoled from side to side along the road; and when the citizens of Venosa beheld the strange knights, they marveled and were afraid. And the Normans seized great flocks which they took with them to Melfi without opposition. The second day they went to Ascoli, where they found the men even more supine. From there they went into fair Apulia and what pleased them they took, what did not please them they left. But they did not combat; for they found no one who opposed them. They divided that which they had taken and they began to seize the wealth of Melfitians and parceled out their women among themselves. They were delighted about the weakness of the men they met, and, confident of their strength and the power of God, believed that they would conquer the cities of Apulia."

The twelve counts were theoretically equal. But for military efficiency one of them was elected war leader and given the title of Count of Apulia, although most of Apulia was still an integral part of the Byzantine empire. At Civitate the war leader was Humphrey de Hauteville, an able soldier and a notable leader of men, as were all the members of his extraordinary family.

A petty Norman baron named Tancred de Hauteville, who lived out his life in complete obscurity near the city of Coutances, is forever famous solely because of his sons. He had twelve, five by his first wife, seven by his second. The first five and four of the second brood made the long journey over the Alps and on to southern Italy to win fame and fortune by their swords. All were tough, courageous, unscrupulous and resourceful. Four, William Iron-Arm, Drogo, Humphrey and Robert Guiscard, were elected successively Counts of Apulia. Two, Robert and Roger, rank among the greatest men of the Middle Ages, as soldiers, diplomats and statesmen. And Roger's son, Roger II, was unquestionably a great man also. Was there ever such an explosion of military and administrative talent in one family?

Humphrey, the commander of the small Norman force of mounted warriors at Civitate, was the least attractive of the brothers. In a cruel age all the brothers committed savage deeds, but Humphrey was conspicuously cruel. Drogo, his predecessor as Count of Apulia, had been assassinated in a church in an unsuccessful conspiracy to eliminate the Norman power in Apulia. In a deliberate program of terror and revenge Humphrey tortured to death everyone implicated in the conspiracy he could capture. The arms and legs of the leaders were torn from their bodies, presumably by horses harnessed to each limb as can be seen in Renaissance paintings of Christian martyrs.

The Norman army which slaughtered the papal troops at Civitate was small, probably less than 1,000 men. The Normans were desperately hungry. According to contemporary chroniclers, they had had nothing to eat for three days. They also had serious qualms about fighting the Pope. The qualms were so grave that the Normans sent an embassy to Pope Leo to see if negotiations might not make the battle unnecessary. But their qualms were not nearly grave enough to induce the Normans to consider for an instant forsaking their hard-won position in southern Italy and their plans for further conquests. And with a Byzantine force on the march to attack them in the rear the Normans knew that they must settle matters quickly—before the Byzantine troops could arrive and before their own strength wasted away because of starvation.

Pope Leo received the small Norman embassy in the presence of the leaders of his Suabian mercenaries. The Normans admitted their many offenses, but they promised amendment and declared their devotion to Pope Leo. Leo said nothing. Ordinarily a masterful man, he seemed completely dominated by his associates. His chancellor, an archdeacon from Lorraine, tried to frighten the Normans with threats and shouted that they should run away. One of the arrogant Suabian commanders even dared to shout at the Pope in the presence of the Norman envoys: "Order the Normans to lay down their arms and leave Italy at once. If they refuse, we do not wish you to accept their treaties or bother with their messages. Not yet have they felt German swords. Let them depart or perish at our hands."

It is possible that Leo and his advisors hoped that a state of suspended negotiations would last long enough for the Byzantine force to arrive. In any case, the Norman deputation, surprised and angered by their reception, returned to their encampment. That night in a council of war the Norman leaders decided to attack the next morning. Their admiring chronicler wrote: "All desired battle so that they might die decently instead of perishing without glory."

Both armies were encamped on a flat plain broken by several sharply rising mounds. The Norman heavy cavalry assembled behind one of these mounds so that the papal troops could not see their preparations. Humphrey de Hauteville commanded the center. Richard of Aversa led the right wing. And the left wing, temporarily held in reserve, was commanded by Humphrey's younger half-brother, Robert, always called Guiscard, which means crafty or wily or wise.

Robert Guiscard, who began his career as a brigand and cattle thief, ended it as the sovereign ruler of southern Italy and of the island of Sicily. At the time of his death, when he was either sixty-nine or seventy, he had recently put to flight the German emperor and the Byzantine emperor, had rescued one of the greatest of medieval popes from his enemies (the same pope who had three times excommunicated Robert) and was preparing to conquer the entire Byzantine empire. His skill as a soldier, his magnetic leadership of men, his insatiable lust for power and his indomitable will were all famous. William the Conqueror is said to have encouraged himself by remembering the courage of Robert Guiscard.

At the time of the Battle of Civitate, Robert Guiscard was only an independent leader living by brigandage in Calabria, the toe of the Italian boot. His older brothers had not welcomed him as their equal. But his power and reputation were rising fast.

The papal troops first learned that they were going to fight a battle when the Norman horsemen trotted out from behind their mound and launched their charge. Richard of Aversa thundered down on the ill-equipped and pitifully non-belligerent Italians and scattered them in ignominious flight. Pursuing their fleeing foes impetuously, Richard and his men were soon far from the din of battle where Humphrey's knights were desperately engaging the Suabians.

The huge, long-haired Suabians were mounted, but they were not comfortable on horseback and had not mastered the art of cavalry combat. Many dismounted so as to wield their long swords more effectively. They fought so well that Robert Guiscard hurried to attack with his reserve force. According to the chronicler of the de Hautevilles, Robert carried a lance in his left hand instead of a shield and a sword in his right, using both with equal skill. But the Suabians held their own. It was the return of Richard of Aversa and his victorious warriors which won the Battle of Civitate. The Suabians, like Harold's housecarls at Hastings, were slaughtered by mounted Normans. Not one of the Suabian soldiers survived.

Pope Leo, watching from the walls of Civitate, must have experienced a shattering emotional shock. A soldier himself in his younger days, he had expected victory. And now before his eyes the best warriors in Europe had not only destroyed his army; they had inaugurated a new era in the history of Italy and of the Papacy. Leo could not possibly know what the near future would hold; but he must have recognized that the world as he knew it would never be the same again.

Without waiting to care for their wounded or count their dead, the triumphant Normans rode at once to storm Civitate and capture the Pope. They burned the huts and hovels outside the city walls and set fire to the immense wooden gates. Leo, wishing to spare the town the horrors of a sack, set out through the streets with a cross carried before him to surrender himself to his exulting foes. But a shift in the wind blew the fire toward the Normans, who pulled back, their fury spent, and seemed content to wait for the next day's events.

Leo spent an anxious night in Civitate. He asked the citizens for asylum, but their fear of the Normans was greater than their piety or loyalty. They demanded that the Pope submit to the Normans. At dawn the following morning Pope Leo IX sallied forth to surrender. An extraordinary scene followed.

The ordinary Norman soldiers prostrated themselves on the ground before the Pope whose army they had so furiously defeated the day before, and the Norman leaders knelt before him and kissed his feet. "My own life," said Leo, "is not dearer to me than those of my friends you have slain." The Norman chiefs, with dust and blood still on their surcoats, wept and promised that they themselves would be his soldiers instead of the dead men. Throughout the Middle Ages tears, violent and capricious emotion and much enthusiasm for dramatic scenes persisted. Norman tears did not mean that those who shed them repented defeating the Pope, only that they wished their enemy had been someone other than the supreme head of the Christian Church.

Walking over the battlefield, Leo prayed for the dead and called out in grief when he recognized the bodies of his friends. Funeral rites for the dead took two days and then the bodies were buried on the battlefield. Pope Leo was solicitously escorted by Humphrey's men back to the papal city of Benevento. And there he remained for nine months, theoretically a free man honored by his recent enemies, actually their prisoner. During this unhappy time the Pope and his conquerors conducted informal negotiations. What they finally agreed on is not known, but historians believe that Leo probably recognized the Norman conquests. He could do no less. He was ill, discouraged and deeply disturbed by charges that a pope should never have abused his sacred office by leading Christians to battle against other Christians. In later times Leo's concern about this issue was not shared by numerous popes.

On his release Leo returned to the Lateran palace in Rome, a sick and exhausted man. Foreseeing his imminent death, he ordered a grave dug for him inside Saint Peter's and had himself carried on a litter to the graveside. While lying there Leo is reported to have seen visions of the dead of Civitate in Paradise. "Truly," he explained, "I rejoiced in our brothers who were killed in fighting for God in Apulia. For I saw them numbered among the martyrs and clad in shining golden robes." Leo died in April of 1054.

Leo IX was a sincere and good man who did his best. He did much to launch the reform of the Church only recently at the nadir of its moral and spiritual fortunes. While he failed to check the Normans, who were the wave of the future for his generation, we can respect him and sympathize with him.

Gibbon did neither: "In the calm of retirement the well-meaning pope deplored the effusion of Christian blood, which must be imputed to his account; he felt, that he had been the author of sin and scandal; and, as his undertaking had failed, the indecency of his military character was universally condemned. With these dispositions, he listened to the offers of a beneficial treaty; deserted an alliance which he had preached as the cause of God; and ratified the past and future conquests of the Normans."

II

Change, Chaos and Civilization

Historical periods may be only a convenience for generalization, but they are a useful and necessary convenience. The Middle Ages began when each historian says they began. The Dark Ages, which began when German barbarians overran the Roman empire, continued through centuries of violent turmoil, of devastating invasions by Saracens, Norsemen and Hungarians, of moral squalor in the Papacy in Rome. Because of these factors it seems reasonable to me to conclude that the Middle Ages began when several changes for the better became noticeable. These were: the establishment of cities and states capable of maintaining a minimum of order in their domains; the establishment of ruling dynasties capable of holding, for at least several decades, the loyalty and respect of their subjects; and the partial reform and civilization of the Church, particularly of the Papacy. Consequently, for the purposes of this book, the Middle Ages in Italy began in the middle of the eleventh century with Pope Leo IX's inauguration of a reform program for the Church and with the Battle of Civitate, which made certain that Norman power would be a major force in Italy for centuries to come.

A start toward a partial understanding of medieval Italy can be made by emphasizing four major factors: the geographical fragmentation of

Italy; the extraordinary physical energy which enabled the Italians not only to survive the manifold miseries of the times, but to build an impressive civilization with one hand while with the other they struggled with pestilence, famine and unending war; the ignorance and credulity which filled the world with a host of supernatural marvels; and the presence of continual change.

Medieval society was not as static as is commonly supposed. Change may not have been as fast and terrifying as it is in the twentieth century. Nevertheless, change was endemic—political, economic, social and cultural change. The changes were so great that Robert de Hauteville, who lived in the middle of the eleventh century, would not have recognized and could not have understood the Italy of Giangaleazzo Visconti, who lived at the end of the fourteenth century.

Throughout the Middle Ages Italy could be described accurately as "a geographical expression"—just as it could in 1849 when Prince Metternich coined the phrase. One might expect a peninsula to impose a certain unity upon its inhabitants. But the Apennine Mountains divide Italy into many regions and in each region independent cities divided the land into small units. Conquests, wars, politics and local patriotism have always fostered an intense Italian regionalism. Of particular importance was the failure of the barbarians who destroyed the Roman empire to make their conquests complete. If they had done so, they might have unified Italy at least as much as the Romans had done.

The barbarians failed to conquer southern Italy, and so in the eleventh century the Byzantine emperor still ruled there. His rule was precarious and often ineffectual, depending as it did on able officials and generals of whom he never had a reliable supply. Rome and numerous coastal cities retained their separate independence. And the areas ruled by the Lombards, the last of the barbarian invaders, had broken up into several independent duchies.

In northern and central Italy were many small and unimportant cities which owed allegiance to local barons and ultimately to the German emperor. As their population and trade grew they acted more and more independently—first overthrowing the rule of the local barons, then imposing their own rule on the barons, then establishing their complete independence, and finally (for most of them) losing it to tyrants and princes. By the thirteenth century these cities had become large, prosperous, vigorous and important.

Other factors contributed to the geographical splintering of Italy. The island of Sicily was ruled by Saracens from 878 to 1091, by Charles of Anjou, a French royal prince, from 1266 to 1282, and by the kings of Aragon for hundreds of years. The Papacy, which was based in Rome, did not effectively rule that city until the fifteenth century. But the popes never ceased trying to exercise as much temporal control as possible. And they never wavered in their claim to rule much of central Italy. This claim was based upon the famous "donation of Constantine" in which the great emperor was supposed to have made a gift of huge territories to the Church. Neither the popes nor anyone else knew that the donation was a gross forgery contrived long after Constantine's death. It was not until early in the thirteenth century that Pope Innocent III temporarily succeeded in establishing papal rule over the so-called papal states.

The existence of so many different sovereign units in Italy made wars so frequent that warfare almost seemed a permanent state. Throughout the Middle Ages neighboring towns fought each other. Alliances of towns fought each other. Local barons, land- and power-hungry adventurers, Moslem raiders, mercenary captains, German and French invaders, and bloodthirsty factions within each city all contributed to the hell's broth of boiling warfare. The Church itself fought countless wars, against the Normans, against the overmighty barons of Rome and the surrounding area, against rulers who defied its temporal or spiritual domination, and against heretics who rebelled against its doctrines.

Many of these wars were caused by the fragmentation of Italy. But other major causes were the fierce ideological passions of the supporters of the Church or of the Empire; the fiery patriotism and lust for conquest of the towns; the ambitions for greater power and rank of individuals; and, perhaps most important of all, the joyful bellicosity of the medieval Italians. Wars caused suffering and devastation and were often waged with brutal ferocity. But they were exciting. They brought color and drama into drab lives. Many medieval Italians seemed to enjoy them.

The population of Italy in the eleventh century was small, but it was growing. Country people were steadily drifting into the towns. In the next three centuries the population soared, the towns grew amazingly, commerce, manufacture, banking and foreign trade all swept ahead on a tide of Italian energy, ingenuity and enterprise. Italians did business all over western Europe, and Italian ships were found in every harbor from the Crimea to London.

As the towns grew they built walls and moats, handsome municipal buildings, cathedrals and palaces for the great. By the fourteenth century most streets in the larger cities were paved. A public water supply was available, but only in wells and fountains. There were no sanitary systems of any kind. The bustling, prosperous towns which looked so impressive smelled dreadful. From gibbets and the windows or battlements of castles hung the decaying bodies of criminals who had been publicly tortured and executed. The lower classes of the towns lived in dirt and darkness, toiling to survive. Every citizen obeyed a host of laws regulating his work, his play, his clothes and his amusements.

Outside the walls in the *contado,* the area ruled by a particular town, there were numerous villages and sometimes subject towns. The peasants grew the food which fed the towns and knew little except poverty, labor, misery and suffering. They were always the principal victims of the wars. All around them were forests. The treeless plains and mountainsides of modern Italy are, historically speaking, the final stage of a process of deforestation which began in antiquity. In the Middle Ages much of Italy was still green and wild. Wolves, bears and wild boars abounded. So did bandits, robbers, outlaws and murderers.

Although the changes between the eleventh and fourteenth centuries were enormous, although gigantic steps were taken in urbanization, commerce and the arts of civilization generally, many aspects of medieval life remained unchanged. Most important of all was the role of religion in everyday life. Men might violate the teachings of the Church, but they rarely doubted the sacred origin of the Church, the sanctity of the pope and the sacraments, the nearness of heaven and hell, and the importance of kindly intercession by the saints. Miracles were commonplace. Even God Himself was very near. So, unfortunately, were Satan and a host of demons, devils and evil spirits.

Writing of the thirteenth century, the nineteenth-century English historian Edward A. Freeman said: "The age was one which could hardly bear to look upon anything in a purely secular way." The remark is perhaps truer of the thirteenth century than of any other, but it certainly applies to all the medieval centuries. Men could not conceive of a world not spiritually dominated by the one true Church, or of a world in which the Church did not play a major and proper role in secular affairs. In their view there were no completely secular affairs. There were exceptions, of course—rulers and their advisors who bitterly opposed the interference of the Church in the internal affairs of their states. The Holy Roman Empire itself, which was ruled by an elected German prince, was sacred in its origin. Several wars were holy before the First Crusade was preached. And crusades continued to be holy even when they were waged for grossly political reasons against fellow Christians who were considered politically sinful and hence religiously sinful, too, by the pope.

In a time when life was short and miserable for most people, when plagues were common, famines frequent and men matured early and died young, people naturally turned to the promise of salvation in paradise; and as naturally feared the punishment waiting for them because of their sins in hell. The fervor of their belief was in no way diminished by the rapacity, ostentatious wealth and vice of the higher clergy, or by the ignorance and flagrant human weaknesses of the local priests. Popes and cardinals might be worldly and covetous; monasteries and convents might be nests of corruption; a cynical anti-clericalism might flourish; but the need for belief never lessened. This need was ministered to by conscientious priests, by the first wave of idealistic Franciscans and Dominicans, and by the popularity of pilgrimages, miracles and relics of the saints.

For nearly 2,000 years devout Christians have denounced the failure of most of their fellow believers to abide by the moral teachings of their faith. The sinful nature of human beings has always ensured that there would be a deplorable gap between Christian morality and the practices of most Christians. That gap was enormous in the Middle Ages. Whether it was larger in the Middle Ages than today is a matter of conjecture. In any case, popes, priests, monks and saints continually lamented the times and seasons, often looking back to an earlier day when virtue was more prevalent; and often predicting the coming of Antichrist and the end of the world.

But if sin flourished, so did faith. Most people believed in every official doctrine and faithfully performed every official ceremony of the Church. Some of those who were disillusioned by the worldly nature of the Church as a powerful organization became hermits or joined the newer monastic orders, which were always reform movements. And some became heretics, finding in new semi-Christian cults a more satisfying faith. In the thirteenth century, heretics were numerous in many Italian cities, particularly in Lombardy.

Medieval Italy was distinguished by an abundance of saints. Several, such as Francis of Assisi and Thomas Aquinas, are world famous. Others, such as Pope Gregory VII, are famous, too, but not for any noticeably saintly qualities. And in many cities at various times local citizens were venerated as saints, sometimes just because they claimed to be saints.

One of the oddest of these was a woman named Guglielma who lived in Milan in the second half of the thirteenth century. During her lifetime she was widely worshipped as an incarnation of the Holy Ghost. Guglielma was particularly revered by members of the wealthy classes. She enjoyed the patronage of the Cistercian monks, and the Archbishop of Milan did not oppose her.

Fra Salimbene, a Franciscan monk who lived in the thirteenth century and wrote one of the most interesting of all medieval chronicles, said that popular devotion to false saints originated among the sick, because they longed to be healed; among the curious, because they desired to see new things; and among the clergy, who were envious of the popularity of the new mendicant orders of Franciscans and Dominicans.

Miracles generally occur among people who expect them. In the Middle Ages nearly everybody expected them and only a few especially intelligent and skeptical persons questioned the authenticity of particular miraculous claims. It was in 1293, according to popular legend, that the Virgin Mary's house in Nazareth flew through the air escorted by angels and landed in the town of Loreto on a hill overlooking the Adriatic Sea not far from Ancona. It became a place of pilgrimage at once and still is. Perhaps it is appropriate that the Virgin of Loreto is a special patroness of aviators.

Less spectacular miracles were almost ordinary. The Virgin and saints were believed to have manifested themselves to many individuals. The Virgin even wrote personal letters which were delivered by angels.

Statues nodded their heads and wept. They still do, if we can judge by the zeal with which pilgrims throng to Siracusa in Sicily to pray before a statue which they believe weeps. The sick were often miraculously healed. And sometimes saints were provoked to violent action.

During the long war between the Emperor Frederick II and the Church in the thirteenth century, local factions were frequently driven out of cities and nearly as frequently returned to drive out their enemies. When exiles stormed the town of Magreba, Salimbene reports:

"Nero da Leccaterra entered the church of the Blessed Virgin and set fire to it that it might be utterly consumed, saying, 'Now, Saint Mary, defend yourself if you can!' Yet even as he spoke these words of malice and insult, a lance hurled by some other hand pierced through his breastplate and entered even into his heart, and suddenly he fell down dead. And, for it is certain that his own men hurled no such lance, especially against their captain, therefore it is believed that the blow was dealt by Saint Mercury, both because he is the wonted avenger of wrongs done to the Blessed Virgin, and also because he slew the apostate Julian with his lance in the Persian war."

It wasn't only the saints who intervened in human affairs. Satan himself, lesser devils and assorted demons were constantly active in their efforts to lure people into sin. In the thirteenth century Saint Dominic, the great founder of the Dominican order of preaching friars, became convinced that a sparrow which had annoyed him by interrupting his studies was an incarnation of the Devil. The opportunity to torment the Devil was too good to lose. Dominic plucked the sparrow alive and is said to have rejoiced in its shrieks. Dominic was a good, pious and intelligent man. But his mind was medieval and so (in some ways) incomprehensible to us. His credulity and his cruelty were normal and representative of his time.

One of the most remarkable manifestations of medieval religious faith was the universal veneration of and credulous belief in the most improbable sacred relics. Relics were so supremely important that they were not only a cult, they were also an industry. Skepticism may have been uncommon in the Middle Ages, but cynics anxious to profit from the simplicity of others were numerous and busy—busy manufacturing false relics or claiming that ordinary objects were sacred.

People believed that the relics treasured in churches all over Europe were genuine and so regarded them with pious awe. But the real significance of the relic cult lay in the conviction of sin and the hope for forgiveness. Sir Kenneth Clark, the distinguished English art critic and scholar, summed it up neatly: "The medieval pilgrim really believed that by contemplating a reliquary containing the head or even the finger of a saint he would persuade that particular saint to intercede on his behalf."

Just when the relic cult began cannot be known—perhaps in the early days of the primitive church. In any case, by the ninth century relics were being stolen in piratical raids. In 828 Venetian sailors stole the body of Saint Mark from Alexandria. In 1087 sailors from Bari stole the bones of Saint Nicholas from the town of Myra in Turkey. The church of Saint Nicholas in Bari, which housed them, became a popular place of pilgrimage.

Crusaders brought back to Europe a treasure trove of relics. After the capture of Jerusalem in 1099 Judas' thirty pieces of silver turned up in Europe and also *two* heads of John the Baptist. Members of the Fourth Crusade looted Constantinople of the True Cross, the Crown of Thorns, some clothes of the Virgin Mary, a tooth of Our Lord, the cup used in the Last Supper, a tooth of Saint John the Baptist, the arm of Saint Stephen and the entire body of Saint Andrew. This particular Crown of Thorns was bought by Louis IX of France, who had the Saint-Chapelle in Paris built to house it. As far as is known, the existence of two other Crowns of Thorns in Paris did not disturb anybody.

Relics were of great official importance to the cities where they were preserved. In times of peril the clergy of Rome used to carry the heads of Saint Peter and Saint Paul in reverent procession through the streets of the city.

To most modern minds probably the most astonishing sacred relics cherished in Rome were some drops of the Virgin Mary's milk which were preserved in the church of Santa Maria Maggiore.

No brief survey of medieval Italy can even list all the elements which made up the life of the times. Some of the religious and political issues, often inextricably entwined together, which provoked controversies and numerous wars will be described in later chapters devoted to individual lords of Italy. Many other topics are ignored because they do not properly belong in a work primarily concerned with the ideas, deeds and personalities of men of power. But one circumstance which dominated all Italy throughout the Middle Ages requires further discussion. It is war.

Familiarity with war as a permanent condition of life is something modern men share with their medieval ancestors. Today we live in a state of controlled terror because of the ever present possibility of nuclear warfare. We have survived two world wars, several lesser wars and are engaged in a disastrous localized war in Indochina. Nevertheless, we regard war as exceptional and unnecessary, as something dreadful which, if men were only less stupid and belligerent, could be eliminated from life.

In medieval Italy wars were not so destructive or so terrifying. But they were far more normal and frequent. They were endemic and omnipresent, a constant part of life in which glory and triumph might be won for individuals and states, or, equally likely, disaster and destruction. Large pitched battles were infrequent; but skirmishes, raids, devastation and loss of life and property were universal. Cities were besieged. Often it was as difficult for the besieging army to maintain its food supply as for the beleaguered townsmen. But occasionally towns were captured and sacked, and always crops, orchards and vineyards were devastated; castles and villages were destroyed. As one historian, L. Elliott Binns, writing of the first decade of the thirteenth century, put it: "The main occupation of the people of Orvieto, as of most Italian cities at this epoch, was warfare with their neighbors, varied by civil strife within their own walls."

These local wars could be merciless. In 1125 the army of Florence slaughtered the entire population of Fiesole and utterly destroyed the town. But usually in battle quarter was given to the defeated. Whether the prisoners gained by this so-called mercy is doubtful. Prisoners were confined in noisome dungeons while awaiting ransom, often in such horrible conditions or subject to such cruel tortures that they died.

The rancorous hatred between neighboring cities is difficult for us to imagine. It was customary for a Florentine to hate a citizen of Siena, Pisa, Lucca or even of Prato, less than ten miles away. Dante, one of the greatest minds of the Middle Ages, and an exile from Florence, nevertheless hated the inhabitants of Florence's enemy cities. The nearer the cities were to each other, the more likely they were to be enemies. Rivals in trade and in economic raw materials, they were often bitter enemies in war. Padua and Vicenza, bloodthirsty enemies, were less than twenty miles apart. Parma and Cremona, equally implacable foes, were only twenty-five miles apart. Perugia and Assisi, some twelve miles apart, were deadly enemies.

Although mercenary troops were present in Italy from early times, they did not come into general use until the fourteenth century. Until then most Italian armies were strictly amateur, comprising the citizens of the particular town that was going to war.

When a medieval Italian city went to war, all men between the ages of fourteen and seventy might be called to arms. Of course, not all of them were. Some of these amateur soldiers had to stay home to run the municipal government, to guard the walls and to keep the local industries and businesses operating. And some men were sick, or crippled, or too old. The majority fought on foot wearing mail shirts and steel caps, wielding spears and pikes as unskilled infantry. The more prosperous citizens, those who could afford to keep horses and the elaborate equipment of a mounted knight, fought on horseback.

Medieval Italian warfare was little concerned with strategy and only occasionally with tactics. The Norman charge from behind a concealing mound at Civitate was unusual. The commanders were prominent citizens believed to be brave. They were not expected to be skillful generals. By the thirteenth century a local war would commonly begin with a shrill blast of trumpets and an ear-piercing ringing of bells, with the assembly of troops and a grand parade. Then the army would march toward the enemy city, destroying everything possible once they had crossed the enemy's border. If the hostile army marched out against the invaders, there might be a pitched battle. If it remained behind its protecting walls, there might be a siege.

Many cities used a *carroccio* as an emblem of civic pride and as an almost sacred symbol that must be protected at all times by the troops. The *carroccio,* an enormous wagon drawn by oxen, was surmounted by masts flying the brightly colored banners of the city. The earliest known appearance of a *carroccio* was in 1093 in Milan. Giovanni Villani, the great Florentine chronicler, described Florence's ceremonious going to war against Siena in 1260:

"The people and commons of Florence gathered a general host against the city of Siena, and led out the *carroccio*. And you must know that the *carroccio* which the Florentines led out to war was a car upon four wheels all painted red, and on it were raised two great masts also red, upon which was spread to the wind the great standard with the arms of the commonwealth, half white and half red, as to be seen to this day in San Giovanni; and it was drawn by a pair of oxen of great size, covered with a cloth of red, which were kept solely for this purpose, and the driver was a free man of the commonwealth. This *carroccio* was used by our forefathers in triumphant processions and on high occasions; and when it went out with the host, the lords and counts of the country round and the noble knights of the city fetched it from its quarters in San Giovanni and brought it onto the Piazza of Mercato Nuovo; and having stationed it beside a boundary stone, carved like the *carroccio*, which is still there, they handed it over to the keeping of the people. And it was escorted to the field of battle by the best and bravest and strongest of the foot-soldiers of the people of the city, who were chosen to guard it, and round it was mustered the whole force of the people. And when war was declared, a month before they were to set out, a bell was hung on the archway of the gate of Santa Maria, which was at the end of the Mercato Nuovo, and it was rung without ceasing night and day; and this was done out of pride, in order that the enemy against whom war was declared might have time to prepare himself. And the bell was called by some the Martinella, and by others the Asses' Bell. And when the Florentine host set out, the bell was taken from the archway and was hung in a wooden tower on a wagon, and the tolling of it guided the host on its march. And by this pomp of the *carroccio* and the bell was maintained the masterful pride of the people of old and of our forefathers when they went to battle."

In the thirteenth century Milan's *carroccio* was drawn by six oxen draped in white cloths decorated with red crosses. The Milanese *carroccio* had a mast shaped like a cross from which flew a white banner with red crosses. For a city to lose its *carroccio* was a shameful disaster.

Sometimes medieval Italian wars were occasions for gaiety, for crude humor and for efforts to shame and humiliate the enemy. The chronicler of Parma wrote: "Then the Milanese besieged the Cremonese; they blew upon their trumpets before the walls and called: 'Come out then, you miserable rabbits, and stand to battle.' But the Cremonese dared not come out." At other sieges it was considered an admirable joke to catapult the carcasses of dead and decaying donkeys over the wall into the city streets. And as a demonstration of complete contempt members of a besieging army would organize horse races around the circuit of the beleaguered city's walls.

During the thirteenth century, when the war between the Emperor Frederick II on one side and the Lombard League and the Papacy on the other dragged on for many years, conditions in Lombardy and in Romagna became almost unbearable. Fra Salimbene, the Franciscan monk who was an eyewitness of this war, wrote a pitiful account of the general suffering:

"I must not omit to tell how the Church party in Modena was driven forth from the city, while the Imperial party held it. So it was also in Reggio; and so also, in process of time, in Cremona. Therefore in those days was most cruel war, which endured many years. Men could neither plough, nor sow, nor reap, nor till vineyards, nor gather vintage, nor dwell in the villages: more especially in the districts of Parma and Reggio and Modena and Cremona. Nevertheless, hard by the walls, men tilled the fields under guard of the city militia, who were mustered quarter by quarter according to the number of the gates.

"Armed soldiers thus guarded the peasants at their work all day long: for so it must needs be, by reason of the ruffians and bandits and robbers who multiplied beyond measure. For they would take men and lead them to their dungeons, to be ransomed for money; and the oxen they drove off to devour or sell. Such as would pay no ransom they hanged up by their feet or their hands, and tore out their teeth; and extorted payment by laying toads in their mouths, which was more bitter than any death. For these men were more cruel than devils, and one wayfarer dreaded to meet another by the way as he would have dreaded to meet the foul fiend. For each ever suspected that the other would take him and lead him off to prison.

"And the land was made desert, so there was neither husbandman nor wayfarer. For in the days of Frederick, and especially from the time he was deposed from the Empire [by the pope] and when Parma rebelled and lifted her head against him, 'the paths rested and they that went by them walked through byways.' And evils were multiplied on the earth; and the wild beasts and fowls multiplied and increased beyond all meas- ure—pheasants and partridges and quails, hares and roebucks, fallow deer and buffaloes and wild swine and ravening wolves. For they found no beasts in the villages to devour according to their wont: neither sheep nor lambs, for the villages were burned with fire. Wherefore the wolves were gathered together in mighty multitudes around the city moats, howl- ing dismally for exceeding anguish of hunger; and they crept into the cities by night and devoured men and women and children who slept under the porticoes or in wagons. Nay, at times they would even break through the house walls and strangle the children in their cradles."

Commenting on this story, the medieval scholar G. G. Coulton pointed out that in many thirteenth-century towns the houses were built of wat- tles and clay. The walls would decay and be left unrepaired, so that it was easy for burglars or wolves to break through.

Salimbene continued: "No man could believe, but if he had seen it as I have, the horrible deeds that were done in those days, both by men and divers beasts. For the foxes multiplied so exceedingly that two of them even climbed one Lententide to the roof of our infirmary at Faenza, to take two hens which were perched under the roof tree: and one of them we took in that same convent, as I saw with my own eyes. For this curse of wars invaded and preyed upon and destroyed the whole of Romagna in the days when I dwelt there. Moreover, while I dwelt at Imola, a certain layman told me how he had taken twenty-seven great and fair cats with a snare in certain villages that had been burned, and had sold their hides to the furriers; which had doubtless been house cats in those villages in time of peace."

The horrors of Italian medieval warfare were not all caused by military operations on land. The naval powers, Venice, Genoa and Pisa, fought each other with equal fury. In the thirteenth century Genoa decisively defeated a Pisan fleet. Salimbene left a vivid account of the fate of the Pisans:

"At last the Pisans finding themselves worsted, yielded themselves to the Genoese, who slew the wounded and kept the rest in prison: and even the victors had no cause for boasting, since fortune was cruel to either side; and there was such weeping and wailing in Genoa and Pisa as was never heard in those two cities from the day of their foundations to our times. For who without woe and bitter weeping can consider how those two noble cities, whereby all plenty of good things come to us in Italy, destroyed each other from mere ambition and pomp and vainglory, whereby each desired to overcome the other, as though the sea were not wide enough for the ships of both! I care not to write here the number of captives and slain from either side, for they were diversely told. . . .

"After the fight of the Pisans and Genoese, many women of Pisa, fair ladies and noble and rich and mighty, gathered together in companies of thirty and forty at a time, and went on foot from Pisa to Genoa, to seek out and visit their captives. For one had a husband there, another a son or a brother or a cousin. . . . And when the aforesaid women sought out their captives the jailors would answer them, 'Yesterday thirty died, and today forty. We cast them into the sea, and thus do we daily with the Pisans.'

"So when those ladies heard such news of their dear ones and could not find them, they fell down amazed with excessive grief, and could scarce breathe for utter anguish and pain of heart. Then after a while, when their breath was come again, they rent their faces with their nails and tore their hair, and raising their voices wept with great wailing until their fountain of tears was dried. For the Pisans died in prison of hunger and famine, and poverty and misery, and anguish and sadness. . . . Moreover, when the aforesaid ladies of Pisa were come home, they found others dead whom they had left safe in their homes. For the Lord smote the Pisans with a plague that year, and many died; nor was there any house without its dead."

The devastation of fields, orchards and vineyards, the destruction of villages and castles, the loss of life and waste of money in medieval Italy's wars were so great that it is difficult to understand how in the thirteenth and fourteenth centuries a high civilization could emerge from such violent chaos. Yet in the thirteenth century trade expanded, towns grew, churches and cathedrals were built and men of genius flourished in Italy who rank among the greatest men of the entire Middle Ages.

Among them were Saint Francis of Assisi, Saint Thomas Aquinas, Pope Innocent III, the Emperor Frederick II, Marco Polo, Dante and Giotto. Also at work in the thirteenth century were three of the most notable of medieval artists: Cimabue, Duccio and the sculptor Giovanni Pisano.

This seemingly miraculous flowering of an urban civilization in the midst of universal violence can be explained, at least in part, by the facts that the wars were generally fought by only a small part of the population, and that the warfare which seemed permanent was actually sporadic, intermittent and localized. While one region suffered, another might enjoy comparative peace.

Much of the adult male population of a city might march gaily off to conquer a neighboring town; but usually victory or defeat came soon and the survivors could then return to their jobs and customary pursuits. When factions in the same city fought each other in bloody vendettas the ordinary citizen remained neutral and little concerned. Let the bellicose aristocrats slaughter each other and tear down one another's towers and houses; *they* were busy earning their daily bread. And by the fourteenth century so many mercenaries were employed that the inhabitants of most cities were no longer participants in wars. They had become spectators only. Fighting was left to the professionals.

The great Italian inventions of the later Middle Ages were international banking; drafts payable at branch banks in other cities and countries so that currency did not have to be transported in wagons protected by armed guards; marine insurance; double-entry bookkeeping; and the minting of honest gold coins. Silver coins were notoriously debased. To bring some kind of monetary order into being, in the year 1252 Florence established the gold standard and minted the gold florin, which soon circulated over much of Europe. Another Italian invention of the later Middle Ages was spectacles.

Also a late medieval development was the personal despotism imposed on a city or on several cities by a leader who combined military force with force of personality. Numerous despotisms were established in the thirteenth century. In the fourteenth they had become the norm. Dante complained that "all the towns of Italy are full of tyrants." Boccaccio, writing in the 1350s, in his *Fates of Illustrious Men* protested against the cruelty and vicious self-indulgence of the Italian tyrants:

"People should not be threatened with force, trampled underfoot, nor tortured. Rulers should always remember that people are not slaves but fellow servants of God. Because it is the sweat of the people that makes the royal eminence shine, the king should be diligent to guard peace and the welfare of his people. How rulers perform this today, God knows. Rule has been transformed into tyranny. Rulers despise the feelings of their subjects. They want to glitter with gems and gold; they want to be surrounded by great bands of servants, to build palaces into the sky, to spend their time with groups of parasites, prostitutes and fools. They feast their eyes on obscenities. They spend their nights in endless debauchery, drunkenness, and scandal. Their days they pass in the deepest sleep while the people guard their well-being.

"They make wars not justly, but in reprisal for personal injury. Believing themselves infallible, they reject the counsel of the wise and believe only themselves. They put aside whatever is good and take up whatever is evil. They burden the city with taxes, torture the citizens, exile and massacre them, trample them into the mud under their feet.

"What shameful wickedness!"

Boccaccio disapproved of torture and so did Salimbene. But torture was commonplace and largely taken for granted throughout the Middle Ages. Criminals were tortured regularly, often in public for the amusement of the law-abiding populace and as a warning to potential miscreants. Prisoners of war were tortured, sometimes in the emotional hysteria of victory over enemies, sometimes to hasten the payment of ransoms. Few doubted that a criminal deserved whatever torment he was forced to suffer. Torture was also officially approved by the Church, which, after condemning heretics, turned them over to secular authorities to be burned. Bandits and robbers tortured their victims, and individual citizens of good repute used torture in the course of personal or family vengeance.

It was all part of the violence and insecurity of the times. When most of mankind suffered from hunger in the recurrent famines, from diseases which the ignorant doctors could not even identify, from plagues, from natural disasters of all kinds and from the horrors of war, torture must have seemed only a somewhat more extreme example of the miseries to which men were born.

And orthodox religious doctrine cultivated a stoical resignation when catastrophes struck. Giovanni Villani wrote: "All pestilences and battles, ruins and floods, fires and persecutions, shipwrecks and exiles, occur in the world by the will of God for the cleansing of our sins."

The dark aspects of medieval life are so striking there is a danger of overemphasizing them. We should remember that life was good for the fortunate few much of the time, and for most people some of the time. A monk piously serving God in a monastery, a bishop ruling a city in splendor, a merchant growing rich by enterprise and calculated risks, a courtier enjoying the munificence of an emperor or tyrant, a craftsman lovingly designing jewelry or a reliquary, carving a statue or building a cathedral—they all enjoyed life and lived it zestfully.

The laborers in the cities and the peasants in the *contados* knew fewer pleasures and far greater hardships. But the urban worker could delight in the spectacle of a tournament or pageant, could rejoice with patriotic fervor when his city worsted a neighbor, and could feel part of all the swarming bustle and intimate communal activity of Italian medieval city life. The peasant, denied such humble pleasures, could at least know the perennial satisfactions of labor close to the land, of seed time and harvest, of worshipping a local saint not very different from the tutelary spirit worshipped by his pagan ancestors before him, of surviving day to day and year by year with the stubborn, patient courage which is perhaps the commonest of human virtues.

The civilization which emerged in medieval Italy was intensely urban. The cities were the centers of power, the bases of economic life, the magnetic attractions for industry, talent, ambition and creativity of all kinds. By the end of the thirteenth century Milan was the largest city in western Europe. Its population may have been as much as 200,000. In 1288 a Milanese schoolmaster wrote a book in praise of his native city, *De Magnalibus Urbis Mediolani*, which may be translated as "Concerning the Greatness of the City of Milan." Milan, he boasted, had 12,500 houses. Its *contado* included 50 towns and 150 villages with a population of 500,000. The city itself had 40,000 men capable of bearing arms, 400 notaries, 400 butchers, 400 bakers, 200 doctors, 80 schoolmasters, 50 copiers and sellers of books, 100 towers on the city walls, 6,000 wells, 3,000 millwheels and 1,000 taverns.

"The people are friendly," wrote the schoolmaster, "affable and honest." Life in Milan, he said, "was excellent for anyone who has enough money." There was work for all. And he claimed that there were cities in Italy whose population ate less food than did the dogs of Milan!

After Milan in size came Florence, Venice and Genoa. Estimates of their populations vary, with 100,000 the average figure. In Florence in the fourteenth century between 8,000 and 10,000 children attended elementary schools. There were 110 churches in the city and its suburbs and 30 hospitals with more than 1,000 beds. Medieval hospitals were numerous, but what care they could provide beyond food and lodging is not clear. Florence had 80 banks, 600 lawyers, 100 apothecaries and 60 physicians and surgeons. Five sixths of the city's annual revenue were devoted to the defense budget, one sixth to normal municipal expenditures. Even in times of peace Florence maintained a standing army of 700 to 1,000 mounted mercenary troops.

Venice, with its great wealth from international trade and its secure oligarchical republican government untroubled by the civil strife which beset the other Italian cities, was admired and envied. Salimbene wrote bitterly:

"The Venetians are greedy men and stubborn and outrageous, and they would gladly subdue the whole world to themselves if they could; and they treat boorishly the merchants who go to them, both by selling dear, and by taking tolls in diverse places from the same person at the same time. And if any merchant carries his goods thither for sale he may not bring them back with him: nay, but he must needs sell them there, will-he, nill-he. And if by mishap of the sea any ship other than their own is driven to them with its merchandise, it may not depart thence except it have first sold all its cargo: for the Venetians say that this ship has been driven to them by God's will, which no man may gainsay."

Many lesser cities in Lombardy, Tuscany and Umbria were important and locally powerful. Naples was the metropolis of the Kingdom of Sicily. And Rome, the capital of Christendom, the most famous city in Europe, was only a den of robber barons. Miserable mobs lived in squalor among the ruins of the Eternal City.

Rome was still surrounded by the third-century walls built by the Emperor Aurelian. Inside the walls were huge open spaces where goats and cattle grazed. The massive ruins of ancient splendor constantly grew smaller because their stones were used by the Roman barons to build their towers and fortresses. As early as the tenth century the local barons had built 181 private fortified towers and 46 private fortresses. By the thirteenth century there were said to be 500 towers, each a monument to the pride and habitual pugnacity of the noble families.

The barons who fought each other for power within the city owned huge estates and many castles in the surrounding countryside. Brutal, barbarous and arrogant, they made Rome ring with the clash of arms and spattered the streets with the blood of their enemies and of their followers. The people of Rome, who considered themselves the worthy heirs of the patricians of antiquity, were famous for their villainous rapacity, their dishonesty and their addiction to violent rioting. They lived by providing food and lodging to pilgrims at extortionate rates and were despised as scum by their contemporaries.

A remarkable letter written by a priest describes conditions in Rome about the year 1240: "How can you enjoy safety in the city, where all the citizens and the clergy are at daily strife for and against both opponents? The heat is insufferable, the water foul, the food is coarse and bad; the air is so heavy that it can be grasped with both hands, and is filled with swarms of mosquitoes; the ground is alive with scorpions, the people are dirty and odious, wicked and fierce. The whole of Rome is undermined, and from the catacombs, which are filled with snakes, arises a poisonous and fatal exhalation."

The fourteenth-century biographer of the Roman demagogue and dictator Cola di Rienzo, writing about the Rome of the 1340s, did not record much evidence of improvement: "The city of Rome was sunk in the deepest distress. There was no one to govern. Fighting was of daily occurrence; robbery was rife. Nuns, even children, were outraged; wives were torn from their husbands' beds. Laborers on their way to work were robbed at the very gates of the city. Pilgrims were plundered and strangled; the priests were evil-doers; every sin was unbridled. There was no remedy; universal destruction threatened. There was only one law—the law of the sword. There was no remedy other than self-defense in combination with relations and friends. Armed men assembled every day."

Yet, in spite of the prevailing chaos, Rome as a city continued to display enormous energy. The populace fought German emperors, popes, whom they repeatedly drove out of the city, and, in the customary manner of the times, numerous neighboring cities.

In the thirteenth and fourteenth centuries, while wars raged and thoughtful people despaired, the cities grew and prospered. Privacy was unknown and undesired. Houses were crowded and the people spent as much time as possible outdoors. They congregated in the handsome piazzas, meeting their friends, insulting their enemies, gossiping, ogling the girls, picking up the latest news. Everyone seemed to know everyone else. Daniel Waley in his *The Italian City Republics* quotes from a fourteenth-century book in praise of Pavia, then a city of about 50,000: "They know each other so well that if anybody inquires for an address he will be told it at once, even if the person he asks lives in a quite different part of the city; this is because they all gather twice a day, either in the court of the commune or in the cathedral piazza."

Slaves were still common in Italy in the thirteenth century. There were slave markets in Venice, Florence and Rome. Also common were astrologers, necromancers and beggars, many of them deformed or mutilated.

In the thirteenth century rich or noble Italians wore scarlet tunics, fur robes, gold chains and rings and usually a long, flowing gown called a *guarnacca*. This was sometimes lined or trimmed with bright-colored silk or fur, and decorated with gold embroidery and silver clasps. In 1240 the ladies of Tuscany, Lombardy and Romagna were much upset by the sumptuary laws of a papal legate who prohibited the wearing of long trains of which "a cubit and a half" swept the streets. Sumptuary laws regulating clothes and jewels were commonplace in the Middle Ages. Many cities imposed them. They were intended to prevent waste and extravagance, and also to prevent the lower orders from dressing as grandly as their betters.

The gowns of both men and women came in many colors—rose, ruby, scarlet, bright blue, green—with gold and silver buttons, silver belts, or gilt or enamel belts. Purses were of silk with silver or gold thread. Women wore chaplets or crowns made of silver or beaten gold. Gregorio Zuccolo described the fashions popular among the ladies of Faenza: "They wore on their heads a chaplet of gold and silver thread; had the necks all bare without any ornament to the point where the bodice begins. The *veste* itself was girt above the flanks with a golden girdle, often adorned with gems. Some had the bodice adorned with gold and the rest of the dress with purple or crimson silk, with open sleeves hanging halfway down the leg and usually reversed over the shoulders, as were also frequently the sleeves of the *chemisette,* which were open, allowing the bare arms to be seen. The arms were artificially whitened, and were adorned with ornamental chains or bracelets of gold."

Amusements were few: tournaments, fairs, pageants, bullfights, hunting, falconry, horse racing, chess, dice. Sometimes a peaceful sporting event went badly awry. In the thirteenth century the city of Treviso held a celebration in honor of a momentary peace. The people of neighboring cities were invited to attend the festival. In the principal piazza a wooden replica of a miniature castle was erected. Gorgeous hangings of fur and silk decorated its battlements. Inside the little castle was a garrison composed of the twelve most beautiful ladies of Padua. They were attended by maidens and armed for defense with flowers and fruit.

Young men from other nearby cities attacked the castle. The ladies showered them with violets and lilies, pears and apples, and perfumed water. Presumably the male warriors threw similar missiles at the girls. Finally a band of Venetians "fighting prudently and delectably" managed to plant the banner of Saint Mark upon the castle wall. But a group of young men from Padua, patriotically incensed to see the ladies of Padua defeated, rushed into the wooden castle and in an instant Venetians and Paduans were fighting. In the melee the Paduans captured the Venetian banner and tore it to pieces.

The Trevisans suppressed the riot and drove both Venetians and Paduans out of town. But the insult to the banner of Saint Mark had to be avenged. Venice declared war on Padua and, in a real battle instead of a mock one, triumphed. The peace terms required the twenty-five Paduans who had desecrated the Venetian banner to go as prisoners to Venice. They were treated courteously and sent home. But henceforth Padua sent Venice an annual tribute of thirty hens. These were regularly let loose in the Piazza San Marco so that the people could enjoy catching them. The event was known as "the festival of the Paduan hens."

III

Terror of the World

In the eleventh century a highly intelligent, cultivated and talented Byzantine princess wrote a history of her father's reign. Anna Comnena's book is called *The Alexiad* because the emperor, her father, was named Alexius Comnenus. In her book the Princess had occasion to refer to Robert de Hauteville many times. After all, he was the greatest soldier of the age, an adventurer who had made himself ruler of southern Italy and of Sicily, who had not been content only to drive the Byzantines out of Italy but had even dared to invade the empire itself, to defeat and nearly capture her august father.

Anna knew personally many people who had known the great Guiscard, had negotiated with him, fought against him or for him. She hated Robert for his "insolent and overweening presumptuousness" in attacking the Byzantine empire. She called him a braggart, tyrannical, crafty, an arch-villain and an arch-schemer, a sly fox and a versatile barbarian. But Anna was too shrewd not to recognize that Robert was no petty brigand. She wrote of him:

"On the one hand he was very courageous and adventurous, and on the other full of bitterness. Wrath ever sat on his nostrils, and his heart was overflowing with anger and fury. . . . The man was a firm upholder of his own designs and conceptions and would never willingly give up anything he had once planned—in a word, he was undaunted and thought he ought to be able to accomplish anything at the first attempt. . . .

"Robert was a most exceptional leader, quick-witted, good-looking, courteous in conversation, ready too in repartee, loud-voiced, easily accessible, very tall in stature, his hair always close-cut, long-bearded, always anxious to maintain the ancient customs of his race. He preserved his perfect comeliness of countenance and figure until the end, and of these he was very proud, as his appearance was considered worthy of kingship. He showed respect to all his subordinates, more especially to those who were well disposed toward him. On the other hand, he was very thrifty and fond of money, very businesslike and greedy of gain, and, in addition to all this, most ambitious. And since he was a slave to these desires, he has incurred the censure of mankind."

The princess was mistaken in this last comment. Robert certainly incurred the censure of those whom he attacked, defeated and conquered. But mankind usually forgives the faults and misdeeds of mighty warriors and conquerors. Victories rarely fail to charm. Power is nearly always respected.

Although all the brothers de Hauteville were valiant, only two were genuinely great, Robert and Roger. Both were totally unscrupulous, coldly calculating, occasionally cruel, rapacious, selfish and ruthlessly ambitious. Both were magnetic leaders of men who inspired devoted admiration in their followers. By the standards of their time both were often merciful. In their personal conduct both were entirely amoral and yet, without hypocrisy, both were sincerely religious. They believed in the teachings of the Church and whenever possible conformed to its rites and sacraments. But these descendants of Viking raiders lived in a barbarous age of such universal violence that it probably never occurred to them that their personal conduct should be restrained by the religion they professed.

Robert, the oldest of Tancred's sons by his second wife, was sixteen years older than Roger, the youngest of the brothers. Primarily a soldier of superb skill, he knew how to impose discipline; how to organize food, transport and supporting forces; and how to negotiate with wonderful guile. Roger was almost as redoubtable a soldier as Robert and was a statesman with a broader view. It was Roger who was chiefly responsible for seeing that the de Hauteville conquest of Sicily acquired some of the religious aura of a crusade; and who established the wise policy of tolerance toward the Moslem religion which made the Norman rule in Sicily unique in the Middle Ages.

Robert Guiscard arrived in southern Italy in 1046. He is said to have ridden down from Normandy alone. He was thirty years old, almost penniless, without a job. His half-brother, William Iron-Arm, the first Norman elected Count of Apulia, had recently died. William's successor to the informal title was his brother Drogo, who soon obtained a genuine and much grander title. The German Emperor Henry III in an impressive investiture ceremony made Drogo "Duke and Master of Italy and Count of the Normans of All Apulia and Calabria." Whether the title meant anything was not quite clear. Since the Roman emperors no one except Mussolini has been master of all Italy. And the Normans did not yet rule more than the northern end of Apulia and did not yet rule any of Calabria.

Drogo could have made smooth the way for Robert. He refused to. So Robert briefly served the Count of Capua as a mercenary knight and then went into business for himself as the leader of a band of Norman horsemen in Calabria. They dealt in brigandage, cattle rustling and general marauding. Robert proved so daring, wily and successful that his followers multiplied. He controlled more and more strongpoints. It was apparent that this younger de Hauteville would make a name for himself.

Seven years after his arrival in Italy Robert Guiscard played a crucial part in the Battle of Civitate. Four years later, in the spring of 1057, Humphrey de Hauteville died. With swift efficiency and brutal selfishness Robert seized for himself all Humphrey's lands which had been left to his son Abélard, who was Robert's own ward. No one seemed to object to this treacherous performance which made Robert Guiscard one of the most powerful of the Norman leaders. As if to confirm his increased stature, the Norman counts of Melfi elected Robert their new duke. It had taken Robert only eleven years to rise, without aid from his powerful brothers, from obscure mercenary to eminence as the Duke of Apulia.

To be elected Duke of Apulia was a considerable distinction, but an equivocal one. The Norman counts of Melfi had established themselves only in the northern part of that province. Most of Apulia had yet to be conquered from the Byzantines. In addition, the Norman counts regarded Robert as their elected war leader only, not in any way as their feudal superior. Even Pope Nicholas II's ceremonial investiture at Melfi in 1059 of Robert as Duke of Apulia, Calabria and Sicily did not change their minds. The official approval of the Church immensely strengthened Robert's position, but it did not diminish the pride and independence of the counts.

Robert Guiscard successfully led his fellow Norman chieftains in their conquest of Apulia. With the aid of his brother Roger he waged a strictly de Hauteville war of conquest in Calabria and Sicily. But he never succeeded in convincing the counts that he was their lawful feudal lord. Consequently, various alliances of Norman barons continually revolted against Robert, often when he was busy fighting somewhere else. The conquest of Sicily took thirty-one years because Robert could never devote his full strength to the project. His brother Roger fought brilliant campaigns in Sicily with astonishingly few troops. Once Robert was so hard-pressed while besieging the important port of Bari on the Adriatic that he had to recall Roger from Sicily to help him capture the city.

Young Roger de Hauteville seems to have arrived in Italy in 1057 at about the time that Robert was elected duke. Robert sent him off as his subordinate but virtually independent commander in Calabria. There Roger made as promising a start as Robert had, but soon the brothers quarreled and Roger, following precedent, set himself up as an independent brigand and even raided Robert's territories. Geoffrey Malatera, a monk employed by Roger to write a laudatory chronicle of the de Hauteville conquests, said that when Roger was a young man fighting in Calabria he had to live off the country and, "finding poverty unpleasant," he and his followers supported themselves by robbery.

Although Robert could be arrogantly dictatorial and selfish, although

Roger could be stubbornly independent and arrogant, too, it was obviously foolish for the two talented brothers to remain enemies. There was too much to be done. The conquests of Apulia and Calabria must be completed, that of Sicily begun. The Lombard duchy of Salerno and the independent seaports of Amalfi and Gaeta waited to be united to a Norman state ruled by de Hautevilles. The brothers arranged a reconciliation. But four years later, in 1062, they quarreled again over the division of Calabrian lands. Robert even besieged Roger, and Roger chivalrously rescued Robert from some confused rebels who had captured the Duke but who did not know what to do with him. After some negotiating and even a renewed outburst of fighting, the two arranged a second and final reconciliation. For the rest of his life Roger served loyally as Robert's feudal subordinate, and after Robert's death as the feudal vassal of Robert's son.

The continuous wars of the de Hauteville brothers with their battles, sieges, raids, their conspiracies, revolts, treacheries, their diplomacy, propaganda and politics, present far too intricate a tangle for unraveling here.* Sometimes they had to wage several wars at once, trying to conquer foreign foes with one hand and to suppress rebellious barons with the other. Inevitably, many of their campaigns were small and sporadic.

Robert de Hauteville's long march to glory was seldom interrupted by a peaceful moment. In 1060 Robert captured the city of Reggio on the toe of the Italian boot, which meant the completion of the conquest of Calabria. That same year Roger commanded an exploratory raid into Sicily. It was the beginning of a war against the Moslem rulers of Sicily which did not end until 1191 with the capture of Malta. In 1071 Robert and Roger together captured the city of Bari in Apulia on the Adriatic coast, the last stronghold of the Byzantines. The city was so well fortified and the Byzantine troops fought so stubbornly that the siege lasted for two years and seven months.

The conquest of Sicily was difficult. The Saracens had ruled there for 200 years. If they had not been divided among rival emirates the

---

* A clear, fascinating and detailed narrative of the Norman conquests in Italy and Sicily may be found in John Julius Norwich's splendid books, *The Other Conquest* and *The Kingdom in the Sun.*

conquest might not have been possible. The Normans first landed as the ally of the Emir of Siracusa. But soon afterward Robert and Roger were emphasizing their divine mission to rescue the Christian inhabitants of Sicily from Moslem rule. For ten years the Normans made little progress. In spite of their spectacular victories and their heroic courage, they were too few.

After one of his most brilliant victories Roger had these words inscribed on his shield:

> The right hand of God gave me courage.
> The right hand of God raised me up.

Finally in 1072 Robert and Roger together captured the city of Palermo, then one of the great Moslem cities of the world. At a victory mass held in the cathedral of Santa Maria, which had been hastily stripped of the symbols of Islam which had transformed it into a mosque, the Normans felt such deep religious emotion that they believed a miracle took place. A monk of Monte Cassino wrote: "There were some good Christians who heard in this church the voices of the angels in dulcet chanting . . . and at times the church appeared illuminated by the light of God, more resplendent than any worldly light."

Palermo was more splendid and civilized than any Christian city in Europe at that time, except perhaps Constantinople. In the Arab world it was surpassed in size and importance only by Cairo and Cordova. It was both a commercial and a cultural center. Palermo had 300 mosques, palaces, markets, financial exchanges, streets devoted to various crafts, a fine harbor and one of the first paper mills in Europe. The population may have numbered as many as 250,000.

Into this magnificent city Robert and Roger rode in triumph. Robert Guiscard had promised not to molest the persons, property, religion or laws of the Moslems. He kept his promise. There was no massacre. There was no discrimination against Moslems who accepted the new regime. Robert de Hauteville, for thirteen years Duke of Sicily only in name, was now the ruler of Sicily in fact. He reserved Palermo for his personal rule and had coins minted whose inscriptions in Arabic read, "King of Sicily." Robert gave most of Sicily to Roger as his personal feudal fief.

The Great Count of Sicily, as Roger became widely known, was a statesman who knew how to establish a regime which did not discriminate against anyone because of his religion. Roger permitted all the mosques to remain open as places of Moslem worship except those which originally had been Christian churches. Islamic law and Islamic courts were left undisturbed. Arabic was declared an official language, and so were Latin, Greek and Norman French. Roger also took care to employ the labor and craftsmanship of Moslems and to make use of the brains and experience of Moslem government officials.

So enlightened, tolerant a policy would be remarkable at any period in the world's history. In the eleventh century, when hatred of Moslems was almost an article of religious faith, it was extraordinary.

From the conquest of Palermo the Norman victory in Sicily was certain. But in several districts Moslem resistance was so desperate, and so few were Roger's troops, that the final conquest took nineteen more years. One other factor added to Roger's troubles. It was a revolt of Norman barons granted estates in Sicily. Robert and Roger had prudently refrained from granting them dangerously large domains. But a powerful faction of ambitious barons revolted anyway. The participation of Roger's bastard son, Jordan, whom he loved, in the rebellion made it all the more painful to Roger.

At first Roger tried to be calm and temperate, saying that Jordan's treason was merely youthful folly which should be forgiven. So Jordan wisely surrendered to his affectionate father. Then Roger summoned Jordan's twelve chief accomplices. These, naïvely thinking that they would share the mercy granted to Jordan, with fatuous folly answered Roger's summons.

Until then Roger had never been responsible for any particularly notable deed of cruelty. Now he was remorseless. The property of all twelve guilty rebels was confiscated in a declaration which was implemented later. Then one by one each man was thrown to the ground and held there while red-hot irons were thrust into his eyes. Roger even threatened to do the same to Jordan if he should participate in any further revolts. In the eleventh century blinding was a common, if terrible, punishment for traitors. If knights, whose only skill was war, were deprived of their lands and then blinded, they had no way of supporting themselves except to beg at some church door.

Roger built many castles and monasteries in Sicily. On the mainland Robert did the same. And the cities of southern Italy also built admirable churches. The number of Norman churches still standing in southern Italy and in Sicily is a wonder and a delight. In Apulia alone the traveler finds them in Lucera and Troia, in Ruvo and Bitonto, and like jewels on a string along the Adriatic coast in Barletta, Trani, Bisceglie, Molfetta and Bari. To those not expert in the niceties of Romanesque architecture they seem surprisingly similar to the Norman Romanesque churches of England. The beautiful rose window of the cathedral of Troia would seem appropriate in many an English church. But the severe simplicity and pure white stone of the Trani cathedral seem unique unto themselves. And the site of the cathedral of Trani, within a few feet of the blue waters of the harbor, is so unusual and lovely that cathedral and harbor together remain vivid in the memory. There are so few cathedrals right beside the sea.

The Norman cathedrals of Italy are always simple in their overall design, but they are ornamented with a host of stone statues, some of them grotesquely amusing in the medieval fashion. Superbly carved bronze doors distinguish a few of the cathedrals, tokens of the time, money and loving care which went into their construction. Some of the finest, of course, were built later, in the reign of Roger's great son, Roger II, and of his sons. The Normans may have been poor Christians; nevertheless, their Christianity inspired them to build cathedrals of enduring beauty.

Just before undertaking the long siege of Bari, Robert Guiscard completed the suppression of a four-year revolt led by three of his nephews. Shortly after the capture of Palermo, Robert quelled another baronial revolt. His merciful forgiveness of the leaders he considered traitors displayed Robert's character at its best. Always genial, cheerful and confident, the Duke of Apulia possessed a kindly charm which was almost sunny.

In 1073 the important city of Amalfi voluntarily acknowledged Robert Guiscard as its lord. In the same year a fiery monk and ecclesiastical reformer and politician named Hildebrand became pope as Gregory VII. One of Gregory's first decisions was to break the Church's alliance with Robert, to excommunicate him and to wage war against him. The curious story of the bizarre relations between the mighty Duke of Apulia and the domineering Vicar of Christ will be told in the chapter devoted to Gregory.

As Robert Guiscard grew older, neither his astounding physical energy nor his insatiable lust for conquest diminished. In 1076 he attacked the city of Salerno and captured it the following year. Thereafter he made Salerno his capital. In 1078 and 1079 he suppressed yet another rebellion of his Apulian barons. And in 1080 Pope Gregory switched his policies again and made peace and an alliance with Robert, who then began preparations for an amphibious operation across the Adriatic to attack the Byzantine empire.

In May of 1081 Robert ferried his large army across the Adriatic and besieged Durazzo. The Emperor Alexius Comnenus led an army all the way from Constantinople to drive out the invaders. In a fiercely con- tested battle outside the walls of Durazzo, Robert Guiscard defeated the Byzantine army so completely that the Emperor Alexius was forced to flee virtually alone. But Durazzo stubbornly held out until the following February before it was forced to surrender. Robert led his triumphant army eastward, intent on capturing the imperial city of Constantinople itself. But in April of 1082 frustrating news reached him. All over south- ern Italy Norman barons, probably bribed by Alexius, were in revolt, some of them for the fourth time. And in Rome Pope Gregory was be- sieged by the German emperor.

The Duke of Apulia's temper was famous. His fury at such news must have been monumental. But he had no choice. Leaving his army under the command of his capable son Bohemund, Robert hurried back to Apulia, collected a small force and rode to Rome. There he found that the Germans had retired to Tuscany and his aid was no longer needed. So Robert marched back to Apulia and once again began the familiar and wearisome task of suppressing rebels. It took him until June of 1083. It would have taken longer if Roger had not come from Sicily to help his brother.

For nearly another year Robert was busy restoring proper order in his extensive domains and in gathering an army large enough to drive the Germans permanently away from Rome. How Robert rescued Pope Gregory from the clutches of the German emperor will also be told in Gregory's chapter. It wasn't until the autumn of 1084 that Robert Guiscard could sail for Greece to resume his interrupted war with the Byzantine empire. It was high time that he came. Bohemund had won several victories, but he had lacked pay for his men and adequate supplies. Many of his troops had deserted, lured away by Alexius' bribes. Bohemund had lost one major battle and most of the territory conquered by the Normans.

After suffering two naval defeats by a combined Venetian and Byzantine fleet, Robert Guiscard won his last great victory, in which he completely demolished the enemy fleet and captured the island of Corfu. Robert spent the winter on Corfu and watched in dismay while a large part of his army sickened and died because of an unnamed epidemic— probably dysentery or typhoid. And in July of 1085 the great Duke of Apulia, Calabria and Sicily succumbed to the dread disease himself and died on the island of Cephalonia.

He was either sixty-nine or seventy years old. His body was taken back to the country he had conquered and ruled with such indomitable determination and buried in the town of Venosa beside the tombs of his famous brothers, William Iron-Arm, Drogo and Humphrey. An inscription carved over Robert's tomb said, "Here lies Guiscard, terror of the world." The tombs and the inscription are gone today. But Robert de Hauteville is not forgotten. His sins were many, but his abilities and achievements were so amazing that his legend lived on for hundreds of years in Italy.

Giovanni Villani, the Florentine chronicler, writing in the fourteenth century, told this story about Robert Guiscard and the leper:

"This Robert Guiscard, Duke of Apulia, was once on a hunting excursion, and he followed the quarry into the depths of a wood, his companions not knowing what had become of him, or where he was, or what he was doing; and then Robert, seeing the night approaching, leaving the beast which he was pursuing, sought to return home; and turning, he found in the wood a leper, who importunately asked alms of him; and when he had said I know not what in reply, the leper said again that the anguish he endured availed him nought, yet him were liefer to carry any weight or burden; and when Robert asked of the leper what he would have, he said, 'I desire that you will put me behind you on your horse'; lest abandoned in the wood, peradventure the beasts would devour him.

"Then Robert cheerfully received him behind him on his horse; and as they rode forward, the leper said to Robert—great baron as he was— 'My hands are so icy cold, that unless I may cherish them against thy flesh, I cannot keep myself on horseback.' Then Robert granted the leper to put his hands boldly under his clothing, and comfort his flesh and his members without any fear; and when yet a third time the leper bespoke his pity, he put him upon his saddle, and he, sitting behind him, embraced the leper, and led him to his own chamber and put him into his own bed, and sat him in it with right good care to the end that he might repose; no one of his household perceived aught thereof.

"And when the banquet of supper was spread, having told his wife that he had lodged the leper in his bed, his wife incontinent went to the chamber to know if the poor sufferer would sup. The chamber, albeit there were no perfumes therein, she found as fragrant as if it had been full of sweet-smelling things, such that neither Robert nor his wife had ever known so sweet scents, and the leper, whom they had come hither to seek, they did not find, whereat the husband and the wife marveled beyond measure at so great a wonder; but with reverence and with fear, both one and the other asked God to reveal to them what this might be.

"And the following day Christ appeared in a vision to Robert, saying, that if He had shown Himself to him in the form of a leper, it was to make trial of his piety, and He announced to him that by his wife he should have sons, whereof one should be emperor, the next king and the third duke."

This edifying story is a fine example of the way the medieval appetite for marvels and miracles inspired legends about famous men. The story-teller who first credited this miraculous appearance of Christ to Robert Guiscard did not know and would not have cared that none of his sons became either a king or an emperor.

How much Dante knew about the character and career of Robert

Guiscard is unknown. But in the eighteenth canto of the *Paradiso* Dante put the mighty conqueror, who fought against two popes and even sold Roman citizens into slavery, in paradise in the company of Charlemagne, Roland and Godfrey of Bouillon, the leader of the First Crusade. Perhaps Dante remembered only that it was Robert and his brother Roger who destroyed the Moslem rule over Sicily and restored the island to its proper place in Christendom.

IV

The Holy Satan

He was a little man, swarthy and ugly, with short legs, a protruding stomach and a weak, whispering voice. His origin was humble and obscure and his learning was much inferior to that of many of the great prelates of his time. But Hildebrand, the powerful advisor to six popes, who reigned on Saint Peter's throne for twelve years as Pope Gregory VII, bestrode his narrow world like a Colossus. He transformed the character and pretensions of the Papacy, he tried heroically to reform the Church and the clergy according to his own fiercely held opinions, he instigated numerous wars and unsuccessfully planned others, he engaged in a furious propaganda and military campaign against the German emperor, he excommunicated scores of persons, and he played a spectacular role in the politics of Italy.

The demonic force of Hildebrand's personality dominated those around him. The awesome power of his inflexible determination was a force of revolutionary impact.

The facts about Hildebrand's birth, parentage and childhood are lost in the dark confusion of the eleventh century. He was probably born about the year 1023. A doubtful tradition has it that he was born in the village of Sovana near Siena, the son of a peasant carpenter named

Bonizo. A somewhat more doubtful tradition has it that Hildebrand was a child prodigy and that miraculous flames sprang forth from his head.

Hildebrand was educated in the monastery of Santa Maria on the Aventine in Rome and thus began life as a monk. Whether Hildebrand ever formally joined a monastic order is uncertain. But his contemporaries believed that he had been a monk.

As a young man he was warned by Peter Damian, a fiery and contentious saint, not to eat too many onions. Many years later, after Hildebrand as pope had plunged much of the medieval world into controversy and war, Damian called him "my holy Satan." Writing to Hildebrand in a vein which curiously foreshadows the famous words Shakespeare put into the mouth of Cardinal Wolsey, Damian said: "Thy will has ever been a command to me—evil but lawful. Would that I had always served God and Saint Peter as faithfully as I have served thee."

While Hildebrand was an adolescent and a young man in his early twenties the Papacy was disgraced by several of the worst popes in its long history. Their conduct was so shameful that it seemed as if the Papacy itself was only an important office for which dissolute and avaricious Roman nobles contended. Finally the man known to history as Gregory VI actually bought the Papacy from a notoriously evil pope for the sole purpose of reform. But the wicked pope changed his mind and a rival pope also claimed the papal throne, so that there were three contending popes at once. Such a spectacle must have made a powerful impression on the devout and ambitious Hildebrand.

Nor could Hildebrand have been any the less shocked by the arrival in Italy in 1046 of the young, pious and powerful German Emperor Henry III for the express purpose of reforming the Church by force of arms. Henry briskly deposed all three popes and installed a pope of his own choice. Hildebrand, who had been associated with Gregory VI in some unknown capacity, accompanied that well-intentioned man into his German exile.

Before he was done, Henry III installed four reforming German bishops as popes. The third was Leo IX, whom we have already met, who brought Hildebrand back with him when he went to Rome. The reason why Henry could so cavalierly make his own friends pope lay in the chaotic methods by which popes were elected. In theory they were chosen by the Roman clergy and the Roman people with the consent of the emperor. Since the emperor was usually far away in Germany, popes were often chosen by rioting mobs or by the armed might of a noble Roman faction. Hildebrand may have acquired his violent prejudice against German emperors presuming to choose bishops when he saw Henry III depose and install popes with such dispatch.

For twenty-five years, from 1048 and the coronation of Leo IX until 1073 and his own coronation as pope, Hildebrand was an important executive in the papal establishment. He profoundly influenced policy and is generally credited with responsibility for major decisions and reforms. He was particularly influential during the reign of Pope Nicholas II (1058–1061), whose election Hildebrand had been instrumental in arranging. Nicholas began his reign under difficulties and had to drive out of Rome a rival pope, Benedict X. Benedict took refuge in the nearby fortified town of Galeria and defied Nicholas. Something had to be done and it was probably Hildebrand's idea to enlist the military aid of the Normans.

In any case, Hildebrand journeyed to Capua and obtained help from the Norman leader Richard of Capua. Hildebrand returned to Rome with some 300 Norman knights and by March of 1059 Pope Nicholas and Hildebrand were in command of an army besieging Benedict in Galeria. The Normans systematically laid waste all the territory around the city, but were unable to capture it. Finally Benedict surrendered after he had been promised that he could live freely in Rome and keep his property there.

But once the rival pope was humbly back in Rome as a mere bishop, Hildebrand had him dragged to the church of San Giovanni in Laterano. There poor Benedict was arrayed in full pontifical robes and before the high altar stripped of them. He had to sign a confession of his sins and was deposed from his rank as a bishop. And then after his public humiliation he was thrown into a dungeon, where he languished until his death twenty years later. Hildebrand, whose courage never failed, who was an idealist and a sincere reformer of a fanatical medieval sort, could be as ruthless and treacherous as any secular ruler.

In August of the same year, 1059, Pope Nicholas journeyed to the Norman stronghold of Melfi in northern Apulia and officially invested

Robert de Hauteville with the duchy of Apulia, with Calabria and with the island of Sicily, on which Robert had not yet set foot. Nicholas and Hildebrand, who had negotiated this investiture, had no right to do anything of the kind. These territories had never even been claimed by the Papacy because they were ruled by Byzantine emperors or Moslem emirs. Nevertheless, the formal ceremony had its sound expedient reasons. Robert, a conqueror with no proper title to his conquests, received the official approval of the Church in a sacred ceremony. Nicholas conferred a favor on the most powerful of the Norman leaders, secured an ally far more conveniently situated than the distant German emperor, and established a claim of feudal suzerainty over southern Italy and Sicily.

Also in 1059 came the most important event in Nicholas' reign and the first major reform accomplished by Hildebrand. At a council in the Lateran, rules were decreed for the election of popes. Thenceforth the only voters would be cardinals. The Papacy would be a Church office only, theoretically removed from the partisan violence of the Roman nobles and people and from the interference of German emperors. The historical importance of this declaration of papal independence was enormous. But the decree was soon violated—when Hildebrand himself became pope.

During the twelve-year reign of Nicholas' successor, Alexander II, Hildebrand, a cardinal and an archdeacon, completely dominated the Pope. Saint Peter Damian wrote bitterly to Hildebrand: "You made him pope; he made you a god." Hildebrand was even commonly called "The Lord of the Lord Pope."

Near the end of Alexander's reign Hildebrand demonstrated how strongly he believed in religious discipline by publicly applauding a notorious bishop who had punished some rebellious monks by blinding them and cutting out their tongues. Hildebrand's approval of such cruelty is not so surprising in a churchman, who soon would become pope and centuries later a saint, as it might first appear. It is really only an example of the prevailing attitude of the times, the universal acceptance of cruelty as a matter of course in the eleventh century.

After the death of Pope Alexander in April of 1073 Hildebrand conducted the funeral service in the Lateran church. In the midst of the ceremony many in the crowd of priests and prelates began to shout: "Hildebrand is pope! Saint Peter chooses the archdeacon Hildebrand!" Hildebrand tried to mount the pulpit and decline the honor—whether sincerely will never be known. Some historians believe he connived in a scheme for a clerical *coup d'état;* others believe his own protestations of reluctance.

Suddenly a cardinal, Hugh the White, who had been excommunicated for simony by Alexander and who therefore should not even have been present at a sacred service, shouted above the clamor: "Well know ye, beloved brethren, that since the days of the blessed Leo this tried and prudent archdeacon has exalted the Roman see, and delivered this city from many perils. Wherefore, since we cannot find anyone better qualified for the government of the Church and the protection of the city, we the bishops and cardinals, with one voice elect him as the pastor and bishop of your souls."

The crowd shouted again: "It is the will of Saint Peter. Hildebrand is pope." They rushed upon Hildebrand, hurried him along to the Church of San Pietro in Vinculi, threw the scarlet robe over his shoulders, crowned him with the papal tiara and enthroned him in the sacred chair. Hildebrand wept—perhaps, as he claimed, out of humble reluctance, more likely out of excitement. Several days after his uncanonical election Hildebrand referred to "this burden imposed upon me against my will and with great reluctance on my part." He wrote, "They rushed upon me like madmen and with violent hands forced me into the seat of apostolic government."

The new pope took the name of Gregory VII and immediately set to work. Gregory, whose will was adamant, whose pride was monumental, who could not conceive that anything could be said for an opponent's point of view, was subject to fits of depression and to transient spasms of humility. Shortly after his coronation he wrote:

"For we perceive what cares surround us, what a load the burden we have assumed presses on us, so that when the consciousness of our own weaknesses begins to trouble our soul we desire rather the repose of death in Christ than to live in the midst of such dangers. The very thought of the duties entrusted to us weighs upon us so that were we not supported by confidence, first in God and then in the prayers of spiritually minded men, our heart would fail us under the burden of our responsibilities."

Two years later Gregory was complaining of his hard lot: "What anxiety oppresses me, what toil renewed day by day wearies and disturbs me . . . my misery . . . my great suffering. . . . A vast and universal grief and sadness walls me about. . . I am crushed by a thousand woes and suffer a living death."

Without much interest in theology, with little tact or insight into politics or into individual character, Gregory never hesitated to do what he thought right. What he thought right was always the glorification of the Papacy and of the pope (who just happened to be himself), the reform of the Church and the expansion of the temporal power of the Church. All this was to be done in the name of the freedom of the Church and of righteousness.

The reforms Gregory imperiously proclaimed had been advocated before, but never so emphatically. There were three of them, each of revolutionary impact. The first reform was to abolish simony, which was the purchase or sale of ecclesiastical offices. Since the Church was enormously wealthy with abbeys and bishoprics owning huge areas, since abbots and bishops were often worldly and ambitious aristocrats, it was inevitable that simony should flourish. Men did not go into the Church solely for religious reasons; as often they became priests because they coveted the wealth and power available to the more successful careerists. Bishops ruled cities, commanded armies and advised kings.

Gregory's second reform was to abolish clerical marriage, or concubinage as he called it. In the eleventh century many priests were married and many others lived with women who were in effect common-law wives. It was customary, normal morality and shocked hardly anybody. But Gregory was determined that Church revenues should not be spent to support priests' families, and that the children of priests should not inherit Church funds or Church offices. The clergy must be a separate caste morally superior to ordinary mortals and completely subservient to papal commands. So Gregory commanded all members of the clergy to repudiate their wives or mistresses and to live celibate lives.

In a synod held in March of 1074 only a few months after his coronation Gregory declared invalid all sacraments performed by simoniacal or married priests. Here was a revolutionary doctrine, one that has never been officially accepted by the Church: that the efficacy of the sacraments required the priests who performed them to be free of sins denounced by the current Pope.

All over Europe the clergy protested that they would not repudiate their wives, heartlessly declaring them concubines and their children bastards. In Germany a synod of married clergy assembled in October of 1074 at Erfurt and formally declared:

"The pope must be a heretic or a madman. Has he forgotten the saying of the Lord? All cannot fulfill his word. The apostle says, 'Let him that cannot contain marry.' He would compel all men to live like angels. Let him take care, while he would do violence to nature, he break not all bounds which restrain from fornication and every uncleanness. They had rather abandon their priesthood than their wives, and then let the pope, who thought men too groveling for him, see if he can find angels to govern the Church."

The third reform Gregory furiously championed was the abolition of lay investiture of bishops. Gregory's dedication to what he called "the freedom of the Church" required that bishops should never be invested by secular rulers. The symbolism of the investiture ceremony must be entirely religious and bishops must be responsible solely to the pope. This was even more controversial than his other reforms because for centuries bishops had been appointed by kings and had ruled large areas as feudal vassals of kings. If they were not subject to their secular rulers, no medieval monarch could rule; too much of his kingdom would be ruled directly by bishops and indirectly by the pope. What made it worse from the monarch's point of view was that Church property paid no taxes to the king, but paid substantial taxes to the pope. No medieval ruler could accept such a devastating blow at his authority as the abolition of lay investiture, and none did.

A singularly provocative comment on Gregory's position in the lay-investiture controversy was made by the great German nineteenth-century historian Ferdinand Gregorovius: "Gregory desired to deliver the Church from her dependence on the State and yet maintain her in her enormous possessions. He would not have understood had a well-meaning idealist informed him that the shortest way to the emancipation of the priesthood from the political power would have been to make it again poor and spiritual as the apostles had been." Later popes did not understand such an idea either when Saint Francis tried to apply it in the rules of his order.

Before telling the dramatic story of Gregory's effort to prohibit lay investiture in the lands ruled by the German emperor, we must consider two of Gregory's political decisions which directly concerned Italy. He had scarcely settled himself comfortably on the papal throne before he repudiated the alliance with Robert Guiscard, which he had negotiated in Nicholas' reign, and made one with Richard of Capua, who was not as powerful as Robert. The reason for this reversal of policy is unknown. But it was foolish. It involved Gregory in a war with Robert which he could not possibly win and which Robert could easily win whenever he wished to devote the time and effort necessary. Historians have speculated whether some raids on Church territory made by Robert's brother and nephew could have provoked Gregory to such a folly, or whether he just disliked having so powerful and unscrupulous a ruler as a neighbor.

More probable was Gregory's sense of security caused by his firm alliance with Matilda, Countess of Tuscany, who ruled much of the Po valley as well as Tuscany. In any case, Gregory excommunicated Robert three times, in 1074, 1075 and 1078.

In 1074, the year after his coronation, Gregory sent letters to dukes, marquises and counts in Burgundy, Savoy and Italy and to the young German Emperor, Henry IV, summoning them to join him in a crusade which would free the Byzantine empire from the threat of the Seljuk Turks and would also deliver Jerusalem from Moslem rule. But before these worthy goals could be achieved the crusaders would help Gregory conquer Robert Guiscard. There were two unusual aspects to this call for a crusade. It was the first crusading appeal ever made by a pope, twenty-one years before Pope Urban II launched the First Crusade with his celebrated oration at the Council of Clermont in France. And Gregory, who was habitually bellicose and delighted in war, proposed to lead the crusade himself as its military commander.

Although few foreign volunteers responded to Gregory's summons, enough Italian troops assembled for Gregory to feel confident. He sent a message to Robert demanding that he meet him at the town of Benevento to humble himself before papal authority. Robert, as suave a diplomat as he was mighty a warrior, accepted the invitation to a conference, saying that his conscience was clear and that it would be an honor to meet the Pope. He went to Benevento and encamped outside the city for three days. But Gregory never appeared. His crusading army had broken up in inter-city squabbles and had dispersed. For Gregory it was a disaster and a humiliation. His wars had a way of turning out badly.

Gregory VII's reforms and his politics were all inherent in his conception of the Papacy and its role in Europe. With passionate conviction he believed that the Church was a divine institution and that the pope was a divinely chosen successor to Saint Peter. All clerics were the pope's direct subjects. All secular rulers were inferior to the pope, whose duty it was to judge them, chastise them, or depose them if they were contumacious. Gregory dreamed of a theocratic autocracy ruling all Europe: the pope would not rule directly, but through secular rulers of whom he approved, and who would act according to his instructions.

This grandiose conception was not entirely new; but Gregory was the first pope who persistently tried to implement it. As the vice-regent of God, Gregory claimed that he had the right and duty to depose bad kings and to choose among rival rulers. "Who," wrote Gregory in a fiery letter to the Bishop of Mentz, "is ignorant that kings and princes had their origin in those who, ignorant of God, and covering themselves with pride, violence and perfidy, in fact nearly every crime . . . claimed to rule over their peers in blind lust and intolerable arrogance?"

Gregory's determination to be an absolute monarch over the clergy and, because of his power to depose, as good as an absolute monarch over secular rulers inspired violent protests all over Europe. "This dangerous man," wrote the Archbishop of Bremen, "wants to order the bishops about as though they were servants on his estates; and if they do not do all his commands, they have to go to Rome, or else they are suspended without due process of law." Other German bishops said they "disliked being ordered about like bailiffs."

Gregory's thoughts about the Papacy were summed up in a collection of twenty-seven statements included in his official register. Among the most interesting are these:

That the Roman Church was founded by God alone.

That the pope may depose persons in their absence.

That the pope may depose or reinstate bishops.

That the pope may depose emperors.

That the pope is the only man whose feet shall be kissed by all princes.

That the pope must not be judged by anyone.

That the Roman Church has never erred, nor, as witness Scripture, will it ever do so.

That the pope can absolve the subjects of the wicked from their fealty to him.

Gregory's claim to be the feudal as well as the spiritual lord over every European ruler was accepted by a number of the lesser states: Dalmatia, Hungary, Capua and Saxony. But William the Conqueror refused Gregory's request for an acknowledgment of fealty: "I have not, nor will I swear fealty, which was never sworn by any of my predecessors to yours." William created bishops and abbots to suit himself and was absolute lord of the English and Norman prelates. This was just the issue of lay investiture which Gregory fought stubbornly to abolish in the Holy Roman Empire.

Gregory could be expedient, cynical and inconsistent. William was powerful and far away. The German emperor was much less powerful, only a feudal overlord opposed by many of his powerful vassals. And Germany was nearer. So Gregory discreetly ignored lay investiture by William in England and Normandy and plunged Germany and Italy into terrible wars over the lay investitures of the Emperor Henry IV.

Henry IV was the son of the Henry III who had so casually deposed and appointed popes—reason enough for Gregory to detest him. But he was the second most important and sacred man in Europe. The Holy Roman Empire, of which Germans had been emperors since Charlemagne, was universally considered the direct inheritor and continuation of the ancient Roman empire. In the Middle Ages men yearned, at least in theory, for unity. Just as there had to be one Church ruled by one supreme pontiff, so there had to be a vague unity called Christendom and one secular ruler superior to all others. The Empire did not include such important states as England and France. Nevertheless, the emperor outranked every other ruler in Europe.

A mystical, indefinable aura of sanctity enveloped the concepts of Empire and emperor. The emperor was supposed to maintain peace (a naïve and impossible notion) and somehow represent God in secular affairs. The Empire and emperor were not nearly as holy as the Church and the pope, but in an inferior way they were holy, too. So when Gregory VII tried to enforce the abolition of lay investiture in the Empire, to depose the emperor, and to establish his own feudal superiority over the Empire, he was deliberately attempting to eliminate the traditional sanctity of the Empire.

Gregory became pope in 1073 at the age of fifty or thereabouts. Henry IV was then a young man of twenty-three. He had been elected King of the Romans by the German princes when he was only four years old and his father still lived. That was the title assumed by the elected king of Germany who would become emperor. The king could not rightly be called emperor until he had been crowned in Rome by the pope. Yet he was emperor in fact if not in ceremonial anointing and was often incorrectly called emperor.

An orphan at six, Henry endured a miserable childhood and adolescence, bullied by imperious bishops, forced at sixteen to marry Bertha, daughter of the Marquis of Turin, much against his will. Henry disliked his wife and in youthful protest maintained a bevy of concubines and caused much scandal. Why is mysterious. Most medieval monarchs were joyfully promiscuous and no one objected. When he was nineteen Henry tried in vain to obtain a divorce and then suddenly reformed and became a faithful and loving husband. By then he was ruling, but not very effectively.

Tall, handsome, clever, eloquent and brave, Henry was the very model of a medieval monarch. Yet he was cast by the fates in a tragic role. It was his misfortune to be the contemporary of Gregory VII and to come into conflict with him when he was still young, hot-tempered and rash. Henry was to know defeats, failures and betrayals. But he was as courageous and obstinate as Gregory himself and a lot craftier. In unscrupulousness the two men were evenly matched. Henry fought stubbornly to maintain the freedom of the imperial monarchy from the temporal power of the Church, a cause which was to be fiercely defended by two of Henry's most celebrated successors, the emperors Frederick Barbarossa and Frederick II.

Henry IV had a stronger reason to oppose the abolition of lay investiture than any other ruler. In Germany half the land and half the wealth were controlled by bishops and abbots. If the prelates owed no allegiance to him for their huge domains, but were to be subjects of a papal monarchy, then his title would be meaningless and his authority destroyed.

Henry raised no objection to Gregory's first decrees deposing all simoniacal clerics and forbidding married priests to celebrate mass. He did not dare. The Saxons had been in revolt and had just imposed a humiliating peace upon him. But in 1075 the Saxons revolted again and in June Henry won a tremendous victory. His position in Germany seemed secure. Now he could reply to the hateful decree against lay investiture Gregory had promulgated in February:

"If anyone in future receives a bishopric or abbey from the hands of any layman, he is under no circumstances to be ranked among the bishops, and we exclude him from the grace of Saint Peter. . . . And if any emperor, king, prince or any lay power presumes to invest anyone with a bishopric or any ecclesiastical office, let him know that he will therewith incur the sentence of excommunication."

Gregory VII challenged Henry IV further by excommunicating for simony five bishops who were Henry's trusted advisors. Gregory suspended or deposed other bishops and removed the Bishop of Bamberg. In his turn Henry defied Gregory by investing a court favorite as the new Bishop of Bamberg in flagrant violation of the new decree. Henry also appointed other bishops to sees in Italy. Finally, in December Gregory sent Henry a letter of protest accompanied by a verbal message threatening to excommunicate him if he did not submit. The year ended in ominous tension between Pope and Emperor and in an extraordinary crisis for Gregory in Rome.

The crisis is sometimes called "the outrage of Cencius." Cencius Crescenti was the Prefect of Rome, at that time the highest municipal office. A friend of the Normans, Cencius had been commander of the Castle of Sant' Angelo. But when Gregory turned on Robert Guiscard and excommunicated him Cencius tried to hold the castle, was captured, condemned to death and then reprieved. He hated Gregory, as did many others. Whether he acted in concert with partisans of Henry's, or whether he hoped to surprise and please Henry and win a great reward, is not known.

Henry Hart Milman, Dean of Saint Paul's and distinguished Victorian historian, wrote in his *History of Latin Christianity* an account of the Cencius episode which deserves quotation in full:

"On the eve of Christmas day the rain had poured down in torrents. The Romans remained in their houses; the Pope, with but a few ecclesiastics, was keeping the holy vigil in the remote Church of Santa Maria Maggiore. The wild night suited the wild purpose of Cencius. The Pope was in the act of administering the Holy Communion, when a fierce shout of triumph and a shriek of terror sounded through the church. The soldiers of Cencius burst in, swept along the nave, dashed down the rails, rushed to the altar, and seized the Pontiff. One fatal blow might have ended the life of Hildebrand and changed the course of human events; it glanced aside, and only wounded his forehead. Bleeding, stripped of his holy vestments, but patient and gentle, the Pope made no resistance; he was dragged away, mounted behind one of the soldiers, and imprisoned in a strong tower. The rumor ran rapidly through the city; all the night trumpets pealed, bells tolled. The clergy, who were officiating in the different churches, broke off their services, and ran about the streets summoning the populace to rescue and revenge; soldiers rushed to the gates to prevent the prisoner from being carried out of town. At the dawn of morn the people assembled in the Capitol, ignorant whether the Pope was dead or alive. When the place of his imprisonment was known, they thronged to the siege; engines were brought from all quarters; the tottering walls began to yield. Cencius shuddered at his own deed. One faithful friend and one noble matron had followed the Pope into his dungeon. The man had covered his shivering body with furs, and was cherishing his chilled feet in his own bosom; the woman had staunched the blood, had bound up the wound in his head, and sat weeping beside him. Cencius, as cowardly as cruel, had no course left but to throw himself at the feet of the Pontiff, and to implore his mercy. In the most humiliating language he confessed his sins, his sacrilege, his impiety. The Pope, thus insulted, thus wounded, thus hardly escaped from a miserable death, maintained throughout the mild dignity and self-command of a Christian Pontiff. His wisdom might indeed lead him to dread the despair of a ruffian. 'Thine injuries against myself I freely pardon. Thy sins against God, against His mother, His apostles, and His whole Church must be expiated. Go on a pilgrimage to Jerusalem, and if thou returnst alive, present thyself to us, and be reconciled with God. As thou hast been an example of sin, so be thou of repentance!' Christ himself might seem to be speaking in his Vice-regent.

"Gregory was brought out; he made a motion to the people to arrest the fury with which they were rushing to storm the tower; it was mistaken for a sign of distress. They broke down, they clambered over, the walls. Gregory, yet stained with blood, stood in the midst of his deliverers; he was carried in triumph to the church from which he had been dragged, finished the service, and returned to the Lateran. Cencius and his kindred fled."

Milman's pious rhetoric may seem quaintly Victorian, but he told his story well. Yet other details are worth recording. During Gregory's night-long ordeal Cencius' two sisters shrilly denounced him and repeatedly shouted obscenities at him. And Cencius, whose life had been saved by Gregory's mercy, who had promised to make a pilgrimage to Jerusalem in expiation of his crime, continued to behave like the old-fashioned villain he was. When he reached the first milestone out of Rome, Cencius mockingly repudiated any idea of going to Jerusalem, holed up in one of his castles, and began a series of unopposed raids on the lands of the Church.

Early in January of the new year, 1076, Gregory sent Henry a patronizing letter: "This decree (however some may presume to call it an insupportable burden or intolerable oppression) we esteem a necessary law; and Christian kings and people are bound directly to observe it. As thou art the highest in dignity and power, so should thou surpass others in devotion to Christ. If, however, thou didst consider this abrogation of a bad custom hard or unjust to thyself, thou shouldst have sent to our presence some of the wisest and most religious of thy realm, to persuade us, in our condescension, to mitigate its force in some way not inconsistent with the honor of God and the salvation of men's souls. We exhort thee in our parental love, to prefer the honor of Christ to thine own, and to give full liberty to the Church, the Spouse of God."

At the same time, or perhaps a day or two thereafter, Gregory peremptorily summoned Henry to appear in Rome to answer for all his offenses before the tribunal of the Pope, and before a synod of ecclesiastics. If Henry refused to come or if he delayed he would be excommunicated.

This was too much for the proud young Emperor-elect. For a year the conflict between the arrogant Gregory and the hot-tempered Henry had been smoldering. Now it broke out in open flames. Gregory had not even specified what Henry's offenses were. They were, of course, maintaining simoniacal bishops at his court, continuing to invest bishops and refusing to submit on the issue of lay investiture. So Henry in his wrath and the overconfidence inspired by his victory over the Saxons summoned his own synod of German bishops to meet in haste at Worms on Sunday, January 24, 1076. Henry was so furious he forgot to consider that many of the greatest princes of Germany resented his imperious ways and would welcome a promising opportunity to revolt. An older and wiser man might have remembered that Gregory was twenty-five years older than he, with a life expectancy of some ten or twelve years, and that diplomatic letters, dignified protests, arguments about trifles and procedural delays might postpone a final rupture indefinitely. Time and change might prove valuable allies.

At Henry's council at Worms a Roman bishop made a series of false and ridiculous charges against Gregory: licentiousness, cruelty, witchcraft and obtaining the Papacy by bribery and violence. With more pertinence he reminded the bishops quite truly that ancient custom required for the election of a pope the consent of the German emperor—for which Gregory had not even asked. Then Henry proposed that Gregory be deposed. The bishops all signed a deposition decree, and so did the bishops of Lombardy assembled at another council at Piacenza.

His anger still raging, Henry then dictated, or perhaps only signed, one of the famous letters of history:

"Henry, King not by usurpation but by God's ordinance, to Hildebrand, not Pope but false monk.

"By craft thou hast got money, by money influence, by influence the power of the sword; by the sword thou hast mounted the throne of peace, arming subjects against their rulers, bringing bishops appointed by God into contempt, and exposing them to the judgment of the laity. Us, too, consecrated by God, amenable to no judge but God, who can be deposed for no crime but absolute apostasy, thou hast ventured to assail, despising the words of that true pope Saint Peter, 'Fear God! Honor the King!' Thou that honorest not the King fearest not God! Saint Paul held accused even an angel from heaven who should preach another Gospel; this curse falls upon thee who teachest this new doctrine.

"Thus accursed then, thus condemned by the sentence of all our bishops, and by our own, come down! Leave the apostolic throne which thou hast usurped. Let another take the chair of Saint Peter, one who preaches not violence and war, but the sound doctrine of the holy Apostle. I, Henry, by the grace of God King, with all the bishops of my realm, say unto thee, 'Come down! Come down!'"

Seldom has such an insulting letter been addressed to a pope, and this particular pope held perhaps the most exalted conception of his office of any pope in history. Gregory VII identified himself with Saint Peter to the point where he claimed that any injury done, even in thought, to the pope was an injury to Saint Peter. "While we sit in his seat and exercise his power, he himself receives the letters or speeches that are addressed to us." Gregory believed that he acted with all Saint Peter's sacred powers and that it was an act of heresy to oppose him. His favorite biblical quotation was from Jeremiah: "Cursed be the man that keepeth back his sword from blood." Gregory usually added (not at all convincingly) that he did not actually refer to a real sword and to real blood, but to the "rebuking of carnal men."

Before Henry's insolent letter could reach Rome, Gregory called a council of his own which assembled in the Lateran in February. Into that solemn synod over which Gregory was presiding stormed a priest from Parma bringing Henry's abusive letter. He shouted: "The King and bishops of Germany send this mandate. Come down at once from the throne of Saint Peter! Yield up the usurped government of the Roman Church! None must presume to such honor but those chosen by the general voice, and approved by the Emperor."

Turning from the Pope to the horrified prelates, the messenger shouted: "Ye, my brethren, are commanded to present yourselves at the

Feast of Pentecost before the King my master, there to receive a pope and a father; for this man is no pope, but a ravening wolf."

The rash priest would have been lynched on the spot by the papal guards if Gregory had not rushed between him and their drawn swords. Gregory then read aloud Henry's letter and replied to it in an eloquent speech in which he assumed that his decree on lay investiture was that of the entire Church and of Christianity itself.

The synod of some 110 bishops and abbots enthusiastically approved excommunicating Henry and adjourned for the night so that the excommunication could be drafted in suitably righteous language. On the following day a number of letters from German and Lombard bishops arrived apologizing and imploring forgiveness for what they called their enforced assent to Henry's decree deposing Gregory. Then Gregory rose in the council and read aloud Henry's excommunication, which was cast in the form of a prayer to Saint Peter:

"O blessed Peter, Prince of the Apostles, mercifully incline thine ear, we pray, and hear me, thy servant, whom thou hast cherished from infancy and hast delivered until now from the hand of the wicked, who have hated and still hate me for my loyalty to thee. Thou art my witness, as are also My Lady, the Mother of God, and the blessed Paul, thy brother among all the saints, that the Holy Roman Church forced me against my will to be its ruler. I had no thought of ascending thy throne as a robber, nay, rather would I have chosen to end my life as a pilgrim than to seize upon thy place for earthly glory and by devices of this world. Therefore, by thy favor, not by any works of mine, I believe that it is and has been thy will, that the Christian people especially committed to thee should render obedience to me, thy episcopally constituted representative. To me is given by thy grace the power of binding and loosing in Heaven and upon earth.

"Wherefore, relying upon this commission, and for the honor and defense of the Church, in the name of Almighty God, Father, Son and Holy Spirit, through thy power and authority, I deprive King Henry, son of the Emperor Henry, who has rebelled against thy Church with unheard-of audacity, of the government of the whole kingdom of Germany and Italy, and I release all Christian men from the allegiance they have sworn or may swear to him, and I forbid anyone to serve him as king. For it is fitting that he who seeks to diminish the glory of thy Church should lose the glory which he seems to have.

"And, since he has refused to obey as a Christian should or to return to the God whom he has abandoned by taking part with excommunicated persons, has spurned my warnings which I gave him for his soul's welfare, as thou knowest, and has separated himself from thy Church and has tried to rend it asunder, I bind him in the bonds of anathema in thy stead and I bind him thus as commissioned by thee, that the nations may know and be convinced that thou art Peter and that upon thy rock the Son of the living God has built His Church and the gates of Hell shall not prevail against it."

Few formal documents written in the Middle Ages are more typical of the religious ideas of the time than this excommunication written in anger and with absolute certainty of the rightness of the position taken. Gregory represented Saint Peter, who represented Jesus. His decisions were divine laws. If his decisions often applied to secular politics, they were no less divinely inspired.

So Gregory launched a war of words against Henry, and his eloquent words were more persuasive than Henry's, for they invoked all the supernatural powers of the religion which molded the minds of men in an age of general belief in, and fear of, the miraculous authority of the Church and of the pope.

Henry replied by arranging that the bishops who supported him in Germany and Italy excommunicate Gregory. But the force of Gregory's excommunication and the ineffectiveness of Henry's soon became plain. Many of the important princes of Germany deserted Henry, or openly revolted. Most of the German bishops turned against him. Henry, the proud conqueror of the Saxons, was now an outcast in danger of losing his throne.

Pope Gregory grimly kept up his propaganda campaign against Henry in numerous letters, always insisting on his supremacy over kings and emperors: "Why is the king alone excepted from the universal flock committed to the guardianship of Saint Peter? If the pope may judge spiritual persons, how much more must secular persons give an account of their evil deeds before his tribunal? Think they that the royal excels the episcopal dignity?—the former the invention of human pride, the latter of divine holiness; the former ever coveting vain glory, the latter aspiring after heavenly life."

Young Henry IV when he defied Gregory's decrees and his excommunication badly misjudged public opinion, particularly the doubtful loyalty of his principal nobles. On October 16, 1076, the German nobles assembled in the town of Trier on the Rhine, registered their approval of Henry's excommunication and proclaimed that if Henry did not win absolution from Pope Gregory by February 22, 1077 (only four months and a week), they would elect a new German king and emperor-designate to take Henry's place. They also decided to reassemble at Augsburg on February 2, 1077, and invited Gregory to be present. Gregory could then tell them whether he would absolve Henry from his excommunication. If he would not, the princes would proceed to elect someone else with Gregory's personal approval.

Henry was encamped with a few followers across the Rhine at Oppenheim. His plight seemed desperate. The German princes and the Pope were united against him. No emperor had ever been excommunicated before. In southern Italy the mighty Robert Guiscard blandly ignored his excommunications. But Henry's excommunication was much more serious. It provided the German princes with a fine pretext and justification for deposing him. So if Henry were not to lose his throne in February he had to persuade his personal enemy, the Pope, to grant him absolution.

Henry wrote Gregory and offered to go to Rome as a penitent. Gregory replied that he was about to start for Augsburg and would settle Germany's and Henry's affairs there. That would never do. If Gregory, already an enemy, were surrounded by Henry's German enemies, his justice was not likely to be tempered by much mercy. So Henry gambled his crown and his life on the chance that he could intercept Gregory and wrest absolution from that stubborn and angry man before he reached Germany.

Most of the Alpine passes were guarded by Henry's German foes. The winter was exceptionally severe. Both the Rhine and the Po were frozen over from November to April. Nevertheless, Henry, accompanied by his Queen, his baby son and one loyal servant, fled from Oppenheim into

Burgundy, whence he might cross the Alps into Italy by the unguarded Mont Cenis pass. Henry hired some local mountaineers to serve as guides and in frightful cold ascended the pass. A slippery crust of snow was not strong enough to bear the weight of the men and horses. At the most dangerous places the guides had to cut a path through the snow.

The descent was even more difficult. On their hands and knees, clinging to each other, the party crawled down the steepest slopes. And always the Queen and the baby had to be dragged along wrapped in ox hides which slipped over the snow and ice. Some of the horses fell off cliffs to their deaths. Others, with their feet tied together, were successfully rolled down frightening ledges. Yet, in spite of the extreme cold, danger and exhausting hardship, the little party descended into northern Italy without any serious accident.

Henry IV's crossing of the Alps in winter, although much less well known, may have been as difficult an achievement as Hannibal's. While Henry was struggling through the mountains Gregory VII was traveling north through Italy toward Augsburg. Somewhere in Tuscany he was met by Matilda, Countess of Tuscany, with an armed escort. Together they proceeded as far as Mantua, where they were astounded to learn that Henry was in Italy. Suspicious of Henry's intentions, ignorant of his lack of soldiers, and fearful that the rebellious bishops of northern Italy might assemble troops in Henry's support, Gregory and Matilda turned back and for safety locked themselves up in her fortress of Canossa.

Matilda, the most powerful feudal lord in Italy north of Robert Guiscard, was Gregory's intimate friend and loyal supporter. Her father, Boniface, had ruled much of the Po valley with cruel efficiency and had been made ruler of Tuscany by the Emperor Conrad. He called himself Duke and Marquis of Tuscany. But in eleventh-century Italy titles had little specific meaning. Matilda, who inherited her father's domains, was always called The Great Countess.

Too little is known about the remarkable Great Countess. Her adoring biographer, Nora Duff, has called her with no possible justification "a grand immortal figure in the world's history." Matilda was no such thing, but she was a lady of parts, a warrior and a ruler. Fluent in four languages, German, French, Italian and Latin, she was able to write letters in Latin without the aid of a learned clerk. She collected manuscripts. For thirty years she fought as an ally of the Papacy against various emperors.

As a girl she learned to wield spear and pike, sword and battle-ax. She was said to wear armor and to wage war in person. Such accomplishments did not prevent her from being considered beautiful. When Matilda was about twenty-four she married Godfrey of Lorraine, the hunchbacked, ugly son of her stepfather. Godfrey was famous for his courage and wisdom, but the marriage, not surprisingly, was unhappy. The couple lived apart and Matilda even considered becoming a nun.

The castle of Canossa was Matilda's greatest military stronghold. Surrounded by three concentric rings of formidable walls, it was situated high on a spur of the Apennines. Looking north over the Po valley from the castle on a clear day, one could see seven cities: Modena, Reggio, Parma, Mantua, Guastalla, Carpi and Correggio. Within the walls of Canossa were a church and a monastery, barracks for troops, stables for horses, storage rooms and accommodations for hordes of servants. The central castle building had rooms for many guests.

Henry left his wife and baby in Reggio and rode on toward Canossa, stopping partway there, probably at one of Matilda's outlying forts. The Great Countess rode down from Canossa for a preliminary meeting with Henry. Somebody had to be the mediator between the intransigent Pope and the seemingly abjectly humble Emperor-elect. Henry was handsome and charming. Matilda returned to Canossa and pleaded with Gregory that Henry be received as a penitent sinner.

Gregory VII had no interest in Henry's possible repentance. What he really wanted was to establish his supremacy over emperors, his right to depose them if they were not properly submissive. Gregory demanded: "If he is truly penitent, let him send me his crown and insignia of royalty in token that he deems himself unworthy to wear them." This was much too severe and so considered by a number of Gregory's associates. No medieval ruler could make such an admission. He could be a sinner, but he could not be unworthy to rule.

While Matilda was in Canossa pleading with Gregory, Henry waited for news in a little chapel. Matilda returned, found him there and presumably delivered Gregory's arrogant and humiliating demand. Henry knelt before the Great Countess and said, "Plead for me, Cousin, plead for my forgiveness with the Holy Father." Matilda went back to Canossa and again urged the Pope to forgive Henry and admit him to his presence. Again Gregory refused. "Let him appear on the appointed day at Augsburg," he said, "and he shall receive rigid and impartial justice."

Then occurred one of the most celebrated episodes of history. Henry IV, King and Emperor-elect, went up to the castle of Canossa dressed in the rude woolen robe of a penitent, bareheaded and barefoot. He knocked on the gate of the third, inner wall of the castle and pleaded for admission. He was refused. The snow was deep in the courtyard. The cold was intense. And for three days the highest-ranking monarch in Europe, a ruler who was to some extent holy also, stood like a beggar outside the castle door. A Christian and a sinner, publicly humbling himself and demonstrating his penitence, mutely appealed for mercy and forgiveness from the supreme head of the Christian Church. And he did not get them.

Many thousands of words written by scores of historians have been devoted to the spectacular drama of Canossa. Since no one can know for certain, authorities differ about such questions as: Was Henry really barefoot, or did he wear sandals? Was his robe woolen or linen? Did he stand there at night also, or only by day? But these are trivial questions compared to the crucial one: Was Henry sincere in his repentance, or was he only acting a dramatic role with enormous skill, forcing Gregory to grant him absolution so that he could return to Germany rid of the stigma of excommunication, reconquer his throne and thereafter ignore the deplorable ideas of a revolutionary pope? Knowing both Henry's obstinate courage and his unscrupulous craft, it seems reasonable to believe that his repentance was a sham and his whole performance a masterpiece of hypocrisy.

While Henry stood humbly in the snow and cold outside the castle gate, Gregory, seated inside beside a crackling fire, must have been, in an emotional sense, almost as uncomfortable. Henry had put him in an impossible situation. If he stubbornly refused to absolve the royal sinner whose abject repentance was being so theatrically dramatized in the castle yard, he would seem cruelly harsh. Mercy and forgiveness were Christian virtues. Could the Pope deny them before the eyes of all

Christendom? But if Gregory did absolve Henry he would betray the German princes who were his allies in his conflict with Henry. He had previously agreed not to make peace with Henry without first consulting them.

For three days Gregory struggled with his dilemma. While he did so an unknown member of his court is reported to have said: "This is not apostolic severity, but rather the cruelty of a tyrant."

Finally Gregory decided that he must absolve Henry, but the conditions he exacted were rigorous: Henry must face a trial before the German princes, who were his enemies and his rebellious subjects, and answer any charges they chose to make against him. If he wished, Gregory himself would preside at this mock trial. If Henry refuted the charges, he would receive his kingdom back from the Pope, a condition which would make him the acknowledged feudal vassal of the Pope. If Henry was found guilty he was peaceably to resign his throne. Until the trial Henry was not to act as king in any way, and until then his subjects were free of all allegiance to him. And if Henry should regain his throne he must henceforth act according to Gregory's instructions and obey particularly the new decree about lay investitures.

Henry was a proud and intelligent man; yet he accepted these humiliating, insulting conditions which would destroy the entire basis of his monarchy. His acceptance proves his desperate need of absolution. His subsequent actions confirm that he was cynically acting a hypocritical role. Henry had no intention of becoming a subservient puppet ruler obeying instantly when Gregory jerked the strings.

So Henry solemnly swore an oath to obey Gregory's unreasonable conditions. Could Gregory really have believed that Henry or any other emperor would abide by them? Then Gregory formally absolved Henry from his excommunication. Henry attended a banquet as Gregory's guest and listened to much grave advice. That banquet must have been difficult to endure. The two men detested and distrusted each other. No matter what they said or what they signed, they were committed to a collision course. As long as Gregory and other popes were determined to establish papal supremacy over secular rulers, and as long as Henry and other monarchs were determined to maintain the independence of their states, there would be wars of words and wars of battles.

Gregory reported to the German princes in a dispatch: "Henry came in person to Canossa . . . bringing with him only a small retinue. . . . He presented himself at the gate of the castle, barefoot and clad only in wretched woolen garments, beseeching us with tears to grant him absolution and forgiveness. This he continued to do for three days, while all those about us were moved to compassion at his plight, and interceded for him with tears and prayers. . . . At length we removed the excommunication from him, and received him again into the bosom of Holy Mother Church."

Henry IV went back to Germany absolved by the Pope of all his sins and so in the minds of many of his countrymen once again the rightful King. The princes who opposed him, however, did not change their minds. They continued to oppose him and were furious with Gregory for his betrayal. And in northern Italy the princes and bishops who had supported Henry, who had hoped to depose Gregory, were equally disgusted with Henry. Politics has always been an emotional business.

Gregory remained at Canossa until September, waiting for a German military escort to come and fetch him through his enemies in Lombardy to Germany to attend a trial which never took place. When he was certain that no guard would come, Gregory returned to Rome. The Canossa episode was finished. Today the ruins of that famous castle lie bleak and deserted. Curious tourists are rare and it is difficult to recreate imaginatively the historic drama which took place there 900 years ago.

Gregory VII spent the next two years in Rome devoting most of his time and effort trying to enforce clerical celibacy. Indeed, he acted as if German affairs were no longer pressing. A savage civil war was raging, but Gregory, whose support of either side would have materially helped to settle the conflict, kept silent.

Henry, safely back in Germany, found that the princes who had tried to depose him were as stubborn as he. In the same year as Canossa, 1077, they elected an anti-king of their own, Rudolf of Suabia. For three years Henry and his supporters fought Rudolf and his supporters while Gregory leisurely considered which was the rightful king and emperor-elect.

Finally, in March of 1080, Gregory proclaimed Rudolf the rightful king and excommunicated Henry for the second time. Since Gregory's decision for Rudolf was a foregone conclusion it is difficult to find a reason why he waited so long. Gregory forbade all Christians to serve Henry and offered absolution for their sins to all who fought for Rudolf. Gregory, who enjoyed making prophecies with absolute confidence, now tried to make Henry's position as bad as possible by proclaiming his most famous prophecy: If Henry did not repent he would be deposed or dead before August. Gregory was so totally certain of his prophetic powers that he recklessly said that if his prediction did not come true men could cease to believe in his authority as pope!

One of the maddening mysteries of the Middle Ages is our ignorance of what the principal actors in many great crises thought or felt. Medieval monarchs did not keep intimate diaries or write chatty, informal letters. Henry IV, obviously, was enraged by excommunications which gave his subjects excuses to revolt. But whether he felt any genuine religious alarm because Gregory's anathemas theoretically cast him out of the Christian community, or whether he was cheerfully indifferent, is unknown. Centuries later monarchs were still finding excommunications exasperating nuisances, but many of them seem to have been personally unmoved and untroubled.

Gregory's second excommunication of Henry lacked the effect of the first. To excommunicate him so soon after absolving him seemed too much like personal spite. It caused no further desertions. And in retaliation Henry called a council of German bishops at Mentz which excommunicated and deposed Gregory. Then at another council of Italian bishops held at Brixen in the Tyrol the bishops were equally cooperative. They confirmed the excommunication and deposition of Gregory and elected an anti-pope, Archbishop Guibert of Ravenna, who took the name of Clement III. At Brixen they were eloquent:

"We, assembled by the authority of God in this place, having read the letter from the synod of nineteen bishops held at Mentz against the licentious Hildebrand, the preacher of sacrilegious and incendiary doctrines; the defender of perjury and murder; the worshipper of divinations and dreams; the notorious necromancer; himself possessed by an evil spirit; him we adjudge to be canonically deposed and expelled from his see, and unless, on hearing our judgment, he shall descend from his throne, to be condemned for everlasting."

August came and went and Henry was neither deposed nor dead.

Gregory made no public remarks about the failure of his rash prophecy. And soon the wrong king died. In October of 1080 Rudolf's army defeated Henry's army in a great battle in Saxony, but Rudolf was killed in action. His death confounded Henry's foes, who for a long time could not agree on a substitute anti-king. While they debated, discussed and dithered, Henry hurried off to Italy for the second time. Less than four years before he had been publicly humiliated there. Now he was intent on settling his score with Gregory.

Rudolf seems to have had some qualms about his role as anti-king. His hand had been cut off by a sword blow and lay on the ground beside him on the battlefield. Gazing at his severed hand, the dying Rudolf is said to have lamented: "With this hand I ratified my oath of fealty to my sovereign Henry. I have now lost my life and kingdom. Bethink ye, ye who have led me on, in obedience to whose counsels I have ascended the throne, whether ye have guided me aright."

On the same day that German supporters of the rival emperors were slaughtering each other in Saxony an army of anti-Gregory Lombards fought and won a battle against the troops of the Countess Matilda.

Although Pope Gregory had proclaimed Rudolf the rightful king and emperor-elect in March of 1080, he was far from certain that he had backed the winning horse. If Henry should defeat Rudolf it would not be long before he marched on Rome to force Gregory's deposition and to be crowned emperor by his own anti-pope. Gregory's alliance with Countess Matilda no longer seemed sufficient. The only ruler strong enough to protect the Pope was Robert Guiscard, whom Gregory hated only a trifle less than he hated Henry. Gregory had refused to renew Robert's papal investiture as Duke of Apulia, Calabria and Sicily originally granted by Pope Nicholas II. He had tried to lead a crusade against Robert. And he had excommunicated him three times. Imagine, then, the humiliation to Gregory's terrible pride when in June of 1080 he journeyed to the little town of Ceprano to cement an alliance with Robert by formally investing him with all his lands as a feudal vassal of the Papacy.

At that time Robert was preparing his attack upon the Byzantine empire. Such daring aggression against a Christian state may seem to us hardly a suitable project for papal approval. But needs must, and Gregory had to find someone capable of fighting Henry. So Gregory wrote letters to the bishops of Apulia and Calabria commending the war against Constantinople and "our most glorious son Duke Robert." And he ordered that all those who followed Robert to his war of conquest should bear themselves fittingly as soldiers of Christ.

Gregory's public repudiation of his thrice-repeated excommunication of Robert Guiscard was pathetic. It was an admission that some, at least, of the major moral and religious decisions he made as pope were subject to reversal for expedient political reasons. Overnight Robert, that fire-breathing monster, became a good son of the Church.

In the spring of 1081 Henry invaded Italy with a large army. He besieged Rome. Gregory took refuge in the Castle of Sant' Angelo, a custom harried popes would follow well into the sixteenth century. But Henry lacked siege equipment and a force large enough to blockade Rome effectively. In July he was compelled to retreat, driven off by Rome's most reliable allies: summer heat, malaria, typhoid and dysentery. If Henry could not then capture Rome and Pope Gregory he could spend his time agreeably fighting his rebellious vassal, Countess Matilda. By Christmas of 1081 Henry was again outside the walls of Rome. He remained there until Easter of 1082 and then once more discreetly retreated to Tuscany before Rome's deadly summer allies could attack his troops.

During Henry's second siege of Rome Gregory wrote Robert Guiscard, then happily fighting in Greece with the intention of crowning his life of conquests by making himself Byzantine emperor, and pleaded for aid: "Remember therefore the Holy Roman Church your Mother, who loves you above all other princes and has singled you out for her special trust. Remember, for her you have sworn an oath; and in what you have sworn—that which, even had you not done so, would still be your Christian duty to perform—you will not fail. For you are not unaware how much strife has been stirred up against the Church by Henry, the so-called King, and how urgently she needs your aid. Wherefore act now; for just as the son will desire to fight against iniquity, so will the Church his Mother be grateful for his devotion and succor."

Whether Gregory gagged when he dictated that bit about the Church loving Robert more than all other princes, we cannot know. If he did not, he ought to have. Gregory, like many popes and most rulers, never doubted that the ends justify the means.

Robert was understandably annoyed at the necessity of interrupting his Byzantine campaign. Nevertheless, he left his son Bohemund in command, set out for Italy and swore "by the soul of his father Tancred to remain unbathed and unshaven until he could return to Greece." This oath is perplexing because Robert is said to have worn a huge beard. But perhaps he grew it then and wore it only for the last years of his life. By the time Robert reached Rome Henry had retreated to Tuscany for the second time. His help was no longer needed.

With stubborn persistence Henry led his army back to Rome and besieged the city for a third time. This six-month siege lasted from Christmas of 1082 until June of 1083, when Henry's troops captured the so-called Leonine city, that part of Rome on the northern or right bank of the Tiber. Gregory, shut up in the Castle of Sant' Angelo there, held out obstinately and so did the larger part of Rome on the left bank of the river.

Not unnaturally Henry now thought that the time had come when he could negotiate with Gregory, probably hoping that some compromise might be reached. If he gave up his plans to depose Gregory would Gregory consent to crown him emperor? Henry is reported to have said that if Gregory would even hand him the crown on the end of a stick from one of the windows of Sant' Angelo he would consider that a coronation.

But Gregory, a virtual prisoner in his fortress, refused to negotiate at all. With sublime arrogance he demanded unconditional surrender from Henry, saying: "Let the King lay down his crown, and give satisfaction to the Church." Pope Gregory VII is not one of the more attractive characters in history, but one must admire such heroic fidelity to his convictions. He could be self-contradictory and crassly expedient, as when he embraced his enemy Robert Guiscard. But he would not budge an inch in his claims for the Papacy's right to choose, approve or depose emperors.

The Romans, tired of being besieged, now switched sides, turned against Gregory and declared for Henry. This was gratifying to Henry, but once again Rome's summer heat and assorted diseases drove him away. Leaving a token force behind him to control the Leonine city and to keep Gregory cooped up in Sant' Angelo he marched off to Tuscany. Henry left just in time. His garrison became so sick it fled, leaving Gregory free to do what he liked. Robert Guiscard, who had been too busy suppressing a revolt of his barons to help the Pope, now sent him a gift of 30,000 gold pieces. With these Gregory bought back the fickle support of the Roman populace. Rarely has money been so wasted! In December of 1083 the Romans switched sides again and proclaimed themselves Henry's allies. And again Gregory locked himself up in Sant' Angelo. With the gates open to welcome him Henry IV marched triumphantly into Rome.

On Palm Sunday of 1084 Henry's personal anti-pope, Clement III, was consecrated as pope in Saint Peter's. And on Easter day he obligingly crowned Henry as emperor. Henry may not have been crowned by the true pope. But at least he had been crowned in Rome by a pope and that was what mattered to him. His satisfaction did not last long. News came that Robert Guiscard was marching on Rome with 6,000 mounted knights and 30,000 foot soldiers to rescue Gregory and to drive out the invaders. Henry did not have nearly large enough a force to fight such an army commanded by the finest soldier in the world. He fled. Three days later the Norman army arrived.

The Romans, worried about their guilt as betrayers of the Pope, refused to open their gates to the Norman army. Four days after his arrival outside the walls Robert launched an attack. After a savage but brief resistance the Normans entered the city, released Gregory from his fortress-refuge and respectfully escorted him across the city to the Lateran palace. Gregory gave them his blessing.

And then Robert's troops, particularly the numerous Saracen recruits from Sicily, proceeded to sack Rome for three days. Goaded to fury, the Roman population fell upon the plunderers and more than held their own until the Normans set fire to the city. While much of the city burned, the terrible sack continued with murder, massacre, torture and rape. The Romans were totally defeated and the great Duke of Apulia, Calabria and Sicily sold many thousands of his Roman prisoners as slaves.

When the Norman army, burdened with loot, marched back to

Robert's domains Pope Gregory VII went with it. He did not dare remain in Rome, where the people held him responsible for their suffering. Had not Gregory persisted in waging war with Henry and involved Rome in three sieges? Had he not invited Robert Guiscard and his terrible soldiers to protect him? Was he not guilty? Because of his pride, his refusal to compromise, his determination to maintain his theological position at no matter what cost to thousands of innocent persons. The Roman people blamed Gregory and so have a number of historians.

To what degree was Robert Guiscard guilty? He had barbarous Saracens in his army. He failed to stop the looting and sack and probably did not try to. That was the custom. Cities which resisted besiegers could expect to be sacked. As for the fire, it is unlikely that Robert ordered it. But he could have. There was little that amoral hero could not do. And Robert certainly bears the blame for the sale of the Romans, his fellow Christians, as slaves.

Henry Hart Milman, the Victorian historian we have already quoted, points out that there is no record of Gregory protesting Guiscard's crime, so hideously worse than anything Henry IV ever did. But Gregory was in no position to excommunicate Robert for the fourth time. He was Robert's guest, dependent upon his hospitality, almost his prisoner. An embittered exile from Rome, Gregory accompanied Robert to Monte Cassino, then to Benevento and then to Salerno, Guiscard's capital.

In Salerno Pope Gregory lived in the archbishop's palace. If he knew regrets or feelings of guilt he did not record them. Perhaps he thought that the Romans had betrayed him and so deserved their punishment. He did not change his mind about Henry. He excommunicated him for a third time. After the completion of the Norman cathedral which Robert Guiscard built in Salerno, Gregory officially consecrated it. Today the austere building with its large courtyard in front of the main doorway surrounded by a cloistered colonnade is almost lost among the modern buildings of a bustling city. But those who look closely can find an inscription on the façade which states that the cathedral was "built by Duke Robert, greatest of conquerors, with his own money."

Gregory VII lived on for another year and finally died on May 25, 1085, a disillusioned but still proudly arrogant old man of approximately

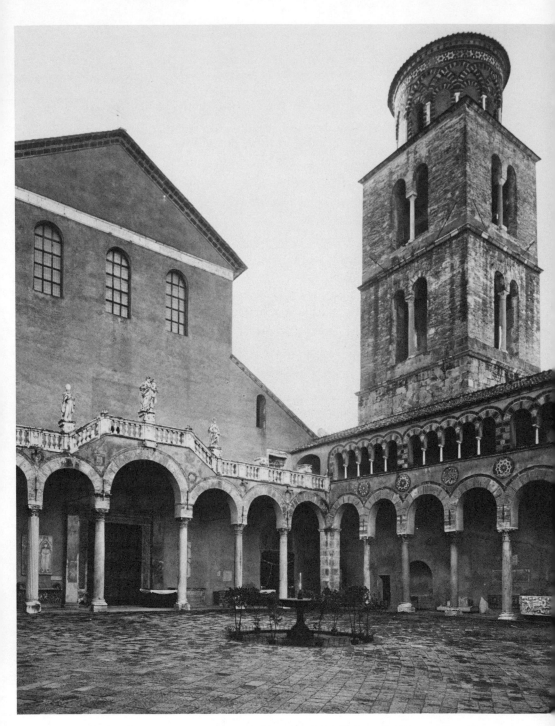

The cathedral and campanile of Salerno, built by Robert de Hauteville. *Alinari*

sixty-two. By any material reckoning he was a failure. He died in exile. He failed to establish the Papacy's supremacy over kings and emperors. He failed to depose Henry IV. He failed to make the entire clergy celibate and to eliminate simony.

But Pope Gregory raised the power and influence of the Papacy to heights it had never known before. He dramatized the issue of papal supremacy so effectively that it would have to be refought again and again by other popes and other monarchs. He made celibacy for the clergy the rule and the ideal so that thereafter only human weakness would bring violations of the new moral standard. And if he failed to eliminate simony, he at least reduced it and made it seem sinful and not just ordinary custom.

During his last years Gregory continually lamented that the world was turning against him. On his deathbed Gregory quoted a text from the Psalms, slightly amended to fit his own conception of his career: "I have loved righteousness and hated iniquity, *wherefore* I die in exile." He was buried in the south apse of the Salerno cathedral, where his tomb may still be seen.

Gregory's great antagonist, Henry IV, also died in exile, in Liège, betrayed and driven out by his own son. Both men were failures in their political ambitions. Both set crucially important precedents. Men never forgot Canossa. Henry's championship of the right of monarchs to control the domestic affairs of their states without supervision by popes was the first important milestone on the long road which led to the separation of church and state.

Gregory VII has been called the greatest of medieval personages and the greatest of popes. Many scholars and historians would challenge such a verdict. But there is no doubt of his courage, his determination, his dedication to what he considered righteousness and his towering importance in his own time.

The dispute over secular investiture was finally settled with a compromise in 1122 at the Concordat of Worms. Henceforth popes would invest bishops and abbots with their spiritual authority and kings and emperors would invest them with their lands. If Gregory and Henry could have reached so sensible a compromise at Canossa, Germany and Italy would have been spared untold suffering.

V

"The Best and Most Celebrated Among Monarchs"

In the great cathedral of Palermo on the south side of the building near the doorway four medieval tombs stand clustered close together. In few sacred buildings do so few tombs symbolize so much worldly power and glory, for these tombs contain the mortal remains of three extraordinary men whose fame once resounded across all Europe, and of the unhappy woman who was related to all three. Beneath a canopy supported by four pillars elaborately decorated in a mosaic pattern of gold, red, black and white is the red porphyry sarcophagus of Roger II, King of Sicily, the most enlightened and one of the most powerful monarchs of the twelfth century. Beside it, beneath a similar canopy supported by six vaguely Corinthian columns, is a porphyry tomb resting on four stylized lions. Here lies Frederick II, Roger's grandson, King of Sicily and Emperor of Germany and Italy, the most remarkable ruler of the entire Middle Ages. An adjoining tomb similar to Frederick's is that of Henry VI, Roger's son-in-law and Frederick's father, the cruel German emperor known as "the Hammer of the Earth." The fourth tomb is that of Constance, Roger's daughter, Henry's wife and Frederick's mother.

Sicilians worshipping in the cathedral rarely pause to glance at the four tombs as they come and go. Tourists politely obeying their guides' instructions dutifully stare at them with small curiosity and scant interest in who those mighty men may have been. Time is a cruel enemy to fame. Only a few of the world's celebrated men escape the obliteration of time's remorseless passage. The rest, who made so much noisy history while they lived, remain known only to historians.

Roger II was the son of Roger I, the Great Count of Sicily, and of his third wife, Adelaide, a Lombard princess from Savona near Genoa, whom Roger I had married in 1089 when he was nearly sixty. At that time he had a dozen daughters and two sons. But Jordan was illegitimate and Geoffrey was a leper confined in a monastery. Jordan's bastardy might not have kept him from succeeding his father. The conqueror of England had been a bastard, too. But Roger wanted a legitimate heir. And so in 1093 Countess Adelaide bore a son, Simon, and in December of 1095 another son, Roger.

The Great Count himself died in 1101, aged seventy. A great soldier, a great and tolerant statesman and a shrewd diplomat, Roger I had never stooped to such treachery as Robert Guiscard did when he robbed his nephew Abélard of all the dominions he inherited from his father, Duke Humphrey. Roger faced the same temptation and resisted it. Robert Guiscard's heir, Roger Borsa, was a weakling, an inept ruler and a poor soldier. How easy it would have been for Roger to usurp his ducal throne! Instead he loyally supported Roger Borsa, although sometimes he bargained greedily for territorial concessions.

Roger I died in Mileto, the capital of his mainland domain in Calabria. Adelaide ruled there as a surprisingly able regent, and there at the age of twelve the boy Simon died. Roger was nine when he became the Count of Sicily. His mother moved the capital of the young lord's domains to Palermo. And in Palermo Roger II grew up surrounded by Greek and Moslem tutors, secretaries and officials.

In 1112 Roger came of age and assumed the direct rule of his state. He was only sixteen and a half. Boys matured early in the Middle Ages. We may be sure that the new ruler of Sicily was no mere boy. He was an astute and ambitious young man. Like all de Hautevilles, Roger craved power and glory; but, unlike the other members of his family who rejoiced in warfare, Roger preferred to obtain his ends whenever possible by diplomacy and intrigue. Roger waged his wars with none of the personal enthusiasm and none of the flair for military leadership of his father and uncles.

The Count of Sicily and of half Calabria spent the first six years of his reign quietly establishing his personal rule. Not until 1118 did he launch his first foray outside his realm, an unsuccessful attack on the city of Gabès in Tunisia. Five years later Roger sent a fleet to attack the Tunisian city of Mahdia. Everything went wrong and the expedition had to be written off as a humiliating fiasco.

But in 1125 Roger contrived the first of many triumphs. His cousin, Duke Roger Borsa, had died in 1111 and been succeeded by his son William, also a weakling but a man of considerable charm. Poor incompetent William, beset by revolts, feuds and private wars, presented Roger with the Guiscard family's share of Calabria in 1125 and formally recognized Roger as his heir. Now the way was clear for Roger to claim the rule of all southern Italy as his right. William died without a son and Count Roger inherited his duchy of Apulia. Unfortunately, with typical incompetence (or perhaps maliciously?) William had not formally recorded his recognition of Roger as his heir. And in his efforts to please he seems to have recognized several others also. Chaos reigned and Roger had to make good his title as Duke of Apulia by force of arms.

He did so, but it took him four years and two military campaigns. During the first two years Roger remained in Sicily and took no active steps toward claiming his duchy. Presumably he was organizing his expeditionary force and dickering with Pope Honorius II for full papal confirmation of his succession. Honorius was not anxious to cooperate. As feudal overlord of Apulia, Calabria and Sicily (the claim first established by Pope Nicholas II when he invested Robert Guiscard as duke of those territories), Pope Honorius thought that Roger was quite powerful enough as Count of Sicily and Calabria without the increase to his power which recognition as Duke of Apulia would bring.

In August of 1127 Roger sailed for Italy with a fleet of only seven ships, a force so small it is apparent that he did not intend to wage war seriously. After ten days of negotiation Salerno welcomed Roger as its ruler and the local bishop (assuming powers he did not possess) anointed Roger as Duke of Apulia. Amalfi also surrendered to Roger.

Pope Honorius had come down to the papal town of Benevento only some thirty-five miles from Salerno to investigate the situation personally. As soon as he heard what his insubordinate bishop had done he wrote Roger and forbade him to assume the title of Duke of Apulia. If he did Honorius would excommunicate him. Undismayed by this threat, Roger rode to Benevento with 400 horsemen. What he intended is not clear because it is not known if he hoped to capture the Pope or the city or both. The gates of Benevento were shut fast. Honorius refused to have any communication with Roger. Frustrated in his hopes of a papal investiture as Duke of Apulia, Roger left some local barons behind to encourage the Pope by raids on the lands of Benevento and went off on a triumphal progress through Apulia and Calabria. Since nobody opposed him Roger soon went cheerfully back to Sicily.

That may have been a mistake. Roger's absence made it easy for Honorius to organize a league of Norman barons pledged to defy Roger's claim to be their duke. Roger II was now confronted with the same sort of baronial revolt which his Uncle Robert had suppressed so often. In May of 1128 Roger landed in Italy with an army of 2,000 knights and 1,500 archers. Pope Honorius, following the examples of those militant popes Leo IX and Gregory VII, personally led an army of rebellious barons against Roger.

For a month in the summer heat of southern Italy the two armies faced each other across a river without fighting. Roger had no illusions about the glory of risking all in an uncertain battle. If time, bribes and diplomacy could gain his ends, so much the better. Pope Honorius, evidently doubtful of the loyalty of his supporters and persuaded that he had better confirm Roger's claim after all, made an agreement to invest Roger as Duke of Apulia, Calabria and Sicily if Roger would come to Benevento for the ceremony. The Norman barons, disgusted by so shameless a betrayal, dispersed.

Roger II journeyed to Benevento, but refused to enter the city. Did he fear betrayal and imprisonment in a papal dungeon? So, shortly after sunset, Roger of Sicily and His Holiness Pope Honorius II met on neutral ground, a bridge over the little Sabato River. And there on the bridge, in the light of hundreds of flaring torches and in the presence of an enormous crowd composed of Roger's troops, the Pope's retinue and the citizens of Benevento, Roger was formally invested as Duke of

Roger II of Sicily being crowned by Christ; mosaic in Martorana Church, Palermo. *Alinari*

Apulia, which meant that he was also Duke of Calabria and Sicily.

The powerful new Duke was thirty-two years old, an intellectual with a strong interest in geography, mathematics and the sciences of his time. Roger was patient and subtle. He loved luxury, ostentation and display and liked to wear imperial robes similar to those worn by the Byzantine emperor. In the small Martorana church in Palermo there is a contemporary portrait of Roger done in mosaic. It is obscured by near darkness, and one has to ask an attendant to illuminate it for inspection. This he will do for a small fee and for only a few minutes at a time.

The portrait shows Roger being crowned by Christ Himself. Roger is dressed in a green robe and a gold dalmatic. The background of the two figures is entirely gold. Roger's face is not that of a blond Norman. Rather, it looks as if he were a Sicilian or a Levantine. His brown hair falls upon his shoulders. His long mustaches meet a neatly trimmed and pointed beard which runs from ear to ear. This highly stylized mosaic cannot be a realistic portrait, but it probably is a faithful suggestion of Roger's superficial appearance.

Stiff and conventionalized as this portrait may be, it is interesting for several reasons. In the barbarous early Middle Ages, portraits of any kind were rare, and reliable contemporary portraits were rarer still. But in the civilized Norman court in Palermo a portrait was considered desirable and mosaic wall decorations were considered essential. Roger II was sufficiently wealthy so that he could import artists in mosaic from Constantinople. They decorated the cathedral Roger built at Cefalù some forty miles east of Palermo on the Sicilian north coast; the Martorana church built by Roger's great admiral, George of Antioch; Roger's private room in the palace at Palermo; and, most important of all, the royal Palatine Chapel in the palace.

Cefalù is a small town on a small peninsula which juts into the sea just below a spectacular cliff. Seen from a distance, it is one of the most picturesque towns in Sicily. Roger himself saw it from a distance under dramatic circumstances. He was sailing back to Sicily from Italy and encountered a terrible storm. Convinced that he was in danger of shipwreck and drowning, Roger swore to build a cathedral wherever he came ashore if his life was spared. He landed at Cefalù, built the cathedral there and installed his tomb in the cathedral while he was alive.

The cathedral of Cefalù. *Alinari*

Cefalù cathedral is a handsome Norman Romanesque building with two simple towers, similar but not identical, and an attractive loggia in front of the doorway. Its glory is one of the finest mosaics in the world, a picture of Christ *Pantocrator* (Ruler of the World) situated in the half-dome of the apse. Its majestic dignity and melancholy compassion are extremely moving.

Roger I began and Roger II continued the reconstruction of a Saracen castle into a Norman palace. Today it is difficult to imagine what it was like in Roger's day because so many deplorable alterations have been made, including an assembly room for the Sicilian parliament and state rooms in the eighteenth-century manner. But the royal chapel and Roger's private room survive in all their original splendor.

The chapel is a blaze of beauty. Mosaic illustrations of Bible stories, religious themes and secular diversions ornament every wall, their bright colors standing out sharply against the shining gold of their backgrounds. The Islamic element in the culture of Roger's state is strikingly present in the ceiling's fantastic wooden stalactites.

Roger's private room is hard to find and most tourists are unaware of its existence. It is worth finding. Its mosaics are as splendid as those in the chapel, with equally lavish gold backgrounds. But the subjects of the pictures are strictly secular. Interspersed among a variety of decorative palm trees are hunting scenes with centaurs among the hunters, lions, leopards, deer, swans and peacocks. In the twelfth century most kings moved from one crowded, uncomfortable, dismal castle to another. Roger II lived in a palace amid splendors suitable to enhance the glory of a powerful autocrat.

Roger II was highly intelligent, clever, sometimes devious, sometimes vindictively cruel. He knew the value of patience and of generosity. He knew how to organize an efficient autocratic state, and how to obtain the most in taxes and services from the various peoples in his polyglot kingdom. His army included a regiment of Moslem archers. These went with Roger in the spring of 1129 when he led a force of 3,000 knights and 6,000 infantry to suppress a rebellion in southern Apulia. The resistance was perfunctory and Roger defeated the rebels with little trouble. He was generous in victory, granted the baronial leaders of the revolt full pardons and permitted them to keep their fiefs.

Christ Pantocrator, Cefalù
Cathedral. *New York Public
Library Picture Collection*

Mosaic wall decoration in King Roger II's chamber in the Palazzo Reale,
Palermo. *New York Public Library Picture Collection*

In the autumn of the same year Roger held a great council at Melfi at which all the Norman counts and barons, bishops and abbots formally swore allegiance to him as their feudal overlord. They were required also to refrain from feuds and private wars (their favorite occupation) and to turn over all thieves and brigands to the ducal courts.

In 1130 Pope Honorius II died. As so often happened in the Middle Ages, two rival candidates were elected to succeed him: Innocent II and Anacletus II. Most European rulers and nations recognized Innocent. Anacletus needed support where he could find it. Roger, duke of three important duchies, yearned to be a properly anointed king. A mutually advantageous bargain was not difficult to arrange. The Duke and the minority Pope met in the little town of Avellino near Naples and came to terms. In return for Roger's military support Anacletus would invest him as King of Sicily, Apulia and Calabria. In September Anacletus was back in Benevento. There he issued a bull confirming the bargain and permitting Roger to be crowned in Palermo by a Sicilian bishop.

Roger II, the son and nephew of adventurers who began their careers as brigands and cattle thieves, was crowned in a sacred ceremony by the Archbishop of Palermo on Christmas day of 1130. The enormous, gorgeously dressed cavalcade of nobles and notables which escorted Roger to and from the cathedral rode in saddles decorated in silver and gold. At the magnificent banquet which followed the ceremony all the dishes and goblets were either silver or gold. Even the servants and waiters were dressed in cloth of silver.

It was a fine thing to be a king, but Roger never gave Pope Anacletus any thanks. He always referred to himself as crowned by God. He may even have regretted his bargain. His support of a pope generally regarded as schismatic involved Roger in years of warfare and encouraged his own barons to revolt. Bernard, Abbot of Clairvaux, an eloquent, influential and pugnacious saint, championed Innocent II and helped organize an alliance against Anacletus and Roger. In a violent propaganda campaign he called Roger a usurper, a tyrant and a "half-heathen king."

If Roger wore his new crown uneasily, he did his best not to show it. He fought stubbornly to subdue a third revolt of his mainland barons. He besieged and captured the rebel towns of Bari and Conversano, and then suffered a disastrous defeat in July of 1132. More than 700 of Roger's knights were captured. The King himself, accompanied by only four knights, escaped and rode hard for Salerno. The great gates of the city slammed behind him just as his triumphant pursuers appeared outside the walls. It was the nadir of Roger's fortunes. He was a king, but he now ruled only the city of Salerno and the island of Sicily. Yet so composed and cheerful was Roger's demeanor in Salerno that men were amazed by such serenity in misfortune. They were soon to be more amazed by Roger's ferocity and calculated cruelty in triumph. He took only two years to reconquer his mainland territories.

The loose coalition of Norman nobles which had defeated Roger did not hold together firmly. Roger returned to the war with a fresh Sicilian army including many Saracens and methodically reduced town after town, fortress after fortress. He took Venosa and his troops massacred every man, woman and child in the city. He recaptured Troia, whose inhabitants had surrendered and meekly pleaded for mercy, and then hanged the five leading citizens and burned the town to the ground. After the siege of Montepeloso Roger massacred the garrison and the population and burned down the abbey. Roger suppressed the rebels of Apulia so savagely that a contemporary chronicler, Falco of Benevento, wrote that his use of terror made the people "wonder and shudder, and pray that God would resist so great a tyrant and man of blood." By 1134 Roger had not only reimposed his rule on all his domains; he had also conquered Naples and Benevento.

Roger II's combination of enlightened tolerance with horrible cruelty was deplorable but not unique. Other tyrants have ruled by the same contradictory means. In the Middle Ages, when cruelty was rampant and commonplace and men passionately pursued what they regarded as their rights, horrible vengeance was always a possibility. Roger had forgiven the leaders of the second revolt. His mercy had not won him loyalty. So now he tried terror. And that did not serve him much better. There would be a fourth rebellion.

The fourth baronial revolt against Roger II came in 1135 and proved to be the most serious of all. The persistent determination with which first Robert Guiscard and then Roger II fought to suppress these revolts is so impressive that one tends to overlook the equally impressive persistence of the Norman nobles' determination not to endure the rule of the upstart de Hautevilles. At first Roger prevailed against his rebellious subjects. But Pope Innocent II and Saint Bernard persuaded the German emperor, Lothair II, to intervene. In October of 1136 Lothair marched into northern Italy and was temporarily delayed there fighting several cities which refused to acknowledge his supremacy. The following year Lothair led his army down the Adriatic coast and invaded Roger's kingdom. As the Emperor advanced on Bari his troops killed, blinded or mutilated all prisoners who had fought for Roger. Bari fell to the conquering Germans and the garrison of the citadel, mostly Arabs, were blinded, multilated, hanged or flung into the sea in chains.

Roger either lacked enough troops to challenge Lothair or he discreetly preferred to avoid the risk of a pitched battle. While he kept out of Lothair's way he had to endure the ignominy of seeing two of the chief Norman cities, Melfi and Salerno, surrender to the Emperor. Roger's fortunes looked nearly as black as they had during the third revolt.

But Lothair, like so many other emperors, could not long maintain a German army away from Germany. Apparently satisfied with his victories, he returned to Germany in the autumn. Almost as soon as the Emperor had departed Roger launched a campaign of reconquest and revenge on all collaborators and traitors. In a few weeks he was again the complete master of the western half of his mainland kingdom. He then marched across the Apennines to deal with the rebels in Apulia.

Saint Bernard, one of the most militant of medieval holy men, was present among Roger's enemies—no doubt exhorting them to a high pitch of righteous indignation against the tyrannical ally of a schismatic pope. In any case, Bernard's presence seems to have been helpful. Roger committed his troops to battle and was soundly worsted. Whether the saint actually watched the fighting is not known. But it is reasonable to suppose that Bernard found the victory gratifying.

Nevertheless, decisive as Roger's defeat seemed, it was singularly inconclusive. Roger retained control of Sicily and the western half of southern Italy. The Emperor was far away in Germany. Only part of Apulia resisted Roger. The stubborn, persistent, subtle King in some mysterious fashion soon seemed more powerful and menacing than ever.

Perhaps if the most eloquent man in Europe could talk to Roger face to face some useful arrangement could be made about that tiresome schismatic, Pope Anacletus. Saint Bernard, who had so often denounced Roger as a tyrant and a heretic, went to meet him.

Bernard of Clairvaux was by birth a Burgundian nobleman. A Cistercian monk, he was the abbot of the most influential religious house of his time and the founder of more than seventy other monasteries. He was the author of the governing statutes of the Order of Knights Templars. Bernard was a poet, a sincere reformer from an orthodox, establishment point of view, and a fanatical foe of heretics. Consequently he was a personal enemy of the controversial religious philosopher Abélard, and of Arnold of Brescia (whom we shall meet in the next chapter), as well as of Anacletus. Bernard frequently wrote dictatorial letters to emperors and popes. His powerful oratory was to be largely responsible for the Second Crusade in 1146. He came to be known as "The Mellifluous Doctor."

Where Roger and Bernard met is not known. At that time, 1137, Roger was a brilliant middle-aged man of forty-one, Bernard a brilliant middle-aged man of forty-six. Bernard's slight, fragile body seemed almost too frail to contain his passionate spirit. He had mortified his body with rigorous austerities. His cell at Clairvaux was so low he could not stand erect in it. His bed was made of planks, his pillow of logs. Jacobus de Voragine, a thirteenth-century Dominican monk who became Archbishop of Genoa, wrote of Bernard in his *The Golden Legend* that at Clairvaux:

"For a long time he lived in exceeding poverty, and many times made his meal from the leaves of the beech tree. The servant of God denied himself sleep to a degree that surpassed human power, being wont to complain that no time was so wasted as the time spent in sleeping. . . . He took no pleasure in eating, but went to take food as to torture, led solely by the fear of fainting. . . . He had so quelled the disorders of the appetite that for the most part he no longer discerned divers tastes." Once Bernard drank oil (presumably olive oil) and did not notice that it was not water.

Although Bernard was a natural leader of men and much concerned with worldly affairs, he was also a mystic who witnessed marvels in religious trances. Once, Bernard believed, while he was reciting the "Ave

Maria Stella" before a statue of the Virgin Mary the Holy Mother Herself appeared to him and put three drops of milk from her breast into Bernard's mouth. Jacobus de Voragine tells of several miracles which were attributed to Bernard:

"An incredible multitude of flies once invaded a monastery which Bernard had built, and they vexed the monks sorely. The man of God then said: 'I excommunicate the flies!' And on the morrow they were found dead, every one."

Bernard also, after considerable conversation with a devil inhabiting a woman's body, drove the fiend out. And he rid another woman from the lustful attentions of an incubus by exorcising the evil spirit.

Saint Bernard was a persecutor of heretics, but he was a protector of Jews. He loved animals and nature. Gibbon wrote of Bernard that he "seems to have preserved as much reason and humility as may be reconciled with the character of a saint."

Bernard's rare combination of warm personal charm, intellectual brilliance, humble piety and absolute certainty of the correctness of his own opinions made him almost irresistible in argument and magically persuasive. Yet this man so superbly armed for negotiation conferred with the wily king of Sicily and concluded an agreement so one-sidedly favorable to Roger that it seems almost incomprehensible. Roger must have been more eloquent, convincing and persuasive than the saint!

Bernard said to Roger, "All Christendom favors Innocent, only you and your kingdom resist him." It was true. And then Roger had the effrontery, the impudence, to offer to mediate between the rival popes. Such an offer from the only important supporter of Anacletus, who had been excommunicated by Innocent for that support, seems ridiculous. Who could be more partisan? But Bernard accepted Roger's offer. Why he did so passes understanding. The fervent champion of Innocent II was willing to leave the decision between the rival popes to the fervent champion of Anacletus! Roger proposed that three of the cardinals who had voted for Innocent and three of the cardinals who had voted for Anacletus should come to Salerno, where they would argue their cases before him. He would then render a verdict.

For four days the dispute was thrashed out before King Roger in Salerno, with Bernard substituting for one of the cardinals as a champion of Innocent. There seemed to be no sound canonical reason for favoring one pope rather than the other. So Roger with consummate prudence and diplomacy declared that the case was too difficult for him to decide without further discussion. Therefore an advocate of each pope should come with him to Palermo and spend Christmas there. Further discussion could take place in the presence of the Sicilian bishops. Saint Bernard even agreed to this! The wicked tyrant had confounded the virtuous saint.

The Palermo conference was never held. Anacletus died on January 7, 1138. The cardinals who supported Anacletus elected one of their number as Victor II. But this Victor with surprising good sense soon realized that there was no need or excuse for further schism. He abdicated in May of 1138 and King Roger then recognized Innocent II as the rightful pope. But Innocent would not absolve Roger from his excommunication; nor would he cease his support of the few diehard Apulian barons still in revolt. In the spring of 1139 Pope Innocent excommunicated Roger for the second time. Somehow this prolonged conflict between the King of Sicily and the Pope and his baronial allies had to be ended.

In May Roger landed at Salerno with a large force. In June Innocent marched south from Rome in command of an army. King and Pope met each other in a crucial personal conference and negotiated for eight days without reaching an agreement. Shortly after their peace conference broke up Roger attacked the papal army and won a brilliant victory. He captured Pope Innocent himself, many cardinals, the papal archives and Innocent's treasure. It was Civitate all over again. Just as Humphrey de Hauteville and Robert Guiscard had captured Leo IX, Roger captured Innocent.

For three days Innocent sulked in the tent his captors provided him with and refused to talk. Finally his helpless position sank in and he signed a treaty granting Roger everything he wanted. The Pope absolved Roger and his two sons from their excommunications and then formally invested Roger as King of Sicily, as Anacletus had done. Now all that remained on Roger's agenda was to finish off the irritating revolt in Apulia. He did so in a few months, hanged some of the more prominent leaders and blinded or mutilated ten others. Roger confiscated the estates of all who had taken part in the revolt and exiled their owners "beyond the mountains," meaning the Alps.

Now at last after ten years of warfare Roger II was firmly established as king of a submissive kingdom and could turn his attention to domestic affairs.

King Roger II appointed and invested his own bishops, to the horror of ecclesiastics who revered the memory of Gregory VII. He promulgated a new code of laws. He minted a new coin valid anywhere in his kingdom called a ducat. The peace Roger now maintained was so novel and so wonderful a contrast to the violent anarchy which had preceded it and which still flourished everywhere else in Italy and in much of Europe that several of Roger's former enemies were much impressed. Among them were Saint Bernard and Peter the Venerable, Abbot of Cluny. In 1142 Peter wrote to Roger:

"Sicily, Apulia and Calabria, before you the refuge and the robber dens of Saracens, have become a magnificent kingdom, ruled by a SECOND SOLOMON. Would that also poor and unfortunate Tuscany, and the lands about it, might be joined to your dominions and enter into the peace of your kingdom."

Once the crisis years of rebellion were over, Roger ceased using terror as an instrument of policy. He did his best to foster trade. He built a large fleet and in George of Antioch employed so able an admiral that Sicily became the dominant naval power in the Mediterranean Sea.

In 1143 the Sicilian fleet began to raid the North African coast, plundering several cities. Tripoli was captured in 1146, Mahdia in 1148. Then came Susa, Sfax and Gabès, and in 1152 Bona. King Roger, who had refused to take part in the disastrous Second Crusade, conquered from the Moslems some 600 miles of the North African coast—from Tripoli in what is now Libya to Bona in what is now Algeria.

Roger was a just and merciful ruler. His reasonable taxes were collected with humane moderation. One Arab historian wrote:

"The enemy of God restored both the cities of Zawilah and Mahdia, furnished capital for the merchants, did good to the poor, confided the administration of justice to a *cadi* acceptable to the people, and ordered well the government of those two cities."

Like his Uncle Robert Guiscard before him, King Roger enjoyed demonstrating his power by attacking the Byzantine empire. His plundering raids took place in the same years as his North African conquests. In 1147 a powerful Sicilian fleet captured the islands of Corfu and Cephalonia. Athens and the island of Euboea were raided. The Sicilian fleet then sailed up the Gulf of Corinth, sacked the city of Corinth and dispatched a force which marched overland and sacked Thebes.

The fleet sailed home to Palermo in triumph, laden deep with plunder. It brought with it a group of silk workers from Thebes who established a silk industry in Palermo. Roger's Viking ancestors would certainly have been impressed by these piratical raids.

In 1149 George of Antioch took the Sicilian fleet through the Dardanelles and across the Sea of Marmara to Constantinople itself. There his archers shot fire arrows against the imperial palace at Damalis. This daring feat was only a gesture of insolent defiance and had no practical significance.

King Roger's efforts to expand his kingdom included persistent attacks on the lands of the Church. These caused more trouble and vexation than anything else and did not add considerably to Roger's domains. But Roger's troops did carry off the treasure of Monte Cassino. The King's genuine piety did not prevent him from looting the most famous monastery in the world any more than it prevented him from fighting popes.

Roger remained a widower for fourteen years after the death of his first wife. He then married two more times. He had five sons and one daughter by his first wife. All of these children died before their father except one son, William the Bad, who succeeded Roger. His second wife had no children. His third bore him a posthumous daughter, Constance. Roger in several ways seemed more an Oriental than a Western monarch. He kept a harem and fathered an unknown number of bastards.

The great King of Sicily died in February of 1154, aged fifty-eight. His red porphyry sarcophagus had been waiting for him for nine years in the cathedral of Cefalù. There in the cathedral he had built as a thank offering after his escape from drowning in a storm at sea Roger was buried as he had wished to be. But sixty-one years later in 1215 his grandson, the Emperor Frederick II, had Roger's tomb transferred to the cathedral of Palermo.

It was said that nobody ever knew what Roger was thinking. He was

Church of San Giovanni degli Eremiti, Palermo, built by King Roger II. *Alinari*

more feared than loved by his subjects. But Roger strove for justice and his justice was respected. He was extremely able in diplomacy and civil administration. He personally checked on everything in the daily operation of his government and "was himself his own chief clerk." He was a superb organizer and a competent if not distinguished soldier. He built many castles and forbade his barons to build any without his permission. In addition to the cathedral of Cefalù, Roger built other churches, of which the best known is San Giovanni degli Eremiti in Palermo, whose five red domes give it a delightfully Oriental look.

The King of Sicily did not enjoy going to war. He much preferred to stay in Palermo in his luxurious palace with his harem and the Moslem poets and scholars whose patron he was. Arabs admired and liked Roger, and Arab poets wrote odes in his praise. The most distinguished Moslem at Roger's court was Abu Abdullah Mohammed al-Edrisi, a great geographer and close friend of the King. Edrisi wrote for Roger a work incorporating all the geographical knowledge then available which is commonly called *The Book of Roger*. Although it is a pioneer book of exact scholarship, it also contains many tall tales and legends:

"England has a shape like the head of an ostrich. The country is fertile. Its inhabitants are brave, active, enterprising; but perpetual winter reigns there."

Edrisi's flattering appraisal of King Roger provides a fascinating glimpse of the impression the conqueror-statesman made on his Arab friends:

"This great King, whom Heaven has loaded with glory and power, is the best and most celebrated among monarchs. His absolute will is the motive of his conduct in state affairs. All the art of government has fixed itself in his person. He unites high intellect and goodness. To these are joined his resolution, sharp understanding, deep spirit, foresight, his skill in all measures, which betray a masterful intellect. He overlooks the whole range of his sovereignty. His sleep is as the awakening of other men. I cannot enumerate his knowledge of the exact and technical sciences, nor set bounds to his wisdom."

VI

Red Beard

"He was liberal and a man of worth, eloquent and noble, and glorious in all his deeds." Some 150 years after the death of Frederick von Hohenstaufen, Giovanni Villani, the Florentine chronicler, thus described the most admired and affectionately remembered of all medieval emperors since Charlemagne. Frederick I, called Barbarossa for his red beard by the Italians, was an emperor who might have strayed into the real world from the pages of some medieval romance. Handsome, courageous, charming and tireless (he took part in tournaments when he was past sixty), Frederick by sheer personality cast a spell over his contemporaries so powerful that it has influenced the imaginations of scholars and storytellers ever since. Somewhere deep inside the Kyffhauser mountain in Thuringia, legends tell, is a cave where Barbarossa sleeps sitting upright in a chair before a table through which his beard has grown. When he awakes he will come forth and make the German empire glorious once again. What does it matter that the story was first told about Frederick's grandson, Frederick II, and by sheer stupidity and confusion became attached to him? For Barbarossa rides down the centuries, his armor shining, his red-gold hair and beard flaming in the sun, a paragon of royal chivalry.

Looked at more closely, with a cold, appraising eye, Frederick von Hohenstaufen does not seem quite so glamorous. He was notably merciful by the bloody standards of the twelfth century, but still capable of deeds of savage cruelty. His ambition to transform his feudal overlordship of Italy into an absolute monarchy was impractical and anachronistic; but he clung to it obstinately and devasted Italy with his wars. His personal pride was great and his pride as German emperor was monumental. He firmly believed that every right ever possessed by Augustus, Justinian and Charlemagne was lawfully his. It followed that if Frederick Barbarossa was a sacred emperor and the legitimate inheritor of all previous emperors, those who opposed him were criminal and sacrilegious breakers of the law. Frederick's uncle, Bishop Otto of Friesling, wrote a history of his nephew's reign in which he expressed the scandalized reactions of the imperial courtiers to the intransigent independence of the Lombard cities of northern Italy:

"Scornful of the old aristocracy, the cities clung to the dregs of their barbaric past; for while extolling the rule of law, they are quite unprepared to submit to it. In effect, rarely, if at all, do they receive their prince with respect, albeit they are in honor bound to show submission and reverence. And never, or hardly ever, do they heed the law unless compelled to do so by force. Thus it frequently happens that their prince, though he comes in peace to claim his rights, is received with hostility. This is harmful to the public weal, since on the one hand the prince needs must waste his substance on military efforts against his own subjects, and on the other hand the subjects will never submit until their wealth is exhausted."

Barbarossa by trying to eliminate the municipal freedoms of the Lombard towns was opposing the ground swell of historical development. He was one of the world's great reactionaries.

Frederick von Hohenstaufen, who spent so many years and so many lives trying to impose his autocratic rule on the cities of northern Italy, was the King of Germany, the King of Italy, the King of Burgundy and the Emperor of the Holy Roman Empire. Although the Empire, as Voltaire so unforgettably said, was "neither holy, nor Roman, nor an empire," it was of immense importance to medieval minds. Its power varied from negligible to enormous, depending on the character and abilities of the individual emperors. But the Empire's significance as a concept fitting medieval notions about the proper organization of the world endured until well into the sixteenth century. "The Empire," wrote James Bryce, "appeared throughout the Middle Ages not what it seems now, a gorgeous anachronism, but an institution divine and necessary, having its foundation in the very nature and order of things."

A German king was elected by the most important princes and prelates. His election traditionally gave him the right to be crowned emperor in Rome by the pope, and to be crowned King of Italy in Milan with the iron crown of the Lombards. But the emperor was rarely as powerful as his titles suggest.

North of the Alps the emperor might be the hereditary ruler of a local domain, but for Germany as a whole he was only the feudal overlord with little actual power over his overmighty nobles. Since the imperial crown was not hereditary, only the most powerful and admired emperors were able to make their sons their successors. This could be done by persuading the princes to elect a child King of Germany while his father still lived as Emperor.

South of the Alps the German emperors were undisputed rulers over most of Italy north of Rome—but only in theory. They lacked the power to rule effectively because the feudal German lords would not fight in Italy for long periods. So local Italian rulers, such as the Countess Matilda, were virtually independent, and many Italian cities by the twelfth century were independent republics in all but name.

When Barbarossa campaigned in Italy during the second half of the twelfth century the cities were intensely proud of the municipal self-governments they had developed and most of them were grimly determined to maintain their virtual independence. Barbarossa realistically recognized that it was beyond his power to organize an autocratic state in feudal Germany. Yet he tried heroically to do just that in Italy and failed. Probably his motive was the wealth and commercial importance of the Italian cities. Their revenues, if he could collect them, would make him a far stronger ruler.

Frederick von Hohenstaufen probably was born in 1122, the son of the Duke of Suabia and the nephew of the Emperor Conrad III. His father headed one of the two most powerful feudal families in Germany.

Frederick I, Barbarossa, a contemporary copper bust from the workshop of Wilbert of Aachen. *The Bettman Archive, Inc.*

His mother belonged to the other. So Frederick was the logical candidate at the imperial election which followed the death of Conrad. His election in 1152 was unanimous.

The thirty-year-old monarch was affable and tactful, patient and astute. His smile charmed his contemporaries, who said that even when Frederick's face was composed he looked as if he were about to smile. His red-gold curls were cut short and he wore a band across his forehead from under which curls fell down almost over his eyebrows. His famous beard was clipped short. His eloquence in German was famous. He learned to speak Italian, but he knew only a little Latin.

Bishop Otto of Friesling described his glamorous nephew: "His person is well proportioned. He is shorter than very tall men, but taller and more noble than men of medium height. His hair is golden, curling a little above his forehead. His ears are scarcely covered by the hair above them, as the barber (out of respect for the empire) keeps the hair on his head and cheeks short by constantly cutting it. His eyes are sharp and piercing, his nose well formed, his beard reddish, his lips delicate and not distended by too long a mouth. His whole face is bright and cheerful. His teeth are even and snow white in color. . . . Modesty rather than anger causes him to blush frequently. . . . He is a lover of warfare, but only that peace may be secured thereby. . . . He is quick of hand, very wise in council, merciful to supplicants, kind to those taken under his protection. . . . In hunting he himself strings the bow, takes the arrows, sets and shoots them. You choose what he is to hit, he hits what you have chosen. . . . He earnestly searches the Scriptures and the exploits of ancient kings. He generally distributes with his own hands alms to the poor and scrupulously divides a tenth of his income among churches and monasteries."

Like his famous contemporary, Henry II of England, Frederick had no capital city, no particular place or palace which he called home, and no well-organized system of bureaucratic administration. Also like Henry, Frederick tried to rule two countries at once. Henry's rule of half of France involved him in constant warfare. Frederick's rule of Italy did the same. He was always traveling. The amount of time medieval monarchs spent on horseback cannot be estimated, but it was prodigious. Frederick's first involvement in Italian affairs came in March of 1153 when he signed an agreement with Pope Eugenius III.

The Pope, as so regularly happened to medieval popes, had been driven out of Rome, then a rebellious commune led by a radical monk called Arnold of Brescia. Frederick agreed to restore Eugenius to Rome and also to fight the King of Sicily, Roger II, whose power worried Eugenius. Frederick would be crowned emperor in Rome and would have an opportunity to arbitrate between the Lombard cities which constantly fought each other. As King of Italy he thought he could rightfully and easily settle matters in Lombardy. It took Frederick thirty years to recognize in a formal treaty that his rule over Lombardy was chiefly honorary and, for all practical purposes, abolished.

The following year in October Frederick led an army across the Brenner pass into Italy. He was joyfully welcomed by a number of Lombard cities, notably Pavia, Cremona, Como and Lodi, which complained bitterly of Milanese aggression. These towns remained loyal to Frederick as their rightful sovereign primarily because of their fear of Milan. But most of the northern Italian cities regarded Frederick as an intruder and an enemy, a menace to their cherished municipal liberties.

No one, however, regarded him as a foreign conqueror. He was the sovereign of all. The dispute and the prolonged war were solely about his right to exercise direct power, to arbitrate local wars, to collect taxes and to appoint local officials.

As Frederick marched farther into Italy he found that feeding his troops was a problem. He was forced to send out foragers to collect contributions from various communities. But some of the towns refused to contribute. So the soldiers looted, which naturally damaged the young Emperor-elect's effort to appear benevolent and impartial. Frederick tried vainly to persuade Milan to accept his arbitration, which would mean giving up her efforts to conquer her neighbors. Milan contemptuously refused. Since he lacked a force large enough to attack Milan, Frederick compromised by placing the city under the ban of the Empire —a sort of imperial excommunication. Unable to punish Milan, Frederick instead destroyed two of Milan's allies, the towns of Asti and Tortona. He then proceeded to march on Rome.

Pope Eugenius, who had asked Frederick to come to his aid, had died in July of 1153. Roger II of Sicily, whom Eugenius wanted Frederick to fight, had died in February of 1154. His successor was his son, William the Bad. The new Pope, Hadrian IV, was an Englishman, the only Englishman ever to become pope. An able diplomat and executive, Hadrian was a firm believer in papal supremacy according to the ideas of Gregory VII.

Hadrian also believed equally firmly that popes should not be bothered by revolutionary republicans in the city of Rome. In the spring of 1155 one of Arnold's tumultuous followers assaulted a cardinal. Hadrian clapped an interdict on the city of Rome in reprisal. The churches were closed. Masses were not said. Marriages could not be performed. In order to persuade Hadrian to remove the interdict the Roman populace drove Arnold out of the city.

Who was this fiery demagogue who led revolts, attacked bishops and challenged popes? He was a monk, a former pupil of Abélard and the abbot of a monastery in Brescia. Austerely virtuous, fiercely eloquent, Arnold was a reformer of the most radical sort. He believed in a republican form of government for cities. He violently denounced the wealth, worldliness and vice of the clergy. Arnold preached that the Church must give up all its property and surrender all its temporal power. He called upon the people to compel the return of the Church to the poverty of the original apostles. No one questioned his personal virtue or the sincerity of his faith. But no pope, the head of the greatest and wealthiest organization in the world, could approve of its dissolution. And no secular monarch could approve of such a rebel against constituted authority.

Arnold's contemporary, John of Salisbury, wrote of Arnold in his *Memoirs of the Papal Court:* He was "one who had mortified his flesh with fasting and coarse raiment; of keen intelligence, persevering in his study of the Scriptures, eloquent in speech, and a vehement preacher against the vanities of the world. . . . He said things that were entirely consistent with the law accepted by Christian people, but not at all with the life they led. To the bishops he was merciless on account of their avarice and filthy lucre; most of all because of stains on their personal lives, and their striving to build the Church of God in blood."

When Arnold was exiled from Rome he took refuge in the castle of a sympathetic baron. Frederick Barbarossa was approaching. Hadrian sent him word that he would be grateful if the Emperor-elect would capture Arnold and turn that arch-heretic over to the justice of the Church. Frederick had no trouble persuading Arnold's protector to surrender his guest. To Frederick, Arnold was a rebel against both Church and state and richly deserved any punishment he might get.

Arnold was promptly tried by an ecclesiastical court, condemned and burned to death by secular officials. To prevent anyone from collecting Arnold's ashes as the holy relics of a martyr they were scraped up and thrown into the Tiber. The spectacle of the great Barbarossa enthusiastically cooperating in arranging the burning of the fanatical idealist is not a pretty one. But such a reaction is strictly modern. By the standards of his time Frederick only did his duty.

Pope Hadrian went out from Rome to meet Frederick. A comedy of errors followed in which the two bickered over protocol and symbolism. If Frederick led the Pope's horse and held his stirrup, would his actions be understood as recognition of the Pope's feudal supremacy or only as a courtesy? If the Pope refused to allow Frederick to kiss his cheek, was that significant or only pique? Soon after these crucial issues had been sorted out a deputation from the rebellious Romans arrived. Ignoring his election by the German princes, the Roman delegation offered to elect Frederick emperor themselves and for so doing asked for a bribe of 15,000 silver pounds. This was the sum popes sometimes distributed to the populace after their coronations. Hadrian had not been able to afford it. Perhaps the Romans thought it only reasonable to try and obtain the money from another source.

"You men of Rome," said Frederick, "make large demands upon our emptied treasury. You will act more advisedly if, by giving up these demands, you try our friendship rather than our arms."

But then the insolence of the Romans' offer to elect him emperor sank in and Frederick exploded: "Is this your Roman wisdom? Who are you who usurp the name of Roman dignitaries? Your honors and your authority are yours no longer. With us are consuls, senate, soldiers. It is not you who choose us, but Charles and Otto that rescued you from the Greeks and the Lombards, and conquered by their own might the imperial crown. That Frankish might is still the same. Wrench, if you can, the club from Hercules. It is not for the people to give laws to the prince, but to obey his commands."

Frederick's angry scorn probably offended the Romans as much as the insolent behavior of his Roman subjects offended him. His words had not been tactful or politic. The Romans held their city and they were determined not to permit Frederick to be crowned within its walls.

Frederick and his army and Pope Hadrian and his escort then proceeded to encamp on the north side of the Tiber outside the walls of the Leonine city, where the Castle of Sant' Angelo and Saint Peter's were located. Across the river lay the greater part of the city, by now largely recovered from the sack by Robert Guiscard's troops. Imperial coronations were traditionally performed on Sundays. If the Romans maintained a guard, or even a watch, upon the walls of the Leonine city, it was singularly inefficient. During the night a detachment of Frederick's German troops filed into the city without opposition and formed ranks surrounding Saint Peter's. Early on the morning of Saturday, June 18, 1155, Pope Hadrian and his cardinals entered the city and took up positions on the steps of the cathedral so that they could welcome Frederick with all proper ceremony.

At eight in the morning the handsome young Emperor-elect rode into the piazza and up to the steps of the cathedral. Pope Hadrian then duly performed the coronation ceremony on a Saturday; but he performed it in a peculiar fashion. Hadrian changed several parts of the traditional ceremony so as to emphasize symbolically the superiority of papal power over imperial power. Hadrian tried to dramatize publicly that Frederick's rank as emperor was *granted* to him by the pope, that he was not just confirming the vote of the German princes.

Frederick Barbarossa was a highly intelligent man. But he knew little Latin and was a crude German warrior compared to the subtle and sophisticated Hadrian. He may not have understood what Hadrian was trying to establish. Or, equally possible, he may have understood it perfectly and not have cared. He wanted to be emperor, and no German king could be officially acknowledged as emperor until he had been crowned in Saint Peter's by the pope. Once he was emperor *de jure* as well as *de facto* he could ignore or repudiate Hadrian's subtle symbolism. The Pope's trickery may seem trivial to modern minds. But it illustrates the importance attached in the Middle Ages to symbolical and mystical ceremonies and to legal and traditional precedents. The reality of power was rarely enough. It could always be strengthened or diminished by intangible rituals and forms.

When an emperor was crowned it was an old Roman custom to fight his German soldiers. But when Barbarossa was crowned the Roman people seemed completely unaware of what was going on. The Emperor and his troops marched peacefully back to his encampment outside the walls. Soon, however, news of the coronation spread across the city and swarms of furious citizens, as angry at the Pope as they were at the Emperor, rushed over the Tiber bridges and began to kill and loot in the Leonine city. Frederick was dining at a banquet held in honor of his coronation when he learned of the ugly riot. He ordered his soldiers to drive the maddened Romans out of the Leonine city. They went to work with enthusiasm and methodically slaughtered the rioters. Many who were not killed in battle were crowded off the bridges and drowned in the Tiber.

Frederick von Hohenstaufen was now a duly consecrated emperor and the victor over a Roman mob. But he did not control the city and he could not remain outside its walls for lack of food for his troops. He marched off and Pope Hadrian went with him. And soon his German nobles insisted on going home to Germany. Frederick, who depended on their good will, could not prevent them. They dispersed and the mighty Emperor was left with only a remnant of his army. Frederick left Pope Hadrian at Tivoli and marched north to Spoleto.

That picturesque hill town imprudently refused to surrender a friend of Frederick's held prisoner there, and equally imprudently paid Frederick a tax in counterfeit money. Understandably annoyed, Frederick laid siege to the city. Still more unwisely, the citizens of Spoleto sallied forth from behind their protecting walls and fought Frederick's small force in open battle. Their confidence was ill-founded. They were soundly defeated and brutally punished. Spoleto was looted and burned to the ground while the inhabitants, who had been allowed to depart, watched from nearby hills.

Frederick returned to Germany. During his year in Italy he had accomplished little: only his coronation. For the next three years the young

Emperor remained in Germany, preoccupied with German affairs. His alliance with Pope Hadrian collapsed. Hadrian annoyed Frederick by making an alliance with King William of Sicily. Frederick annoyed Hadrian by appointing bishops. And then Hadrian enraged Frederick by referring in a letter to the imperial crown as a *beneficium* bestowed at the coronation. The word meant "fief" to the German nobles and seemed to mean that Hadrian considered the empire a feudal fief of the Papacy, which perhaps he did. But so violent was the protest of the German lords that Hadrian apologized, saying that by *beneficium* he meant only a favor. That was better, but still insulting. It suggested that Frederick had no right to be crowned, but was crowned only as a favor.

When Frederick Barbarossa marched down into Italy for the second time in July of 1158 he came at the head of a powerful army and he brought with him a number of legal authorities. The Emperor intended to settle once and for all the problem of those rebellious Lombard cities led by Milan which insisted on their ancient liberties, by which they meant the independent practices they had developed only during the last century. To Frederick such rank rebellion against his own sacred majesty was insufferable. He intended to restore proper order and to install German governors in the rebel cities.

The cities which had welcomed him on his first appearance in Italy did so again, and so did numerous rural nobles and the pro-imperial parties in most towns. Frederick was not just the august and outraged Emperor; he was the leader of an Italian political party. It was his misfortune that his Italian supporters were less numerous than his Italian foes. His foes fought heroically to preserve their independence, which many of them had not used well. They had constantly fought each other. Milan had cruelly destroyed the cities of Como and Lodi. So there was much justification for Frederick's ambition to bring peace and prosperity to Lombardy under his autocratic rule.

The Emperor began his summer campaign by attacking Brescia, Milan's ally, and quickly subdued it. He then besieged Milan itself for five weeks, with brisk fighting and the usual summer outbreaks of disease. But a surprising display of good sense by both sides produced a compromise agreement which granted Frederick many of his imperial rights and yet left Milan considerable freedom. If the agreement had been kept and the precedent had been followed elsewhere, much suffering would have been avoided.

Encouraged by his settlement with Milan, the Emperor marched to Piacenza and camped on the fields of Roncaglia nearby. There he held a formal court with representatives from many cities present. Its purpose was for Frederick's lawyers, some of them from the great law school at Bologna, to find precedents in ancient laws which would justify Frederick's imposing his personal autocratic rule on Lombardy. Instead of bluntly proclaiming his repudiation of many of the cities' independent practices, it was evidently thought tactful to appeal to forgotten laws of the good old days.

The financial "rights" Frederick demanded were comprehensive. Peter Munz in his *Frederick Barbarossa* enumerates them: "They comprised rents from certain estates which had originally belonged to free Lombards; tolls to be levied on public roads and navigable rivers as well as in ports, wharves and markets; the right to coin money, the right to levy fines and to the ownership of estates without lords. Further the right to confiscate the property of persons who had contracted forbidden marriages. The Emperor was allowed to demand horses, ships and wagons as well as extraordinary subventions for the purposes of war. He was declared the sole owner of silver mines and salt mines and of all fisheries, and the half owner of any treasure which was discovered as the result of a search."

The list is impressive. It is small wonder that most of the Lombard cities resisted such sweeping claims. Even more alarming was the assertion that all judges and city magistrates must be approved by the Emperor and must not take office without his consent. The Roncaglia claims were a diagram for autocracy. However, they were left deliberately vague, never put into writing and obviously subject to interpretation and bargaining.

In the following months Frederick acted as if he believed everything was settled and the Roncaglia decrees would be accepted. But Milan, correctly recognizing the decrees' threat to its independence, broke the compromise truce and attacked an imperial fortress. This insolent defiance of his sacred authority enraged the Emperor. In a formal ceremony held in Bologna he again put Milan under the ban of the Empire for high treason and rebellion, and declared that Milan was to be looted and its inhabitants enslaved.

Renewed hostilities began when Frederick besieged the city of Crema, an ally of Milan and an enemy of Cremona, Frederick's ally. The Cremonese had given Frederick a bribe of 15,000 silver marks to destroy Crema. The siege lasted for six months, from June of 1159 until January of 1160, and was conducted with ferocious savagery by both sides.

To protect one of his siege engines the Emperor hung prisoners from it so that archers on the walls of Crema could not shoot at it without killing their friends. They shot anyway and killed them. In retaliation the people of Crema executed some of their German prisoners on the ramparts of the city in full view of the besiegers. When the exhausted city finally surrendered, it was totally destroyed. There was no massacre and no rape. Frederick mercifully permitted the miserable citizens of Crema to depart as homeless refugees.

Shortly after the fall of Crema in 1160 Barbarossa attacked Milan, devastated its surrounding territory and began a siege which, with interruptions, lasted for two years. The Milanese withstood the Emperor's might with obstinate determination until, their strength drained away, their supplies exhausted, emaciated and half starved, they sent emissaries to surrender to the triumphant Emperor. Frederick, who never slaughtered the populations of rebellious towns as Roger II of Sicily had done, could still be cruel in the twelfth-century fashion. Shortly before the Milanese envoys arrived he had demonstrated what kind of justice insolent rebels against his authority could expect. He had sent six Milanese prisoners back to their beleaguered city. Five had been blinded. The sixth led the others. His nose had been cut off.

Barbarossa kept his court in Lodi, his faithful ally and Milan's bitter enemy. There on March 1, 1162, the consuls of Milan prostrated themselves before the Emperor, admitted that they had committed treason and promised unconditional surrender. A few days later the consuls returned with 300 Milanese knights who begged for mercy. Several days after that about 1,000 foot soldiers came to Lodi and surrendered the *carroccio* of Milan. The occasion was ceremonious.

Trumpeters standing on the *carroccio* blew a farewell blast. The tall mast of the *carroccio* was lowered. Barbarossa himself removed the Milanese banner and then all 1,000 Milanese soldiers knelt and asked for mercy. Frederick said nothing. But a high official reminded the kneeling Milanese that their surrender was unconditional. They would hear the conditions the next day.

Frederick told them that as traitors they deserved death, but he would be merciful. The consuls and many other prominent citizens would be held as prisoners. Hostages would be taken from among the knights. The walls and moats of Milan would be destroyed. And all the citizens would individually swear oaths of loyalty to the Emperor.

But even all this was not enough. A week later Frederick gave in to pressure from his Italian allies and ordered the entire population of Milan to leave the city. Then, block by block, building by building, Milan was destroyed. The city's vindictive Italian enemies did most of the demolition work in short order, so great was their hatred and thirst for revenge. "God," said the Archbishop of Salzburg, as he stood among the ruins, "has done unto this city as she did unto others."

It should be pointed out in Frederick's favor that there was no massacre or mass rape, so often the sequels to successful sieges. And also that it was an old Italian custom to destroy the houses and towers of one's enemies. The Emperor, who considered the rebels of Milan villainous traitors and sacrilegious defiers of his imperial authority, undoubtedly thought that he was merciful. He believed, too, with sublime optimism, that with Milan destroyed he could bring about a golden age of peace in Lombardy.

This spectacular triumph of imperial might was not nearly as decisive as Barbarossa thought. In 1162 the German Emperor was still a long way from understanding how passionate was Italian city patriotism and how furious was his foes' determination to preserve their municipal freedoms.

So Frederick made a major mistake. He divided the Milanese refugees into four groups so that they would not be a united force, which was sensible. But he permitted them to establish themselves in four new communities only a few miles from the ruins of Milan. If Barbarossa had scattered the Milanese all over Italy he might have eliminated their capacity to lead the war against him. Instead, he left them so near to each other that they easily communicated and so near to the site of their former greatness that their patriotic fury continued to burn at white heat.

While the Emperor was busy suppressing the rebels of Crema and Milan a new crisis in the Papacy arose. Pope Hadrian, who had made an alliance with Milan against Frederick, died in September of 1159. A tumultuous conclave followed, out of which emerged two rival popes. Alexander III, whose claim to be the rightful pope was the more convincing, followed Hadrian's policy of opposition to Frederick. Victor IV, the anti-pope, was a fiery partisan of Frederick's.

In January of 1160 the Emperor summoned a church council to be held in Pavia, which, he seemed to think, could settle the issue of the rival popes. For Frederick to call such a council was a reckless and impolitic decision. Since the reign of Gregory VII it had been firmly established that ecclesiastical matters and especially papal concerns were not subject to control or interference by any secular power. And here with insolent authority was Barbarossa claiming "that the Emperor has the sole authority to settle a papal election." Only fifty bishops attended Frederick's council at Pavia.

Alexander haughtily refused to be present and thereby demonstrated to most of Europe that he was indeed the rightful pope. The council approved Victor's election and, naturally, so did Frederick. The two rival popes proceeded to excommunicate each other and Alexander excommunicated Frederick.

So, like Henry IV before him, Barbarossa now had his own anti-pope and both of them were excommunicates. And, also like Henry IV, in the rightful pope he had a shrewd and powerful enemy. Alexander was doggedly determined not to permit Frederick to achieve the reality of sovereign power in Italy. If Frederick did so, the temporal power of the Papacy would soon disappear.

Pope Victor lived only four years and was succeeded by a second anti-pope, Paschal III, whose doubtful claim to the Papacy was even less convincing than Victor's. Paschal was a loyal imperialist and a useful servant always ready to obey the Emperor's wishes.

In 1163–64 Barbarossa made his third expedition into Italy, a short and ineffectual one which accomplished little. But in 1166 Frederick marched into Italy for the fourth time and brought with him a large army. He remained for two years, won victories and suffered disasters. Some historians believe that he wanted to capture Pope Alexander. Frederick certainly would have known how helpful the de Hautevilles had found it to capture popes. But what he could have done with Alexander as a prisoner is not clear. He could hardly have forced him to abdicate and recognize Paschal.

Frederick's genuine piety and usual mercy make it seem unlikely that he would mistreat or abuse Alexander. But if Frederick could keep Alexander in some comfortable imprisonment he could cut off his torrent of anti-imperial propaganda letters and cyclicals, and he could stop his leadership of the rebellious Lombard cities.

After wasting considerable time in Lombardy on punitive raids Barbarossa marched on Rome for the second time. He split his army in two, sending one half under the command of Rainald, Archbishop of Cologne, through Tuscany on the shortest route to Rome. Frederick led the other half down the Adriatic coast to attack Ancona. The Romans rashly sent an army out of the city to risk a pitched battle with the Archbishop's troops and were decisively defeated. When Frederick heard the good news of this victory he raised his siege of Ancona and hurried to join Rainald. Their united force then easily captured the Leonine city north of the Tiber. Paschal was installed as pope in Saint Peter's and there he crowned Frederick emperor. Why Frederick wanted this second coronation is baffling. He had already been crowned by Hadrian, a genuine pope without any rival claimant. To be crowned by his personal anti-pope could hardly add any further authority to his position.

Soon afterward the Roman population surrendered the main part of the city south of the Tiber. Frederick celebrated in a solemn "crown-wearing" festival and it seemed as if his triumph were complete.

Unfortunately for Frederick, Pope Alexander had fled and his escape robbed Barbarossa's victory of much of its significance. And the very day after the pompous "crown-wearing" ceremony a terrible pestilence broke out in the Emperor's army. It was August and exceptionally hot. The malaria-infested lands of the surrounding countryside were always a threat to Rome's conquerors. The exact nature of the pestilence which smote the imperial army (like that which destroyed Sennacherib's before Jerusalem) is unknown; but most probably it was malaria combined with dysentery.

Thousands of Barbarossa's soldiers died, including many of his best friends and most important subordinate commanders. Panic spread among the survivors. Their fear of death was compounded by religious guilt caused by their sacrilege in enabling a schismatic anti-pope to be crowned in Saint Peter's and to crown Frederick there. The mighty army which had marched in triumph from Germany to Rome disintegrated. The survivors fled in small groups or alone. Many of the terrified fugitives died in their flight long before they saw the Alps.

"Never since the world began," wrote Thomas à Becket, Archbishop of Canterbury, to Pope Alexander III, "have the power and justice of God been more clearly manifested than in the destruction by so shameful a death of the authors of this great persecution."

Barbarossa himself left Rome with a small escort on August 6, 1167. He had not even set foot in the larger part of the city. He reached Pavia safely on September 9 and learned that many of the northern Italian cities had united against him in an alliance which was to become famous as the Lombard League. With no army to protect him Frederick was in serious danger of capture. He did not dare remain longer in Italy. Flight to his secure base in Germany was essential. But flight was difficult. Most of the Alpine passes were guarded by the troops of enemy cities.

Frederick rode west from Pavia and reached the little city of Susa at the foot of the Alps some forty miles west of Turin. And there the local officials forced him to remain. Their respect for their Emperor was not as great as their fear that if they let him escape, his enemies would take vengeance upon them. But somehow Frederick, disguised as a servant, managed to get away. Behind him he left a loyal friend who briefly pretended to be the Emperor. Frederick crossed the mountains into Burgundy and safety and thence proceeded to Germany.

As early as 1166 Verona, Vicenza, Padua and Treviso, soon joined by Venice, had formed an alliance to resist Barbarossa's domination. And in the spring of 1167 while Frederick was marching on Rome four other Lombard cities formed a league for mutual support against the Emperor: Cremona, Mantua, Bergamo and Brescia. Cremona's membership in the new anti-Frederick organization was ominous. If Cremona, ancient foe of Milan and former stanch ally of Frederick, could not be trusted, what city could? Hardly any.

The rule of the ignorant, brutal governors Barbarossa had installed in the towns he controlled had been too harsh. Backward, feudal Germany just did not have a corps of educated government servants who could serve their Emperor in Italy. So, for lack of better, Frederick had been forced to appoint avaricious, corrupt and violent men who won only hatred for his rule. Sometimes the barbarous German governors demanded seven times as much in taxes as was rightly owed. They extorted unreasonable fines, demanded bribes and raped women and girls. In spite of such provocations the Lombard towns still did not deny that Frederick was their rightful emperor. What they denied was his right to rule them directly. Frederick wanted to be a benevolent autocrat. The Lombards wanted him to be a distant and abstract symbol.

Soon after their alliance Cremona, Mantua, Bergamo and Brescia aided the Milanese to rebuild their city and Milan resumed its former leadership of the war against the Emperor. And in December the two alliances united and formed the Lombard League. By 1174, when Frederick returned to Italy for the fifth time, the league included thirty-six towns.

Pope Alexander made an alliance with the league, sent money to the league, exhorted it and manipulated it with astute diplomatic finesse. Like all medieval popes, he was determined that no German emperor should win enough power in Italy to threaten papal power. He was equally obstinate, of course, in his opposition to this particular emperor who maintained his private anti-pope. But, unlike Gregory VII, who deposed Henry IV, Alexander did not try to depose Frederick.

Pope Alexander did threaten to excommunicate and interdict any Lombard town which dared to make an alliance with any city not a member of the league, or with any other alliance. Compared to many medieval popes, Alexander was a reasonable and moderate man; but he was essentially politically minded and employed spiritual means for political ends as a matter of course.

As a gesture of defiance to Frederick Barbarossa the members of the league built a new fortified city in western Lombardy on a strategic site. And as a gesture of appreciation to Pope Alexander they named it Alessandria. The new city was to prove a major obstacle to Frederick when he returned for his last great effort to subdue his rebellious subjects and to impose his imperial authority on Italy.

In 1174 Frederick von Hohenstaufen was about fifty-two years old, still handsome, vigorous and charming. His personal magnetism was as strong as ever, his reputation as a fine soldier and as a generous foe untarnished. Widely admired as a man of his word, Barbarossa was respected by his enemies and loved by his friends. Although he fought against the political schemes of Pope Hadrian and Pope Alexander, his personal piety was never questioned. A contemporary called him "clementissimus and dulcissimus"—most merciful and most sweet.

A modern historian, T. F. Tout, has written of Barbarossa that his long effort to impose his rule on Italy was "one of the most magnificent failures in history." And that Frederick "with all his faults remains the noblest embodiment of medieval kingship. . . . He was chaste, honorable, just and religious. He was assiduous at divine service, devout in his behavior in church, regularly putting aside a tenth of his income for pious and charitable objects. A mighty warrior, he only rejoiced in battle because victory was the best method of assuring peace." We may doubt that Barbarossa's final goal was peace rather than power, but we cannot doubt that this remarkable man has had an enduring appeal.

For six years Frederick was busy with German affairs. Then in 1174 he marched into Piedmont from the west with an army too small for his needs. Several of the great German nobles had refused to join his campaign. Nevertheless, Frederick was optimistic. He had never lost a battle. Genoa and Pisa now supported him.

His first object was Susa, the town which had dared confine its lawful Emperor as a prisoner. Frederick burned Susa to the ground. He then marched on Alessandria. How could that "city of straw" resist him?

The mere existence of this new fortress city named for his enemy was an insult. And two of his Italian allies, the Marquis of Montferrat and the city of Pavia, felt that they were directly menaced by Alessandria. The siege of Alessandria lasted for six months, from October of 1175 until early April of 1176. The Alessandrians manned their walls with tenacious courage. Some of Frederick's troops, depressed by the hardships of winter fighting and by their lack of success, deserted. Medieval sieges were always doubtful and difficult. At Alessandria supplies were scarce and shelter scanty. Disease sapped the numbers and the morale of the troops.

In desperation Frederick violated the Truce of God, which was supposed to prevail during Lent. He ordered tunnels dug under the walls of Alessandria. On Good Friday night a party of soldiers crawled into the tunnels and some of the men broke into the city. But the alarm sounded while most of Frederick's soldiers were still in the tunnels. The Alessandrians destroyed the tunnels, smothering the men inside them, and those who had emerged were driven back across the walls with heavy losses. The gates, which Frederick had expected to be opened to him, remained closed. Dismayed by this repulse, Barbarossa burned down his camp outside the city and abandoned the siege. His failure to chastise the insolent rebel city was discouraging to him, and gloriously encouraging to his enemies.

Shortly after the Emperor looked his last on the walls and towers of Alessandria the imperial and Lombard League armies encountered each other, formed their lines for battle and then prudently decided not to fight. Instead, a truce was arranged and a long series of complicated negotiations was begun. Frederick offered some concessions, but the negotiations collapsed when the league representatives demanded that the Emperor repudiate his anti-pope and accept Alexander.

The following year Frederick summoned reinforcements from Germany. In the middle of May some 2,000 mounted warriors arrived at Como, which city on the southern end of Lake Como is only about thirty-five miles north of Milan. When Frederick heard of their arrival he was in Pavia, some thirty miles south of Milan. He at once marched forth with 500 mounted knights, circled around the hostile city of Milan, and joined his new recruits at Como. He then set out to march around Milan again and return to Pavia. His force of 2,500 heavily armed horsemen was accompanied by the infantry militia of Como, who served only as a guard for the baggage.

The Lombard League troops marched out of Milan to intercept the imperial army. The Lombard cavalry may have numbered about 4,000. The Milanese infantry, pikemen and crossbowmen, were much more numerous. So Barbarossa's troops, consisting only of mounted knights, were greatly outnumbered. Early in the morning of May 29, 1176, the two armies met near the village of Legnano and fought one of the famous battles of the Middle Ages.

Contemporary accounts of the Battle of Legnano are inadequate and confused. We know far more about what happened at Hastings more than 100 years earlier than we do about Legnano. However, it is certain that the battle began when the Lombard advance guard rounded the end of a wood and unexpectedly saw Frederick's advance guard riding peaceably toward them. There was a sharp skirmish. The Germans fell back upon their main force and the Lombards had time to draw up their horsemen in four battalions. The Milanese infantry, with a special honor guard surrounding the sacred *carroccio,* probably was deployed behind the cavalry.

Frederick Barbarossa was too much the gallant medieval knight to be a prudent general. Although he saw that his army was dangerously outnumbered, he refused to retreat and fight on some more propitious occasion. He is said to have thought it "unworthy of his imperial majesty to show his back" to the enemy. He ordered a charge and rode with his men. All four Lombard cavalry units were driven from the field by the German knights, who then turned and attacked the Milanese infantry.

The struggle was long and bloody. Frederick himself led repeated charges against the Milanese infantry. But when victory seemed possible a number of the Lombard knights reassembled and, joined by fresh horsemen from Brescia, charged the imperial troops in the flank. Frederick's horse was killed and he himself was flung to the ground before the enemy pikemen. The Germans panicked. They fled and many were slain as they fled. Many others drowned in the Ticino River. The Lombard-Milanese triumph was complete. The Emperor himself was believed to have perished on the battlefield.

Three days after the Battle of Legnano Frederick von Hohenstaufen turned up safely in Pavia, where his death was being mourned. How he escaped and what adventures he may have met with in his flight are unknown.

The news of Legnano spread swiftly across Italy and great were the rejoicings over the defeat of the mighty Barbarossa. The triumphant Milanese wrote in a dispatch to Bologna: "Glorious has been our triumph over our enemies. Their slain are innumerable as well as those drowned or taken prisoner. We have in our hands the shield, banner, cross and lance of the Emperor, and have found in his coffers much gold and silver, while the booty taken from the enemy is of great value; but we do not consider these things ours, but the common property of the Pope and the Italians. In the fight Duke Berthold was taken, as also a nephew of the Empress and a brother of the Archbishop of Cologne. The other captives are innumerable and are all in custody in Milan."

For twenty-two years Frederick Barbarossa had not wavered in his determination to impose his rule on Lombardy. Now after this disastrous defeat, and after the refusal of some of the most powerful German nobles to support his Italian war, he was forced to recognize that he lacked the power to subdue the indomitable Italians. Always a shrewd judge of possibilities, Frederick knew that he did not have to surrender or flee the country. He could divide his enemies by making a separate peace with the Pope. Late in October imperial envoys were talking to Pope Alexander in the papal city of Anagni some thirty-five miles southeast of Rome.

The negotiations at Anagni were delicate and devious. Pope Alexander cared more about ending the schism and persuading the Emperor to recognize him as the true pope than he did about the war in Lombardy. Frederick cared more about salvaging what he could from his untenable position as an emperor who could not rule an important part of his empire than he did about papal politics. Finally a preliminary truce called the Peace of Anagni was agreed upon. Its most important provisions were that Frederick would recognize Alexander as the true pope and that Alexander would make a separate peace. But nothing would be final until a more formal peace conference could be held with the Lombard League towns participating.

That conference was held the next year in Venice from May to July, 1177. All important questions were laboriously settled through intermediaries while Barbarossa remained on the mainland. Only after it was fixed that Frederick and Alexander would make peace and that Frederick and the Lombard League would sign a six-year truce did the Emperor enter Venice.

On Sunday, July 24, the Emperor crossed over to the Lido, riding in the Doge's special galley. There three cardinals absolved him from his excommunication, and only then did the Doge himself arrive and escort Frederick across the lagoon to Venice. The Pope was awaiting the

Emperor, seated on a temporary throne erected in front of the great cathedral of San Marco. An immense crowd packed the entire piazza.

A contemporary chronicler wrote that when Frederick "approached the Pope, inspired by the Holy Spirit and venerating God in Alexander, he put aside his imperial dignity and insignia and prostrated himself at the feet of the Pope. With tears in his eyes Alexander cordially raised him, embraced and blessed him. Presently with voices raised the Germans intoned the Te Deum. The Emperor then took the Pope by the right hand and led him into the church, and when he had again received the Pope's blessing he returned with his retinue to the Doge's palace."

Unlike Henry IV during his famous humiliation at Canossa, Frederick I wore no special garb of penitence and did not admit any papal superiority over his imperial power. He made no public recantation. The nearest he came to an admission of his error in supporting schismatic popes was when he haughtily said: "Let it be known to the entire world that although we are clothed in the dignity and glory of the Roman Empire, this dignity does not keep us from ignorance."

The night of his arrival in Venice Barbarossa sent word to Pope Alexander that he would like to hear him say mass the next day. So on the following morning Frederick escorted the Pope into the cathedral. He was angered to see the choir stalls occupied by curious spectators and in a fit of righteous fury drove them out—no doubt consciously aware of the famous precedent when Jesus drove the moneychangers out of the temple. Frederick listened politely to Alexander's sermon and could not understand a word of it because of the Pope's accent. But a distinguished cleric translated in a whisper as Alexander spoke. We are not told whether Alexander spoke Latin with an Italian accent, or an Italian too fluent and colloquial for Frederick to grasp.

Historians have differed over the question whether Frederick or Alexander came out the better from the Venice peace conference. Alexander got what he wanted. But Barbarossa also obtained much. He made a dignified peace with the Pope. He made a six-year truce with the Lombard League towns which left him still their sovereign, although without much actual power. And he even made a crafty and ambiguous agreement with Alexander which left him full control of Tuscany for the next fifteen years.

In the pavement of the porch of San Marco cathedral in Venice are three red slabs of marble which mark the spot where the Emperor Frederick von Hohenstaufen prostrated himself in humble reverence before the shrewd and courageous old man who was His Holiness Alexander III.

After the Peace of Venice the Emperor remained in Italy, progressing from city to city, diplomatically displaying himself as an affable and benevolent ruler who bore no grudges after twenty-two years of savage, although intermittent, warfare. Resigning himself to the inevitable, Frederick with astonishing cheerfulness made the best of his disappointing situation. If his ultimate sovereignty was accepted, if the fiercely rebellious little republics recognized him as their emperor only in an abstract and symbolical sense, he would (at least in public) be content.

The truce with the Lombard League lasted until 1183 when in a treaty signed at the city of Constance in what is now Switzerland Frederick formally recognized the league and surrendered the various rights he had once so imperiously claimed. The league cities in their turn formally acknowledged his feudal supremacy as emperor. All that the Treaty of Constance really accomplished was to ratify the *fait accompli* previously achieved at Venice.

In January of 1185 Frederick Barbarossa returned to Italy for the sixth and last time. But instead of marching at the head of an army, instead of denouncing the impudent rebels who defied his authority, he came as an honored guest and was welcomed with popular enthusiasm in Milan (of all cities!). And in Milan, for so many years his implacable enemy, Frederick presided at the wedding of his son Henry to Constance, posthumous daughter of King Roger II of Sicily and aunt of the reigning king of Sicily, William II (the Good). The son born of that diplomatic marriage, Frederick II, was to win even more fame than his grandfather Frederick I, without winning any of the admiration and affection which Barbarossa enjoyed throughout his life.

On July 5, 1187, Saladin, the great Kurdish Sultan of Egypt and Syria, utterly defeated the ineptly led army of the crusading Kingdom of Jerusalem at the Battle of Hattin. Three months later Saladin captured the holy city of Jerusalem. Pope Gregory VIII summoned the Kings of France and England and the Emperor of Germany to a new crusade to deliver Jerusalem from the infidel. Philip Augustus of France and Richard Coeur de Lion probably felt no genuine religious enthusiasm for the crusade in which they thought it expedient to take part. But Barbarossa, who had considered going crusading several times before, embraced the cause with heartfelt sincerity. The Emperor's clear duty was to protect the Church and Christendom from their Moslem foes. Frederick had been a warrior all his life. Now here was a holy war which would make a glorious climax to his long career. At Pentecost late in the spring of 1188 Frederick took the crusader's cross in a grand ceremony in the city of Mainz. According to one estimate, 13,000 others also took the cross on the same day.

A year later, in May of 1189, Barbarossa set sail down the Danube to join his army assembled at Vienna. Medieval chroniclers with their credulous love of mouth-filling round numbers wrote that he led 100,000 men. It is unlikely that he had even a third as many.

The German crusaders marched across the Balkans and Asia Minor on a long and dangerous trek. They fought Turks in numerous battles and suffered horribly from hunger, thirst and disease. They crossed the Taurus Mountains and in June of 1190 reached the Christian Kingdom of Armenia. The elderly Emperor, riding ahead of the main body of his army, dismounted at the river Saleph. And there, in an unhappy accident whose exact nature is not known, Barbarossa drowned. The great Frederick von Hohenstaufen was sixty-eight years old when he died. His army, deprived of its magnificent commander, disintegrated. Barbarossa's heroic effort late in life to crown his career with a glorious crusade was as total a failure as were his Italian wars.

VII

The Man Who Never Laughed

When Frederick Barbarossa's son Henry married King Roger II's post-humous daughter Constance in Milan in 1185 the groom was twenty years old, the bride thirty-one. Constance, who had spent many years in convents, was not a bit enthusiastic about her marriage. But her nephew, King William II (the Good), wanted the German alliance and insisted upon Constance's cooperation. As an unmarried daughter of a royal family it was her duty to do what she was told. William was only thirty-two himself, married and still childless. Presumably, he believed that he would have a male heir who would inherit the Kingdom of Sicily. But if he should have no heir, or if an infant heir should die as so many babies did in the Middle Ages, Constance would be the heir and her husband would be King of Sicily.

We may be sure that Frederick Barbarossa considered such an alluring possibility when he agreed to the marriage. His own popularity and supremacy as emperor made it reasonable to suppose that Henry would be elected to succeed him as King of Germany and Emperor-elect. And if Henry could add the Kingdom of Sicily to his other territories, that would be a major diplomatic triumph and an ironic revenge upon the popes who had struggled so persistently to destroy imperial power in Italy.

William the Good, by ignoring such a possibility, committed a blunder of statesmanship of enormous proportions. He ensured the end of the de Hauteville dynasty in Sicily and southern Italy and its replacement by the Hohenstaufens. But time robs many political mistakes of their contemporary urgency and significance. Today William is chiefly remembered as the builder of the glorious Benedictine abbey and cathedral at Monreale a few miles outside Palermo.

And Henry? He lived long enough to achieve a fearsome reputation and to terrify much of Italy and Sicily, but not long enough to win enduring celebrity. His slight, sinister figure seems dim today, cast into the shade by the fame and glory of his great father, Barbarossa, and equally obscured by the fame and brilliance of his great son, Frederick II.

Yet Henry was remarkable, too, an exceedingly able, intelligent and utterly ruthless ruler obsessed by love of power. Henry was short and almost puny compared to the magnificent Barbarossa. He was learned in Latin, law, and history and even wrote verses. He was a good soldier and a crafty politician. His ambition was without limit, his greed insatiable, his cruelty far greater than the customary cruelty of his time. Henry's cold-blooded ferocity was carefully planned and methodically, horribly executed.

In 1189 William the Good died without heirs. He was only thirty-six. So Constance and Henry became the lawful rulers of the Sicilian kingdom. In the same year Barbarossa had left Germany on his crusade after appointing Henry regent during his absence. Consequently Henry was too busy in Germany to claim his Sicilian throne immediately. The prospect of a German king did not please the Sicilian nobles. By now they were used to de Hautevilles and wanted another. So William's cousin Tancred, an illegitimate de Hauteville, was crowned king in Palermo.

After word of his father's death reached Germany, Henry was busier still. The German princes elected him king and emperor-elect. So it was not until January of 1191 that Henry could leave Germany and march into Italy to be crowned emperor in Rome. His coronation took place on April 15, 1191.

Two weeks later Henry invaded the Kingdom of Sicily, intent on driving out the usurper Tancred and imposing his own lawful rule. Capua,

Aversa and Salerno all surrendered to him without fighting. He besieged Naples, but so many of his German soldiers fell sick with malaria Henry had to raise the siege. With his army greatly reduced in numbers Henry prudently returned to Germany.

German affairs again occupied Henry's full attention so that he could not take up his unfinished business with Tancred until 1194. But Tancred died in the same year. Consequently when Henry arrived the opposition was so ineffectual that he easily conquered his kingdom. Henry imprisoned Tancred's widow, Queen Sibylla, cruelly murdered many of her loyal supporters, and probably murdered her infant son, who disappeared. On Christmas day of 1194 Henry von Hohenstaufen had himself crowned King of Sicily in the cathedral of Palermo.

The Empress Constance was not present at her husband's coronation as King of Sicily. She was traveling at a leisurely rate from Germany to Palermo because Henry wanted the child she was expecting to be born in Sicily. Constance had reached the city of Jesi in the March of Ancona when she realized that her child would have to be born there. The Empress was now forty years old. She had been married for nine years and had not borne a child. She was determined that no political enemies or scandalmongers would be able to cast doubt on the authenticity of the imperial birth about to take place. So she had a large tent erected in the piazza of Jesi. Into that tent during the accouchement crowded nineteen cardinals and bishops and as many matrons of the town as could find room. They witnessed the birth of a male child on December 26, 1194. The child was named Frederick after his paternal grandfather.

Immediately after his coronation as King of Sicily, Henry arrested all the nobles and clergy present on a charge of conspiring against him. He might as easily have arrested them before the ceremony, but Henry probably took a sadistic pleasure in contemplating the fate he planned for them while they respectfully watched his crowning. Henry then had all those who had attended the coronation of Tancred burned alive. Tancred's body and that of his eldest son, Roger, were dug out of their graves and beheaded. And it was rumored that Tancred's second son, William, aged seven, who had disappeared, was blinded and castrated.

Henry's government in both Germany and the Kingdom of Sicily was harsh and efficient. Perhaps thinking that he could succeed where his father had failed, Henry made elaborate plans for a crusade and even sent a contingent of troops to Palestine. But in 1197 when he returned to Sicily Henry discovered evidence of a widespread conspiracy against him in which both Pope Celestine III and the Empress Constance were implicated. That Constance should have detested her brutal husband is only natural. That she should have dared to conspire against him is proof of her exceptional courage.

Two brief excerpts from biographies of Frederick II show the nature of the vengeance Henry took upon the leaders of the conspiracy. Ernst Kantorowicz wrote: "The Emperor had the captured ringleaders done to death with the most cruel tortures, and he compelled his wife to be present at the ghastly execution of her guilty countrymen, while the court jesters played their grisly pranks with the still quivering bodies."

Georgina Masson wrote: "Count Giordono was put on a red-hot iron throne, and a red-hot iron crown was hammered with nails into his head, an allusion, apparently, to Henry's suspicion that he had planned to succeed him in the sovereignty of the island."

The young Emperor who ordered such torments and who punished his wife by forcing her to watch them was a psychopathic monster. No man, it was said, ever saw him laugh.

In August of the same year, while his fleet and his crusading army were being assembled at Messina on the northeast corner of Sicily, Henry went hunting in the woods of Linari near Messina and caught a fever. A month later on September 28, 1197, while he was riding back to Palermo Henry died of dysentery. He had reigned for only seven years and was only thirty-two years old.

After Henry's death the redoubtable Constance seized power in the Sicilian kingdom and made an arrangement with the new Pope, Innocent III. She had herself and her three-year-old son, Frederick II, crowned in Palermo, thus ensuring that, no matter what troubles occurred during the boy's minority, he would be the undoubted King of Sicily. Unfortunately, the courageous Empress died in Palermo the next year, in November of 1198, leaving her little son to the guardianship of the Pope. Anarchy followed in Sicily with Henry's German officials, Norman barons and Saracens all fighting each other for power. Pope Innocent, far away in Rome and much preoccupied with other matters, could not do much about it.

The child Frederick grew up in Palermo, running wild in the streets, somehow learning several languages and becoming an athlete, sometimes being fed by the charity of those who pitied the neglected royal boy. He came of age at fourteen and with Innocent's support assumed the rule of his unhappy kingdom.

VIII

"Lower Than God, Higher Than Man"

Long after a medieval pope had been consecrated in Saint Peter's, other customary ceremonies continued. Lothario Conti, a brilliant member of an aristocratic Roman family who had been a cardinal since he was twenty-nine, became Innocent III on February 22, 1198, when he was only thirty-seven. If he conformed to the usual procedures described by Gregorovius, the young Pope came out of the cathedral, walked to a wooden platform and seated himself on a throne. An archdeacon then removed from his head the papal miter and replaced it with a crown symbolizing his temporal rule, saying: "Take the tiara and know that thou art the father of princes and kings, the ruler of the world, the vicar on earth of Our Savior, Jesus Christ, whose honor and glory shall endure through all eternity."

Dressed in splendid robes glittering with jewels, Innocent then mounted a white horse covered with scarlet trappings and took his place in the middle of a magnificent cavalcade, which proceeded in the following order:

One of the Pope's horses (presumably unmounted and led by a groom); next the cross-bearer; then two horsemen bearing gold cherubim on lances; two prefects of the marine; the advocates and the judges in their long black robes; the school of singers; the deacons, sub-deacons, foreign abbots, bishops, archbishops; the abbots of the twenty-nine Roman abbeys; the patriarchs and cardinal-bishops; the cardinal-presbyters and cardinal-deacons. Some of these worthies were so old they could barely stay on their horses. Only then came the Pope on his white horse, accompanied by the prefect of the city. Behind the Pope came the members of the civic guilds, the militia, and the knights and nobles of Rome in full armor carrying the heraldic emblems of their houses.

The procession filed at a stately pace through applauding crowds, through triumphal arches specially erected for the occasion and through the ancient Roman arches of Titus and Septimius Severus. Chamberlains scattered coins among the crowds. The parade passed by the Colosseum and finally arrived at the piazza in front of the Lateran church. The journey had taken at least an hour. The clergy of the Lateran welcomed the new Pope with hymns and then escorted him to the portico of the church.

Here Innocent took his seat on an ancient marble chair, the *stella stercoraria*, which was a pierced chair like a modern toilet seat. The symbolism of this may have been to remind the Pope of the virtue of humility. Cardinals raised the Pope from the lowly seat, reciting the biblical verse: "He taketh up the simple out of the dust, and lifteth the poor out of the mire." Innocent then took three handfuls of gold, silver and copper and threw them to the crowd, saying: "Gold and silver are not mine, but what I have I give thee."

Then Innocent went into the Lateran church and prayed. When he had finished his prayers he received the homage of its clergy. From the church he went to the Lateran palace and in an elaborate ceremony took possession of the building. The officials of the palace kissed Innocent's foot. More prayers and more ceremonies followed, with the cardinals participating and the Senate of Rome swearing homage. A banquet concluded the exhausting day. The Pope sat alone at a table raised above the others. The clergy and nobles, officials and judges sat at lower tables. The greatest nobles present waited on the Pope.

The entire performance is a fine example of the medieval delight in symbolism and in ostentatious display. It also demonstrated the wealth and worldly grandeur of the Church, which contributed so much to the anti-clericalism of the time. The eighteen-year reign of Innocent III included so much corruption, venality and greed in the Church hierarchy that Innocent himself protested against it and instituted numerous reforms; the years of Innocent's reign also included a great wave of sincere religious feeling which manifested itself in popular demonstrations, in the creation of the mendicant orders of Saints Francis and Dominic, in the building of cathedrals and in the proliferation of heresies.

The secularization of the Church, its concern with organization, administration, finances and temporal power, offended many devout persons at the end of the twelfth century and the beginning of the thirteenth. The rapacity, greed and sexual license of high Church prelates shocked, and the moral corruption in many monasteries and convents disgusted. Innocent himself admitted that fire and sword alone could heal the corruption within the Church. A contemporary said of the officials of the Roman Curia: "They are stones for understanding, wood for justice, fire for wrath, iron for forgiveness; deceitful as foxes, proud as bulls, greedy and insatiate as the minotaur." Bishops extorted money from priests. Among the bishops' sources of revenue was the right of *collagium*, a payment with which clerics bought the right to keep a concubine in brazen defiance of the reform decrees of Pope Gregory VII. Gregory, who had died embittered more than 100 years earlier, would have been bitterer still if he could have seen the sad results of his furious insistence on clerical chastity!

Confronted by such a situation, a newly elected pope might be expected to devote his entire time and energy to reform, or to despair. Innocent did neither. He was a sincere reformer, but his reforms occupied only a small part of his attention. Innocent's principal goal was to increase the power and glory of the Papacy by making the pope the feudal superior of all secular rulers in a more efficient and universal way than was dreamed of by Gregory VII. He hoped to accomplish this at a time when no pope was able to rule the riotous city of Rome and most popes, including Innocent, were periodically driven out of the city by the malice of the nobles or the fury of the mobs.

Lothario Conti was born in the papal town of Anagni in 1161. He studied in Paris and in Bologna, became a canon lawyer and a theologian. In 1190 he was made a cardinal. As a cardinal Innocent wrote four quite

Pope Innocent III, fresco in the Sacro Speco at Subiaco. *Alinari*

undistinguished works of theology. But Innocent's sharp and logical mind, his legal and theological learning, his ability as an orator, organizer and diplomat were so outstanding that in the conclave of January 1198 he, the youngest of the cardinals, was unanimously elected pope. He was not a priest. So on one day he was ordained and on the next he was consecrated and crowned in Saint Peter's.

The new Pope was small, with a round, clean-shaven face and noticeably protruding ears. His complexion was dark and his expression stern. His masterful personality, his limitless ambition for the Papacy and for himself, and his colossal arrogance were to make his reign spectacular. Some historians consider Innocent the greatest pope who ever lived. But Innocent was so much the worldly politician that he never achieved canonization as a saint as, rather surprisingly, did that somewhat similar character, Gregory VII. Innocent was admired but not loved. Saint Lutgardis believed that Innocent could only escape damnation to hell by a narrow margin.

Formidable personality though he was, Innocent had his softer side. He had a sense of humor. He sang well and composed poems. The beloved Latin hymn *Veni Sancte Spiritus* has been attributed to him. He was honest and incorruptible most of the time. But he stooped to devious trickery in his politics and a number of times employed unworthy means for what he considered the worthy ends of the Church. Sometimes, but not always, he was kind, patient and tolerant.

In his first sermon as pope Innocent III preached on the text: "See, I have this day set thee over the nations and over the kingdoms, to pluck up and to break down, to destroy and to overthrow, to build and to plant." This was his conception of the pope's "plenitude of power," which he was to elaborate and insist on throughout his reign. The spiritual power, argued Innocent, was supreme over temporal power:

"The Lord Jesus Christ has set up one ruler over all things as His universal vicar, and as all things in heaven and earth and hell bow the knee to Christ, so should all obey Christ's vicar, that there be one flock and one shepherd. . . . No king can reign rightly unless he devoutly serves Christ's vicar. . . . Princes have power on earth, priests over the soul. As much as the soul is worthier than the body, so much worthier is the priesthood than the monarchy."

Repeatedly Innocent insisted on the supreme majesty of his own position. "The pope, although the successor of the prince of the apostles, was not *his* representative on earth, not the representative of any man, but *the representative of Christ himself, and through him the representative of God.*" Innocent claimed that he was a mediator between God and man, "lower than God, higher than man; less than God but more than man." He even said, "God is honored in us, and in us is God despised when we are despised."

Inspired by this awful mandate, Innocent plunged into his tasks with enthusiasm. His plans were made easier to implement by the death of the Emperor Henry VI three months before his election, which left Italy and Germany in a state of total confusion. The way was open for Innocent to make himself felt in international politics as well as in ecclesiastical affairs.

The new Pope began his reign by inaugurating several reforms in the papal court. He drove out the moneychangers who conducted their business in a passage near the Lateran palace kitchen. He dismissed numerous porters and janitors who had regularly demanded bribes of everyone who wanted an audience with the pope. And he sternly shut down a flourishing business which manufactured forged papal letters. Unfortunately, some of the forgers contrived to continue their profitable specialty elsewhere. Three times a week Innocent presided over a papal court of justice called a public consistory. Innocent displayed such legal skill and wisdom that a contemporary chronicler wrote:

"All were amazed at these qualities, and many learned men and jurisconsults would frequent the Roman Church simply to listen to him, and learned more in his consistories than they would have in the schools, especially when they heard him giving judgment; for so subtle was his statement of the case on either side that each party hoped for victory when it heard his presentation of its position; and no advocate, however skillful, appeared before him but did not acutely dread his objections to the points pleaded."

Innocent frequently said that he was morally obliged to do justice to fools as well as to wise men. "Mercy is higher than justice," he said, an idea he often ignored in his political decisions.

Innocent began his political maneuvers to increase the power and security of the Church by arranging to increase his own influence in the city of Rome. Innocent was Bishop of Rome, but he was not its ruler as the Renaissance popes were to be. Medieval popes had to recognize the distasteful fact that Rome was a free city with its own parliament, its own finances, its own army and its own right to make war and peace. Because of the murderous factions which so frequently fought each other, it was thought expedient and peaceful at times to have only one senator. Innocent somehow persuaded the Senator to swear an oath of loyalty to him; and he persuaded the imperial Prefect, an administrative official theoretically subordinate to the emperor, to switch his allegiance to him.

Innocent then turned to the pleasing task of driving what he called "the detestable German race" out of Italy. These were the German governors appointed by the late Emperor Henry VI. Innocent's intention was to impose papal rule and authority on the areas claimed by the Church because of the famous "donation of Constantine," but which the Church had never actually controlled: Umbria, part of Tuscany, the Romagna and the March of Ancona. In those regions the local populations were already in full revolt against Henry's tyrannical appointees. With their aid papal troops drove out the Germans. When Innocent visited Spoleto, Todi, Assisi and Perugia he was enthusiastically hailed as their deliverer and acknowledged as their sovereign.

Also in 1198 Pope Innocent issued a summons for a crusade to redeem Jerusalem from the infidels. And he began a campaign against heretics which continued throughout his pontificate. In April he wrote an archbishop in southern France urging him to wage war on heresy: "The prelate and his brethren are ordered to extirpate it by the utmost rigor of ecclesiastical censures, and if necessary by bringing the secular arm to bear through the assistance of princes and people. Not only are the heretics themselves to be punished, but all who have any dealings with them, or who are suspect by reason of undue familiarity with them."

In spite of the Pope's scheme to control Rome indirectly through friendly officials, that ever rebellious city broke into violent revolution in 1203. With much of the city in flames, Innocent was compelled to flee to nearby Palestrina. Ten months later he returned. A faction favorable to Innocent, joined by the Pope's own troops, fought bloody battles in the streets against the more radical party. Innocent bribed some of the opposition leaders to desert their cause, and the temporarily cowed municipality granted the Pope the right to appoint or depose the senator, which was in effect the right for the time being to rule the city. But this settlement, of course, endured for only a short while. Four years later the imperious Pope, who gave orders to kings, again had to flee from the city.

No other pope has ever involved the Papacy and himself in so many controversial issues, interfered in the affairs of so many nations, excommunicated so many monarchs or written so many pungent, dictatorial letters as Innocent III. Six thousand of his letters survive! Innocent did not claim direct rule over foreign countries. He claimed a general feudal overlordship and the special obligation to act on occasions of sin, or to maintain peace.

If a monarch sinned Innocent's duty was to reprove him and, if he proved contumacious, to excommunicate him. If there were rival monarchs, as was the case in Germany, Innocent had the duty to choose the better candidate. He interpreted sin so widely that he acted on any political question he chose. So in the normal course of his supervision of royal morals Innocent excommunicated the King of England, the King of France, the Emperor of Germany, the King of Navarre, the King of León and the King of Aragon.

Innocent's letters show him often being devious and evasive, sometimes being deliberately ambiguous, sometimes taking a firm moral stand, sometimes equivocating and for cynical political reasons supporting villainous bishops who ought to have been excommunicated and deposed.

An example is the Pope's support of Waldemar, Bishop of Schleswig in Denmark. It is unlikely that Innocent personally approved of the nefarious bishop, but to Innocent the all-important issue was that no cleric should be tried or punished by a secular court. No matter what his offense, a priest was only subject to the jurisdiction of the Church. Bishop Waldemar, a bastard son of King Cnut V of Denmark, had committed treason by leading a revolution against the reigning king of Denmark, had been defeated, captured and thrown into prison. Innocent, insisting on the privileges of the Church and ignoring Waldemar's flagrant guilt, demanded his liberation. The Danish king demurred, but subsequently agreed to release Bishop Waldemar in Hungary on Innocent's promise that the traitor would cause no more trouble.

But the criminal Bishop refused to stay quiet in Hungary and appealed his case to Rome. His case was unusual. As the bastard of a double adultery he was ineligible for holy orders in the first place. Danish emissaries testified that in addition to treason he was also guilty of adultery, apostasy, perjury and dilapidation (damaging or destroying Church property). Nevertheless, Innocent restored the wicked prelate to his bishopric in Denmark and permitted Waldemar to send a deputy to represent him if he feared for his safety in his native land.

Innocent III's concern for the Church's privileges caused him to support scoundrels. His concern for the spiritual welfare of the Church caused him to support saints.

In the summer of the year 1210 a young man of twenty-eight, dressed in a shabby brown robe with a rope tied around his waist, arrived in the city of Rome accompanied by twelve other young men similarly dressed. The leader of the group requested an audience with the Pope. Just how he obtained it under what circumstances is unknown because the whole episode is confused by differing accounts and contradictory legends. According to one story, the leader, who came from the Umbrian hill town of Assisi, stationed himself in a passageway where the Pope could be expected to pass. Innocent soon appeared, but mistook Francis for an ordinary beggar and ordered him to go away. Nevertheless, Francis persisted and was interrogated at length by a committee of bishops and cardinals.

The cardinal who was most thorough in this investigation, Giovanni di San Paolo, was deeply impressed. He went to Innocent and said: "I have found a man of the highest perfection, who desires to live in conformity with the Holy Gospel and observe evangelical perfection in all things. I believe that by him the Lord intends to reform the faith of the Holy Church throughout the world."

That night, or perhaps the next, another tale tells us, Pope Innocent had a vision in a dream. In his vision he beheld the Lateran church in danger of collapsing, but being held up by the pious efforts of one man.

The Dream of Innocent III, in the upper church of St. Francis in Assisi. *Alinari*

And this man was he who had stood in the passageway, to whom Innocent had refused to speak. Clearly, the Church in danger would be supported and strengthened by Francis.

So on the next day Cardinal Giovanni presented Francis of Assisi to Innocent III. And Francis asked the Pope's approval of the preaching he and his disciples were engaged in and of the rules he had chosen for his little order. The total poverty which was the basic tenet of Francis' order and the rigorous asceticism which Francis and his followers practiced seemed to Innocent excessive.

"My dear children," he said, "your life appears to me to be too severe. I see indeed that your fervor is too great for any doubt of you to be possible; but I ought to consider those who shall come after you, lest your mode of life be beyond their strength."

Innocent's comments were entirely reasonable from the point of view of a practical man of the world. But they were irrelevant to Francis, who, like many saints, was not a reasonable man.

At a consistory held shortly thereafter most of the cardinals agreed that Francis' new order was a dangerous innovation and that its dedication to absolute poverty without any possessions whatever was beyond human power. They were, of course, absolutely right for most men, but they were not right for Francis and his original disciples. "But," argued Cardinal Giovanni di San Paolo, "if we hold that to observe gospel perfection and make profession of it is an irrational and impossible innovation, are we not convicted of blasphemy against Christ, the author of the gospel?"

Pope Innocent was impressed by this argument. And he must also have been impressed by the character and personality of Francis, whose simplicity, piety, joy in God and in all the works of God, and radiant charm made him the most lovable and most beloved of saints. Innocent did not formally authorize the Franciscan Order, but he gave Francis his verbal approval and encouraged him and his disciples to continue preaching after first gaining the consent of their local bishops. At that time only bishops were allowed to preach. Parish priests were confined to celebrating mass and the various sacraments.

Innocent also recognized Francis as the responsible head of the order,

Saint Francis of Assisi; fresco in the Sacro Speco at Subiaco. *Alinari*

insisted that the order be under the direction of the Papacy and that its members assume the tonsure.

Although little enough is known about that fateful meeting of the great pope and the great saint, not even how often they may have met, the contrast between the two men of religion is imaginatively provocative. Innocent, for all his sincere piety, was arrogant, legalistic, a champion of the Church as a worldly organization, a lover of power and of pomp. He was able, tireless and intelligent. But he did not love and he did not inspire love. When he died many rejoiced.

And Francis? Millions of words have been written about him, nearly all of them written with admiration and affection. No final word on Francis' character and mission can ever be said. Both are subject to personal interpretation and opinion. What seems certain is that the prosperous merchant's son from Assisi, who dedicated his life to poverty and to as faithful an imitation of Christ as the world has seen, by his example and by his teaching did much to renew the religious life of the Middle Ages. At a time when masses of men were repelled by the worldly nature of the Church, Francis ignored doctrine and ritual and preached repentance and the love of God to the ordinary people of Italy. Francis brought Christianity out of the churches and into the hearts of men.

The tragedy of his mission was that Francis' message did not reach enough men and did not influence enough of those it did reach to cause any permanent change for the better in the conduct of most of mankind.

Francis of Assisi was a remarkable and a peculiar person. He was a mystic who believed that in his religious ecstasies he experienced direct revelation from God. He was an extremist who did not recognize the practical realities of the world. His gentle humor, his unfailing courtesy, his usual cheerfulness and his loving heart are irresistible. One can't help liking Francis of Assisi. But our affection for him cannot obscure the fact that this lovable poet and saint was not only childlike, he was also childish.

Maturity frequently recognizes the necessity to compromise with the ways of the world. Francis did not compromise. Some of his neighbors in Assisi thought he was mad. They did not think so because he heard Christ's voice and struggled with a personal devil. Such marvels might happen to anybody. They thought Francis was mad because of his repudiation of all material ends, all practical considerations, all comforts and normal pleasures. His excessive emotionalism, his fits of gloom and more frequent ecstatic raptures were certainly abnormal. If Francis lived today he would probably be diagnosed as a manic-depressive.

Giovanni Bernardone was called Francesco because his parents had taught him French. He was born in Assisi about 1182. His father was a rich cloth merchant who made frequent trips to France. Francis is supposed to have spent a dissipated youth. In 1202 he took part in a battle against the Perugians, was captured and spent a year in prison. After his release he was seriously ill and his thoughts turned to religion. On a pilgrimage to Rome when he was in front of Saint Peter's, Francis exchanged clothes with a beggar.

Some years later when Francis was praying in San Damiano, a small chapel in a bad state of disrepair on the outskirts of Assisi, he thought he heard the crucifix speak to him, saying, "Francis, go and repair my house, which as you see is wholly a ruin." Francis went home, selected a bundle of fine cloth from his father's shop, sold it at the market in nearby Foligno and gave the money to the priest of San Damiano. Not surprisingly, Francis' father was annoyed. When Francis refused to return the money, his father hailed him before the Bishop of Assisi, who ordered Francis to return the money.

Again he refused and this time he took off the clothes he was wearing, saying that they were his father's, too, and henceforth he would no longer recognize his father. Some commentators have called this rather theatrical gesture an example of Francis' sense of humor. It seems more likely that it was a solemn, symbolical dramatization of his forswearing property and adopting a life of total poverty. In any case, Francis began rebuilding the chapel of San Damiano with his own hands, begging food for himself and stones for the chapel.

Francis' personality was so appealing and his example of self-sacrifice so striking that soon disciples gathered around him. Francis demanded that they live as austerely as he did. They owned no property of any kind except their ragged robes. They lived by begging and occasional labor for food. They preached to the common people outdoors. They did not preach religious doctrine or criticize the established Church.

Francis taught repentance for sins, hope of heaven, joy in the love of God and loving kindness. He himself tried, and he expected the friars who were the members of his order to try also, to lead a life of absolute conformity with the example set by Jesus—including Jesus' so-called "difficult" sayings such as "Sell all thou hast and follow me" and "Take no thought for the morrow." When the number of Francis' disciples reached twelve he led his little band to Rome to ask Pope Innocent's approval of his new and revolutionary order. Hitherto most monks had lived in monasteries, where they toiled and prayed and worshipped to save their own souls. Now Francis intended to live in the world and do his best to save the souls of others.

The response to Francis' mission was enormous. Within eleven years the twelve original Franciscan friars had been joined by thousands of enthusiastic recruits. While he lived Francis was widely regarded as a saint. He continued to live as simply as before. He knew little Latin and wrote so badly he rarely tried. His letters and his beautiful religious poems were dictated. Francis scorned books and learning and believed that books were a form of property his followers should do without. Stories about him multiplied. After his death the stories increased and were written down. Many miracles were attributed to him, and quaint and charming legends tell of his preaching to birds and fishes, of his asking animals to be quiet so his sermons could be heard, of his converting the wolf of Gubbio.

In 1219 crusaders were besieging the city of Damietta in Egypt. Francis and a few of his friars journeyed to Egypt and were shocked by the demoralized condition of the Christian army. Francis predicted a major defeat and saw his prediction come true. And he witnessed the capture of Damietta. In his naïve simplicity and his ignorance of the power of the Moslem religion, Francis was certain that if he could only talk to the Egyptian sultan he could convert him to Christianity. He managed to cross the military lines and did talk to the sultan, but he failed to make a convert.

Back in Italy, Francis was distressed to realize that his order had grown so large it had to be organized. It had to have written rules and an administrative center. The order did not seem able to avoid property. The friars had to have somewhere to live. Rich men bequeathed them money and estates. There had been rules before, but not written ones. The rule on poverty is interesting: "The brethren shall appropriate to themselves nothing, neither house, nor place, nor other thing, but shall live in the world as strangers and pilgrims, and shall go confidently after alms. In this they shall feel no shame, since the Lord for our sake made himself poor in the world. It is this perfection of poverty which has made you, dearest brethren, heirs and kings of the kingdom of heaven. Having this, you should wish to have nought else under heaven."

Unhappy about the necessary organization of the Franciscan Order, Francis resigned the leadership to another and resumed his life as a simple ascetic and preacher. He suffered a serious infection of the eyes. Increasingly ill and almost blind, he retired to a mountain hermitage and there received the wounds of the stigmata. He died in 1226 at the age of forty-four. Two years later he was canonized by Pope Gregory IX.

Thirty years after Francis' death the Franciscans of Reggio nell' Emilia bought a former imperial palace with the cash they obtained from the sale of their old convent. Pope Innocent was right about the ideal of absolute poverty being too severe, at least for most of those who came after Francis.

Ninety-two years after Francis' death Pope John XXII excommunicated the Spiritual Franciscans, a splinter group whose members stubbornly clung to the saint's ideal of absolute poverty.

Innocent III concerned himself with scores of matters of small importance as well as with six of major consequence, which overlapped so confusingly in time that no chronological account is possible. These were: the Fourth Crusade; Innocent's war on heresy, which included the Albigensian Crusade; the rival emperors of Germany; the matrimonial troubles of the King of France; the religious and political troubles of the King of England; and the Fourth Lateran Council.

One of the Pope's first actions was to summon a new crusade to drive the Moslems out of Jerusalem. "It needed but perfect faith, more holiness," he said, "and one believer would put to flight twelve millions" (one Rebel can lick ten Yankees!). Crusaders who sincerely repented their sins, Innocent promised, would have their sins forgiven and be granted eternal life.

The Fourth Crusade, which was launched in response to Innocent's appeal, has been universally denounced as a cynical war of conquest and plunder and as a complete perversion of the crusading ideal. Instead of expelling Moslems from Jerusalem, the crusaders attacked the Christian city of Constantinople, looted it, drove out the Greek emperor and installed the Count of Flanders in his place. Innocent certainly did not plan the crusade that way; but he seems to have suspected fairly early what might happen and he rejoiced in the result—a good Catholic emperor in Constantinople instead of a Greek Orthodox one.

In May of 1201 envoys of the French counts and barons who led the crusade made an agreement with Venice for transportation of their army to Palestine at a cost of 94,000 silver marks. In the same year Alexius, exiled son of the imprisoned and blinded Emperor Isaac, whose throne had been lost to a usurper, visited Innocent in Rome. Alexius said that if the crusaders would restore the legitimate imperial family to power, a reunion between the Roman and Greek churches might be arranged. This suggests that Innocent knew an attack on Constantinople was at least being discussed as a possibility.

Somehow the usurping emperor, Alexius III, heard of the possible threat to his throne and wrote to Innocent imploring him to prevent such an outrage. Innocent in an equivocal and threatening reply dated November 16, 1201, wrote that he had tried to discourage the idea, but that the Emperor should use not words but deeds and hasten to "extinguish the fire while it was still far away" lest it should reach his own country. This letter confirms that Innocent knew of the possible attack on Constantinople. But the letter is also a threat that unless Alexius took an active part in the crusade he might himself be attacked. The Pope, who longed to see Jerusalem liberated, seems to have considered an attack on Constantinople as a reasonable alternative.

The crusading army assembled in Venice could not raise the promised 94,000 marks. So the Venetians offered to postpone payment if the crusaders would join them in an attack on the Dalmatian city of Zara, ruled by the Christian King of Hungary. Innocent heard of this (his sources of information were excellent) and at once forbade it. He was ignored. The crusaders and Venetians captured Zara in November of 1202, sacked the city thoroughly and then spent the winter there.

Pope Innocent was justly incensed. A crusade, which he himself had summoned, had defied his explicit prohibition and had attacked a Christian city. He excommunicated the entire expeditionary force. But shortly thereafter he absolved the crusaders, who had had little choice, but continued the excommunication of the Venetians.

If Innocent III had continued his excommunication of the crusaders, if he had declared them unworthy of fighting for the holy cause and called off the crusade, his moral position would have been better. Having seen and condemned the crusaders' attack on one Christian city and knowing of the threat to another, Innocent still did not explicitly forbid an attack on Constantinople. Instead, he equivocated and ordered that no more Christians were to be attacked unless they were actively hindering the holy war. This was too ambiguous and too subject to interpretation to be of any use. In 1204 Constantinople was captured and savagely sacked, and Baldwin IX, Count of Flanders and Hainaut, was crowned emperor in Saint Sophia.

Innocent's response to the diversion of the Fourth Crusade to attack the capital of a Christian empire was vague and contradictory. He wrote a letter of hearty congratulations to Baldwin, who, Innocent said, had served as an instrument of divine justice in bringing the Greek empire under the rule of good Catholics. It was "a miraculous event." But in spite of his relish in the expansion of papal influence, Innocent had troublesome doubts. He wrote:

"We do not mean to judge rashly the means employed by Providence. It is possible that the Greeks have been punished justly for the sin they committed against God; but it is also possible that you had not the right to punish them, and are guilty of hating your neighbor. But can we apply the word neighbor to these schismatics who rejected the love of their brethren? Who knows but that, in making you the instruments of his justice, God has given the legitimate recompense of your efforts?"

Later, when Innocent heard of the bloody horrors of the sack of Constantinople, he was furiously angry and depressed. "They who are supposed to serve Christ rather than their own interests, who should have used their swords only against the pagans, are dripping with the blood of Christians. They have spared neither religion, nor age, nor sex, and have committed adultery and fornication in public, exposing matrons and nuns to the filthy brutality of their troops. For them it is not enough to exhaust the riches of the Empire and to despoil both great and small; they had to lay their hands on the treasures of the Church, and what was worse its possessions, seizing silver retables from the altars, breaking them into pieces to divide among themselves, violating the sanctuaries and carrying off crosses and relics."

Innocent probably did not admit to himself that he had failed to take the firm moral position which his duty required; but it was shockingly clear to him and to all Europe that the crusade he had preached had been perverted into a brazen act of cynical aggression.

Disillusioned as he must have been with the ignoble Fourth Crusade, Innocent nevertheless never gave up his efforts to launch another crusade to liberate Jerusalem. He failed because crusading zeal was dying. Only the moral fervor of a much admired and beloved king, Louis IX of France, who while he lived was considered a saint, kept the crusading spirit alive a little longer.

Eight years after the capture of Constantinople occurred the most pitiful and absurd of all crusades. Hordes of children in France and Germany, inspired by the preaching of boys who claimed divine inspiration, marched across Europe. They were sublimely convinced that where sinful adults had failed, their own childish innocence would prevail. They expected ships to appear miraculously to transport them to Palestine, or that the sea itself would part before them as the Red Sea had done before Moses and the Israelites. Many of the French children who reached Marseilles did find ships. They joyfully went abroad and were sold as slaves by the ship captains to the Arabs.

Some of the German children arrived in Rome and were received by the Pope. Innocent admired their faith and was touched by it. But as a practical man who had learned something about crusades he was appalled by their foolish credulity. He urged the children to go home. When they grew up would be time enough for them to become crusaders. Little is known of the children's fate. Probably few of them reached home.

Innocent III was responsible for another crusade, the Albigensian, which to modern minds seems even more inexcusable than the Fourth. Albigensians is the name given to the heretics of southern France who are more properly called Cathari. In the thirteenth century most right-minded people looked upon heretics with horror and loathing, regarding them as rebels against true religion and also as rebels against society and decent folk. No one recognized that the heretics were as sincere as Franciscans in protesting against a worldly church; no one granted them the right to their own kind of semi-Christian or non-Christian religion. The crisis seemed terrible because the Cathari and several other varieties of heretics were numerous and multiplying. There were many in the towns of Lombardy and central Italy.

The Cathari were the most numerous of the heretical sects. They were concentrated in southern France, particularly in the cities of Albi, Béziers, Carcassonne and Toulouse. They also flourished in Milan, Florence, Bologna, Verona, Orvieto and Viterbo—the last only some forty miles from Saint Peter's. The Cathari believed in perpetual war between good and evil. The good was spiritual, the evil fleshly and material. The Cathari strove for purity because the spirits of pure souls were united after death with the universal spirit.

They believed that the world was so dreadful that there was no need of hell. The souls of evil persons were punished by being reincarnated and forced to live again in the world, perhaps as animals. Since all matter and sex were evil, the elect of the sect ate no meat or eggs and abstained from sexual intercourse. Chastity was the ideal for all Cathari; but only those who were certain of their ability to remain chaste experienced the rite of *consolamentum*, which meant that they were numbered among the perfect ones.

The Cathari, of course, were religious fanatics of the most extreme sort. Most of them were simple people who fervently believed in their peculiar religion and died bravely fighting for it, or as martyrs condemned by the Inquisition. In France they were exterminated in horrible massacres; or, after they were interrogated and condemned by Dominican inquisitors, they were executed by secular officials. In Italy the Cathari were eliminated chiefly by the Inquisition, although there were military campaigns against them there also. The extermination of the Cathari was so complete that their religion was utterly rooted out of Europe and our knowledge of what they actually taught and believed is scanty and unreliable.

Early in his pontificate Innocent III wrote to the papal city of Viterbo urging severe penalties against all who sympathized with heretics. He was ignored. In 1205 the heretics of Viterbo carried a municipal election and an excommunicated heretic was elected the city's chief executive. Innocent was incensed. He wrote that if Viterbo were destroyed and the slaughtered citizens were only a shameful memory, their punishment would still be inadequate. Innocent ordered the heretical city administration thrown out, the exiled bishop reinstated and all laws against heretics enforced. If these laws were not obeyed, the surrounding towns must make war on Viterbo.

However, so little was done that two years later, in February of 1207, the Pope himself led a military expedition against the heretical city. At Innocent's approach all the heretics fled. Innocent saw to it that their houses were demolished and their property confiscated.

The terrible story of the Albigensian Crusade in southern France is too long and complicated for retelling here. It began when Innocent sent papal legates empowered to force local bishops to rid their dioceses of heresy. The bishops were reluctant to persecute a large minority (in some cities perhaps a majority) of the population. So Innocent issued sterner orders to his legates. He offered greater rewards and complete remission of sins to those who exposed heretics and confiscated their property. He urged the King of France in vain to participate in the holy work.

"Action ranks higher than contemplation," wrote Innocent in a letter urging his deputy in southern France to continue fighting heretics and not to retire to a monastery as he was anxious to do. "Exterminate the heretics," Innocent wrote. The word he used, *exterminare*, was ambiguous. It can mean "to exile" or "to execute." Judging by their actions, we can presume that many of the Albigensian crusaders interpreted the word as "execute."

Finally, in 1208, the Pope issued a summons to a holy crusade. The attractions of a crusade fought conveniently near in a rich and pleasant country and offering remission of sins for its members were great. Nobles from northern France, avid for loot and for confiscated estates, waged war with bloodthirsty ferocity. Various papal legates urged them on with mad fanaticism. There were desperate sieges, horrible massacres, betrayals and treacheries. It was Innocent himself who authorized Dominican friars to interrogate heretics and to turn those guilty over to the secular arm for punishment, sometimes death by burning. This was the beginning of the Inquisition, which did not receive full official status until the pontificate of Pope Gregory IX.

Innocent's devious and shifty politics during the Albigensian Crusade are the darkest chapter in his entire pontificate. It is only fair, of course, to remember that the idea of religious tolerance was unknown at the time and that the idea of religious unity was paramount. Innocent undoubtedly believed that he was doing God's will.

While the armies which answered his call ravaged a large and beautiful area, while they destroyed much of the civilization of southern France, Innocent did little to limit the atrocities of one of the cruelest wars ever waged. He did make several ineffectual protests. But he did not take a strong stand. One historian has written that his legates "forced his hand or disobeyed his instructions." This may be so. But Innocent could have recalled his disobedient legates; he could even have excommunicated them. He did not. The guilt for the horrors of the Albigensian Crusade is partly his.

In 1213, with many heretics dead, Innocent tried to end the war. In vain. He was persuaded to renew the crusade. It continued intermittently until 1244, twenty-seven years past Innocent's death. Not until then was the last obstinate outpost of resistance taken and the last property assigned to one of the conquerors.

In 1198, the year Innocent III became pope, the princes of Germany elected a German king and emperor-designate to succeed the recently deceased Henry VI. They chose Henry's younger brother Philip. Unlike the psychopathically cruel Henry, Philip was a gallant and likable man with some of the charm of his great father, Frederick Barbarossa. Philip was thus the third Hohenstaufen elected emperor. It seemed likely that he would continue the Hohenstaufen policy of enforcing imperial rights in Italy wherever he could in order to rule as much of Italy as he could.

Nevertheless, another candidate was elected by a defiant minority faction of the German princes. This was Otto, a son of the Duke of Saxony and a nephew of the English king, Richard Coeur de Lion. Otto was a tall, powerful and brave soldier. He was also proud, stupid, obstinate and tactless. Otto was a hereditary foe of the Hohenstaufen dynasty. Princes who shared his opposition to the Hohenstaufens were encouraged to vote for him by bribes from King Richard. Evidently Richard thought it would be politically convenient to have his nephew, who had grown up at the English court, become emperor. So once again there were rival emperors and a ferocious civil war which devastated much of Germany for ten years.

One of the pope's duties which Innocent stressed was to maintain peace. His support would have greatly helped Philip, the more popular candidate, win the civil war and restore peace. But Innocent was determined to maintain the Church's rule over the Italian cities he had snatched from Henry VI's governors. If Philip triumphed he might try to reconquer those cities. So while the war raged in Germany for three years Innocent made no public choice—just as had Pope Gregory VII in somewhat similar circumstances.

But as early as May of 1199 the Pope secretly told Otto's ambassadors that he would support Otto if Otto was sufficiently devoted to the Roman Church. The ambassadors swore oaths in Otto's name. In public Innocent still pretended to be neutral. Then in the summer of 1200 Otto said that he would confirm anything his ambassadors had agreed to.

Otto had not been doing well in the civil war and so desperately needed Innocent's support. In return for his support the Pope was determined to bind Otto to exacting terms. In June of 1201 Otto formally signed a treaty with Innocent which was so one-sided that he could not have intended to keep it—just as Henry IV had done at Canossa. Otto swore to surrender all imperial rights in Italy; to recognize all conquests and annexations Innocent had already made and to aid him in making more; to allow imperial relations with France to be controlled by the Pope; and to repeat these pledges when he had been crowned emperor.

One month later Pope Innocent III publicly and formally recognized Otto as German king and emperor-elect after more than three years of delay and secret negotiation. Innocent tried hard to make it appear that he supported Otto for principles of pure justice. He issued an edict in which he set forth arguments for Otto. It was, wrote a caustic critic of Innocent, the German historian Johannes Heller, "the partisan work of a pettifogging lawyer, a web spun out of willful distortions." And Innocent excommunicated Philip.

The Pope's official blessing enabled Otto to keep on fighting. But not all Innocent's propaganda letters, legates and maledictions against Otto's enemies could win the war for him. Philip persisted and prospered. So, only two years after he embraced Otto, Innocent began secret negotiations with Philip. He discussed possible terms for switching his support from his own candidate to the man whom he had excommunicated. While thus engaged Innocent continued his public support of Otto. Such treacherous and dishonest diplomacy shows that the Pope really did not care which man became emperor. What he cared about was the power of the Papacy, his right to choose an emperor and the precedent of having done so, and the security of the papal temporal rule in Italy.

The civil war in Germany dragged on and Philip continued to be victorious. Finally Pope Innocent decided that he must back the winning horse. He renewed negotiations with Philip, who swore, as Otto had done, to respect the Church's conquests in Italy and to be properly subservient to the Pope. Innocent then solemnly absolved Philip from his excommunication and announced his intention to betray Otto and proclaim Philip the rightful king and emperor-elect. Innocent's repudiation of his own choice must have been humiliating and embarrassing. But he was spared the ignominy of a formal declaration for Philip. In June of 1208 one of Philip von Hohenstaufen's own followers murdered him!

The Pope wrote the German princes that heaven had decided in favor of Otto. The princes, who were tired of war, agreed. In May of 1209 Otto was unanimously elected by fifty-five German princes. In the same year the burly, boorish Otto journeyed to Italy to be formally crowned in Saint Peter's. Pope and Emperor-elect met in Viterbo, embraced and wept tears of joy "in remembrance of their common trials, in transport at their common triumph." On October 4 Innocent III duly crowned Otto in Saint Peter's in a grand ceremony. Otto said, "All I have been, all I am, all I ever shall be, after God, I owe to you and the Church."

Within a few months Otto demonstrated that his signature on the treaty he had made with Innocent was a perjury and that his gratitude to Innocent was a myth. Otto reimposed imperial rule on the papal states in Tuscany, Umbria and the Romagna. He seized Perugia and Orvieto. He blockaded Rome and even robbed ecclesiastics on their way to the papal court. And then Otto went to war to conquer the Kingdom of

Naples and Sicily, which since the days of Pope Nicholas II and Robert de Hauteville had been a papal fief.

As soon as he was crowned, Otto, who was supposed to be a humble and loyal partisan of the Pope, became as aggressive an imperialist as the Emperor Henry VI. Innocent's rage at this brazen betrayal by the man he himself had intended to betray was terrible. He had made a disastrous error. In Rome there was furious resentment against Innocent's bungling. While Innocent was delivering a sermon one of the Roman nobles shouted at him: "Thy mouth is as the mouth of God, but thy works are like the works of the devil."

It was inevitable then that the Pope would excommunicate the Emperor he had raised up to be his own enemy. He did so on November 18, 1210, just a year and two weeks after he had crowned him. Although Otto was a monumental perjurer, he protested against his excommunication and defended himself, reasonably from the imperial point of view: "I have sworn to preserve the majesty of the Empire and to recover all the rights which it had lost. I did not deserve the ban. I will not meddle with the spiritual power; on the contrary, I will rather protect it. But as Emperor I will be judge of all temporal matters throughout the Empire." The hereditary anti-Hohenstaufen here sounds just like Barbarossa, who would have agreed with these sentiments.

Once more a Roman pope was at war with a German emperor. Innocent sent monks into Germany to wage a propaganda war against Otto. And, with what painful emotions we can only guess, Innocent wrote letters confessing his mistake in supporting Otto to the same German princes he had a short time before urged to elect Otto.

The Pope's campaign against the Emperor was rewarded by a revolt in Germany. It came when Otto was about to invade Sicily. Instead, he was forced to return to Germany, where he arrived in the spring of 1212. As another measure against Otto, Innocent summoned out of Sicily Henry VI's teen-age son, Frederick, who through his mother, Constance, was King of Sicily. Innocent sent the young man off to Germany under his own sponsorship to be a rival claimant to the imperial throne. It is proof of the intensity of Innocent's rage against Otto that he should even consider aiding another of the hated Hohenstaufens to become emperor.

As for Otto, he was so badly defeated in the great Battle of Bouvines in 1214 by King Philip Augustus of France that he retired to a private life of piety and good works. He died in 1218.

"Every man of sound mind is aware that it belongs to our office to snatch any Christian away from any mortal sin, and, if he scorns to be corrected, to coerce him by means of ecclesiastical sanctions," wrote Pope Innocent III to the bishops of France. The sinner he had in mind was Philip Augustus, the most astute and powerful king to rule France in many generations. The interesting problems of Philip's marital situation had caught Innocent's disapproving attention shortly after his coronation.

Philip's first wife, Isabella of Hainaut, had died. He had subsequently married a Danish princess called Ingeborg. Of all the unfortunate princesses who have married cruel or callous kings for reasons of state, poor Ingeborg was surely one of the most miserable. The royal couple, already married by proxy, met for the first time in the city of Amiens on August 14, 1193. That night they retired together as at least conventionally happy newlyweds. The following morning, during Ingeborg's coronation as Queen of France, King Philip went ghastly pale and shuddered conspicuously.

After the coronation Philip said that he had suddenly found Ingeborg physically repugnant and that he disliked her so much he could have nothing to do with her. Scandalous rumors soon titillated the courts of Europe. Was Ingeborg deformed by some loathsome abnormality? Did the King suspect her of some previous misconduct? Or did he fear that she was a witch?

The reason for Philip's strange behavior is unknown and presents a fascinating psychological mystery. A political reason could hardly have turned up overnight. At that moment the King was not enamored of anyone else. If he had been horrified during the night he need not have permitted the coronation ceremony to proceed. If he truly did form his celebrated repugnance during the coronation as he claimed, it must have been some mysterious psychological aberration. He didn't know the poor princess well enough yet to have grounds for shuddering dislike.

Queen Ingeborg spoke no French. The King and his courtiers spoke no Danish. Ingeborg's manners were uncouth. Something had to be done. A court of French bishops was most cooperative. It annulled the royal marriage on the grounds of consanguinity. To do this the bishops had to be resourceful and imaginative. To find a blood relationship between Philip and Ingeborg they would have had to trace their pedigrees back past the reign of King Clovis.

Ingeborg, alone, bewildered and publicly repudiated, somehow managed to appeal to the Pope in Rome, the final authority on morals and marriage. She insisted that the marriage had been consummated. Philip denied it. One of them lied. It is far more likely that the cynical, unscrupulous King was the liar than the pathetically unhappy young Queen from Denmark. All of this occurred five years before Innocent became pope.

Three years after his separation from Ingeborg, considering himself legally unmarried, Philip married Agnes, daughter of the German Duke of Meran, and, surprisingly, fell passionately in love with her. Agnes was beautiful and charming. Ingeborg was a nuisance, always writing letters to Rome. So Philip made Ingeborg's life even more miserable, dragging her from convent to convent, from castle to castle. Innocent's predecessor, Pope Celestine III, sent a legate to France to look into the canonical legality of Philip's marriage to Agnes. The King told the legate that his marriage was no business of the Pope's. Celestine died and the problem was left to Innocent.

In September of 1198 Innocent wrote a sanctimonious letter to the bishops of Paris expressing his grief that his beloved son Philip had shut up his lawful wife in a cloister and thereby endangered his reputation and his hope of salvation. The King's crime was clearly the cause of the famine then afflicting France. The Pope obviously considered the French bishops' annulment null and void.

So Innocent sent a legate to France with stern instructions: "If within one month after your communication the King of France does not receive his queen with conjugal affection, and does not treat her with due honor, you shall subject his whole realm to an interdict: an interdict with all its awful consequences."

The interdict was proclaimed at Dijon in December of 1199. It was a curious situation. Neither the government of France nor the people of France was charged with any wrongdoing. The King by repudiating the woman the Pope considered his lawful wife had committed a purely private sin. To punish Philip, Innocent deprived everyone in his kingdom of the sacraments of religion (except baptism of infants and extreme unction for the dying). He was to impose interdicts on other nations similarly. No better example could be found of the difference between medieval and modern thought. Innocent unquestionably believed that he was doing God's will, defending the sanctity of marriage. Today most people would think that he was cruelly punishing the innocent. He could have excommunicated Philip as an individual sinner.

The King was furious. He swore he would rather lose half his dominions than part with Agnes. He expelled many bishops and priests from their benefices for obeying the interdict and confiscated their property. He removed Ingeborg from a convent and shut her up in a castle. And he sent a delegation to Rome to protest to Innocent.

"He knows our decree," said the inflexible Pope. "Let him put away his concubine, receive his lawful wife, reinstate the bishops he has expelled, and give them satisfaction for their losses. Then we will raise the interdict."

King Philip became even more angry. "I will turn Mohammedan! Happy Saladin, he has no pope above him!" Philip convoked a parliament of nobles and asked what was to be done. He was bluntly told to submit to the Pope, dismiss Agnes and take back Ingeborg.

Agnes was also in a painful situation. She wrote Innocent a touching letter: "She, a stranger, the daughter of a Christian prince, had been married, young and ignorant of the world, to the King, in the face of God and the Church. She had borne him two children. She cared not for the crown. It was on her husband that she had set her love. Sever me not from him." Innocent never answered her letter.

While all this was going on Pope Innocent wrote friendly letters to King Philip concerned with other matters. His official disapproval of Philip's sin against marriage, with its necessity for punishment and reproof, did not alter his desire to maintain cordial relations with the powerful King of France.

In September of 1200 Philip conferred with a papal legate at his castle of Saint Léger at Sens. Evidently concluding that the Pope would not remove the interdict and that nearly a year without sacraments was as much as he could ask his subjects to endure, the King surrendered, repudiated Agnes and formally received Ingeborg back as his wife. The interdict was removed. "The Pope does me violence," Philip said to Ingeborg. "His Holiness only requires justice," she replied.

Agnes left the court to live in the chateau of Poissy and died there in childbirth early in 1201. Her child died a few days later. Philip still would not have anything to do with Ingeborg. He tried again to have their marriage annulled, writing Innocent that witchcraft must be the cause of his aversion. The Pope recommended prayers, alms and sacraments to remove the evil spell. Denied an annulment, Philip soothed his frustration by shutting up Ingeborg in a prison. She had no friends there, was fed with scraps of wretched food and lived in miserable squalor. And under these conditions the Queen of France remained for eleven years.

Meanwhile Pope Innocent had become involved in a furious dispute with John of England. He deposed him and invited King Philip to invade England as the champion of the Church. In order to play this role suitably, the next year Philip released Ingeborg from prison and had her escorted to court. The gesture was meaningless, but appearances had to be preserved by a king who proposed to conquer England in the name of the Church as William of Normandy had done.

But Innocent changed his mind and decided that he did not approve of the English invasion after all. England was now under the Pope's protection because John had acknowledged Innocent's feudal overlordship and had made England a papal fief. Under these changed circumstances Philip decided he had better not invade England. But in 1216 he permitted his son Louis to do so. Innocent was incensed. In the year of his death still brandishing excommunications like thunderbolts, he excommunicated Louis and was preparing to excommunicate Philip when he died.

The King of France submitted to Pope Innocent III only when he judged it temporarily expedient and deliberately ignored the Pope whenever he thought it opportune. The first time he took back Ingeborg it was only a formal pretense. After the death of his beloved Agnes, Philip persecuted Ingeborg with no pretense at all that he had accepted her as his wife and with no concern for the Pope's disapproval. And Innocent knowingly let Philip get away with his persecution. A powerful and crafty king did not need to take the Pope's fulminations too seriously.

Innocent's celebrated power over kings was never as great as it seemed. This was notably true of his relations with King John of England.

John, younger brother of Richard Coeur de Lion, was one of the two great religious skeptics of the thirteenth century. The other was the Emperor Frederick II. According to one of John's biographers, he was entirely indifferent to religion. Needless to say, Pope Innocent III could not conceive of such an attitude. Numerous medieval monarchs bore the stigma of excommunication with surprising equanimity. But to have no interest whatever in religion was incomprehensible. Innocent, who was himself a treacherous opportunist when it suited him, never had a glimmer of what kind of man he confronted in the cynical King of England.

It all began in 1205 when the Archbishop of Canterbury died and a group of rebellious monks elected a candidate of their own as archbishop and hurried him off to Rome to obtain papal approval. But another candidate, approved by King John, was elected by a majority of the monks. The King sent a delegation representing this group to Rome to prevent the Pope from approving the minority candidate and to secure approval for their own. A third deputation was also in Rome, this one of bishops, to protest both elections because they claimed the right to elect the archbishop themselves.

To such an expert canon lawyer as Innocent a trifling dispute like this should have presented no problems. But for some inexplicable reason he withheld his verdict and announced in the last week of December that he would deliver it on December 21, 1206, nearly a year later. The delay must have enraged the three delegations, but they were helpless. It would be interesting to know how they paid for their food and lodging in the extortionate city of Rome and how they passed their time for a year amid its daily dangers. At last, right on schedule, Innocent delivered his decision in a full consistory.

Innocent told the delegates that he had great solicitude for the see of Canterbury, which may have surprised them. Then he said that they should forthwith elect a candidate of his own choosing, Cardinal Stephen Langton. The delegates demurred. Innocent, who was always an absolute monarch within the Church, ordered them to elect Langton or be excommunicated. They did so.

Langton was an Englishman who had lived long at the Court of Philip Augustus as the French King's confidential advisor, and Philip was King John's great enemy. No wonder the delegates hesitated to elect him. Langton was also the man who conceived the excellent idea of dividing the Bible into chapters to make it easier reading.

Still in no hurry, Innocent did not write King John to inform him of Langton's election until spring. He praised the Cardinal's learning and his exemplary virtue. Such a man, Innocent pointed out, would be helpful for the salvation of King John's soul. Innocent, still in no hurry, consecrated Stephen Langton as Archbishop of Canterbury in June. John, whose reputation for wickedness was probably well deserved, was shrewd and stubborn. He had no intention of permitting an intimate friend of his enemy Philip of France to become the head of the English church.

Three English bishops, those of London, Ely and Worcester, wrote the Pope that they had tried and failed to persuade John to accept Langton. But John by interfering in Church affairs had angered the Pope far more than Philip had done by his marital misbehavior. So Innocent commanded the three bishops to put all England under an interdict. Once again a whole nation would be punished for the individual sin of its sovereign. The interdict was imposed on March 23, 1208. Immediately after they had obeyed the Pope's command the three bishops, joined by two others, fled across the Channel to safety. Even if Innocent did not, they knew John's vindictive character.

John showed what he thought of Innocent's interdict by ordering all clerics to leave England at once. How many did leave is unknown. Then John confiscated all Church property and appropriated all Church revenues for his own treasury. It was a financial windfall for John and for the English people, too. There was no need for any general taxes for the duration of the interdict. By law and custom John was in the right. Popes had no right to appoint archbishops of Canterbury. They had the right to confirm or reject elections, just as John had the right to approve or disapprove them.

Since the interdict did not seem to inconvenience John and was actually profitable for him, Innocent excommunicated him the following year. Two years later, in 1211, Innocent officially absolved all John's subjects from their fealty and allegiance to him. And the year after that Innocent issued a formal decree which declared that John was deposed from his throne so that "another, more worthy than he, to be chosen by the Pope, should succeed him."

Although Innocent could not appoint a mere Archbishop of Canterbury, he intended to appoint a king of his own choosing! In theory the Pope may have claimed only to be a feudal overlord and the proper judge and punisher of sin. But in fact he was trying to act as the supreme ruler in temporal affairs as well as in spiritual. Innocent, of course, would have denied this. He would have argued that he was merely ridding England of an incorrigible sinner and choosing a worthier monarch.

Such an argument seems hollow because the monarch Innocent chose was Philip of France, who had been so unworthy a few years before that Innocent had excommunicated him!

John was now in serious trouble. Philip was a much better soldier than he. Many of John's treacherous and rebellious barons would probably join Philip when he landed on English soil. So in 1213 John surrendered to Pope Innocent, accepted Langton as Archbishop of Canterbury, and acknowledged that the Pope was the feudal overlord of England. John T. Appleby, one of John's biographers, has explained John's decision concisely:

"John conceived a scheme for placing himself under the direct protection of the Pope, an act that would change the nature of Philip's invasion from a holy war called by the Pope into an unlawful and sacrilegious attack on the Pope's own domain. . . . This act gave Innocent the suzerainty of England that William the Conqueror had stoutly denied to Gregory VII. . . . To surrender the kingdom to the Pope and to hold it of him as a feudal fief was a brilliant stratagem, designed to free John from his present dangers; it had little practical effect on the government of England, and John's son later repudiated it."

John's surrender of England as a feudal fief absolutely delighted Pope Innocent. He wrote the King enthusiastically: "Who but the Divine Spirit that 'bloweth where it listeth and who knoweth not whence it comes or whither it goeth' directed and guided you, at once so prudently and so piously, to consult your own interests and provide for the Church? . . . Come then, exalted prince, fulfill the promises given and confirm the concessions offered, so that God Almighty may ever fulfill any righteous desire of yours and confirm any honorable purpose, enabling you so to walk amid temporal blessings as not to fail of winning the eternal."

Innocent in his total ignorance of John's character believed that he was sincerely penitent!

Later that year Innocent wrote his legate in England to get on with the job of restaffing the bishoprics and abbeys, specifying that the King's consent be previously obtained. This is just the issue which John had insisted on and which had prompted Innocent to wage ecclesiastical war against him. But now, with John an exalted prince in good standing with the Church, with England a papal fief, Innocent no longer seemed to care who appointed or approved English bishops. But with his usual deliberation Innocent waited until June 29, 1214, before lifting the interdict on England. It had lasted for six years, three months and six days.

As King John's troubles with his rebellious barons grew he ingratiated himself with Pope Innocent further by taking the crusader's cross, thus indicating that he would go crusading as his elder brother Richard had done before him. We may be certain that John had no intention whatever of doing any such thing. After his barons had forced him to sign the celebrated Magna Carta, John sent a copy to Innocent, hoping that the Pope would absolve him from his oath to observe that revolutionary document. Innocent was deeply shocked: "Are the barons of England trying to depose a King signed with the Crusaders' Cross and placed under the protection of the Apostolic See and to transfer to another the dominion of the Roman Church? By Saint Peter, we cannot let this injury go unpunished!"

This was gratifying to King John. Even more satisfying were dispatches from the Pope which reached England early in 1216. In these Innocent excommunicated by name the leading barons in revolt against John and put an interdict on the city of London because it supported the barons. John could not have asked for more. Far craftier than Innocent, he had converted a pope who was his furious enemy into a pope who was his partisan champion.

During the momentous years in which Innocent III played his starring role in the major matters just narrated he found time to scatter widely other excommunications and interdicts and to accept the submission of other nations as feudal fiefs of the papacy: Portugal, Aragon, Hungary, Bohemia, Poland, Galicia, Serbia, Croatia and Bulgaria. Such a list is more impressive in theory than in fact. The rulers of the various nations were motivated by local political conditions. The actual independence of their countries was not seriously impaired.

And Innocent continued his efforts to reform the Church. He instituted a system of regular inspections of convents and monasteries. He set up a fund to aid needy priests. And he tried to improve the education of the clergy. He continued his efforts to launch a crusade. And he convoked a great council of ecclesiastics which assembled in Rome in the autumn of 1215 and is known as the Fourth Lateran Council.

The purpose of the council was to combat heresy, clarify doctrine and inspire a new crusade. Various committees under Pope Innocent's direction drafted reports and declarations in advance. Some 1,500 archbishops, bishops, abbots, priors and representatives of religious orders convened in the Lateran church. There on the first day the crowd was so great that the aged Archbishop of Amalfi fell to the pavement and was trodden underfoot to his death. Others also died, crushed to death by the crowd.

Innocent told the delegates that "the corruption of the people has its chief source in the clergy. From this arise the evils of Christendom: faith perishes, religion is defaced, justice is trodden underfoot, heretics multiply, schismatics are emboldened, the faithless grow strong, the Saracens triumph."

The canons against heresy approved by the council were fierce: "If any temporal lord fails to purge his land of this heretical foulness after being required and warned to do so by the Church, he shall be bound with the fetters of excommunication by the metropolitan and other bishops of the province. And if he refuses to make amends within one year, the Supreme Pontiff shall be informed of this, that he may declare the lord's vassals free from fealty to him, and lay his land open to occupation by catholics, who, after exterminating the heretics, shall possess it without any opposition and preserve it in the purity of the faith."

During the council Innocent authorized the Dominican Order of Preaching Friars. He declared that Jews must wear a distinctive dress and must not appear on the streets on festive days. He insisted once again that the clergy must not be taxed by secular authorities. And he proclaimed that laymen must pay tithes to the Church as well as taxes to the state. New orders of monks were prohibited—in vain. Many new orders have been founded with full papal approval since Innocent's time. Confession at least once a year was made compulsory. And the doctrine of transubstantiation (that bread and wine miraculously become the flesh and blood of Christ in the sacrament of mass) was proclaimed an official doctrine of the Church.

The Fourth Lateran Council lasted less than a month. There were only three general sessions. In these the delegates listened to sermons and approved the prepared resolutions.

Except for his nepotism in securing money, lands and a title for his ambitious brother, Pope Innocent III was a personally virtuous and conscientious pontiff. He was a sincere reformer. He displayed wisdom and generosity in encouraging Saint Francis. The energy and industry he devoted to his tasks were exceptional. The ruthless cruelty he advocated toward heretics was not a purely personal fault; it was the prevailing attitude of his time.

His efforts to enhance the power and glory of the Papacy, to exalt it over all the monarchs of Europe, was entirely in conformity with the convictions and aspirations of many medieval popes. Innocent's success was more spectacular than theirs; but it was flashy and ephemeral. His methods in pursuit of his ends were those of a secular statesman. Legalistic in argument, inconsistent in tactics, Innocent shifted his ground as opportunity or expediency suggested. In many of his letters he told deliberate falsehoods.

Like many other medieval and Renaissance popes, Innocent III believed that the end justifies the means. We may regret that the supreme head of the Christian Church, the arbiter of morality, did so believe; but popes are only men. Their characters are not transformed when they are crowned. The greatness generally credited to Innocent was genuine, but it was strictly limited. Although he certainly was not spiritually great, Innocent III was a great personage in the history of the Church and a great figure in the pageant of medieval history.

Few major historical personages have aroused more controversy or more widely divergent opinions than Innocent. Depending upon their religious convictions, their political beliefs and the times in which they lived, various historians have described Innocent as an unscrupulous opportunist and as virtually a saint. Historians agree on what Innocent did and said. They differ on what were his motives and intentions, and on the significance of his writings, which were usually full of biblical quotations and symbolical phrases. They also differ by stressing or omitting mention of various aspects of Innocent's pontificate. Consequently, everyone who writes about Innocent III expresses only a personal judgment. The ambitious Pope remains, as he was throughout his own lifetime, a controversial and enigmatic figure.

Gibbon's verdict was spiteful, but so concise and deft it demands quotation: "Innocent may boast of the two most signal triumphs over sense and humanity, the establishment of transubstantiation and the origin of the inquisition."

In the summer of 1216 Pope Innocent III set out on a journey to Pisa and Genoa, intending to make peace between those hostile cities so that their combined fleets could be used in the crusade he planned. He stopped in Perugia on the way and died there of malaria complicated by a paralytic stroke. A French pilgrim, Jacques de Vétry, who was present in Perugia, wrote that Innocent's body was left unwatched in a church, as was the custom, and that thieves entered the church at night and stole the rich garments in which the body was wrapped, and left it "almost naked and stinking."

IX

Stupor Mundi

"If the Lord had known about Sicily, he would not have made such a fuss about Palestine." The remark is flippant, irreverent and mildly humorous. In the thirteenth century there was only one man who could have made it, and every reasonably well-informed person would have known at once who it was. No orthodox Catholic could conceivably say anything so perilously close to blasphemy. No heretic could say it because heretics were exceedingly solemn. It had to be someone who enjoyed making skeptical and shocking remarks, who had no need to fear papal disapproval or angry public opinion. It had to be Frederick von Hohenstaufen II, King of Sicily and Holy Roman Emperor, a man whose ideas, character, behavior and public career were all so extraordinary that he was known in his own time as *Stupor Mundi*, the Wonder of the World.

Fra Salimbene, the pious Franciscan friar whose fascinating chronicle we have already quoted, deplored Frederick, as was only to be expected of a devout believer; but Salimbene had known the Emperor personally and recognized his charm:

"Of faith in God he had none; he was crafty, wily, avaricious, lustful, malicious, wrathful; and yet a gallant man at times, when he would show his kindness or courtesy; full of solace, jocund, delightful, fertile in devices. He knew how to read, write, and sing, and to make songs and music. He was a comely man, and well formed, but of middle stature. I have seen him, and once I loved him, for on my behalf he wrote to Brother Elias, Minister General of the Friars Minor, to send me back to my father. He knew how to speak with many and varied tongues, and, to be brief, if he had been rightly Catholic, and had loved God and His Church, he would have had few emperors his equals in the world."

Frederick II, some historians have argued, was the ablest and most versatile monarch who ever lived. This may be true. But Frederick's faults of character and mistakes of policy were so great that he failed to achieve most of the ends for which he stubbornly contended. A failure he was, but a great and fascinating failure. To some Frederick was a hero, to many more he was anathema and Antichrist. His career was a parade of paradoxes. A tyrant, he fought against the tyranny of the Church. A religious skeptic, he professed orthodoxy and persecuted heretics. A crusader who liberated Jerusalem, he was excommunicated for his achievement. The enigmatic Emperor was also a poet, a scholar, a scientist, a linguist fluent in six languages, a soldier, a statesman who conceived and created the first modern autocracy, and a ruler who became so maddened by opposition and treachery that he committed unspeakable atrocities.

Everyone who knew Frederick recognized his charm. When young he was handsome, with the red-gold hair of the Hohenstaufens. When older he was fat, but still magnetically charming. But the charm was ephemeral, blighted by the snake-like gleam said to shine in his eyes and by the fear he inspired. No one ever really trusted Frederick. He was too strange, a man whose mind was a bizarre combination of medieval and modern ideas. Proud as Lucifer, arrogant as Rameses, Frederick tried to exalt himself as emperor to divine heights. He never condescended to tact or compromise. In an age of general religious faith, he made sarcastic jokes which provoked furious offense. In an age of passionate hatred of Moslems, he made Saracen troops the mainstay of his army and aroused a hurricane of prejudice. In an age of strongly established city-states and of papal temporal power, Frederick waged war persistently upon both.

So, like his own contemporaries, we can only wonder at this man of brilliant intelligence who was right on many issues, but who defeated his own ends by his defiance of the most dearly cherished convictions and prejudices of his time. What could he not have achieved if he had used craft and diplomacy in Italy as he did in Palestine to appease (instead of outraging) the religious beliefs of the most religious century in history?

Little is known of Frederick's childhood and youth. On his fourteenth birthday, December 16, 1208, his minority ended and he assumed the rule of the Kingdom of Sicily. The age at which young rulers in the Middle Ages came of age differed from time to time and from country to country. Frederick's maternal grandfather, Roger II, came of age at sixteen. Although precociously intelligent, Frederick was confronted by so much near-anarchy that he was not an effective ruler for a number of years. When he was fifteen Frederick married a bride of Innocent's choosing, Constance of Aragon, the widow of the King of Hungary, aged twenty-four. In 1212 the young couple had a son they named Henry.

In the same year ambassadors from the German princes arrived in Palermo with the news that the princes had voted to depose the Emperor Otto and had elected the seventeen-year-old Frederick in his place. Evidently the princes thought that the son of Henry VI and the grandson of Barbarossa would make a better emperor than the hated Otto. Pope Innocent III, who was doing everything he could think of to eliminate the ungrateful Otto, thought so, too. He summoned the young King of Sicily to Rome and there the two met for the first and only time.

The imperious, worldly Pope was fifty-one, famous, powerful, vastly experienced in the wicked ways of the world. Frederick was not yet eighteen, brilliantly talented but untried. He had left his kingdom of Sicily in a state of violent turmoil in order to risk all on a wild gamble that the German princes meant what they said and that he could in fact become the King of Germany and emperor-elect. Innocent was gambling, too. Could he trust this sleek, affable teen-ager? If Frederick should become a popular and powerful emperor, would he threaten papal temporal power in the traditional Hohenstaufen manner?

Innocent asked a high price for his support of Frederick. Everything he asked for, Frederick promised: to make his infant son Henry king of an independent Kingdom of Sicily as soon as he himself became emperor; to respect Innocent's territorial conquests; and to lead a crusade. Frederick had no more intention of keeping these promises than had Henry IV, Otto and Philip to keep theirs. He particularly had no intention of surrendering the throne of the Kingdom of Sicily to his child. That kingdom, he said later, was the apple of his eye.

Even this early in his career it is probable that Frederick realized that as emperor he would only be a feudal overlord of Germany. Sicily he intended to make the secure base of his power—that is, Sicily and the mainland portion of the Sicilian kingdom. So Frederick lied to Pope Innocent in the immemorial tradition of political dishonesty and expediency, a tradition honored by all the monarchs and by all the popes of his time.

Innocent gave Frederick some money for traveling expenses, but not enough, and Frederick sailed from Ostia for Genoa. At that time he spoke little German. Otto was still powerful. Frederick had no armed escort. In Genoa he was delayed by lack of money and by enemies who lay in wait for him on the roads of Lombardy. The Milanese and their allies intended to prevent still another Hohenstaufen becoming emperor. But Frederick was able to raise a loan in Genoa. Hurrying from one friendly city to another, he managed to escape capture and to cross the Alps into Germany.

Pope Innocent had instructed the German bishops to support Frederick. In compliance to his commands the bishops of Chur and of Saint Gall in what is now Switzerland supplied him with a small force of mounted knights. With these Frederick hurried to the important city of Constance. He arrived on time, but only just, for Constance was preparing an elaborate welcome for the Emperor Otto, who was approaching from the other direction and whose servants were already inside the city's walls. Otto's cooks were preparing his dinner and the Bishop of Constance was superintending the final arrangements for Otto's official welcome.

But instead of the expected guest the young Frederick rode up to the city gate and demanded admission as emperor-elect. The Bishop of Constance refused to open the gate to Frederick. Fortunately for Frederick, a papal legate was with him. The legate forcefully reminded the

Bishop of Constance that the Pope had excommunicated Otto and that he had commanded all bishops to support Frederick. The Bishop reluctantly obeyed the legate and ordered the gate opened. The young King of Sicily rode into the city, whose buildings were decorated with banners hung in honor of Otto. Three hours later Otto arrived at Constance. But the gates remained shut and he had much too small a force with him to attack the city. Presumably Frederick ate Otto's dinner.

Frederick's youth, good looks and charm won him many supporters in Germany. They called him *"das Chint von Pulle,"* the child of Apulia. The phrase was affectionate but mistaken. Frederick was born in the March of Ancona and at that time had probably never been in Apulia. On December 9, 1212, Frederick von Hohenstaufen II was crowned King of Germany and emperor-elect at Mainz. Three years later he was crowned all over again at Aix and in a formal ceremony took the cross as a crusader.

What was his motive? By then he was twenty, cynical, calculating. Perhaps he intended to make a popular gesture, to emphasize his importance as emperor and to ensure papal protection of himself as a ruler who had sworn to lead a crusade. Innocent was still pope and Frederick thus dramatized his intention to keep at least one of the promises he had made in Rome.

The new Emperor-elect remained in Germany for eight years. His supremacy over the Emperor Otto was established in 1214 when Otto was decisively defeated by King Philip of France at the Battle of Bouvines. Four years later Otto died, obscure and powerless. As he lay dying Otto tried to expiate his sins by having several priests scourge him. While he painfully recited the words of the *Miserere* he repeatedly paused and urged the priests to lash him harder. In the Middle Ages the deaths of kings and emperors frequently offered edifying examples of the fickleness of human fortune.

In April of 1220 Frederick persuaded the German princes to elect his eight-year-old son, Henry, as king. That meant that Germany as well as Sicily had two kings, father and son. But Frederick did not worry about the high rank of his child. He expected to be crowned emperor in Rome soon. In Germany, as his grandfather Barbarossa had found it necessary to do, Frederick granted so many privileges to the bishops and princes that his rule there was more ceremonial than actual. It was regrettable, no doubt, but Frederick knew that his vast schemes would have to be carried out south of the Alps.

Pope Innocent III's successor on the papal throne was Honorius III, old, frail and obsessed with a new crusade. He crowned Frederick emperor in Saint Peter's on November 22, 1220. In return for Frederick's renewal of his oath to go crusading he agreed that Frederick, contrary to his oath to Innocent, could continue as King of Sicily for his lifetime. Frederick promised to depart for Palestine by the following August. So early a departure date was clearly impossible. Before he could leave, Frederick had to subdue a host of rebellious barons and a major Moslem revolt. If Honorius did not realize that such a program could not be completed in a few months, Frederick certainly did. In any case, he at once began his campaign to restore order in his Kingdom of Sicily and to create his own conception of an efficient, benevolent tyrant state. It took him five years and numerous postponements of his crusade.

Rarely has any monarch accomplished so much in so little time. Frederick soundly defeated the Norman rebels and conquered the Saracens of Sicily. He reorganized the administrative, military, legal and economic systems of the kingdom. And he began a propaganda effort, which he kept up for the rest of his life, to glorify himself and his new imperial autocracy.

Two of Frederick's military reforms were revolutionary. He confiscated all the castles in Sicily and on the mainland and transformed them from private fortresses and residences into government forts operated by the department of defense and occupied by small garrisons. He forbade the building of new private castles and during his long reign he himself built some sixty new castles at strategic locations.

And he solved the problem of what to do with the defeated Saracens of Sicily by transporting some 16,000 of them to the mainland. These he established as a military colony at Lucera, fifteen miles northwest of the present city of Foggia. Lucera is situated on a commanding height overlooking the Apulian plain to the south. The Saracen troops were archers and horsemen, an elite corps fanatically loyal to their Sultan Frederick. Isolated in a Christian country, they felt dependent on Frederick. And, of course, they were immune to papal or any kind of Christian influence. At Lucera mosques and minarets were raised and several times a day the muezzin called the faithful to prayer. No wonder that Lucera was called *Lucera dei Pagani*.

Today Lucera is a small, bustling town. The mosques and minarets were destroyed long ago. On the outskirts of the town is the site of the fortress-castle Frederick built. It was blown up in the eighteenth century to provide building stones for a new courthouse. But the massive wall built by a later conqueror, Charles of Anjou, still stands, a majestic monument to medieval might. It surrounds a large area, so large that troops could assemble, camp and drill inside the enclosure.

Frederick's Saracens were reliable and efficient and served him faithfully until his death. At first glance his use of them seems an imaginative and practical military scheme. Nevertheless, it was a major propaganda and psychological blunder. The Saracens' mere presence in Italy inspired shock waves of pious and scandalized horror. They seemed to justify every accusation made by Frederick's enemies, who called him the "Sultan of Lucera," said that he was a Moslem and an enemy of all good Christians. No matter how useful they were as soldiers, Frederick's use of Saracens in a crusading age was a fine example of his fatal refusal to recognize the importance of contemporary religious feeling.

Frederick II's reorganization of the state was designed to restore the autocracy of King Roger II and to make it more enlightened, comprehensive and efficient. The basic idea behind his many innovations was to eliminate the monarch's dependence on the violent caprices of the feudal nobility and on the uncertain cooperation of the cities. Frederick preserved the privileges of the nobles as a fighting class. He used them in his army. But he reduced their local power by greatly increasing the power of royal courts. And he did not employ them in his government.

Frederick made all state officials bureaucrats responsible to himself. Inefficient state servants were dismissed. Corrupt ones were mutilated or executed. The state was supported by customs dues, taxes and economic monopolies. Agriculture was fostered. A merchant marine and a navy were created. The currency was reformed. A university was founded at Naples for the express purpose of training government officials. No subject of the kingdom was permitted to attend a foreign university. And there was a serious and idealistic effort to promote justice, particularly to look after the rights of widows and orphans.

Justice included the minute regulation of morals and private behavior. Dice and other games of chance were forbidden. Subjects had to be in their houses before the third evening bell. Jews had to wear a distinctive dress. Prostitutes had to live outside city walls and were forbidden to frequent public baths with honest women.

Frederick's new state was an absolute autocracy. In 1231, when Frederick had recently won several notable triumphs, he published his famous *Constitutions of Melfi,* a code of laws presented in a volume called *Liber Augustalis.* This was a compilation of old laws dating back to Roger II and of new ones drafted to implement Frederick's ideas of justice and good government. The Emperor introduced his code of laws by saying that his state "should be a mirror of perfection for all who look therein, the envy of every prince, the model for every kingdom."

The *Liber Augustalis* is much concerned with legal procedure, with the powers of royal courts, with the duties and privileges of the nobles, with the rights of women. It included many enlightened provisions: a guarantee of personal liberty, a monopoly of criminal justice for the crown, protection of the vassal against the baron and of the weak against the strong, the protection of foreigners, and the admission of female inheritance. It abolished trial by combat, except in some cases of murder by poison and of treason. There were laws to prevent pollution and to improve sanitation.

Many of the specific laws are interesting. Only royal servants could wear swords. There were severe punishments for blasphemers, frequenters of taverns and preparers of love potions. Adulterous wives were to have their noses slit, and their husbands, if indulgent to the wives' adultery, were to be publicly whipped. No one could practice medicine without a government license and a university degree:

"Since we are aware of the serious expense and irrecoverable loss that can occur because of the inexperience of physicians, we order that, in the future, no one may dare otherwise to practice or to heal, pretending the title of physician, unless he has first been approved in a convened public examination by the Masters of Salerno. The person appointed should approach our presence with testimonial letters concerning his trustworthiness and sufficient knowledge both from the masters and from those appointed by us, or, when we are absent, he should approach the presence of the person who remains in our place, and he should obtain the license for healing from us or him. The penalty of confiscation of his goods and a year in jail is commanded for anyone who dares in the future to practice contrary to this edict of our serenity."

Several laws regulated weights and measures, and others prohibited frauds: "So that the frauds of individual artisans may not go unpunished, if they have been found to have turned to trickery in their crafts against our prohibition and ordinance, anyone apprehended in a fraud for the first time, if he makes counterfeit works or sells forbidden or corrupt food or watered wine for pure, will pay one pound of purest gold to our fisc. If he cannot pay because of his poverty, he should be beaten. If he is apprehended in the same crime again, he should lose a hand. If he is apprehended committing the same crime a third time, he should undergo the penalty of death on the forks, which he has fully merited by committing illegal acts and not correcting the things he has done."

Whatever death on the forks may have been, we may be sure that it was a peculiarly unpleasant method of execution.

In imitation of the Byzantine empire and in open rivalry with the papacy, Frederick exalted his state and himself into a sort of sacred cult. His state itself was holy and the Emperor was infallible, a divinely inspired ruler. "As God the father is manifested through Christ, so is Justice manifested through the Emperor. As Christ has founded His Church, so the Emperor has founded his State." One of the decrees issued at Melfi said: "Discussion of any judgment, decision or disposition of the Emperor is sacrilege."

Because the *Constitutions of Melfi* were the culmination of Frederick's reorganization of the Kingdom of Sicily, we have jumped forward a decade and now will return to several of the events of that decade. In 1222 the Empress Constance died. She had lived in Palermo guarded by eunuchs like a sultan's most important but not favorite wife. Frederick neglected all three of his wives in the same fashion. Their only role was to bear him legitimate children. But in spite of the harem Frederick kept and took around with him, women did not play important roles in his life.

Frederick's principal interests were learning, scientific inquiry and his struggle to impose his imperial authority on northern Italy and to supplant the temporal power of the Church in Italy with the sacred power of his own state.

In 1223 Frederick began to build a castle-palace at Foggia which became his favorite residence. Nothing is left of it today save one gateway. But several of Frederick's most important military fortresses still stand, notably those at Barletta and Bari in Apulia and at Enna and Catania in Sicily.

Frederick married for the second time in 1225. The bride was Yolanda, the fourteen-year-old daughter of Jean of Brienne, and Queen of Jerusalem in her own right by inheritance. In August Frederick sent fourteen galleys to Palestine to escort Yolanda to Brindisi in southern Apulia. The cynical, scheming, self-indulgent Emperor and the naïve child were married by proxy in the church of the Holy Cross in Acre. When the imperial fleet sailed into the harbor of Brindisi, Jean and the Emperor Frederick were there to welcome the little Empress. A second wedding ceremony was performed in the cathedral of Brindisi. Jean had renounced his regency of Jerusalem during his negotiations to marry his daughter to the Emperor. Of course Yolanda's royal title was merely honorary because she headed a government in exile at Acre. The Egyptian sultan ruled Jerusalem. But by marrying Yolanda Frederick secured a claim to the throne of Jerusalem which might serve him well if he ever made that often promised crusade.

Early in the morning on the day after the Brindisi wedding ceremony the Emperor left the city with Yolanda without informing his father-in-law of his departure. Jean hurried after the bridal couple in high dudgeon. When he caught up with the early risers Frederick showed no pleasure at seeing him. The brutal selfishness of his imperial son-in-law was made clear to Jean when Yolanda in tears told him that during the night Frederick had seduced Jean's niece. Jean's disillusion and frustrated rage became even more painful when several of Frederick's soldiers robbed him of the money King Philip of France had left him for a crusade to recapture Jerusalem. Jean fled for solace to the court of Pope Honorius and another startling tale about Frederick began to circulate.

The incident reveals one of the worst aspects of Frederick's character, his utter indifference to the feelings of others. The man who could so treat a fourteen-year-old bride was obviously incapable of winning the affection of his subjects. For all his intellectual brilliance and superficial charm, there was something cold and repellent about Frederick.

Poor unhappy Yolanda was bundled off to Palermo to lead a life of strict seclusion. In 1228 her son, Conrad, was born. Six days after her baby's birth the pitiful little Empress died. She was only sixteen. With Yolanda's death Frederick ceased to be King of Jerusalem and the baby Conrad became king. But such a trifling legal technicality did not stop Frederick from continuing to call himself King of Jerusalem in addition to his other titles.

While Frederick was reorganizing his state in Sicily and southern Italy he did not forget his oath to go crusading. Pope Honorius was annoyed by Frederick's repeated postponements, but Frederick knew how to pacify the old gentleman. Other matters weighed on the Emperor's mind. In 1226 Frederick held an imperial diet at Cremona in Lombardy to discuss three things: preparations for the crusade; means of extirpating heresy; and the restoration of imperial rights in Italy. In all probability Frederick was perfectly serious about all three.

In private he may have been a religious skeptic, but a successful crusade would immensely increase his fame and authority and strengthen his hand in the conflict with the temporal power of the Papacy which was brewing. Frederick's persecution of heretics has seemed to some historians the supreme hypocrisy and cruelty of a cynical villain. Another theory is more probable. It is that Frederick regarded heresy as a kind of rebellion against the state, an exercise of personal choice in religion when such a choice was not permitted. Religion was a state institution. No subject had a right to choose his religion any more than he had a right to question any law, policy or decision of his ruler.

By restoring imperial rights Frederick II meant what his grandfather Barbarossa had meant—imposing his direct rule on those insolently independent Lombard cities of northern Italy. Those cities suspected as much and were just as determined to fight Frederick for their municipal liberties as they had been to fight Barbarossa. It was inevitable that the Papacy should support them in every way possible. If Frederick should establish effective personal rule in northern Italy as he had done in the south, the independence of the papal states sandwiched between the two regions would be precarious indeed.

So in 1226 many of the northern cities organized a new Lombard League. They closed the Alpine passes and prevented Germans from attending Frederick's diet at Cremona. Not yet prepared to use force, Frederick diplomatically arranged a postponement of the issue and swore another oath to Pope Honorius to depart for Palestine in August of the next year, 1227. Although Frederick had often postponed his departure, he certainly intended to go crusading someday, whenever he had the time and it was convenient.

In March of 1227 Honorius died. He was succeeded by Pope Gregory IX. The new pope was the former Cardinal Hugolino da Conti, a relative of Innocent III, perhaps a cousin, perhaps a nephew, although he was fourteen years older than Innocent. Gregory had been the friend and protector of Saint Francis of Assisi. A handsome, proud and bad-tempered old man of about eighty-five, Gregory was a passionate persecutor of heretics and a vehement champion of the supremacy of the pope over all secular rulers. It was Gregory who officially inaugurated the Inquisition in Rome and authorized the burning of hundreds of heretics. Although he was a powerful and influential pontiff, Gregory was driven out of Rome by hostile citizens five times in his fourteen-year reign.

Faithful at last to his promise, Frederick assembled a large army at Brindisi in August, a much larger army than he could adequately provide for. An outbreak of malaria or dysentery swept through the crowded camp, but, notwithstanding, several thousand men sailed in late August. Frederick himself sailed on September 8. His ship was not far out of the harbor when an important noble, the Landgrave of Hesse, came down with malaria. Frederick ordered his ship to call at the port of Otranto and there the Landgrave died and the Emperor himself became ill. While his fleet sailed to Palestine without him, Frederick went to Pozzuoli to convalesce. He sent a message to Pope Gregory to explain the unfortunate delay.

Since the distance from Otranto to Pozzuoli near Naples is more than 250 miles, much of it through mountainous country, it is understandable that Gregory was convinced that Frederick lied and was not sick at all.

He excommunicated the Emperor. Frederick recovered and made plans to sail the following year. Gregory was furious. An excommunicated man could not lawfully go on a crusade. Frederick sailed anyway in June 1228. Gregory, who had excommunicated Frederick for not going on crusade, now excommunicated him a second time for going.

Frederick von Hohenstaufen II, who had associated with Moslems from childhood, who was intellectually interested in all religions but did not believe in the doctrines of any, who was under the ban of the Christian Church, was a strange crusader. But he had prepared the way by establishing diplomatic relations with the Sultan al-Kamil of Egypt, who had recently conquered Jerusalem from his own nephew. In Palestine Frederick and the Sultan conducted courteous and devious negotiations. Frederick's little crusading force was much too small for any major conflict. The Sultan was a reasonable man. The two rulers respected each other and wisely avoided war—as two earlier rulers who also respected each other, Richard Coeur de Lion and Saladin, had failed to do. They concluded a peace treaty.

The treaty gave to the Christian Kingdom of Jerusalem the city of Jerusalem and the villages of Bethlehem and Nazareth, plus a corridor to the sea at Jaffa. In Jerusalem the Moslem holy places were left under Moslem control and all Moslems were granted the right to enter the city and worship according to their faith. The treaty was a triumph of diplomacy for Frederick, who gained without shedding a drop of blood all that the Christians of Europe had dreamed of gaining. Unfortunately, in the thirteenth century the world was not yet ready to accept so reasonable and humane a settlement.

Moslems everywhere were horrified at this servile surrender to the unbelievers. Christians everywhere were enraged. To redeem the Holy City without unsheathing a single sword seemed an unspeakable outrage, a profanation of the crusading ideal itself. A diplomatic triumph was no triumph at all. How much more satisfying to Christians it would have been to slaughter thousands of Moslems in battle and to massacre thousands more afterward! Frederick's enormous service to Christendom earned him little gratitude among Christians.

And almost at once Frederick further infuriated the Christian barons of the Kingdom of Jerusalem. He was only the father of the rightful infant king and an excommunicate to boot. Yet he announced that he would go to Jerusalem to be crowned king. On Saturday, March 18, 1229, the Emperor marched triumphantly into Jerusalem. On Sunday he went to the church of the Holy Sepulcher for his illegal or at least highly questionable coronation. Not a priest was in the church, only his own soldiers. No priest dared be present at any ceremony crowning an excommunicated person. Undismayed, Frederick had a crown placed upon the altar and then placed it himself upon his own head.

Six days after Frederick entered Jerusalem Pope Gregory IX excommunicated him for the third time. Gregory was nothing if not thorough. Three excommunications were obviously better than one.

While he was in Jerusalem Frederick inspected the Moslem shrines with lively interest and the Moslems of the city inspected him. The outlandish Christian Emperor, who was known for skeptical remarks about Christianity, did not make a favorable impression. Popular opinion was summed up in a sentence which became famous: "He would not be worth 200 dirhems in the slave market, with his smooth red face and myopic eyes."

Frederick's high-handed behavior made him hated throughout the Christian Kingdom of Jerusalem. When he rode through the streets of the city of Acre on his way to the harbor to sail for Italy, mobs in the streets flung animal entrails and dung at him. In June of 1229 the Emperor landed at Brindisi and learned that during his absence redeeming Jerusalem Pope Gregory IX had organized an army and had invaded the mainland portion of his Kingdom of Sicily.

When Frederick defied the Pope and sailed for Palestine he had taken a dangerous, calculated risk. He did not know how long he would be gone. If his crusade was a failure his power and influence would be severely undermined. And in Pope Gregory IX he had left behind him in Italy a relentless enemy who would stop at nothing to destroy him. Gregory would have hated Frederick even if he had kept his crusading promises. To the bitter old Pope the Emperor was a sinister enemy who could never be trusted, whose intention to rule northern Italy was a fearful threat to the Papacy.

Aware of this, Frederick can hardly have been surprised by his third excommunication. But even the cynical Emperor must have been surprised when he read an intercepted letter in which Gregory urged the Sultan not to let Frederick secure Jerusalem. Equally underhanded was Gregory's dispatch of Franciscan monks throughout the Kingdom of Sicily to spread the news that the Emperor was dead.

But the living Emperor at the head of an army in his own kingdom was more than the papal troops cared to face. They fled back across the border into the papal states. In the summer of the following year, 1230, Pope and Emperor made peace. Gregory removed the ban of excommunication and called Frederick "a beloved son of the Church." Only a short time before, he had called Frederick a "disciple of Mohammed." Frederick visited Gregory at his paternal home in Anagni, where, Frederick reported afterward, they sealed their peace treaty with "holy kisses." For three days the unscrupulous, fierce old Pope and the unscrupulous, cynical Emperor dined and talked together, dissembling their mutual hatred. The peace they made lasted for nine years, during which Frederick aided Gregory with armed force in his wars with the people of Rome.

Frederick was now thirty-five, the undisputed autocrat of the Kingdom of Sicily, the Emperor of Germany and Italy. In the north of Italy numerous cities opposed him; but, just as in Barbarossa's wars, other cities loyally supported him. It is time now to pause in our narrative of Frederick's career and to consider the character, mind and manner of life of that extraordinary man.

The nineteenth-century English historian Edward A. Freeman wrote of Frederick: "It is probable that there never lived a human being endowed with greater natural gifts, or whose natural gifts were, according to the means afforded him by his age, more sedulously cultivated, than the last Emperor of the House of Swabia." Freeman went on to call Frederick "the most gifted of the sons of men" and to say that he was "one who in mere genius, in mere accomplishments, was surely the greatest prince who ever wore a crown."

Such praise sounds excessive, particularly when we remember Frederick's cruelties and failures. But if we remind ourselves that by accomplishments Freeman meant talents or abilities, then his judgment seems almost just. Perhaps we should list Frederick's outstanding abilities in order to understand their range and diversity:

Frederick von Hohenstaufen II was a diplomat, statesman and lawgiver.

He was a soldier of considerable tactical skill who, in the medieval fashion, frequently fought bravely in the front ranks.

He spoke Italian, French, German, Arabic, Latin and Greek.

He was a scientist learned in mathematics, anatomy and zoology. His favorite possession was a silver planetarium sent him by the Sultan of Damascus. He wrote the most authoritative book on falconry ever written, *The Art of Falconry*, which was the first book written in Europe based on strictly scientific observation and investigation.

He was a poet who surrounded himself with other poets, who wrote love songs in vernacular Italian two generations before Dante made Tuscan the literary language of Italy.

He was a builder of many castles and is believed to have been the architect of one, the Castel del Monte, which is unique in the history of castle architecture.

He was a speculative thinker who doubted many of the orthodox beliefs of his time and conducted experiments to prove or disprove them.

Frederick was an eccentric and flamboyant individualist who conformed to no standards save his own, who kept a harem, who traveled with as many animals as a modern circus, who delighted in astounding mankind.

In his opposition to the temporal power of the Church, Frederick never publicly questioned its spiritual power, and he never championed an antipope as his grandfather and other emperors had done.

Although he could make sarcastic or humorous remarks, Frederick had no real sense of humor and no understanding of the public opinion of his time, or of the importance of public opinion in politics. Frederick's conception of his own lofty eminence as emperor was even more inflated than Barbarossa's had been. He believed that anyone who opposed him was a traitor and sacrilegious, too. Consequently, his terrible rage provoked by opposition caused him to perpetrate atrocious cruelties.

The Art of Falconry, which Frederick wrote late in his life, is an astonishing work absolutely crammed with specific facts and technical information. It discusses feeding, breeding, reproduction, anatomy, capture, housing, care and training of falcons. A modern reader with no particular interest in falcons would find *The Art of Falconry* tedious. Nevertheless, it is impressive. Frederick's introduction is especially interesting:

"With the object of bequeathing it to posterity, we now offer a true and careful account of those matters between the covers of this monograph. . . .

"We have investigated and studied with the greatest solicitude and in minute detail all that relates to this art, exercising both mind and body so that we might eventually be qualified to describe and interpret the fruits of knowledge acquired from our own experience or gleaned from others.

"For example, we, at great expense, summoned from the four quarters of the earth masters in the practice of this art of falconry. We entertained these experts in our domain, meantime seeking their opinions, weighing the importance of their knowledge, and endeavoring to retain in memory the more valuable of their words and deeds.

"As the ruler of a large kingdom and an extensive empire we were very often hampered by arduous and intricate governmental duties, but despite these handicaps we did not lay aside our self-imposed task and were successful in committing to writing at the proper time the elements of the art. *Inter alia,* we discovered by hard-won experience that the deductions of Aristotle, whom we followed when they appealed to our reason, were not entirely to be relied upon, more particularly in his descriptions of the characters of certain birds. . . .

"Entire conviction of the truth never follows mere hearsay. . . .

"The author of this treatise, the august Frederick II, Emperor of the Romans, King of Jerusalem and of Sicily, is a lover of wisdom with a philosophic and speculative mind."

Frederick's interest in falcons and other birds was equaled by his interest in animals. On his various estates he kept vast herds of water buffalo, 500 cows in Sicily, 6,000 sheep in Calabria, camels in Malta, and quantities of pigs, goats, horses, pigeons, peacocks and bees. He maintained a huge park for wild game near Foggia. And he delighted in his private menagerie, which he took with him on his various campaigns in Italy.

Frederick's imperial progress must have been worth watching. His long caravan plodding along the dusty roads of Italy was led by an advance guard of his Saracen mounted archers. Next came camels carrying Oriental dancing girls guarded by Negro eunuchs. Then appeared the members of the court, splendidly dressed and riding magnificent horses, with the Emperor among them mounted on his favorite black horse, Dragon. Pages followed, and falconers with their falcons perched upon their wrists, grooms leading hounds in couples and other Saracen grooms riding horses with hunting leopards (cheetahs) seated on the cruppers. The imperial menagerie caused immense excitement everywhere with its white elephant on whose back was a wooden tower with Saracen archers inside it. Almost as astonishing as the elephant was the giraffe, the first ever seen in Europe. There were lynxes, lions (presumably in cages), bears and monkeys. Finally there was a train of mules and pack horses carrying scribes, secretaries, notaries, musicians and other servants as well as baggage, books, government documents and the imperial treasury. To feed and house such a procession must have been difficult, but an absolute emperor can arrange such matters.

The Castel del Monte, which Frederick began to build in 1230, crowns a hill which rises out of the flat Apulian plain about twenty miles south of Barletta. It is constructed of limestone which seems pinkish-gray in some lights and yellow in others. It is two tall stories high. Its shape is an exact octagon with eight large trapezoid rooms on each floor. At the exterior angles of the octagon are eight octagonal towers, each with two rooms, one above the other. In the middle of the interior courtyard there used to be an octagonal bath of white marble. The only entrance door is trimmed with marble and so are the second-story windows. Lavatories were supplied with water by lead pipes from cisterns on the flat roof.

Such a building seems too small to be a fortress, too strong to be just a residence. Historians guess that it may have been a hunting lodge. Whatever it was, it is the creation of an original mind, a mind completely indifferent to the precedents established by hundreds of years of traditional castle building. Frederick II, of course, had just such a mind.

Today Castel del Monte is surrounded by a circle of decorative trees. Somewhat lower down on the hill is a pleasant inn and restaurant recently built to accommodate tourists who come to see Frederick's unique castle. Comparatively few come, but those who do find much to stimulate

Castel del Monte. *Alinari*

their imaginations. It is easy to fancy that these strange trapezoidal rooms are furnished with the fine tapestries and ivory and gold and silver objects which Frederick is known to have collected; easy to fill the room with courtiers and servants and to listen while the Wonder of the World recites one of the poems which Dante is said to have admired, or while he discusses mathematics with a Moslem scholar, or while he makes one of the flippant witticisms which shocked so many of his contemporaries.

Not all of Frederick's witticisms were shocking. At least one is still provocative in its insight. Frederick defined *gentilezza* (the attributes of a gentleman) as "hereditary wealth *plus* good manners."

Among the learned men at Frederick's court were a mathematician named al-Hanfi, sent to him by the Sultan of Egypt, and the greatest Christian mathematician of his time, Leonardo Fibonacci. A Greek from Egypt named Theodore served as a secretary and ambassador, but he was also a translator, scientist, physician and astrologer. The most learned and famous man at Frederick's court was Michael Scot, an astrologer, philosopher, zoologist and translator.

Scot was a Scotsman from Fifeshire who had studied at Oxford and in Paris. A scholar who knew Arabic, Hebrew and Latin, he translated three important works into Latin: al-Bitruji's *Astronomy,* Aristotle's *Zoology* and Averroës' *Commentaries on Aristotle.* Scot also wrote three books on astrology. He had a great reputation as a wizard. He claimed to know in advance how he would die, but, knowing, he tried anyway to prove his own prognostication wrong and to prevent his death by always wearing an iron cap to protect his head. Nevertheless, he was killed by a falling stone. Dante put Scot in hell as a false prophet with his head turned backward on his shoulders.

Frederick, who could charm people easily but only briefly, had few friends. He was too arrogant, too selfish and too suspicious. His important official and courtier Pietro della Vigna probably was his friend also, but their relationship is not certain. Pietro was nearly as talented and versatile as Frederick. He was a judge, a drafter of laws, letters and propaganda circulars. He was also a scholar, a poet, a philosopher and a soldier. For many years he served Frederick faithfully, but in 1248 Frederick accused Pietro of bribery and embezzlement and had him blinded. Expecting further torture, as he was led into a dungeon Pietro asked his guards if there was anything between him and the wall. They said no. Pietro then lowered his head and rushed at the wall so violently that he caused his own death.

Frederick, although quite plump, usually ate only one meal a day. He bathed every day. The chronicler John of Winterthur wrote that this proved "that he had no regard for the commandments of God or for the feasts and sacraments of the Church."

Frederick's inquiring mind made him wonder what proof there might be of the immortality of the soul, and his casual cruelty made him conduct an experiment which is celebrated. He had a dying man nailed inside a cask so that his soul could not escape. After the poor wretch had died, the cask was opened and no soul was found.

Fra Salimbene described another of Frederick's experiments: "He fed two men most excellently at dinner, one of whom he sent forth to sleep, and the other to hunt; and that same evening he caused them to be disemboweled in his presence, wishing to know which had digested the better; and it was judged by the physicians in favor of him who slept."

Salimbene described another of Frederick's experiments in which he gathered together a group of orphaned babies, "bidding foster mothers and nurses to suckle and bathe and wash the children, but in no wise to prattle or speak with them; for he would have learnt whether they would speak the Hebrew language (which had been the first), or Greek, or Latin, or Arabic, or perchance the tongue of their parents of whom they had been born. But he labored in vain, for the children could not live without clappings of the hands, and gestures, and gladness of countenance, and blandishments."

In an age when cruelty was universal and largely taken for granted, such experiments did little to blacken Frederick's reputation compared to the most celebrated of the flippant remarks attributed to him: that the world had been deceived by three impostors—Moses, Jesus Christ and Mohammed.

In the summer of 1235 the Emperor married for the third time. The bride was Isabella, sister of King Henry III of England, a girl of only twenty-one. Isabella was a beauty and her dowry of 30,000 silver marks was impressive. Her extravagant trousseau included a gold crown, a magnificent necklace, a chest full of jewels, a dinner service of gold and silver plates, and even some cooking pots of silver whose impracticality caused much talk. Isabella brought with her from England robes and silks for her bed and a train of fine horses. Frederick followed the advice of his astrologers and did not consummate the marriage until the day after the wedding. His faith in the astrologers, or in his own prowess, was so great that he immediately told Isabella she was pregnant of a son. Frederick also wrote King Henry this good news.

Unfortunately, Frederick was mistaken. Isabella's son was not born until the autumn of 1237. He was called Henry Secundus because Frederick's first child by his first wife, Constance, was also a Henry. Isabella also bore a daughter, Margaret. Shortly after the wedding Isabella was handed over to the care of Saracen eunuchs, the dismal fate of all three of Frederick's wives. Isabella died in 1241. Her son, Henry Secundus, died at the age of fifteen, two years after his father's death.

Frederick never loved his wives and, although he had at least nine illegitimate children, he never loved other women. He was sensual but not affectionate. The only people he ever loved were the two ablest and most attractive of his bastard sons, Enzio and Manfred.

In order to consider Frederick the Wonder of the World, we have gone forward in time. Now we return to Frederick the Emperor and his wars and politics, picking him up in 1231, the year after he had made peace with Pope Gregory IX. Frederick called an imperial diet to be held in Ravenna. It was time that he got on with his program of imposing his imperial rule on northern Italy. While he waited for the delegates to assemble, Frederick conducted an archaeological dig and excavated the beautiful tomb of Galla Placidia, the fifth-century Roman empress, from underneath a pile of dirt and rubble. This gives Frederick a strong claim to having been the first archaeologist.

The Lombard League cities, suspicious as ever, again closed the Alpine passes. Some German princes arrived by circuitous routes, but Frederick's deputy in Germany, his son Henry VII, was not among them. Henry was nineteen, stupid, stubborn and weak. Frederick announced that a second session of the imperial diet would be held at Aquileia at the northern end of the Adriatic Sea and commanded Henry to come and stay in the nearby town of Cividale. Frederick was furious with his son for his disobedience in not being present at Ravenna. Now he refused to see Henry until he accepted several harsh conditions for his better behavior, including Henry's signature on a letter to the Pope saying that he "would be prepared to accept his own excommunication if he did not obey his father."

Frederick, for all his brilliance, was not a good judge of men. His severity to Henry shows that he did not know how to handle a rebellious teen-ager any better than do many fathers today.

To subdue the stubbornly defiant cities of the Lombard League, Frederick needed soldiers from Germany. But the league members still blocked the Alpine passes. So in 1232 Frederick made an alliance with Ezzelino da Romano, an ambitious nobleman from the northeastern province of Italy called the March of Treviso. With Frederick's backing, Ezzelino seized the important city of Verona and opened the Brenner pass. German soldiers could now answer Frederick's summons. Unfortunately for the Emperor, he was never able to enlist enough of them. At no time in his prolonged war against the Lombard rebels did Frederick have an army of more than 15,000 men. It was always too small. Frederick could win victories, but he could not win the war. On the other hand, while he lived and enjoyed the support of numerous sympathizers the Lombard cities could not win either.

Two years later foolish young Henry VII led a revolt of the Rhineland cities against his father and, what was worse in Frederick's opinion, made an alliance with his bitterest enemies, the Milanese. Such treachery seemed worse than Absalom's. Pope Gregory excommunicated Henry, a favor he granted in return for Frederick's aid against the Romans. It was the last time Gregory cooperated helpfully with Frederick. Thereafter, although nominally at peace with the Emperor, Gregory encouraged the Lombard League members to fight and launched a virulent propaganda campaign against Frederick. Gregory had always hated and distrusted Frederick and now he was delighted to be busy again in the congenial task of trying to destroy him.

In 1235 Frederick marched across the Alps to suppress his son's rebellion and with superb confidence did not take an army with him. Instead, he took large sums of money for useful political bribes and his traveling menagerie. The German princes supported Frederick, and

Henry's allies deserted him. As he had done in Palestine, Frederick achieved his purpose without fighting a single battle. He insisted that his traitorous son surrender unconditionally.

In July of 1235 in the city of Worms Henry VII surrendered to his father and prostrated himself on the floor, sobbing out his penitent appeal for pardon. For a dreadful interval Frederick did not deign to reply. Finally he forced Henry to renounce his title as King of the Romans and all his possessions. Frederick tortured and executed other traitors and rebels, but he spared his son's life. Henry was imprisoned in Heidelberg castle and later he was transferred to the castle of San Felice near Melfi in Apulia. Later still he was kept in protective custody at Nicastro near Cosenza in the foot of the Italian boot.

In 1242 when he was thirty Henry committed suicide by riding his horse over a cliff. When the news was brought to Frederick he commented: "The pity of a tender father must yield to the judgment of the stern judge. We mourn the doom of our firstborn. Nature bids flow the flood of tears, but they are checked by the pain of injury and the inflexibility of justice."

At Mainz in the next year, 1236, Frederick held another diet, the last he ever held in Germany. Frederick appealed for military aid. He denounced the intolerable state of affairs in rebellious Lombardy. "Pilgrims and beggars pass there freely; only I, the Emperor, may not cross my own dominions." Shortly thereafter Frederick marched into northern Italy and began a war which lasted for fourteen years, from 1236 until 1250. In January of 1237 the princes of Germany elected Frederick's son Conrad to be King of the Romans. Conrad was only seven years old.

The war began as an effort to impose imperial rights on Lombardy. It never ceased to be that, but Pope Gregory's commitment to aid the northern Italian cities became so great that the war changed its emphasis and became more and more a war between the temporal power of the Papacy and imperial power. Steven Runciman, the distinguished English medieval scholar, has summed up the political significance of the ferocious fourteen-year war so concisely his remarks deserve quotation:

"In the course of his reign there emerged in most Italian cities an imperialist party usually called Ghibelline, after the Hohenstaufen castle of Weibeling, in opposition to the papalist party, usually called Guelf, after the Welf Saxon dynasty which the popes had supported against the Hohenstaufen. The pope by now had become merely the head of the Guelf faction in Italy; and similarly the emperor had become merely the head of the Ghibelline faction."

The Lombard League cities were, of course, ardently Guelf. Their enemy cities, such as Pavia, Cremona and Verona, were Ghibelline. It was the support of these Ghibelline cities and of factions in other cities which enabled Frederick with his inadequate army to prosecute the war. But these Italian Ghibellines usually fought only their Guelf neighbors. Most of Frederick's regular army came from his southern kingdom; the rest were Germans.

The war dragged on for years because thirteenth-century castles and city walls were strongly fortified and in that pre-gunpowder age the defense was usually successful. When cities were captured treason was likely to be the cause. There were only a few major battles, but destructive raids and skirmishes were almost continuous. Psychological propaganda was as important as military action.

Pope Gregory IX, long before he excommunicated Frederick for the fourth time and went formally to war against him, bombarded the Emperor with denunciations and invective, rhetorical outbursts which were circulated all over Europe. Frederick replied in kind, exalting his own sacred role as emperor far beyond any claims Barbarossa had ever made.

Gregory said of Frederick: "The Beast is rising from the sea, whose name is infamous, whose claws are of a raging bear, and teeth as of a lion; he is cunning as a panther, and never opens his mouth but to curse the name of God." He called Frederick the Antichrist and accused him of sodomy.

So violent were Gregory's encyclicals that they actually aroused sympathy for Frederick. In 1238 Matthew Paris, a monk in the English monastery of Saint Albans, wrote in his great chronicle of contemporary history:

"The fame of the Emperor Frederick was clouded and stained by his envious enemies and rivals; for it was imputed to him that he was wavering in the Catholic faith, or wandering from the right way, and had given utterance to some speeches, from which could be deduced and suspected that he was not only weak in the Catholic faith, but what was a much more serious crime, that there was in him an enormity of heresy, and the most dreadful blasphemy, to be detested and execrated by all Christians. For it was reported that the Emperor Frederick had said (although it may not be proper to mention it) that three conjurors had so craftily led away their contemporaries as to gain for themselves the mastery of the world: these were Moses, Jesus and Mohammed; and that he had impiously put forward some wicked and incredible ravings and blasphemies respecting the Holy Eucharist. Far be it, far be it, from any discreet man, much less a Christian, to unlock his mouth and tongue in such raving blasphemy. It was also said by his rivals that the Emperor agreed and believed in the law of Mohammed more than that of Jesus Christ, and that he had made some Saracen harlots his concubines. A whisper also crept among the people (which God forbid to be true of such a great prince), that he had been for a long time past in confederacy with the Saracens, and was more a friend to them than to Christians; and his rivals, who were endeavoring to blacken his fame, attempted to establish this by many proofs. Whether they sinned or not, He alone knows who is ignorant of nothing."

The next year Paris wrote: "The knavery of the Roman Church was so deservedly execrated by all that the Pope's authority was respected by few, if any. The Pope most eagerly thirsted after the Emperor's blood and favored the rebellious, heretical Milanese."

To counter papal propaganda Frederick and his staff of eloquent ghost-writers produced circulars and letters which claimed that the Emperor and the Empire were even more sacred than the Pope and the Papacy. In a formal ceremony in the cathedral of Pisa Frederick declared: that the Empire was a divine institution and that God had appointed the Emperor to maintain peace and justice; that imperial rights, laws and courts were all sacred; that everything pertaining to the Emperor was sacred; that the Emperor was Christ's heir and successor; and analogies were drawn between the Emperor's long struggle as prince of peace and the life of Jesus.

Frederick's propaganda argued that it was not he who was the heretic, but Pope Gregory, who went to war as the friend and ally of heretics, meaning the Milanese. The biblical language and analogies of Frederick's proclamations are absurd but interesting:

"And know ye of us, your prince and gracious possessor! Prepare ye the way of the Lord, make his paths straight! Take the bars from off your doors that your Caesar may come in, gracious unto you and unto rebels terrible, at whose coming the evil spirits shall be silent which have long oppressed you."

In a letter to the town of his birth, Jesi, Frederick wrote: "Noble town of the March, the place of our illustrious birth, where our Divine Mother brought us into the world, where our radiant cradle stood: that thy habitations may not fade from our memory, that thou, our Bethlehem, birthplace of the Caesar, may remain deep-rooted in our heart. Thou, O Bethlehem, city of the March, art not least among the cities of our race: for out of thee the Leader is come, the prince of the Roman Empire, that he might rule the people and protect thee and not suffer that thou be in future subject to a foreign hand."

We will never know how much, if any, of this inflated rhetoric Frederick took seriously. He wanted to eliminate all Church influence in temporal affairs and endow his state with the same kind of divine authority as that of the Byzantine empire. Although a skeptic who doubted personal immortality and the virgin birth, Frederick believed so fervently in the autocratic state he was trying to create that his own person acquired sanctity in his mind.

Nevertheless, such pompous propaganda did not convince. More people believed the Pope's propaganda than Frederick's.

The great war began well for Frederick. In 1236 with the aid of Ezzelino da Romano he captured the important city of Vicenza. He then appointed Ezzelino to be his vicar there. A story is told of Frederick and Ezzelino walking and chatting in the garden of the bishop's palace in Vicenza. The Emperor drew his dagger and said: "I will show you how you can without fail maintain your rule," and then Frederick cut off the tops of all the taller flowers. Ezzelino remarked: "I shall not fail to note the Emperor's instructions." Nor did he, as we shall see when we consider Ezzelino's spectacular career.

The only trouble with this story is that Herodotus told it first about Thrasybulus, tyrant of Miletus, who cut off the highest stalks of wheat to demonstrate the safest way to rule. Still, since the lesson taught is one most tyrants learn, the story could originate separately in different times and places.

Early in 1237 Ezzelino captured the cities of Padua and Treviso. Frederick arranged a marriage between his bastard daughter Selvaggia and Ezzelino, evidently thinking so valuable a subordinate and ally would make a fine son-in-law. We are not told what his daughter thought of her marriage to one of the cruelest monsters known to history. Frederick's own reputation, of course, was damaged by this expedient alliance. How could the divinely appointed guardian of justice be also the friend and father-in-law of the nefarious Ezzelino?

In the following November the Emperor won the victory of Cortenuova, one of the greatest battles fought in the Middle Ages. Earlier Frederick had secured possession of Mantua and Ferrara. He knew that winter was nearing and the campaigning season nearly over. He had hoped to capture Brescia also, but it was too late in the autumn and a large Lombard League army was nearby. So Frederick employed an elaborate stratagem. He dismissed some of his loyal Ghibelline contingents and announced that he was going to take up winter quarters in Cremona. But instead of doing so he marched southwest to Soncino, a village on the road to Milan, and lay in wait for the league army, which would pass there on its own return to winter quarters. His army numbered only some 10,000 men—German and mercenary mounted knights, Saracen archers and Italian troops from his Kingdom of Sicily.

On November 27 the Lombard League army marched by, strung out in a long procession: first heavy cavalry, then the infantry with the great Milanese *carroccio* and then the baggage train. Frederick, warned of the enemy approach by a smoke signal, attacked the center of the long column. The league knights were scattered and driven off. Many were killed or wounded and more were captured.

The league infantry had time to draw themselves up around the *carroccio* with a ditch and some hedges partly protecting them. The imperial cavalry charged the massed Lombards repeatedly and the Saracen archers discharged thousands of arrows. The battle lasted until dark. During the night the surviving league troops fled, abandoning their baggage, weapons and even their sacred *carroccio*.

Frederick's triumph was enormous. Some 3,000 enemy infantry and 1,100 knights were made prisoner, including the podesta (governor) of Milan.

Never were Frederick's fortunes so high as after Cortenuova. Now was his opportunity to make peace with Milan on favorable terms, to grant the obdurate city a limited freedom which would still maintain some of his imperial prerogatives. Instead, Frederick demanded unconditional surrender. It was the greatest political mistake of his career and ensured that the war would continue indefinitely. The Milanese undoubtedly remembered what had happened to their city when they surrendered unconditionally to another Hohenstaufen, Barbarossa. They knew well that the grandson was not as generous in victory as the grandfather. To Frederick's demand for surrender the Milanese replied: "We fear your cruelty which we have experienced; so we prefer to die under our shields by sword, spear and dart, rather than by trickery, starvation and fire." The mention of fire admitted that many of the Milanese were heretics.

The Emperor celebrated his victory at Cortenuova by entering the Ghibelline city of Cremona in a triumphal parade, with his famous white elephant drawing the Milanese *carroccio*. Tied to its mast was the podesta of Milan. Frederick dispatched the *carroccio* to Rome as a trophy of his victory.

Two years later came Pope Gregory's enlistment in the war against the Emperor, and a year later, in 1240, the Pope declared the war a crusade. And he summoned a general Church council to be held in Rome in 1241. Its unannounced but widely understood purpose was to arrange the deposition of the Emperor. Frederick responded by warning that, since the purpose of the council was purely political, he would prevent the cardinals, bishops and other prelates from attending.

Nevertheless, in May of 1241 more than 100 churchmen sailed from Genoa for Rome. Frederick's Pisan and Sicilian fleet intercepted the Genoese fleet and won a great victory. All the council delegates were captured. For three weeks they remained in chains on shipboard as the imperial fleet sailed southward. Then the churchmen were transferred to filthy prisons in Naples and in Sicily.

By August, in spite of the notorious fevers of the Roman summers, Frederick was attacking Rome itself and his troops had raided up to the very gates of the city. Pope Gregory IX, now nearly one hundred years old, was still fierce and determined, but very weak. When news of the Pope's death reached Frederick he did not try to disguise his hatred for his implacable enemy: "And so he who refused to make peace or to treat of peace, who took upon himself to challenge Augustus, was fated to fall a prey to the avenger August. And now he is dead indeed! Through him the earth lacked peace, the strife was great and how many perished!"

For nearly two years (except for the fifteen-day reign of Pope Celestine V) the papal throne was vacant. Finally, in June of 1243, Innocent IV was elected. As stubborn, crafty and obstinate an enemy of the Emperor as Gregory had been, Innocent continued the papal war against Frederick with unflagging zeal. In 1245 in the city of Lyons in France, where he had fled for safety, Innocent presided over a Church council which excommunicated Frederick again and deposed him as emperor and king.

Until his deposition Frederick had always insisted that he was a loyal Catholic opposed only to the political offenses of the popes. Now he sent a circular letter to the monarchs of Europe in which he denounced the wealth and worldliness of the Church and suggested that he himself would reform it by returning the Church to its original apostolic poverty. And Frederick said to his fellow rulers:

"He has presumed to declare me deposed, and has thereby committed an immeasurable offense against all kings. What can you as individual kings not expect from the audacity of this prince-priest, when he, who possesses no judicial authority over me in temporal matters, ventures to depose me; me, who by the solemn election of princes and with the consent of the entire (and then upright) Church, have been crowned with the imperial diadem? But I am not the first, nor shall I be the last, whom the abuse of the sacerdotal power seeks to hurl from the throne. And you are participators in the guilt, because you obey that hypocrite, whose thirst for power all the waters of Jordan could not wash away."

The war continued with victories and defeats on either side, and with abominable atrocities committed by both sides. For years Frederick had made use of a rationally controlled cruelty. He could be coldly inhuman, but he was no worse than many of his contemporaries. Now, after the deposition, with defiant rebellion still unchecked, Frederick indulged in a kind of irrational frenzy of cruelty. It seems almost as if he had undergone a major psychological change and had become as monstrously cruel as his father, Henry VI, had been, or as was his fearful son-in-law, Ezzelino da Romano.

"Our conscience is pure and therefore God is with us," said Frederick. The Guelf cities and individuals who fought him were not just enemies in war, they were rebels. And rebellion was an infamous abomination. So with a pure conscience Frederick hanged the rebels he captured. Anyone who was found with letters from the Pope on his person had his hands and feet cut off. Hostages were taken from many towns and confined in prisons in Apulia to be promptly executed if their native towns dared to revolt. Some rebels were blinded, others mutilated, others drowned.

Ernst Kantorowicz, a German scholar whose learned and admiring biography of Frederick was published forty years ago, referred rather bafflingly to Frederick's "knightly deeds," and wrote:

"In his manifestos he boasted, for instance, that he had had 300 Mantuans hanged along the banks of the Po, or again that he had prevented the defection of Reggio by publicly beheading 100 revolutionaries. Before the end the word 'mercy' was deleted from his vocabulary."

When the town of Altavilla revolted, Frederick took it by storm, razed it to the ground and had the leaders of the revolt blinded and burned alive.

Some desperate men who formed a conspiracy against Frederick and planned to assassinate him were captured and brought before the Emperor for judgment and condemned as parricides: the Emperor was their father. Each was blinded. Then from each the nose and one hand and one foot were cut off. And then the dying men were slaughtered by various methods—by being burned, drowned, hanged or dragged by horses over stony ground.

Frederick, who tried to maintain his rule by such dreadful methods, was sincerely and deeply shocked by the wickedness of those who opposed him. He was sacred and they were not.

Unable to capture and destroy the hated city of Milan, the principal champion of "abhorred liberty," Frederick made a desperate effort to subdue the defiantly Guelf city of Parma.

Parma had been Ghibelline. But on June 15, 1247, its Guelf exiles seized the city and were promptly and strongly reinforced by troops from other Guelf cities. Within two weeks from the defection of Parma Frederick was at nearby Cremona and two days later he marched up to the walls of Parma.

"Then the Emperor," wrote Fra Salimbene, who lived in Parma throughout the siege, "all inflamed with wrath and fury at that which had befallen him, came to Parma; and in the district called Grola, wherein is great plenty of vineyards and good wine (for the wine of that land is most excellent), he built a city, surrounded with great trenches, which also he called Victoria, as an omen of that which should come to pass. And the moneys which he minted there were called *Victorini*; and the great church was called Saint Victor."

When he called his encampment Victoria and planned to make it a real city to replace the one he intended to destroy, Frederick displayed a rash optimism. More humbly, the people of Parma invoked divine aid.

"The women of Parma (and especially the rich, the noble and the powerful) betook themselves with one accord to pray for the aid of the Blessed Virgin Mary, that she might help to free their city; for her name and title were held in greatest reverence by the Parmese in their cathedral church. And, that they might better gain her ear, they made a model of the city in solid silver, which I have seen, and which was offered as a gift to the Blessed Virgin; and there were to be seen the greatest and chiefest buildings of the city, fashioned of solid silver, as the cathedral church, the baptistry, the bishop's palace, the Palazzo Communale, and many other buildings which showed forth the image of the city.

"The Mother prayed her son: the Son heard the Mother, to whom of right He could deny nothing, according to the word which is figuratively contained in Holy Scripture, 'My mother, ask: for I must not turn away thy face.' These are the words of Solomon to his mother. And when the Mother of Mercy had prayed to her Son to free her city of Parma from that multitude of nations which was gathered against it, and when the night was close at hand, the Son said to His Mother, 'Hast thou seen all this exceeding great multitude? Behold, I will deliver them into thy hand this day, that thou mayest know that I am the Lord."

The deliverance thus promised came, but not for many months. Meanwhile, Fra Salimbene wrote:

"Men went out daily from either side to fight; crossbowmen, archers and slingers, as I saw with mine own eyes: and ruffians also daily scoured the whole diocese of Parma, plundering and burning on all sides: and likewise did the men of Parma to those of Cremona and Reggio. The Mantuans also came in those days and burned Casalmaggiore to the ground, as I saw with mine own eyes.

"And every morning the Emperor came with his men, and beheaded three or four, or as many more as seemed good to him, of the men of Parma and Modena and Reggio who were of the Church party, and whom he kept in bonds: and all this he did on the shingles by the riverside within sight of the men of Parma who were in the city, that he might vex their souls. The Emperor put many innocent men to an evil death, as we see in the case of the Lord Andrea di Trego, who was a noble knight of Cremona, and of Conrad di Berceto, who was a clerk, and valiant in arms, whom he tortured in diverse manners with fire and water and manifold torments."

The siege of Parma lasted for eight months, until February 18, 1248. Early that morning Frederick, his bastard son Manfred and about fifty knights mounted their horses and rode out of Victoria to go hunting with falcons. Several detachments of Frederick's besieging army had been allowed to drift away on unimportant excursions. The Emperor was bored with the dull siege and overconfident. While Frederick was away pursuing his favorite sport the Parma garrison made a sortie and part of the imperial army charged after them. The besiegers were tricked.

Out of the city gate poured a mass of armed men and with them hordes of civilians brandishing every kind of weapon: "women and girls went out with them, youths and maidens, old men and young together." They overwhelmed the surprised imperial troops, looted Victoria of everything worth looting including the *carroccio* of Cremona, and set the buildings on fire.

The Emperor heard the great alarm bell of Victoria tolling. He and his companions galloped back to the encampment and flung themselves into the battle. They were too late. The battle was already lost. Frederick was forced to flee with only fourteen horsemen. It was the worst defeat of Frederick's career and an exhilarating triumph for the Guelf cause. The plunder captured included the imperial treasury with many kinds of jewels, the scepter and the imperial seal, the menagerie, the eunuchs and the harem.

Salimbene described how the imperial crown was found "by a little man of mean stature, who was called Cortopasso (Short-step), and who bore it openly on his fist as men bear falcons, showing it to all who could see it, in honor of the victory they had gained, and to the eternal disgrace of Frederick."

The good Franciscan was fascinated by Frederick's crown. "It was of great weight, for it was all of gold, inlaid with precious stones, with many images of goldsmith's work standing out, and much graven work. It was as great as a caldron, for it was rather for dignity and for great price than as an ornament for his head; for it would have hidden all his head, face and all, had it not been raised to stand higher by means of a cunningly disposed cloth. This crown I have held in my hands, for it was kept in the sacristy of the Cathedral of the Blessed Virgin in the city of Parma."

The blow to the imperial cause was great, but it was not fatal. The war went on and two years later, in 1250, the Emperor won a great victory on the exact site where Victoria had been plundered and burned. His victorious army drove the rebel soldiers back inside the walls of Parma. The city would have been lost, the citizens of Parma believed, except for the intervention of the Blessed Virgin. Ever mindful of her city of Parma, she broke the drawbridge over the moat and drowned Guelfs and Ghibellines together. In this victory Frederick captured the *carroccio* of Parma and 3,000 prisoners.

In the same year as his victory over the Parma Guelfs, in the month of December Frederick II was riding from Foggia to his castle at Lucera when he fell gravely ill of dysentery. So he stopped for the night in the castle of Fiorentino. And there, two weeks before his fifty-sixth birthday, he died. Frederick had made a pious will in which he left his Kingdom of Sicily to his legitimate son Conrad and vast estates in Apulia to his bastard son Manfred. As Prince of Taranto, Manfred was to govern all Italy until Conrad could come from Germany and assume his rightful rule.

When Pope Innocent IV heard the glad tidings of Frederick's death he was so pleased that he wrote to the faithful Catholics of Sicily: "Let the Heavens rejoice. Let the earth be filled with gladness. For the fall of the tyrant has changed the thunderbolts and tempests that God held over your heads into gentle zephyrs and fecund dews."

Frederick von Hohenstaufen II was the most determined foe of its temporal power that the Church ever knew. He died an excommunicate. Nevertheless, he died an officially orthodox Catholic. At his own request, his body was dressed in the humble robe of a Cistercian monk and transported to Palermo in a solemn procession. There it was clothed in royal robes and buried in the cathedral, close by the tombs of his father, Henry VI, and his grandfather, Roger II.

Shortly thereafter a rumor swept over Italy. The great and cruel Emperor who had inspired so much fear, so much shuddering awe and so much amazed wonder could not die like ordinary men. The marvelous story told how a pious friar had been praying on the Calabrian coast near the strait which divides Italy and Sicily. At the moment of Frederick's death he had seen a great procession in the sky, with the Emperor at the head of 5,000 mounted knights. And he had seen Frederick lead his ghostly army down into the crater of Mount Etna.

X

The Hero in Arms

And so Pope Innocent IV, merely by outliving the Emperor Frederick II, appeared to be the victor in their prolonged conflict. The worldly Pope, always an unscrupulous political opportunist, had never wavered in his passionate hatred of the strange Emperor. Innocent was justified in his rejoicing because the Hohenstaufen dynasty would never again be a serious threat to the cities of Lombardy and so also to the temporal power of the Church itself. But the Pope's victory was only half won. Frederick's brilliant bastard son Manfred would dominate Tuscany and even cast his long shadow over Lombardy. The Church had need of a champion who could destroy Manfred—not just some mercenary soldier, but a great leader who could rally thousands of warriors to the holy cause, and who could find hundreds of thousands of marks, florins and ducats to support the continuing crusade against the abominable House of Hohenstaufen. After some delay and much bargaining, the champion was found. He was Charles of Anjou, younger brother of Louis IX, the saintly King of France.

Innocent transferred the papal court from its seven-year exile in Lyons back to Rome. Cardinal Hugh of Saint Cher, a learned and virtuous man, made a farewell speech to the citizens of Lyons in which he frankly acknowledged what had happened there during the court's stay: "We found three houses of ill fame when we came hither seven years ago and now at our departure we leave the whole city one continuous brothel."

The Pope certainly did not approve of such a development. But that is the way things were wherever the papal court was established, whether at Rome, Lyons or later at Avignon. Innocent was far too busy negotiating, threatening, conspiring and fighting to have time to worry about such customary, deplorable circumstances.

In the spring of 1251 Pope Innocent returned to Italy in triumph. It was May when he reached his native city of Genoa. Fra Salimbene, as he did so often, noted down the details: "There he gave a wife to one of his nephews, at whose wedding he himself was present with his cardinals and eighty bishops. And at that feast were many dishes and courses and varieties of meats, with diverse choice and jocund wines; and each course of dishes cost many marks. No such great and pompous wedding as this was celebrated in my days in any country, whether we consider the guests who were present or the meats that were set before them: so that the Queen of Sheba herself would have marveled to see it."

Innocent IV died in December of 1254. Earlier in the same year Frederick's young son Conrad had died. His two-year-old son, Conrad II, called Conradin, was unquestionably the rightful king of the Kingdom of Sicily. But the baby was in Germany with his mother and Manfred was in the kingdom. A beguilingly handsome young man, Manfred was described by Dante as blond, beautiful and of noble appearance. He shared his father's charm and many of his tastes. A poet and a lover of women and the luxurious life, Manfred could spur himself to resourceful action. But he lacked the energy and will to be a successful tyrant.

Nevertheless, Manfred seized power in the kingdom, had himself proclaimed regent for his little nephew and was widely suspected of spreading a rumor that Conradin had died. In 1258, while the rumor was circulating, Manfred had himself crowned king. Later, when the rumor was proved false, Manfred said that he would hold the throne only until Conradin came of age. Neither of them lived that long.

Manfred's power reached its peak in 1260 when he sent a large force to support the Ghibelline city of Siena against Guelf Florence and the

Sienese-Hohenstaufen army won a tremendous victory. Ghibelline cities and despots hastened to ally themselves with King Manfred. Would Manfred become as dangerous to the Papacy as Frederick had been? The new Pope, Urban IV, thought so and began to search for a champion of the Church.

So in 1262 Urban sent an envoy to France to persuade Charles of Anjou to undertake the great cause. He offered a substantial inducement. As the feudal overlord of the Kingdom of Sicily he offered Charles the crown if he succeeded in eliminating Manfred. Charles, whose insatiable ambition gnawed at his liver until he died, was ripe for the bait.

Who was this gloomy and arrogant prince? Giovanni Villani, the Florentine chronicler, who was ten years old when Charles died, described him thus: "This Charles was wise, prudent in counsel and valiant in arms, and harsh, and much feared and respected by all the kings of the earth, great-hearted and of high purpose, steadfast in carrying out every great undertaking, firm in every adversity, faithful to every promise, speaking little and acting much, scarcely smiling, chaste as a monk, catholic, harsh in judgment, and of a fierce countenance, tall and stalwart in person, olive-colored, large-nosed, and in kingly majesty he exceeded any other lord, and slept little and woke long, and was wont to say that all the time of sleep was so much lost. Liberal was he to knights in arms, but greedy in acquiring land and lordship and money, from whencesoever it came, to furnish means for his enterprises and wars. In jongleurs, minstrels or jesters he never took delight. This Charles, when he passed into Italy, was forty-six years of age, and he reigned nineteen years in Sicily and Apulia."

Charles of Anjou was twelve years younger than his elder brother, King Louis IX. He was born in 1226 and in 1249 accompanied King Louis on his first, disastrous crusade to Egypt. There Charles fought bravely and shared captivity with his brother. Charles was always respectful and loyal to his royal brother, but his pride, greed and ambition made him a difficult character. He was Count of Anjou and Maine by inheritance and Count of Provence because of his marriage to Beatrice, youngest daughter and heiress of Count Raymond Berenger.

Although the Count had three older daughters, he left Provence to Beatrice to ensure its independence. The other daughters, like princesses

Charles of Anjou, a contemporary statue, Rome. *Alinari*

in a fairy tale, had all married husbands of spectacular eligibility. Margaret had married King Louis IX of France. Eleanor had married King Henry III of England. And Sancha had married Richard of Cornwall, who was elected King of the Romans. According to several contemporary chroniclers, Beatrice supplied Charles with another reason for wanting to make himself King of Sicily.

Once the English Queen was visiting the French Queen and Charles and Beatrice were present also. Charles returned from hunting and found Beatrice in tears. A contemporary narrative, *The Chronicle of Morea*, translated by Harold E. Lurier in a volume he calls *Crusaders as Conquerors,* continues the story:

"Now the count recognized that the eyes of the countess were swollen from many tears and he said to her with anger, 'What are you crying about, countess?' And she wanted to deny it and not disclose it. Immediately he swore a dreadful oath and said, 'If you do not tell me truthfully, at once, why you are crying, I will give you such a beating that you will really cry.'

"And she, frightened, told him the truth; that she had gone to see her two sisters and had sat with them to chat; 'and because I sat with them as if of equal rank and did not show them deference because they were queens, my sister the Queen of France began to speak to me and said to me: "It is not right that you, my good sister, sit with us as an equal in the same rank nor of the same worth, for it is fitting that we have higher glory and worth, than a countess or a duchess or any other lady." And I, on hearing it, was immediately so sorely grieved that from grief and shame I left there and came here to my chamber and wept many tears.'

"Now when the count heard this, he made a dreaful vow and said to his wife, the countess: 'I swear this to you by Christ and His Mother, that I shall never rest nor be content until I bring it about that you become a queen with a crown.'"

Charles of Anjou had already proved his ability to rule and to wage war by cruelly suppressing several revolts in Provence. He was crafty and ruthless, avaricious and selfish, a French royal prince who never trusted anyone or cared about anyone not a member of the French nobility. He was a pious and orthodox Catholic who sincerely believed that if he destroyed King Manfred and seated himself on Manfred's throne he would be doing God's will. Pope Urban's invitation and his own colossal egotism left him no room for doubts. Charles could hardly have been better qualified for his role as a conqueror and leader of a political crusade.

Pope Urban and Charles conducted prolonged negotiations which came to nothing because the Pope died in October of 1264. The new pope, Clement IV, was a former chancellor of King Louis and a former subject of Charles. As a cardinal he had been called "le Gros" (the Fat). Clement renewed negotiations with Charles and a treaty between them was concluded in April of 1265. Its key points were that in return for being sponsored by the Church in his war of conquest and for being crowned as the ruler of the Kingdom of Sicily, Charles of Anjou would recognize the Pope's feudal overlordship, and that Charles would not hold office or land within the papal states. And Clement promised to declare the war a crusade. Both allies were to raise money for the cause.

They borrowed and taxed. The French clergy contributed a tenth of their possessions. Florentine bankers lent huge sums on condition that they could exploit the financial resources of the Kingdom of Sicily. And Countess Beatrice even pawned her jewels to help raise money for the conquest. The money thus collected was never enough; but at no time have inadequate funds prevented the waging of wars.

In April of 1265 Charles of Anjou sailed from Marseilles with a small fleet which transported 1,000 knights but no horses with which to mount them. He was boldly taking a considerable risk. Pisa was King Manfred's ally and Pisan naval power could easily have intercepted the flotilla and have captured every man on board. Charles might have spent the rest of his life in some Sicilian dungeon—which was exactly the fate of the cardinals and bishops captured by Pisan galleys when they tried to sail to the Church council called by Pope Gregory IX.

But the Pisan fleet never left port. Charles reached papal territory safely. The Pisans were quarreling with one of King Manfred's vicars and did not settle their dispute until it was too late. Charles was lucky then, as he often was.

Charles entered Rome in May and settled down in the Lateran palace as if he were already a king honored as a guest by the Pope. Clement, like so many medieval popes, was not present in the riotous city of

Rome. He was in Perugia. When he heard of Charles's presumption and effrontery in moving into the papal palace of the Lateran without an invitation, he wrote the champion of the Church a letter of rebuke:

"Thou hast made bold to do that which no Christian king has ever permitted himself. Contrary to all decorum, thy followers at thy bidding have entered the Lateran Palace. Thou must know that it is in no wise agreeable to me that the Senator of the city [Charles had been voted that title by the Romans], however illustrious and honored may be his person, should make his residence in one of the palaces of the popes. I desire to prevent future abuses: the precedence of the Church must not be infringed by anyone, least of all by thee, whom I have called to thy exalted station. Thou must not take this amiss. Seek thy abode elsewhere in the city. It has plenty of spacious palaces. Moreover, do not say that I have rudely thrust thee out of one of my palaces. I have, on the contrary, been mindful of thine own dignity."

Charles vacated the Lateran. So proud a man must have been furious, but he probably thought the issue was too small a matter to justify quarreling with Pope Clement, whose wholehearted support he needed.

Although he had been enthusiastically welcomed by the Guelf faction in Rome, Charles was desperately hard up. Where all the money he had raised went is obscure, but in Rome he could not pay the daily living expenses of his 1,000 knights, his numerous companions and his many servants. He begged the Pope for money. Clement protested:

"My treasury is completely empty. The reason whereof is shown by the confusion of the world. . . . How can the Pope find money for himself and others without resorting to Godless means? Never in any undertaking have I found myself in such straits."

In another letter, not to Charles, Clement wrote of Charles's financial plight: "Ask the count himself how wretched his life is. He begs clothing and keep for himself and his people with the sweat of his brow, and always looks to the hands of his creditors, who suck his blood. They make him pay a solidus for that which is not worth two pence, and even this he only acquires by flattery and humble request."

The financial crisis continued and Clement wrote again to Charles: "If thy troops do not come I do not know how thou wilt await them and how thou wilt manage to live, how thou wilt maintain the city, or assist the approach of the army if it be delayed. Should it, however, arrive as we hope, still less do I know how we shall feed so many men."

The Provençal army, whose arrival in Rome the Pope anxiously awaited, crossed the border into Italy in June of 1265. The soldiers, who wore the crusaders' cross, much resembled the conquistadors who followed Cortés and Pizarro. Their religious zeal to destroy the hated and excommunicated Hohenstaufen, King Manfred, was no doubt genuine. But it was far surpassed by their zeal to acquire land and wealth in Manfred's kingdom.

The crusaders marched to Bologna, ravaging the land on their way. They were joined by Italian Guelf recruits. Their numbers are unknown, but historians estimate about 6,000 mounted knights and an unknown number of Italian infantry. The Provençal army took seven months to march to Rome, wasting much time in leisurely stopovers in various cities. Two hundred and twenty-nine years later another French army, that of King Charles VIII, marched to the conquest of the Kingdom of Naples and reached Rome in only four leisurely months. Charles's men arrived in Rome exhausted, in rags, without pay. Since Charles had no money to speak of, he could do little to help them. So he led them promptly off to war. Somehow, in spite of his poverty, he had managed to find horses to mount the 1,000 knights who had accompanied him by sea. The crusading army left Rome on January 10, 1266.

Fourteen days before his departure Charles of Anjou and his wife, Beatrice, had been crowned in Saint Peter's by five cardinals as King and Queen of the Kingdom of Sicily. The fact that Manfred was still king was not considered to have any significance. Pope Clement was not present. He had preferred to stay in Perugia.

Knowing of the preparations for Charles's coronation, Manfred sent a futile letter of protest to Pope Clement, who replied rhetorically: "Let Manfred know that the time for grace is past. Everything has its time, but time has not everything. The hero in arms has issued from the gate; the ax is already laid to the roots."

A mystery haunts the story of Charles's army slowly marching all the way to Rome without Manfred making any major attempt to halt it or delay it. Manfred had many Ghibelline allies in northern Italy. But he did nothing to organize them into a defensive force which could come to his aid. And he did very little to prepare to defend the kingdom itself. Why did this intelligent and able ruler remain so inert and passive? There must have been a fatal flaw in his character, an irresponsible and indolent willingness to leave his fate to chance, which would have horrified his father. Frederick had many faults, but apathy and laziness were not among them.

So Charles was able to march into the Kingdom of Sicily unimpeded, leading his ragged, hungry and desperate soldiers to war against a charming but incompetent enemy. Traitorous cities surrendered their keys to Charles and numerous fortresses yielded without resistance. With much of his kingdom going over to the enemy in panic, aware that some of the barons in his own army were upon the brink of treason, Manfred at the last moment tried to negotiate with Charles. Villani wrote that Charles replied: "Tell the Sultan of Lucera for me that today I will send him to hell, or he will send me to paradise."

That was just before the momentous Battle of Benevento. Manfred had tried to keep his army between Charles and the city of Naples; but he could not maneuver long because of his fear of desertions. His astrologers assured him that the signs were favorable. He knew that Charles's troops were hungry and underfed. If he could have postponed battle for several more days Charles's army would have had to surrender or disperse. But Manfred did not dare delay. If he did, too many of his own barons might be fighting for Charles!

The battle was sharply fought. But many of Manfred's barons did desert, right in the middle of the battle action, and so made a French victory certain. When King Manfred saw that the day was lost he put on his helmet, and as he did so its crest of a silver eagle fell off. "Behold," said Manfred, "the sign of the Lord." Then with no insignia of his royal status he charged to meet his death—just as King Richard III was to do at Bosworth Field 219 years later.

When he was congratulated after the victory Charles was as glum as usual and as ambitious for further conquests: "What do you wish me to rejoice at? To a valiant man the whole world would not suffice."

Charles wrote to Pope Clement: "After a fierce struggle on both sides, with the Divine aid, we caused the first two ranks of the enemy to yield, on which the rest sought safety in flight. So great was the carnage on the field that the bodies of the slain covered the face of the earth. The fugitives did not all escape. Many fell by the swords of their pursuers. Many were taken prisoner and brought to our dungeons. . . . Of Manfred we have as yet heard nothing: whether he fell in battle, was taken prisoner, or escaped. The charger which he rode and which is in our hands seems to imply his death. I inform Your Holiness of this great victory, in order that you may thank the Almighty, who has granted it and who fights for the cause of the Church by my arm."

Two days after the battle a common soldier led an ass with a corpse tied on its back through the camp, shouting: "Who wants to buy Manfred?" The corpse was naked because camp followers had stripped the dead of their clothes as well as of their armor and weapons. Charles had several captive barons led in chains to testify whether the body was indeed Manfred's. They said it was. But only one of them showed any grief. "Oh, my king!" he cried out in anguish and hid his face in his hands and wept.

Charles wrote again to Clement: "Moved by the feelings of humanity, I have caused the dead to be buried with honor, though not with ecclesiastical rites." Because Manfred was an excommunicate he could not lawfully be buried by a priest in consecrated ground. Charles ordered each of his soldiers to throw a stone on the corpse. A large cairn was thus formed.

The victorious soldiers then proceeded to sack the nearby papal city of Benevento. For eight days the Christian crusaders summoned by the Pope and fighting for the Church massacred the inhabitants. Whether Charles of Anjou permitted this horror or tried and failed to prevent it is not known. When Pope Clement heard of the atrocities committed in Benevento he is said to have shrieked in despair.

King Charles's victory was so complete most of the Kingdom of Sicily went over to him and he entered Naples in triumphant state. Applauding crowds flung flowers before him in the streets. The cold, taciturn conqueror did not bother to make himself popular, but he acted on a political maxim which Machiavelli was to recommend 250 years later: a new ruler should eliminate the members of the previous ruler's family. So Charles had Manfred's family captured and imprisoned. Historians have named several different castles as their place of confinement. But

Steven Runciman, one of the most authoritative of modern medieval scholars, says that their prison was the Castello del Parco at Nocera near Salerno. Manfred's young widow, Queen Helena, died there after five years of imprisonment. She was not yet thirty. Manfred's three bastard sons were never released. One was still alive in the castle in 1309, forty-three years after the Battle of Benevento.

Four months after the battle Pope Clement had recovered from the shock caused by the massacre of his own subjects at Benevento. He wrote to his legate in England in a spirit of vindictive glee: "Our dear son Charles is in peaceful possession of all the Kingdom, having in his power the putrid corpse of that pestilential man, his wife, his children and his treasure."

Although by contemporary medieval standards Charles was merciful after Benevento, he imposed severe taxes and his French officials collected them harshly and extortionately. So, soon Charles was hated throughout his newly conquered kingdom. A contemporary chronicler, who was a Guelf and so should have been a partisan of Charles, lamented:

"Oh, King Manfred, little did we know thee when alive! Now thou art dead, we deplore thee in vain! Thou appearedst as a ravening wolf among the flocks of this kingdom; now fallen by our fickleness and inconstancy under the present government, under which we groan, we find that thou wert a lamb. Now we know by bitter comparison how mild was thy rule. We thought it hard that part of our substance must be yielded unto thy hands, now we find that all our substance and even our own possessions are the prey of the stranger."

Charles administered a stern justice to his subjects, but had little other concern for them. "He regarded all commoners," wrote Ferdinand Schevill, "whether in his native France or in Italy, the land of his adoption, as laborious clods whom God in his goodness had provided in order that sovereigns and their barons, the true elect of the earth, might lead an honorable and dignified existence."

Even Pope Clement lost his enthusiasm for his French protégé, who refused to take Clement's advice as he was expected to do. Clement sent letters and personal envoys urging Charles to control the cruelties of many of his officials and to temper the general severity of his regime.

Charles replied with his habitual arrogance: "I know not what the word tyrant means; this I know, that so far I have been protected by God; I doubt not that He will still protect me."

Pope Clement accused Charles of being haughty, self-willed and un-grateful, which he was. In one letter Clement lamented that Charles was "neither visible, nor audible, nor affable, nor amiable."

No one ever thought that King Charles of Anjou was affable or amiable, but many thought that it would be prudent to join the winning side. Charles was the victorious Guelf champion. So, many towns in Lombardy went Guelf and so did others in Tuscany. In January of 1267 Charles led an army into Tuscany and was ceremoniously welcomed by Florence, Lucca, Pistoia and Prato. All four cities humbly elected Charles their podesta, or governor. But Siena and Pisa stubbornly remained Ghibelline. So Charles attacked Siena and besieged its outlying fortress of Poggibonsi for five months before capturing it.

Charles's power was impressive. Nevertheless, many cities and in-dividuals bitterly resented it. As early as 1266, the year of Benevento, envoys from Palermo, Siena, Pisa, Pavia and Verona were in Germany trying to persuade the boy Conradin, Frederick's grandson, to lead an army into Italy and drive out the Angevin oppressor.

At fourteen Conradin had the usual Hohenstaufen good looks and charm. He "was as beautiful as Absalom and spoke good Latin," wrote a contemporary. Conradin was not only attractive, he was clever, courage-ous and ambitious to restore the lost glory of the Hohenstaufens. Even so, there was something feckless and politically naïve in the idea that the handsome boy should command an army in battle against such a mighty warrior as Charles.

Nevertheless, in September of 1266 Pope Clement took the threat so seriously that he announced he would excommunicate anyone who should work to elect Conradin emperor and anyone who should accom-pany him if he came into Italy. And in the following spring Clement wrote letters denouncing the boy king as "a poisonous basilisk arisen from the stock of the dragon."

Conradin's best friend was a young teen-ager a little older than he was, Frederick of Baden, heir to the duchy of Austria. The King of Bohemia had annexed Austria, so Frederick was also an exile from his hereditary domain. When Conradin and Frederick led an army of some 3,000 German knights into Italy in the autumn of 1267 Conradin was only fifteen years old. He arrived in Verona on October 21 as short of money as Charles had been when he first arrived in Rome. In November Pope Clement excommunicated Conradin and all his supporters. Nevertheless, revolts in favor of Conradin broke out in Sicily, Calabria, Apulia and Rome.

Conradin's little army marched slowly from Verona to Pavia to Pisa. And then in April Clement excommunicated Conradin and his supporters for the second time within six months. The first anathema had evidently not been sufficiently efficacious. By June Conradin had reached Ghibelline Siena and in July he was marching on Rome. His route took him a few miles west of the papal city of Viterbo, where Pope Clement was then living as a fugitive from the rebellious and riotous Romans.

From the battlements of Viterbo the Pope watched the great cloud of dust which marked the progress of Conradin's army, now considerably enlarged by Ghibelline Italian recruits. The old man, surrounded by his cardinals, prophesied with utter confidence: "He will vanish like that golden dust." Then remembering how young and inexperienced Conradin was, Clement added: "They are leading him like a lamb to the slaughter."

While Conradin marched down to Rome the revolt in Sicily prospered and spread so widely that only the cities of Palermo and Messina remained faithful to Charles. On July 24 Conradin arrived in Rome and was welcomed by an almost hysterically enthusiastic populace. In the city of the popes an acknowledged enemy of the Pope was greeted with hymns of rejoicing and with showers of flowers. The buildings were hung with silks and satins in his honor.

Conradin spent three weeks in Rome and then marched out to attack the French usurper. At the Battle of Tagliacozzo King Charles won another total victory. He had been merciful after Benevento. Now he was enraged by widespread rebellion and by the presence of Italians in Conradin's army. Charles ordered that the feet of many of his prisoners should be cut off. Someone had the courage to tell him that the sight of so many mutilated cripples would only inspire further hatred against himself. Charles solved that problem by ensuring that the

The walls of Lucera. *Orville Prescott*

cripples would not be seen. He had the miserable men piled like cordwood in a nearby building, which was then burned.

Frederick's city of Lucera persisted in resisting Charles and withstood a seven-month siege before being forced by starvation to surrender. Charles spared the lives of the Saracens, but hanged every Italian found in the city.

From the slaughter of Tagliacozzo Conradin and his friend Frederick of Baden fled to Rome and thence south to the village of Astura on the seacoast some thirty-five miles south of Rome. Conradin and several of his companions tried to escape in a boat, but were captured at sea and handed over to a detachment of Charles's soldiers. These took their prisoners in chains to the Colonna fortress of Palestrina and thence to Naples. There Conradin and Frederick were imprisoned in the Castello dell' Uovo on a little island in the harbor which today is overlooked by tourist hotels.

While Charles deliberated on the most expedient way to dispose of Conradin, Pope Clement, it was widely believed, encouraged him to execute the young prince by sending Charles this message: *"Vita Conradini, mors Caroli; vita Caroli, mors Conradini,"* which may be translated as "The life of Conrad requires the death of Charles; the life of Charles requires the death of Conrad."

But to murder a royal prince captured after a bravely fought battle, and that prince a charming boy of sixteen, would be a gross violation of the medieval code. To justify the execution King Charles had his lawyers prepare an indictment in which Conradin's invasion of his own hereditary kingdom was declared a robbery and an act of treason. Then Charles's judges pronounced Conradin and Frederick guilty and condemned them to death by beheading. A scaffold was erected on the Campo Moricino, the site of the present Piazza del Mercato.

Young Conradin died as bravely as King Charles I of England and, like that unfortunate monarch, denied the right of his captors to try and to execute him. Conradin was playing chess with Frederick in his prison cell when an official named Robert of Bari read him his death sentence. "Slave," said Conradin, "do you dare to condemn as a criminal the son and heir of kings? Knows not your master that he is my equal, not my judge? I am a mortal and must die; yet ask the kings of the earth if a prince be criminal for seeking to win back the heritage of his ancestors. But if there be no pardon for me, spare, at least, my faithful companions; or if they must die, strike me first, that I may not behold their deaths."

When Conradin was led onto the scaffold he fell on his knees and, raising his hands, exclaimed: "Oh, my Mother! How deep will be thy sorrow at the news of this day!" With Conradin also died his loyal friend Frederick of Baden and four Italian nobles who had supported him.

This judicial murder has been execrated for centuries and has blackened King Charles's reputation more than have his far greater cruelties to victims less appealing than the gallant young prince, who failed to win his kingdom, but who succeeded in winning the sympathy of thousands centuries after his pathetic death.

One month after Conradin's execution the Pope, who had cynically advised it, himself died.

The Sicilian revolt was soon suppressed and Charles of Anjou then dominated all of Italy. The absolute monarch of the Kingdom of Sicily was also the Senator of Rome, the Vicar of Tuscany and the podesta or protector of all the Guelf cities. For ten years King Charles, as senator, ruled Rome through vicars of his own. In one year 200 thieves were hanged. So complete was Charles's authority in Rome that he even put his name on the Roman coins.

In addition, of course, Charles was still Count of Anjou, Maine and Provence. But even such extensive dominions were not enough. Charles dreamed of a Mediterranean empire and, like Robert Guiscard and the Emperor Henry VI before him, planned to conquer the Byzantine empire and seat himself upon the imperial throne in Constantinople.

But Charles's dream of Eastern conquests had to be postponed because his royal elder brother, the King of France, planned to go crusading again and demanded Charles's cooperation. Charles could hardly refuse. King Louis was the most admired and beloved monarch in Europe. A crusade was holy. Charles was devoutly orthodox. And besides, Charles was enormously in debt to Louis. He owed Louis 8,000 marks still unpaid out of Queen Margaret's Provençal dowry; 7,000 marks which Charles had borrowed to pay obligations in his father-in-law's will; 5,000 marks which Louis had given Charles when he married, which were to be repaid if Charles acquired greater dignities, which he certainly had; and, worst of all, 30,000 pounds which Louis had lent Charles when they were in the Holy Land after the failure of Louis' Egyptian crusade. Louis forcibly pointed out to Charles that he needed all this money for his new crusade, for the marriages of his children, and for the ceremonial knighting of his eldest son, Philip.

Whether Charles repaid any large part of these debts is doubtful, but he certainly intended to take part in the new crusade. Why the crusade attacked Tunis rather than the Moslems of Palestine and Syria is a question that has perplexed historians. Was it King Louis' idea? Could the ailing King have believed the improbable rumor that the Emir of Tunis wished to become a Christian convert and would welcome a Christian army on his shores? Charles had personal reasons for wanting to attack Tunis, but it is doubtful if Louis would have thought them adequate. Charles was angry with the Emir because he had ceased paying the annual tribute he had formerly paid to Frederick and Manfred for free trade with Sicily. And the Emir had given refuge to several of Charles's enemies.

The decision could have been a compromise. Perhaps Charles agreed to join Louis' second crusade (provided it went to Tunis) if Louis would in his turn support Charles's anticipated attack on the Byzantine empire. In any case, Tunis it was. King Louis intended to sail early in May of 1270, but he was weak and unwell and there were many delays. It was July before King Louis and his crusaders sailed from the port of Aigues-Mortes. They did not land on the arid coast of Tunis until July 17 in the middle of the summer's greatest heat. The lesson of Rome's summer epidemics had not yet been learned. There was very little fresh water and no sanitation. Soon half the French army was laid low with dysentery.

King Louis IX fell fatally ill. As he lay dying King Charles's fleet was seen approaching. Charles landed on August 25 and hurried to his brother's tent. The King of France had just died and his body was still warm. Charles fell on his knees in tears and prayed. The usual medieval public display of emotion would account for this, but it is at least possible that Charles felt some sincere affection for his brother and he may even have felt guilty because of his own late arrival in Tunis.

Charles of Anjou assumed command of the disastrous crusade and advised his nephew Philip, now King of France, to make peace. The Emir was anxious to see the crusaders depart and granted favorable terms, including 210,000 ounces of gold, reparations paid the invaders to defray the expenses of their invasion. Charles sailed away on November 14, taking with him King Louis' heart and entrails, which he piously buried in the Benedictine abbey of Monreale near Palermo. The dead King's bones were taken back to Paris to be buried in Saint-Denis.

In the same year a fleet of Sicilian and Genoese crusaders was wrecked off Trapani on the westernmost point of Sicily. King Charles appropriated for himself everything valuable which could be salvaged from the wrecked ships, excusing his rapacity on the grounds that an old law of King William's and an equally old custom authorized such seizures.

Fra Salimbene tells a story about Charles's foolhardy valor. The best jouster in his newly conquered kingdom was supposed to be a knight from the Campagna district near Rome. Charles, who was considered an expert jouster himself, was much vexed by the champion's great reputation. He arranged to challenge the famous warrior to a joust, using an incognito to conceal his identity. Charles's son, Charles of Salerno, called "the Lame," warned his father that all might not go well. But the King persisted. The joust was held and Charles was knocked unconscious off his horse. When he regained his wits the stubborn King was determined to run another course with his victorious opponent. His son persuaded him not to by saying: "Peace, Father, for the leeches say that two of the ribs of your body are broken."

In addition to his severe enforcement of the laws and his sincere effort to maintain justice, Charles tried in other ways to be an efficient and conscientious monarch. He repaired roads. He encouraged agriculture, protected state forests to conserve a timber supply for ships, and introduced Barbary sheep onto his royal farms. He made Naples his capital. And beside the harbor in Naples he built the formidable Castel Nuovo, which still stands today.

The French officials Charles employed throughout the kingdom regarded the Italians as an inferior subject people and provoked bitter resentment. Charles's gifts to some 700 Frenchmen and Provençals of feudal fiefs in Sicily enraged the Sicilians. And his insistence on making French the official language of his government angered everybody. King Charles, arrogantly confident of his military power, never dreamed of trying to conciliate his new subjects. He was too busy planning further conquests.

In 1271 Charles dispatched an expeditionary force across the Adriatic to attack the Byzantine empire. It captured Durazzo and much of Albania. This was so gratifying that Charles promptly announced that he was now King of Albania. And then he went to war against Genoa. The new Pope, Gregory X, forbade Charles to attack Constantinople directly. Gregory wanted to see if a conference he had called for 1273 in Lyons could make any progress toward the elusive goal of uniting the Roman Catholic and Greek Orthodox churches. To that congress Gregory summoned the foremost living Catholic theologian and philosopher, Thomas Aquinas.

Thomas, a second cousin of the Emperor Frederick II, was King Charles's most distinguished subject. He was born at Roccasecca near Monte Cassino in 1225. He was the youngest and seventh son of Landolfo, Count of Aquino, a nobleman who served Frederick II as a soldier and as a government official. Three of Thomas' older brothers fought in Frederick's army. One of them was a traitor who went over to the papal cause, was captured by Frederick's forces and was executed for treason. In addition to his six brothers, Thomas had five sisters.

Much against his father's wishes, Thomas joined the Dominican Order. His massive body and deliberate manner earned him the nickname "The Dumb Ox." But his achievements as a scholar, teacher and theologian won him such universal admiration that he was called "The Angelic Doctor." Among his many works the most important is the *Summa Theologica*, the greatest of all contributions to medieval scholastic philosophy and religious doctrine. When Thomas received the

The Castel Nuovo, built by Charles of Anjou, Naples. *Alinari*

Pope's summons to come to Lyons he was teaching and lecturing in Naples. Although seriously sick, he obediently set out on the long journey.

He had not gone far when his illness became worse. He was carried to the Cistercian abbey of Fossanuova and there on March 7, 1274, at the age of only forty-nine he died.

Although students of Saint Thomas' life have been unable to find any reason to doubt that he died a natural death, a rumor swept over Italy that King Charles had had Thomas poisoned. Since Charles could have had no conceivable motive to murder the scholar saint, it is reasonable to suppose that the Italians disliked their grim French conqueror so intensely that they were delighted to believe him capable of so horrible a crime.

Giovanni Villani, who was born about two years after Thomas' death, and Dante, who was nine years old at the time, picked up the malicious gossip and repeated it as truth in their famous books. Dante wrote:

> Charles came to Italy, and—for amends—
> Made Conradin a victim, and thereafter
> Drove Thomas back to heaven.

And always Charles's wars continued and multiplied. He fought Genoa until 1276. He fought an alliance of Ghibelline cities in northern Italy and failed to defeat them. He continued to fight the Byzantine empire in Epirus and Albania. And he forcibly intervened in the College of Cardinals to make sure that popes of his personal choice were elected.

In 1276 after the death of Pope Gregory X the conclave was held in the Lateran palace in Rome. Charles ringed the great building with soldiers and permitted food to be taken in to his own supporters among the cardinals, but not to his opponents. Not surprisingly, one of his best friends was elected, who most inconsiderately died five weeks later.

The next pope, John XXI, reigned for only a year and the one after that, Nicholas III, for only two years. The conclave to elect his successor was held in Viterbo and lasted for six months without an election. Early in 1281 the people of Viterbo rioted in protest against the dilatory cardinals. And then for the second time Charles intervened in the election of a pope. Charles marched on Viterbo and occupied the town with his own troops. With the enthusiastic consent of the citizens of the town he imprisoned the cardinals in the papal palace and announced that he would keep them there until they should reach a decision. Thoroughly cowed, the cardinals in February elected a French patriot and ardent supporter of Charles, Simon of Brie, who took the name of Martin IV.

In the same year Charles's army in Epirus was defeated by the Byzantines and he lost most of his conquests across the Adriatic. Also during that fateful year a vast conspiracy was organized to drive the hated French conquerors out of the island of Sicily. The conspiracy was a triple one.

First there were the Sicilians themselves, maddened by the rapacious and corrupt rule of Charles's officials. Second there was the Byzantine emperor, who knew that generous sums of money spent promoting revolt in Sicily were the best possible means of preventing Charles from launching a major assault on Constantinople. Third there was King Peter of Aragon, who by his marriage to King Manfred's daughter, Constance, had as good a claim to the throne of the Kingdom of Sicily as Henry VI had had through his marriage to Roger II's daughter, Constance. Like most medieval kings, Peter could not resist an opportunity to expand his dominions. Now, with so much help, the time seemed opportune.

In the spring of 1282 King Charles was in Naples superintending preparations for his campaign against Constantinople. At the same time King Peter of Aragon was in Barcelona superintending preparations for his conquest of Sicily. Charles received warnings of Peter's intentions, but he did not take them seriously. And then without warning of any kind occurred the remarkable outbreak against a foreign tyranny which is famous as the Sicilian Vespers. Probably it was accidentally provoked. The conspirators would have planned it to coincide with Peter's invasion.

On Easter Monday, March 30, 1282, a crowd of Sicilians gathered to attend the Vesper service at the church of the Holy Spirit outside the city wall of Palermo. While they waited on the piazza for the church bell to summon them inside, a group of drunken French soldiers joined them. The Sicilians glowered but did nothing as the "brutal soldiery" made offensive remarks to their wives and daughters. One swaggering sergeant dragged a young married woman out of the crowd and either said or did something insulting which enraged the girl's husband. He wore a dagger and he used it to kill the sergeant. The other French soldiers rushed upon the murderer; but they were in turn set upon by a crowd of Sicilians, all of them surprisingly well armed. Every one of the French soldiers was killed.

The bells of the church were tolled and men sprinted through Palermo to call the oppressed citizens to battle and revenge. Other church bells tolled throughout the city. Soon the streets swarmed with armed men determined to exterminate the hated French. They slaughtered the French soldiers, their wives and children—even Sicilian girls who had unpatriotically married Frenchmen. They forced their way into convents, dragged out the French monks and friars and slew them in the streets. A few terrified French managed to escape the massacre, but by morning some 2,000 French were dead.

The exulting rebels tore down the flags of Anjou, proclaimed Palermo a free city and sent off a delegation to petition the Pope to become the city's protector.

Messengers carried the news to other Sicilian towns and more massacres of French followed. The French garrisons of two small towns, who had behaved well, were spared and allowed to leave the island. Messina, the second most important city, also revolted, set fire to a fleet of Charles's ships assembled in the harbor and drove most of the French garrison troops into the castle of Mategriffon. Later these troops were permitted to leave Sicily on the condition that they would sail directly to France. One of two shiploads broke the agreement and sailed to join Charles on the mainland. The Sicilians were so enraged by this betrayal that when they intercepted the second shipload of French they flung them all overboard to drown.

When King Charles realized that all Sicily was in the hands of the rebels and that all the ships which had been in the harbor of Messina were destroyed he prayed: "Lord God, if it hath pleased Thee to afflict me with adverse fortune, grant at least that it may come in little steps." The Sicilian Vespers, in which perhaps as many as 4,000 French were slaughtered, meant that Charles had to abandon his cherished plan to conquer Constantinople and that he had permanently lost Sicily, the part of his Italian kingdom which gave it its name. Henceforth Charles and his Angevin successors would be rulers of the Kingdom of Naples.

Charles's rage was terrifying. He gnawed his scepter and swore to take a monstrous vengeance. If he should live a thousand years he would not stop razing Sicilian cities, burning crops and torturing the insolent rebels. He would leave Sicily a desolate, uninhabited desert, a warning of the fate that awaited those who revolted against their rightful God-given kings.

Charles immediately began to plan the reconquest of Sicily. He still had all his ships which had been in mainland ports and the soldiers who had expected to fight the Byzantines. While Charles was reorganizing his resources a Franciscan friar arrived from Sicily and obtained an audience with the King.

"How dare you come to me from that land of traitors?" demanded Charles.

With rash but magnificent courage the friar replied: "I am not a traitor, nor do I come from a land of traitors. I come urged on by religion and conscience to warn my holy brethren not to accompany your unjust arms. You have abandoned the people committed by God to your charge to be torn by wolves and hounds. You have hardened your heart against complaints and supplications. The people have avenged their wrongs. They will defend, they will die, for their holiest rights. Think of Pharaoh!"

Instead of having the friar slaughtered on the spot or having him shut up in a dungeon for life, Charles let him return safely to Sicily. He may have been impressed by the friar's religious fervor; or he may have thought that it would be sound psychological warfare to allow the friar to report how large an army he was assembling.

On July 25 King Charles of Anjou personally led a large force to the reconquest of Sicily, landing near Messina and beginning his operations with a siege of that city. As so often happened in the Middle Ages, the besiegers made little progress. And then came the news that King Peter of Aragon with 600 mounted knights and 8,000 *almugaveri,* guerrilla infantry notorious for their cruelty, had landed at Trapani at the western tip of Sicily on August 30.

Peter of Aragon was welcomed enthusiastically in Palermo on September 2. Two weeks later King Peter's ambassadors arrived at Charles's camp outside the walls of Messina. They were granted an audience and Charles received them inside his royal tent, where he was seated on a bed covered with silk. The envoys stated formally that "The illustrious Peter, King of Aragon and Sicily, commands you, Charles of Provence, to depart from his kingdom; to give him free passage into his city of Messina, which you are besieging by sea and by land; he is astonished at your presumption in impeding the passage of the King of Aragon."

Charles, who regularly treated others arrogantly, did not relish such arrogance addressed to himself. Again he gnawed on his scepter. But Charles knew that many of his troops had succumbed to the usual ailments of campaigning in the Mediterranean summer heat. King Peter was a formidable enemy whose fleet was superior to Charles's. In addition, Charles's many wars had left him deeply in debt. A long war with the King of Aragon would be dreadfully expensive. So Charles replied that he did not admit Peter's claim to be the King of Sicily, but that he might consider leaving the island temporarily. A week later, when he learned that Peter was marching against him, he did so.

And then, instead of waging war against King Peter, Charles challenged him to a duel that would settle the dispute about their rival claims to the throne of Sicily. What are we to think of this outburst of quixotic medieval chivalry? Did King Charles seriously believe that, since his cause was righteous, God would see to it that his arms prevailed? Since the duel was not to be a single combat but a battle between the two kings supported by 100 knights each, its outcome might have been considered unpredictable. Or did the unscrupulous Charles plan some sort of trickery to secure victory? We shall never know. Over the immense gulf of seven centuries it is not possible to understand the medieval mind of the morose, taciturn, arrogant Charles of Anjou.

Pope Martin IV, when he heard of this flamboyant gesture, denounced its flagrant impiety. To allow the dispute to be settled by the lottery of a barbarous duel would cast doubt on the Papacy's feudal supremacy over the Kingdom of Sicily and on the legitimacy of its grant of the crown long since to Charles. Besides, it would be a foolish risk. So Pope Martin sternly forbade Charles to fight the duel. His arguments and his prohibition made no impression on the stubborn King. Peter of Aragon had already been excommunicated for his criminal invasion of Sicily and so he also was indifferent to papal commands and arguments. The two kings chose their companions for the great duel and proceeded with their preparations.

The site chosen was Bordeaux in Gascony. There in the dominions of King Edward I of England no favoritism need be feared by either side, even though Edward had condemned the duel as frivolous. The fact that Charles of Anjou was nearly fifty-six and his opponent only forty-one did not dampen Charles's determination, although it probably influenced the decision to have a battle royal instead of a single combat.

In January of 1283 Charles made his son, Charles of Salerno, regent of the kingdom and then set off on a long, leisurely and roundabout journey to Bordeaux via Naples, Rome, Florence and Paris. The two kings arrived in Bordeaux at the end of May. June 1 was the day appointed for the momentous duel.

June 1 proved to be a pretentious fiasco. King Peter assembled his knights so early in the morning that the chance of meeting Charles and his knights in the lists was nil. Peter rode in great state at the head of his dauntless one hundred. Heralds blew trumpets and proclaimed his presence. With no opponent to fight, he had his victory proclaimed.

King Charles, equally careful to choose a suitably prudent hour, paraded to the lists several hours after Peter had left and likewise found no enemy present. He, too, proclaimed his triumph. Both kings broadcast charges of cowardice and departed from Bordeaux in opposite directions. Never in history was there a more inglorious duel. It may have been arranged in all seriousness. But caution seems to have prevailed and it ended in ludicrous farce.

Charles of Anjou stayed in France for nearly a year, leaving the war for Sicily to be waged by his son, Charles the Lame. During his absence the news of the Sicilian Vespers and of King Peter's conquest of Sicily provoked several revolts on the mainland. In Forli, a small city in the Romagna district and so not properly subject to Charles, hundreds of

Frenchmen were massacred. And in Rome in January of 1284 the powerful Orsini family led a revolt in which all the soldiers of the French garrison were massacred.

Not until the end of May of 1264 did Charles leave France. He sailed from Provence and proceeded cautiously along the Italian coast so as not to encounter the Aragonese fleet, which was commanded by the greatest fighting admiral of the thirteenth century, Roger of Lauria.

Charles the Lame was not as able, intelligent or cautious as his father. Although he had been ordered by his father to avoid a naval battle, on June 5 he recklessly led the Angevin fleet out of the harbor of Naples. Roger was waiting for him. He decisively defeated the younger Charles's fleet and captured Charles himself. When this debacle became known in Naples, another anti-French revolt broke out. Many Frenchmen were slaughtered and their houses were sacked and burned.

Charles of Anjou heard the bad news when he landed at the port of Gaeta some fifty-five miles north of Naples. His anger at his son's disobedience and bungling was so great that he felt no pity for him in his defeat and captivity: "Who loses a fool loses nothing. Why is he not dead for disobeying us?"

In Naples Charles arrested hundreds of persons suspected of participating in the anti-French revolt. He declared that he was merciful to these rebels because he had only impaled one of them. He hanged 149 and pardoned the rest.

Desperately pressed for money, with all his dreams of empire gone and King Peter of Aragon in possession of the Calabrian city of Reggio just across the strait from Messina in Sicily, Charles grimly continued the war. He led an army south from Naples to drive the invaders out of Reggio and besieged that city for two weeks. While he did so the Aragonese fleet raided the Calabrian coast and nowhere met with any opposition. The local population had no interest in fighting for the King from France. So Charles gave up his siege of Reggio, abandoned Calabria and marched east to Brindisi on the Adriatic coast. And there he planned a new campaign to be fought the following year.

Charles of Anjou spent Christmas in the old Norman fortress town of Melfi in Apulia and then went on to Foggia, the favorite city of the Emperor Frederick II. And there King Charles fell gravely ill. On his deathbed the conqueror-king, whose reign was ending so unfortunately, prayed: "Lord God, as I believe truly that Thou are my saviour, I pray Thee to have mercy on my soul for the sake of the Holy Church and not for my own profit or gain. So Thou will pardon my sins."

Charles of Anjou, Count of Provence, Anjou and Maine, King of the Kingdom of Sicily, died on January 7, 1285. He was fifty-eight years old. His body was taken to Naples for burial. Although the island of Sicily was forever lost to them, members of the royal house of Anjou continued to rule the Italian mainland portion of their domain, thereafter called the Kingdom of Naples, until 1442.

XI

The Man Whom Even
the Demons Fear

In the second decade of the fourteenth century there lived in the city
of Padua a poet named Albertino Mussato. He was a patriot who feared
that the Paduans were not sufficiently united and determined to resist
the attacks on their city made by Cangrande della Scala, Lord of Verona.
To remind the Paduans of the horrors of conquest by a foreign despot
and the need for heroic defiance Mussato wrote a play in Latin verse
which he called *The Tragedy of Ecerinis*. This curious drama, written
in imitation of the plays of Seneca, embodied all the horror stories and
gruesome legends which still clung around the name of Ezzelino da
Romano, the thirteenth-century tyrant and ally of the Emperor Frederick II who had ruled Padua with diabolical cruelty.

The play made Mussato famous. The University of Padua crowned
him with a laurel wreath. In the play's first act Ezzelino and his brother
Alberico are told by their mother, Adeleita, how they came to be born.
Their father was Satan, who in the form of a monstrous bull twice
raped Adeleita:

> When the first hour of the night, the universal time of rest,
> Released all mankind from work,
> Behold the earth bellowed from its depths,
> So that its center groaned and chaos was set free.

Heaven on high echoed the sound.
A sulphurous mist invaded the atmosphere
And formed a cloud. Then a giant flash,
Like lightning, illuminated the house and thunder
Followed. A smoky cloud pervaded the bedchamber
And carried with it pollution. Then I am seized and pressed.
Oh the shame! I suffer an unknown adulterer.

EZZELINO:
What sort of adulterer, Mother?

ADELEITA:
                        No less than a bull.
Curved horns arise from the shaggy neck,
And a mane of thick bristles crowns him.
A bloody liquid streams from both eyes,
His nostrils vomit flame with frequent snorts,
Ashes rise from his spreading ears and spew forth
From his mouth. His mouth also belches a thin
Flame and a constant fire licks his beard.
As this sort of adulterer gained his desires,
He filled my womb with the deadly seed of Venus.
Victorious in this slaughter, he withdrew from the bedchamber,
Seeking the depths of the earth and the earth yielded before him.
Alas the too tenacious seed of Venus I received
Burned within as it instantly attacked my vitals.
My womb felt the terrible burden of you,
Ezzelino, you are the true offspring of your father.

After their mother had confirmed in shorter space that Alberico is
also the son of the Devil, Ezzelino turns to his brother and asks exult-
antly:

What more do you wish, my brother? Are you ashamed,
Madman, of so great a father? Do you deny your divine origin?
We are born of the gods. Romulus and
Remus, whose father was Mars, did not enjoy so exalted a lineage.

These lines show perfectly the reputation acquired by Ezzelino da
Romano, a man who was widely believed not only to have had the
Devil for his father, but also to have rejoiced in his paternity.

Such legends show the fear and hatred Ezzelino, often called "the

Monstrous" or "the Unspeakable," inspired in his own time. Like other tyrants, Ezzelino used his absolute power so cruelly that he seems to have been insane. Nero and Caligula belong in his dreadful company and in our own century Hitler and Stalin, who slaughtered millions. To most of mankind it is the killing or torturing of many people innocent of any crime which has always seemed proof of insanity. While it is abominable, but not insane, to kill or torture an individual enemy for revenge or to secure information.

Insane mass murderers can be shrewd and able. Ezzelino da Romano was. He was a brave soldier, a capable general and a commanding leader of men who won and held the loyalty of many faithful followers as well as the terrified loathing of many others. And he may not have been quite so monstrous as his enemies said he was. Fear and hate invariably provoke exaggeration. In the Middle Ages the prevailing cruelty ensured that no atrocity story would be questioned. And the casual medieval habit of scattering eye-popping round numbers about has confused all subsequent historians. Should the doubtful figures be accepted at all, cut in half or reduced by two thirds?

The da Romanos were feudal lords, the hereditary rulers of the town of Bassano and its surrounding district some thirty miles due north of Padua. Ezzelino's father, Ezzelino II, was called "the Monk" because late in his life he retired to a monastery. He did not join a monastic order. Ezzelino III was born in 1194, his brother Alberico a few years later. While the brothers were children their father played an active part in the politics and wars of northeastern Italy, the area called the March of Treviso.

Ezzelino II was a leader of the Ghibelline faction in Vicenza, but was driven out of that city in 1207. In the same year he made an alliance with the Ghibellines of Verona, called the Montecchi (the Montagues in Shakespeare's Romeo and Juliet). Ezzelino II and the Montecchi seized control of Verona, but were soon driven out by the Guelfs led by Bonifacio, Count of San Bonifacio, who considered himself to be also the Count of Verona, and by Azzo VI d'Este, Marquis of Este and Ferrara. Ezzelino III inherited his father's leadership of the Montecchi and also his furious feud with the Bonifacio and Este families.

Little is known about Ezzelino's youth and young manhood. He did not marry until he was twenty-seven, more than ten years older than the usual age of noble medieval bridegrooms. The bride was Zilia, daughter of the Count of San Bonifacio, an alliance made possible only by a temporary truce between the rival houses. To make the precarious peace seem as secure as possible, Ezzelino's sister, Cunizza, was married at the same time to Zilia's brother, Rizardo.

This was the first of Ezzelino's four marriages. The second was to Frederick II's bastard daughter, Selvaggia. He married for the fourth time when he was fifty-six. All four marriages were purely political. Ezzelino's indifference to his wives was even more notorious than Frederick's to his. Frederick, at least, had legitimate as well as illegitimate children. Ezzelino seems to have had none. Yet his enemies, who denounced him with horror and imagination, made no charges of homosexuality against him. Probably Ezzelino's only love was power.

Ezzelino III inherited from his father all his castles between Padua and Verona and so before he ruled any important city he was a major power in northeastern Italy. Alberico received the castles to the east near the city of Treviso. It was not until the year 1226 when he was thirty-two years old that Ezzelino revealed his limitless ambition and consuming lust for power. With the help of the Montecchi he seized Verona and made himself lord of the city. Ezzelino ruled moderately like any capable nobleman and soldier, but in the next year, 1227, a municipal faction recovered so much power that Ezzelino lost his preeminent position. So to regain his position Ezzelino spent the next three years infiltrating the predominant party and building up his own influence.

While he was thus engaged in Verona his power as a rural nobleman remained so great that in 1228 he was able to wage a war against the city of Padua. The following year Ezzelino helped his brother Alberico suppress a revolt of his subjects. The brothers suspected that Franciscan and Dominican friars had instigated the rebellion. From that time Ezzelino hated all friars and refused to allow them in his dominions. This meant that Ezzelino was a protector of heretics, because the Dominicans were the chief inquisitors charged with rooting out heresy.

In 1230 the Bonifacio family tried to seize power in Verona and Ezzelino played a major part in helping the city defeat the putsch.

When the dust settled, Ezzelino III was once again sole Lord of Verona. In the fighting he had captured his brother-in-law, Rizardo di San Bonifacio. Instead of holding Rizardo for ransom or imprisoning him indefinitely, Ezzelino made arrangements to kill Rizardo and some of his other prisoners by slowly starving them to death. This is the first example of the cruelty which was to make Ezzelino infamous. However, his father, Ezzelino II, emerged from his monastery and persuaded Ezzelino not to starve Rizardo and the others; but he could not persuade him to release his prisoners.

During these years Ezzelino da Romano was a member in good standing of the Guelf Lombard League which opposed the Emperor Frederick II. But in 1231 the league interfered in Veronese affairs and demanded the release of Rizardo di San Bonifacio. Ezzelino, all sweet reasonableness, agreed to let his enemy go if Rizardo's chief castle were surrendered to him. Until the transfer of the castle was completed the Lombard League agreed to keep Rizardo under guard in Piacenza. So Ezzelino released his hostile brother-in-law, evidently thinking he had made a good bargain—a strategic castle for one enemy. But the Lombard League had no intention of handing the Bonifacio castle over to Ezzelino and did not do so. The league members did not trust Ezzelino, did not want to increase his power and did not like his being Lord of Verona, which controlled the Brenner pass to Austria. So Ezzelino was betrayed and lost his important prisoner and much of his reputation and influence in Verona.

The da Romano-Bonifacio feud had been personal, a matter of which house should rule Verona. But the Lombard League's hostility to one of its members was a deliberate political repudiation. Ezzelino was incensed and dismayed. At this critical moment the Paduans launched an attack on Ezzelino's castles and estates, and much against his inclination Ezzelino was forced to appeal to the Lombard League for help. It was promised, but was withheld for weeks. Finally the league ordered the Paduans to make peace. Ezzelino was left discredited, defeated by Padua, betrayed by the league, no longer Lord of Verona. It was the nadir of his career.

But if the Lombard League had betrayed him, Ezzelino knew where to find an equally powerful ally. He switched sides, turned Ghibelline and became a feudal subordinate of the Emperor Frederick II. Ezzelino promised to enlist Verona in the imperial cause if Frederick would help him recapture the city. The alliance was concluded in March of 1232. Its terms included a statement that among its declared enemies were not only the Lombard League, but also Ezzelino's personal foes, Rizardo di San Bonifacio and Azzo VII d'Este. Frederick supplied German mercenaries and some Saracen troops, and with these in April Ezzelino recaptured Verona. He was once again securely in power as lord of the city. But only a year later his rule was interrupted by a bizarre interval.

It was caused by a great religious movement which swept over northern Italy. It was called "The Great Alleluia" and seems to have begun in Tuscany with the preaching of a man who always shouted "Alleluia" three times and blew upon a small trumpet to summon the people to his revival meetings. Because of his trumpet he was called Benedictus de Cornetta. Much more celebrated and influential was a Dominican friar, Giovanni of Vicenza, who preached with such emotional eloquence that he was widely worshipped as a saint. Fra Giovanni was believed to work miracles and to raise the dead. From city to city he went and the people who had suffered the horrors of war for so long became hysterical in their enthusiasm for the peace the fiery friar preached.

Fra Giovanni was ecstatically received in Padua and Vicenza. But Ezzelino, who hated all friars, refused to permit him to enter Veronese territory. So the Lombard League, in support of the peacemaker, ravaged the Veronese countryside. In spite of his new alliance with the Emperor Frederick, Ezzelino, the lord of only one city, was not yet strong enough to defy the whole league. In April of 1233 he capitulated to the league's forceful persuasion and allowed Fra Giovanni to enter his domains. Although Ezzelino was Lord of Verona, a faction opposed to him was still very much alive and potentially dangerous. Fra Giovanni by the power of his personality imposed peace on the citizens of Verona. In a fit of rapturous enthusiasm for peace the people of Verona made the preacher their dictator by general acclamation. Bowing before this sudden and humiliating turn of events, Ezzelino swore obedience to his successor as Lord of Verona with tears in his eyes. The tears, if genuine, were probably tears of rage.

To celebrate his triumph and to inaugurate the rule of Christian virtue over Verona, Fra Giovanni immediately ordered that sixty men and women belonging to the leading families of the city were to be burned to death at the stake as heretics. And he prepared to hold a grand international peace festival on the plain of Paquara, three miles outside Verona on the banks of the Adige River. A pulpit for the evangelist was built with its base upon the Veronese *carroccio*. The meeting was called for August 28.

On that day enormous crowds assembled from Verona, Vicenza, Padua, Bologna, Ferrara, Mantua, Parma, Modena, Reggio, Brescia and Treviso. The crowds were so large that contemporary chroniclers made preposterous claims that the entire populations of many towns were present and that the total attendance was 400,000. How many actually responded to the friar's call cannot be known. But it is possible that the peace-festival crowd was the largest ever to assemble in Europe up to that time.

Public frenzy was so intense that a number of nobles and rulers thought it expedient to be present also, among them those two bitter enemies Ezzelino da Romano and Azzo d'Este. Fra Giovanni preached on the text, "Peace I leave with you, my peace I give you." He commanded the people to make peace and to forgive the sins of their enemies. And he announced that Ezzelino and Azzo d'Este had been reconciled, and that the da Romano and Este families would be united by the marriage of Alberico da Romano's daughter, Adeleita, to Azzo d'Este's son, Rinaldo. Tears and embraces swept through the crowd and a new day seemed to have dawned in northern Italy. Unfortunately, only four days later the Ghibelline and Guelf cities went back to fighting each other again.

In addition to Verona, Vicenza also declared Fra Giovanni its Lord. But the eloquent friar soon proved that he had no aptitude for government. He demanded that various castles be handed over to him personally and he enraged the Lombard League members by his friendliness to Ezzelino. Fra Giovanni trustingly went to his city of Vicenza and that good Guelf town threw its friar-dictator into prison. He was soon released and for a month or two longer he tried to play an important political role. He failed, retired to Bologna and disappeared from history. After that interregnum of six months Ezzelino da Romano was once again Lord of Verona. He remained so for the rest of his life.

At the age of thirty-nine the ambitious Lord of Verona was now ready to embark on his spectacular career as a warrior in the imperial cause and as the tyrant of a virtually independent state of his own. Ezzelino was a short man with a dark complexion and a wiry build and, according to unfriendly chroniclers, he was covered all over with black hair like an animal's fur. At this stage of his career Ezzelino was not yet any more cruel than the other rulers of his time. He was still able to control his explosive temper and he did not allow it to influence his political and military schemes. He was a careful and thorough planner and organizer. He could be prudent when it was advisable. And his occasional cruelties were only a deliberate method of ruling by terror.

But, as is so often the case, as was also true of his master, Frederick II, the corruption of absolute power warped Ezzelino's mind and undermined his character. He eventually came to regard any sort of opposition, even a mild verbal complaint, as intolerable rebellion; and he came to regard himself as "a scourge for the punishment of sinners." The sinners were usually aristocrats and notables. The common people cowered meekly under his terrible rule and suffered comparatively little, compared with their betters in the social hierarchy. Toward the end of his life Ezzelino's excessive suspiciousness became completely irrational and the number of victims sacrificed to his blood lust was proof of his insanity.

Ezzelino's expression was habitually ferocious. People were terrified by his mere appearance, and also, of course, by the tales they had heard of his atrocities. His frightful rages were so frequent that it was commonly believed he continuously trembled with wrath.

Fra Salimbene had this to say of Ezzelino: "I believe in truth that no such wicked man has been from the beginning of the world unto our own days: for all men trembled at him as a rush quivers in the water, and not without cause: for he who lived today was not sure of the morrow. The father would seek out and slay his son, and the son his father, or any of his kinfolk, to please this man: he could submit ladies to the foulest mutilations, and cast them into prisons with their sons and daughters to perish of hunger. . . . I believe most certainly that as the Son of God wished to have one specially whom he might liken unto himself, namely Saint Francis, so the Devil chose Ezzelino."

For the next year and a half, until April of 1235, Azzo VII d'Este and various Lombard League cities continued to wage war against Verona and the da Romano castles and lands. Finally the contestants grew temporarily weary of the protracted struggle and patched up a fragile peace. Count Rizardo di San Bonifacio and his followers were permitted to return to Verona. Padua paid Ezzelino a substantial war indemnity. And the wedding of Adeleita da Romano and Rinaldo d'Este, which had been necessarily postponed during the hostilities, was at last celebrated.

The peace meant nothing. The hereditary feuds of these medieval noblemen were so rancorous and Ghibelline-Guelf hatreds were so implacable that no peace could ever be more than a mere armistice. War was certain to begin again soon, not with a formal declaration but with a sudden surprise attack. Such an attack came in less than a year, in the winter of 1236.

Ezzelino da Romano had left Verona to ride northeast to his ancestral city of Bassano. After he had passed the intervening city of Vicenza, Azzo d'Este, who was then the podesta there, led out a mounted force and posted it in the village of Montebello to intercept Ezzelino on his return journey to Verona. And in Verona Count Rizardo led an armed insurrection against Ezzelino's government. All would have been lost if a faithful follower of Ezzelino had not hastened after him with the alarming news. Cut off by Azzo d'Este from the direct road, Ezzelino and a few companions were forced to travel by a mountain path so deep in snow and ice that in places they had to cut their way through. How and with what we are not told. Swords would have been of little use and we can presume that they did not carry snow shovels.

At the precise moment when his loyal supporters were about to turn and flee from their Bonifacio enemies, Ezzelino galloped into the principal piazza of Verona. Shouting his personal battle cry, *"Za Za Cavaler Ecelin,"* Ezzelino charged. His magnetic presence so encouraged his own men and so discouraged his enemies that he drove them out of the city in panic. Azzo d'Este, when he learned that the *coup d'état* in Verona had failed, returned prudently and peacefully to Vicenza.

The following November the Emperor Frederick and the Lord of Verona together attacked the city of Vicenza, from which Azzo d'Este had discreetly fled when he learned of their approach, and encountered little resistance. The imperial troops stormed the town and sacked it with all the customary atrocities. During the sack Frederick and Ezzelino came upon a soldier in the act of raping an unfortunate woman. Ezzelino drew his sword and killed the rapist. The Emperor must have been astonished to see so ruthless a character as Ezzelino reacting so violently to one of the traditional pleasures of soldiers in a sacked town. Ezzelino turned to Frederick and said that he would have done the same to him if he had found him guilty of "so great a scandal."

This surprising story about the monster who at a later time was to imprison, mutilate and torture women and children shows that Ezzelino had not yet succumbed to the furious sadism which overwhelmed him shortly thereafter. He could still be shocked by criminal behavior.

The Emperor Frederick turned the rule of Vicenza over to his valuable ally, who thenceforth governed the city through officials he appointed to carry out his orders. The capture of Vicenza was a great triumph for the imperial cause and also for Ezzelino personally. But less than four months later, in February of 1237, Ezzelino won a far greater triumph. He conquered, without the help of the Emperor, the larger, richer and more important city of Padua. The conquest was surprisingly easy, made so by considerable treason and inertia on the part of the war-weary Paduans. After Ezzelino had made one unsuccessful attack on one of the city gates Padua meekly surrendered.

The following morning Ezzelino da Romano, Lord of Verona, and Count Gebhard von Arnstein, who represented the Emperor, entered Padua in triumph. The Paduan chronicler Rolandini wrote: "So, on the very next day, February 25, 1237, Count Gebhard and Ezzelino with their troops entered Padua peaceably. And many people saw— and I particularly saw it—that as Ezzelino was going through the city gate, he pushed back his iron helmet, and, leaning over from his horse toward the gate, kissed it." The Paduans may have thought that this gesture was a sign of affection for their city. If so, they were mistaken. Most probably Ezzelino was expressing his elation at conquering the city which he had fought for so many years and which now he could rule as he pleased.

Rolandini continues: "The city was handed over to Count Gebhard, who received it in the name of the Emperor and in his stead. And afterward at the general assembly of the councils Lord Ezzelino made a speech and said—but nobody understood the full significance of what he said—that it was true that Padua had been given to Lord Gebhard for the Emperor, but to the representatives of the Emperor as well; and therefore whatever was done or considered thereafter on behalf of the Commune of Padua was of no value, unless it should be done with the advice and consent of Lord Ezzelino."

For the next nineteen years Ezzelino da Romano ruled Padua. He never was Frederick's official vicar, but Ezzelino appointed vicars of his own choosing, made Padua the capital of his virtually independent state and frequently resided there. So absolute was his rule that the Paduans always referred to him as Dominus—"the Lord."

A few weeks later the city of Treviso surrendered without fighting to Ezzelino's lordship. Later still Ezzelino added the cities of Belluno, Feltre and Trento to his dominions. Nominally he was a feudal subordinate of Frederick's. Although Ezzelino was always formally loyal to Frederick, he was so powerful and he acted so independently that he seemed more like a foreign ally.

The capture of Padua for the imperial cause so delighted Frederick that he arranged the marriage of his bastard daughter, Selvaggia, and Ezzelino, whose first wife, Zilia di San Bonifacio, must have died. The wedding was celebrated in Verona on May 23, 1237. The Emperor and the Lord of Verona, Vicenza, Padua and Treviso provided feasts for the entire population of Verona for six days.

In November of the following year, 1238, Frederick II won his greatest victory at the Battle of Cortenuova. Among those present at the battle was Ezzelino da Romano, as was only to be expected. But hardly to be expected was the presence of Azzo VII d'Este fighting in the imperial army. Azzo had spent much of his time in recent years as a Guelf member of the Lombard League waging war on Ezzelino.

But Azzo's politics, like Ezzelino's, were flexible and subject to change without notice. He and Ezzelino were both competing for the favor of the Emperor. It became apparent shortly after the battle that Ezzelino was the more successful courtier. J. K. Hyde in his *Padua in the Age of Dante* commented, "The enmity of Azzo and Ezzelino was, as far as we can tell, absolute, but their Guelfism and Ghibellinism was only contingent." Azzo soon returned to his Guelf allegiance.

For the first two years of his rule over Padua Ezzelino continued to act like any other succesful soldier and despot and committed no acts of notable cruelty. The great change in his character occurred in 1239. This was the year in which his brother Alberico declared himself a Guelf, drove Ezzelino's garrison out of Treviso and made himself lord of the town. The brothers remained enemies, although rather inactive ones, for the next seventeen years.

Ezzelino began his reign of terror when he arrested a knight on mere suspicion of Guelf sympathies and had him promptly executed without trial. Soon afterward Ezzelino executed another prominent citizen and shortly thereafter on the same day he burned one of the canons of Padua at the stake and hanged eighteen less distinguished citizens.

All the noble families of Padua tried to collaborate with their terrible ruler. Their collaboration was useless. Ezzelino's psychopathic suspicion destroyed all these potential supporters save for those who fled from the city. Paduan nobles were hanged, beheaded, tortured, starved to death in prison. When Ezzelino decided to live in Verona he appointed his nephew, Ansedisio de' Guidotti, his deputy in Padua. The nephew was as cruel as the uncle and was constantly goaded on by so-called "death letters" from Ezzelino.

The three prisons of Padua were insufficient. Soon there were eight, all crowded with miserable wretches, some dying of confinement in darkness, filth and fetid air, some starving. Relatives of suspected persons suffered the same dreadful fate as the suspects. And many women and children also suffered and died in the prisons of Padua. The chronicler Monachi wrote:

"Ezzelino had no means of pleasure except the shedding of blood. As in Verona so in the whole March, he eagerly extended his hand to imprison and kill, and he filled cities and camps with a multitude of captives whom he tortured with dreadful hunger. Pressed by hunger and thirst, the wretches ate all sorts of unclean things and were driven to drink urine. The intolerable filth, the corrupt air, the excessive heat and dreadful darkness were such in Ezzelino's prisons that the prisoners were scarcely able to breathe. Many died for this reason.

"In addition, so great was the multitude of human beings in these prisons, as one person was packed against another, that no one was able to sit or lie down; but the weakness of the body allowed no one to stand on his feet. The clamor of those moaning and sighing, and the beating of hands echoed so horribly that one would have thought, not that prisons had been built, but infernal houses of correction, and that just punishment was being inflicted by demons: for there was no rest, no consolation, no hope of redemption from evils past and future. There the greatest wish was for death which would end such great evils."

Padua suffered more than any other city under the tyrant's rule, but even Verona was not spared. There Ezzelino's victims were paraded through the streets on their way to beheading or burning. Ezzelino even had his half-brother, Ziramonte da Romano, imprisoned in one of Verona's dungeons, where he died. Nevertheless, in spite of the ever present terror, Verona remained faithful to Ezzelino until his death. The wonder is that the monster never seemed monstrous to everybody.

And, like other men, Ezzelino could not be consistent. He could not be wicked all the time. On one occasion he wrote a letter in which he professed considerable idealism: "Two things chiefly there are in this life for which, among other things, men are bound to labor: namely, to keep faith with friends and to live with honor." Of course, we do not know what Ezzelino meant by honor. Perhaps he only meant position, rank and power.

Throughout his life Ezzelino da Romano incurred the enmity of the Church, not so much for his manifold crimes as for his protection of heretics and the suspicion that he was a heretic himself. Within the area he ruled, Ezzelino permitted no persecution of heretics. Any persecuting he would do himself for personal and political reasons. In the spring of 1239 Pope Gregory IX excommunicated the Emperor Frederick II and in the autumn of the same year he excommunicated Ezzelino.

Five years later Pope Innocent IV arranged an inquisitorial trial of Ezzelino, who was charged with being "publicly defamed for heresy by reason of his association with heretics." Since the accused was "terrible and powerful," the inquisitor, who was supposed to make public the charges, was permitted to publish them in any place where he could do so safely. The trial itself, with the accused conspicuous by his absence, concluded: that Ezzelino was the son of a heretic, that his relatives were heretics, that under his protection heresy had spread throughout the March of Treviso, and that he did not believe in Christianity.

With all deliberate speed the Pope, after four years, condemned Ezzelino as a manifest heretic. But Innocent assured Ezzelino that he would experience the abundant clemency of the Church if he would present himself in person before the papal court by the next Ascension Day some two months hence. Ezzelino remained in the north and was excommunicated again.

Why the four-year delay and why the promise of clemency? By this time Ezzelino was notorious for his crimes as well as for his support of the Emperor Frederick II and for his Ghibelline politics. We can speculate that the gingerly fashion in which Pope Innocent treated him may have been caused by respect for Ezzelino's power. If Ezzelino could be reconciled to the Church, even if only diplomatically and theoretically, perhaps he might also be persuaded to abandon the imperial cause. The possibility was remote, but evidently not to be overlooked.

And always Ezzelino continued to play an active part in the great Ghibelline-imperial, Guelf-papal war. In 1247 he brought what Salimbene called "a vast army" to Frederick's aid during the siege of Parma. Whether he was present in person when Frederick suffered his disastrous defeat at Victoria is not clear. After Frederick's death in 1250 Ezzelino remained as powerful as ever.

In December of 1255 Pope Alexander IV decided that something drastic must be done to destroy the wicked and flourishing Ghibelline lord. He chose Filippo Fontana, Archbishop of Ravenna, to lead a crusade against Ezzelino and he made Filippo a papal legate. His choice was odd. Filippo had warlike abilities, but there wasn't a churchman in Italy with a worse reputation.

This Filippo was a Tuscan from the district of Pistoia who as a youth had journeyed all the way to the city of Toledo in Spain to learn the black art of necromancy. Although a distinguished necromancer tried to instruct him in his arcane calling, Filippo was not an apt pupil. He personally encountered numerous demons, but nevertheless he did not progress well in his studies. So the master necromancer said to Filippo: "You Italians are unfit for this art; leave it to us Spaniards, who are fierce men, and like unto demons. But thou, son, go to Paris and study in Holy Scripture; for thou shalt yet be a mighty man in the church of God." Filippo went to Paris, studied industriously and began his successful career in the Church hierarchy.

As Archbishop of Ravenna, Filippo took bribes, sold benefices, fathered children and behaved in so worldly and cruel a fashion that he fascinated Fra Salimbene, who wrote: "The said Archbishop was sometimes melancholy and gloomy and furious, and such a son of Belial that none could speak with him." Filippo, Salimbene wrote, was "a mighty drinker and loved not water with his wine" and "he cared more for war than for relics of the saints." Salimbene described the Archbishop's manner of conducting his household:

"There were full forty men-at-arms, whom he ever led with him, to be guardians of his life and person; and they feared him as they feared the Devil. Nay, Ezzelino da Romano was scarcely less feared; for he gave his servants grievous punishments. One day, as he went from Ravenna to Argenta (which is the Archepiscopal palace), he caused one of his servants to be bound with a rope and plunged into the water, and thus they dragged him bound to the ship through the rolling waves, as though he were a sturgeon, because he had forgotten to bring the salt.

"Another time he caused a certain other servant to be bound to a great pole and turned as on a spit, before the fire; and when the men of his household wept for him with pity and compassion, the legate, seeing the cruel sight, said to them, 'Poor wretches! Do you weep so soon?' and he bade that he should be taken away from the fire. Yet the man had already borne bitter anguish of soul and much roasting. Moreover, the legate cast into chains a certain Amanato, his steward, a Tuscan; and the rats devoured him in the prison, for he was accused of having wasted his master's goods. Many other cruelties he practiced on those who were of his household, for his own vengeance and their punishment, and to strike fear into others."

Such was the man chosen by the Pope to enlist an army in the service of the Church and to lead it on a holy crusade against Ezzelino da Romano. Archbishop Filippo proceeded to Ferrara and there from the steps of the cathedral of Saint George he preached a recruiting sermon to a large part of the population of Ferrara and the numerous exiles from Padua. Salimbene sat among a delegation of Dominican friars, although he himself was a Franciscan, and listened to Filippo: "He began to preach in a loud voice, saying briefly that the time for words was now past, and we must keep silence, for the time is come to do those deeds which words do but represent. And he published how he had been made legate by the Lord Pope against Ezzelino da Romano, and how he would fain raise an army of crusaders to recover the city of Padua, and to restore the expelled Paduans. And whosoever would be of his army in that expedition should have indulgence and remission and absolution for all his sins. And let none say: 'It is impossible for us to fight against that man of the Devil whom even the demons fear,' for it shall not be impossible with God, who will fight for us."

In March of 1256 Archbishop Filippo arrived in Venice and requested permission to deliver a recruiting sermon in the Piazza San Marco. It was granted and Filippo preached eloquently. Many enlisted. The various contingents of crusaders assembled at Bebe, a Venetian fortress on the Brenta River. The ragtag-and-bobtail army included English mercenaries, volunteers from Milan, Mantua, Bologna, Ferrara and Venice plus a large number of bellicose clergy who tried to inspire the troops by singing hymns. Venice supplied galleys which carried the crusaders up the Brenta toward Padua.

Ezzelino da Romano was not even in Padua to direct the defense of his most important city. So certain was he of the strength of the city and of the loyalty of the garrison commanded by his nephew, Ansedisio, and so contemptuous of the papal army, that he did not consider the crusade a threat serious enough to distract him from his siege of the Guelf city of Mantua. Ezzelino had assembled a large army from his various subject cities and territories, and his Ghibelline ally Uberto Pallavicini, Lord of Cremona, had joined him with a sizable force of his own.

Rarely has confidence been less justified. Ansedisio was an inept general. The Paduan garrison was not loyal. And the fire and fury of the numerous monks and friars in the crusading army really did much to arouse the enthusiasm and hearten the courage of the papal troops. Ansedisio led part of his garrison out of Padua to attack the crusaders. So many of his own garrison deserted to the enemy that he had to scurry ignominiously back behind the walls of Padua. Then Ansedisio diverted the course of the Brenta to prevent the Venetian galleys from approaching Padua. To no purpose. The crusaders abandoned their ships, marched across the muddy bed of the river and attacked the city.

The papal army was repulsed from the city walls; but the embattled clergy attacked one of the gates with a battering ram from under the protecting roof of a wooden shelter. The defenders set the ram and shelter on fire; but the monks used the flames to burn down the gate. Suspecting that the population would rise against him, Ansedisio fled from another gate on the opposite side of the city and the triumphant crusaders marched into Padua. They had captured the city in one day's fighting.

They were crusaders and all their sins had been forgiven. So for eight days they sacked Padua, the city they had rescued from a cruel tyranny, robbing every house, torturing citizens to force them to reveal where they had hidden money and valuables, raping the women. The terrible prisons of Padua were opened and the surviving victims of Ezzelino's madness staggered out into the light. The pitiful host of several thousand men and women included those who had been blinded, who had had a hand or a foot cut off or a tongue torn out. There were also a number of children who had been blinded and mutilated.

When Ezzelino da Romano heard that the papal army was within a few miles of Padua he changed his mind and hastened off to take charge of the defense himself. He was riding hard at the head of a small mounted troop when the first messenger reached him with the news of the fall of Padua. Ezzelino hanged the messenger. Soon afterward Ansedisio himself rode up to meet his glowering uncle. Ezzelino arrested Ansedisio on the spot and a few days later executed him in Verona.

Although part of the crusading army fled at Ezzelino's approach, he was unable to recapture Padua. He retreated to Verona and there made his plans for revenge and for further warfare. And in the midst of his terrible rage and frustration the monstrous tyrant, never known for his sense of humor, made a joke. In Padua Ezzelino had employed three humble citizens as joint treasurers. The chronicler Giovanni da Nono wrote:

"Enghelfredo, a tailor and secondhand-clothes dealer, was the third treasurer of the noble and powerful Ezzelino da Romano when he was Lord of Padua and the March. He, when he lost Padua, said, 'I am leaving in Padua the richest notary, that is Alberto Bibi, the richest barber and the richest tailor in the whole March of Treviso.' These men divided Ezzelino's treasure into three parts, and each then became a money-lender!"

Ezzelino's rage against Padua for its lack of enthusiasm in his cause and for its prompt surrender to the papal legate led him to commit the most celebrated crime of his nefarious career. In Verona he arrested all the soldiers from Padua who had been serving with him in his siege of Mantua. They were in no way guilty for the loss of Padua, but they were Paduans and that was enough. All of them were imprisoned in the dungeons of Verona and its vicinity. Various chroniclers report that their number was from 10,000 to 12,000. Since medieval armies were small and the men came from only one of Ezzelino's subject cities, such a figure must be a gross exaggeration. We cannot guess how many thousands they were, perhaps only two or three. But three years later, after Ezzelino's death, the prisons were opened and only 200 miserable Paduans were found still alive.

The loss of Padua increased Ezzelino's mad ferocity, but it did not diminish his ability or energy. During the next three years he managed to capture some of the soldiers of the Paduan garrison who had refused to defend the city. Ezzelino burned them to death at the stake. He also recaptured a castle called Montegalda, which, after only a token resistance, surrendered. But the intolerable insolence of the garrison in resisting at all so enraged Ezzelino that he had every captured soldier blinded.

In the following year, 1257, Alberico da Romano, who had been a nominal Guelf and an enemy of Ezzelino ever since he seized Treviso in 1239, switched sides again and became reconciled with Ezzelino. During those eighteen years Alberico had ruled Treviso with such horrible cruelty that his reputation was only a little less dreadful than his brother's. His alliance was welcome and considerably strengthened Ezzelino's position.

The anti-Ezzelino crusade continued in a desultory fashion until the summer of 1258 when Ezzelino and his old ally Uberto Pallavicini, Lord of Cremona, attacked the city of Brescia, which they agreed to rule jointly. Inside Brescia was the papal legate, Archbishop Filippo Fontana, who had conquered Padua. Filippo may not have been a proper Archbishop, but he was a man of action. While Ezzelino and Pallavicini were besieging some outlying castles and had not yet attacked Brescia itself Filippo sailed out and attacked his enemies. He was soundly defeated. His troops panicked and fled. The victors captured some 4,000 prisoners, among them the papal legate himself.

Instead of killing or torturing the man who had deprived him of Padua, as he might have been expected to do, Ezzelino treatd Filippo respectfully. Perhaps his sadistic fury was only vented on those he regarded as rebels. Filippo was an open enemy.

Although Ezzelino da Romano was an obstinate foe of the Church as well as of the Guelf party, he seems to have had some, perhaps only momentary, sincere religious convictions. At least, he did not think that the Pope's crusading army should have sacked Padua. He said to Filippo:

"How is it possible that our holy mother the Church can still survive, when under her wings one Christian can be unjust to another, and her own servants can condone robbery and oppression? You are surely aware that those who came to Padua with you, calling themselves Christians and warriors of Saint Peter, robbed and murdered other Christians, extorted tribute from them, and reduced many to the state of widows, orphans and beggars. And then they make the strange claim that they were acting in the name of the Church, which had given them a free hand and never mentioned restitution of their ill-gotten gains."

These words sound strange indeed from the lips of the terrible tyrant who had ruled Padua with such cruelty for so many years.

A few days later Ezzelino and Pallavicini captured Brescia. Each ruled half of the conquered city. And in Brescia Ezzelino's madness plumbed new depths of insane ferocity. Prisoners of war were tortured and murdered, nobles beheaded, priests burned, women mutilated, children killed, monks and nuns tortured and churches robbed. And in some mysterious manner Ezzelino persuaded his ally and partner Pallavicini to return to Cremona. As soon as he had left, Ezzelino assumed the sole rule of the entire city.

The Lord of Cremona was understandably furious. He had been betrayed and, what was worse, had been made to look like a gullible fool. With reckless folly Ezzelino had driven his only reliable friend and ally into the arms of his enemies. Pallavicini joined Ezzelino's most vindictive foe, Azzo VII d'Este, in a Guelf alliance formed to destroy Ezzelino da Romano.

In the summer of 1259 the anti-Ezzelino allies marched north to attack Ezzelino at Brescia. At the age of sixty-five, which was far gone in old age by medieval standards, Ezzelino marched out of Brescia to confound his enemies in a campaign which was the most ambitious of his life. He intended nothing less than the capture of Milan. A faction of exiled Milanese nobles conspired with Ezzelino to conquer their native city. In return for his aid Ezzelino was to become Lord of Milan. Even in this final spasm of his infamous career Ezzelino da Romano did not seem infamous to everyone. For the satisfaction of returning in triumph to Milan and expelling their enemies, the exiles were willing to accept Ezzelino as their ruler.

But the plan went awry. Sympathizers inside the city failed to open the gates of Milan to Ezzelino and his allies as expected. So Ezzelino attacked the nearby city of Monza instead, failed to capture it and retreated to the bridge at Cassano over the Adda River. And there the indomitable tyrant was outmaneuvered by his numerous enemies, defeated and captured. Deserted by his Brescian troops (and no wonder, considering his terror in Brescia!), Ezzelino was wounded by an arrow through his foot and knocked off his horse by the blow of a club (some chroniclers say of a reaping hook) on his head.

His captors were about to tear Ezzelino to pieces when Pallavicini intervened, had him taken to his tent and his wounds dressed. The Paduan chronicler Rolandini wrote: "Ezzelino when prisoner preserved his menacing silence. He fixed on the ground his savage eyes, and gave no utterance to his deep indignation. From all sides the soldiers and people came together to see this man, once so powerful; this prince, famous, terrible, and cruel above all princes of the earth; and universal joy broke out on all sides."

The fallen tyrant was taken to the nearby town of Soncino. There during the first night of his captivity the bells of a neighboring church rang loudly in celebration of Ezzelino's downfall. He woke up and in a characteristic fury ordered, "Go, cut down that priest who makes such a din with his bells."

"You forget," said one of his guards, "that you are in prison."

Many priests urged the notorious prisoner to repent of his sins. "I repent of nothing," Ezzelino snarled, "except that I have not taken full vengeance upon my enemies; that I have badly commanded my army; and that I have allowed myself to be duped and betrayed."

Ezzelino refused food and medicine and, according to several chroniclers, committed suicide by ripping off his bandages and tearing open his wounds.

He had good cause to commit suicide, because Azzo d'Este and Pallavicini might well have intended to torture Ezzelino to death as was later done to his brother Alberico. But an arrow wound in the foot and a bump on the head don't seem serious enough injuries to make suicide possible by tearing at them. Steven Runciman thinks that his captors murdered Ezzelino. Perhaps they did, after torturing him, and then spread the suicide story.

And so perished the most terrible tyrant in Italian history. Few men have been so feared and hated as the man called by one of his own Veronese subjects "a minister of Satan, the Devil's executioner, drinker of human blood, insatiable enemy of the Church and sedulous inventor of evils." Dante in the *Inferno* condemned Ezzelino da Romano to the river of boiling blood, the punishment for tyrants "who dealt in bloodshed and in pillaging."

XII

The Great Dog

Although those mighty warriors Frederick II, Ezzelino da Romano and Charles of Anjou had died, their deaths did not bring peace to Italy during the latter part of the thirteenth century. Guelf and Ghibelline animosities and rival factions within those parties continued to torment the unhappy land. The greed and ambition of despots precipitated numerous wars. And in the north emerged two of the most magnificent and bellicose dynasties of tyrants Italy ever knew—the della Scala family of Verona and the Visconti of Milan.

Verona, one of the most interesting cities in Italy, lies at the feet of the Alps on the banks of the Adige River fifteen miles east of the southern end of Lake Garda. It was important in Roman times. Its ancient amphitheater is smaller than the Colosseum, but much better preserved and large enough to seat 32,000 people. On the northern bank of the Adige is a picturesque and imposing castle and over the river a handsome bridge, both built by Cangrande II, one of the later members of the della Scala family, commonly called the Scaligeri. There is a Palazzo degli Scaligeri, and in the center of the city, to the east of the church of Santa Maria Antiqua, are the wonderful Scaligeri tombs, intricate and elaborate medieval structures bristling with spires and statues.

Equestrian statue of Cangrande della Scala, Verona. *Alinari*

Oddly situated above the principal doorway of the church is the tomb of the greatest of the Scaligeri, Cangrande I della Scala. On top of the tomb is a copy of an equestrian statue of Cangrande (the original statue is in a museum). It is a somewhat crude fourteenth-century work. Cangrande, dressed in full armor, has pushed his helmet back upon his shoulders, holds his head erect and smiles as broadly as the Cheshire cat. He has just brought his horse to a halt and the horse's cloth trappings still wave in the wind.

In his *Decameron* Giovanni Boccaccio wrote of the most celebrated, admired and powerful member of the Scaligeri: "As very manifest renown proclaims almost throughout the whole world, Messer Cane della Scala, to whom in many things fortune was favorable, was one of the most notable and magnificent gentlemen that have been known in Italy since the days of the Emperor Frederick II."

Cangrande della Scala was a warrior whose joy in battle and campaigning was intense and contagious. He was a generous host to many of the artistic and political exiles of Italy. He was the friend and patron of Dante. His blond good looks, his charm and his personal magnetism were almost as famous as his victories.

We first hear of him in 1294 when he was about three and a half years old. In that year his father, Alberto I, held a *curia*, which was a great and formal celebration of a victory or of the importance and splendor of a ruling house. Guests were invited from great distances and entertained with banquets, festivals and tournaments. Actors, jugglers, acrobats and minstrels swarmed in the streets. As a token of his friendship Alberto della Scala presented his guests with 1,500 cloaks of English woolen cloth, blue, green, scarlet, purple or white, lined with fur. And he made twelve knights. Among them was Cangrande.

Why did Alberto knight so small a child who was not even his eldest son? Alberto's affection for the little boy was well known. But could there have been something humorous in the accolade? Knighthood was never taken as seriously in Italy as in France or England. Cangrande had been christened Francesco. *Cane* means "dog." The child's uncle, the founder of the Scaligeri dynasty, was named Mastino, which means "mastiff." Why dogs' names were popular in the family is another mystery. Little Francesco's name was changed to Cangrande, which means "the great dog." According to contemporary chroniclers, Cangrande's mother while expecting his birth dreamed that she would bear a dog whose bark would be heard throughout the world. This sounds fanciful, but dreams and omens were serious matters. It could be the reason why Alberto called his youngest son Cangrande. Anyway, Cangrande and his successors used a dog as the crest upon their helmets. *Scala* means "ladder" or "stairs." The official Scaligeri arms were a five-rung white ladder on a red field surmounted by a black eagle.

In 1259, after the death of Ezzelino da Romano, Cangrande's uncle, Mastino della Scala, became the *de facto* Lord of Verona. He was a popular and successful ruler and for the next eighteen years he was loyally supported by his younger brother, Alberto. But on October 26, 1277, as he rode through the principal piazza of Verona, Mastino was assassinated. On the following day a mass assembly of Verona's citizens elected Alberto della Scala the *de jure* lord of the city and granted him every possible governmental power. Alberto promptly demonstrated his gift for government by beheading 200 persons implicated in Mastino's murder.

Alberto was even abler and more popular than Mastino. He was devout and conventionally orthodox. Verona had been a Ghibelline city since Ezzelino da Romano seized power, and so it lay under a papal interdict. To propitiate the Papacy, Alberto arranged the burning of 200 heretics. These had been arrested by Mastino, but their lives had been spared. Alberto had them dragged out of their dungeons and burned alive in a spectacular ceremony in Verona's Roman amphitheater. This act of exemplary piety mollified the Pope, who then removed the interdict. Alberto, although still a Ghibelline, thus became a loyal son of the Church. By this time the Guelf and Ghibelline names had become almost meaningless and were only local party or faction labels.

The traditional hatred between Verona and Padua, so virulent in Ezzelino's time, continued during Alberto's reign. In 1294 the republic of Padua formally condemned the Lord of Verona to death. Untroubled by this meaningless gesture, Alberto continued to rule successfully and securely. The order and justice he provided were much appreciated—as they were in many other cities where the people preferred the rule of absolute lords to incessant internal strife.

On September 3, 1301, Alberto della Scala died after a long illness. A contemporary Veronese chronicler called him "sublime in soul, perfect in his ways, far-seeing in council, pious, merciful, sagacious." In fact, he continued, every virtue abounded in Alberto. Another chronicler wrote that Alberto was "high-minded, virtuous, prudent, merciful and wise, that he governed Verona in the fear of God, suppressed tumults and quarrels, and protected the poor and weak from the rich and powerful, whereby he won the love of his people."

Alberto was succeeded by Bartolomeo, the oldest of his three sons. Bartolomeo was entrusted with the guardianship of his younger brothers. He was the most exemplary character the Scaligeri produced. To his father's virtues of wisdom and justice he added benevolence and love of peace. Since hardly any ruler in medieval Italy loved peace, Bartolomeo seemed strange and wonderful. Unfortunately for Verona and for all northern Italy, Bartolomeo died on March 7, 1304, after a reign of only two and a half years. He was twenty-seven years old.

It was during Bartolomeo's brief reign that a Florentine exile with a saturnine disposition and a genius for poetry arrived in Verona and became a guest of the Scaligeri court.

Scholars cannot agree on the precise dates of Dante Alighieri's sojourns in Verona, but most believe that Dante's first visit was in 1302 or 1303. At that time Cangrande was either eleven or twelve. Some seventeen or eighteen years later, when Dante was completing his *Divine Comedy* in exile at Ravenna, he wrote in the *Paradiso* a prophecy about Cangrande supposedly delivered in 1300 when Cangrande was only nine years old:

> One stamped at birth with valor by the stars,
> So that his goodly deeds shall be renowned.
> The nations are not yet aware of him
> Because his age is tender; for nine years
> These spheres have wheeled about him and no more. . . .
> For he will spurn both money and intrigue.
> So widely will his great magnificence

Be known that even his enemies
Will be unable to hold still their tongues.
Look thou at him, and to his benefits;
By him will many people be transformed,
And rich and poor put in each other's places.

It was hindsight, of course, but nevertheless a nice, typically medieval compliment to the poet's friend and former host.

Bartolomeo della Scala was succeeded by Alboino, the second of Alberto's sons. A weak character with none of the Scaligeri talents for government and war, Alboino would have liked to play a passive role, but he was forced to spend much of his time at war. After four years as the sole Lord of Verona, in 1308 Alboino wisely and generously made his younger brother joint lord with him. Cangrande was then only seventeen or eighteen, but he was already known as a promising soldier.

In the same year Henry, son of the Count of Luxembourg, was elected German king and emperor-elect. The Scaligeri brothers were among the first to send ambassadors to the new Henry VII with promises of military and financial aid whenever he came to Italy to be crowned King of the Romans in Milan and Holy Roman Emperor in Rome.

Henry VII was a handsome, attractive man from so small a state that he had little military power of his own. An idealist, he dreamed of restoring the power and influence of the emperor in Italy, something Barbarossa and Frederick II had been unable to do by force of arms. Henry somewhat naïvely hoped to function as a *rex pacificus,* as he called himself. By diplomacy and charm he would compose feuds and establish peace so that the Guelf lions would lie down with the Ghibelline lambs, or vice versa. Henry marched into Italy in 1310 with an entirely inadequate force.

Most of the traditionally Ghibelline cities welcomed Henry warmly, but the Guelf King of Naples and the Guelf city of Florence bitterly opposed him. Alboino and Cangrande della Scala invited Henry to come to Verona, but Henry passed the city by on his way to Milan. The Scaligeri were disgusted with Henry anyway because they had learned that the Emperor-elect thought he could make peace in Verona between them and the members of the exiled house of San Bonifacio, whose current count still claimed to be Count of Verona as had his ancestor in Ezzelino's time.

A small pro-Bonifacio faction persisted in Verona, and to keep them firmly suppressed the Scaligeri passed laws against any kind of reconciliation. If anybody should dare cry, "Peace! Peace!" he would be considered a Bonifacio traitor and could be punished by death. Gentlemen would be beheaded, common folk hanged. But ladies received special consideration. Since it was ungentlemanly to touch a lady, she had the privilege of being burned.

Because of their irritation with Henry the Scaligeri brothers did not attend the ceremony in Milan in which he was crowned with the iron crown of the Lombards. They were represented by ambassadors. Annoyed in his turn, Henry appointed a citizen of Pisa to be imperial vicar of Verona. This affront, of course, only added to the resentment of the Scaligeri. But in 1311 some delicate diplomacy and a promise that Verona would contribute generously to Henry's expenses persuaded the Emperor-elect to change his mind. Henry dismissed the Pisan and appointed the Scaligeri brothers imperial vicars of Verona. The formal title gave their absolute power as Lords of Verona a pleasant additional confirmation.

The defiance of the Guelf cities led by Florence completely blasted Henry VII's hopes of being accepted as a general feudal overlord and benevolent peacemaker. Prominent among his foes were Padua and Brescia. Padua had recovered completely from its sufferings under Ezzelino in the previous century and was a large, prosperous and powerful republic. The city of Vicenza was ruled by Padua and its citizens furiously resented what they considered Paduan tyranny. So, as a blow against Padua, Henry VII sent an army to liberate Vicenza commanded by Cangrande della Scala. It was his first important military command and he was only twenty years old.

Cangrande seems to have arranged matters with masterly guile. On April 15, 1311, Ghibelline partisans inside Vicenza revolted and displayed imperial flags. At the same time they opened the gates and Cangrande led his troops into the city. The easy triumph was a bitter humiliation to Padua and the foundation of Cangrande's reputation. Vicenza became a free city loyal to the Empire, but within the city Cangrande organized a pro-Scaligeri party. His own loyalty to the Empire was always officially correct, but it was only official. Cangrande's real purpose was to conquer, and to make the Scaligeri the rulers of as much of northern Italy as possible—the same purpose as Ezzelino's.

Henry himself, the frustrated peacemaker, was busy besieging Brescia. Cangrande and Alboino joined him and pitched their tent beside the Emperor-elect's. Henry then made young Cangrande commander of all the Italians in his little army. But in August a pestilence of an unknown kind broke out in the imperial camp. Alboino della Scala succumbed to it, but recovered partially. Nevertheless, he was too weak to remain on active duty. Cangrande escorted his brother back to Verona and then returned to the siege with Veronese reinforcements. He personally led numerous attacks on the walls of Brescia.

In September after a four-month siege Brescia surrendered. One of the few military successes Henry enjoyed in Italy, it was celebrated by a triumphal victory procession into the city. Cangrande rode in the procession at the head of 300 knights.

Henry VII then moved on to the traditionally imperial city of Pavia and there convoked an assembly of all the cities of northern Italy. But Henry rather fecklessly changed his mind and went off to Geneva. Various embassies, with Cangrande among them, followed him there. Henry's absence from Italy encouraged the Guelf cities to form an alliance against him. It also encouraged the Guelf faction in Brescia, which recaptured the city and drove out Henry's Ghibelline supporters.

Cangrande's presence at the imperial court was expensive because he wanted to be appointed imperial vicar of Vicenza, and that required a substantial bribe. Before the bargaining was concluded a messenger from Verona arrived with the news that Alboino was desperately ill. With the decisive impetuosity for which he became famous, Cangrande left Geneva at once and by a remarkable feat of hard riding reached Verona in five days. He arrived in time to be present at Alboino's death on November 29, 1311. Cangrande della Scala was now sole Lord of Verona.

Shortly thereafter, with help sent by Henry VII and by Cangrande, the Ghibelline exiles of Brescia recaptured the town and again drove out the Guelfs. In some Italian cities in the fourteenth century government was as subject to change without notice as the weather.

In Verona Cangrande adroitly established his rule. The treasury was nearly empty, a nuisance which time and taxes would eliminate. To increase his legal powers Cangrande persuaded the city council to grant him additional prerogatives, including the *arbitrium,* which made him above the laws and able to do anything he pleased. Seldom has absolute power been so freely granted and explicitly approved by the ruled.

In February of 1312 Henry VII appointed Cangrande della Scala, already imperial vicar of Verona, imperial vicar of Vicenza. Cangrande went to Vicenza on February 11 and informed the municipal government of his appointment. Several of the local officials dared to oppose their new ruler. But on the following day Cangrande made an eloquent oration full of specious promises and expressions of his high-minded intentions and persuaded the Vincentines to accept his rule without overt opposition. In theory Cangrande represented Henry VII in Vicenza. In fact Vicenza became an integral part of his state and he was as much its lord as he was Verona's. At the age of twenty-two or thereabouts the young warrior was also a wily politician.

The long rivalry between Padua and Verona was now more envenomed than ever. They had always fought each other. Padua as a republic was a natural enemy of Verona, a despotism. And Cangrande's annexation of their former subject city, Vicenza, enraged the Paduans. So without bothering to declare war Padua attacked Verona. It was the first of a cluster of four wars fought by the neighboring cities during the reign of Cangrande.

In April of 1312 Cangrande evidently thought that his rule over Vicenza was sufficiently well established for him to leave. He went back to Verona. During his absence the Paduans attacked Vicenza and won a gratifying little victory outside the walls of the city. Cangrande returned to Vicenza convinced that there had been treachery. He arrested many citizens he suspected of Guelf sympathies, fined some, tortured some, and hanged or beheaded others. The charming young hero with his noble appearance, his unfailing courtesy and generosity (he was said to scorn money) was already a cruel and suspicious tyrant. If absolute power corrupts absolutely, it had not taken long to corrupt the young Lord of Verona and Vicenza.

So the people of Vicenza, who had hated the Paduans, now hated Cangrande and the Veronese, and longed for the good old days under

Padua. Thenceforward Cangrande had to keep a careful watch to make sure that Vicenza did not revolt and join Padua.

The war was waged in typical medieval fashion. Paduan troops raided up to the walls of Verona and Veronese troops marched up to the walls of Padua, with nothing much accomplished in either case. But hostilities picked up in August of 1314 when the Paduans again attacked Vicenza and captured a suburb just outside the walls called San Pietro. The commander of the Veronese garrison in Vicenza set fire to San Pietro so as to leave no cover or shelter for the Paduans.

Cangrande was in Verona attending a wedding when he heard the news of the attack and of the loss of the suburb. With a few knights he is said to have galloped all the way from Verona to Vicenza, some thirty-five miles. Since no horse can gallop that far we can presume that Cangrande walked his horse frequently to rest it, or that he was able to change horses several times. At any rate, immediately after his arrival in Vicenza Cangrande led a hastily improvised charge on the Paduans, who panicked and fled. Cangrande certainly displayed no particularly brilliant generalship; but his impetuous action was highly successful.

In some respects the small affray was a typical medieval battle. Only seven of Cangrande's knights and thirty of his foot soldiers were killed. But they captured nearly 1,500 of the fleeing Paduans! Some were hunted down with dogs as they tried to hide in the fields and woods. Some of the women of Vicenza, supposedly sympathetic to Padua, joined in the brutal sport. Long files of Paduan prisoners were roped together and marched off to Verona through heavy rain and deep mud.

They had been so confident of capturing Vicenza that they had brought with them goblets and dishes of gold and silver, beds and pillows with silk coverings, and baskets of food and medicine. Cangrande treated the nobles among his prisoners as honored guests. Among them was Albertino Mussato, the Paduan historian and poet whose play about Ezzelino da Romano we have quoted.

Peace between Padua and Verona was signed on October 4, 1314, eighteen days after the battle. During the two-and-a-half-year war Cangrande had spent most of the time on the defensive and had displayed no notable military skill to match his courage and powers of leadership. But this total victory established his reputation as a great soldier.

Either in the following year, 1315, or in 1316, Dante Alighieri returned to Verona and remained as a guest of Cangrande for a considerable time. During most of Dante's twenty years of exile, where he was for how long is unknown. So scholars do not agree whether his stay at Cangrande's court was in 1315 or in 1316, or in parts of both years, or perhaps even in 1317. In any case, it is time to consider Cangrande's most famous guest, the most famous of all medieval Italians.

The author of *The Divine Comedy* was born in Florence in May of 1265. His father, a member of a noble family in reduced circumstances, worked as a notary and moneylender. Dante was the only child of his father's first wife. He had a half-brother and two half-sisters. His father died when Dante was about eighteen. He left Dante a modest country property whose income supported Dante as a gentleman of leisure until his exile. Dante was a scholar, a poet and a politician whose passionate interest in politics was nearly as strong as his passionate interest in poetry.

Some time in the 1280s when he was in his twenties Dante fell romantically, chastely and distantly in love with Beatrice, the daughter of Falco Portinari. Dante idealized her as a symbolical representative of personal and theological virtue, and after her early death in 1290 he wrote a collection of poems about her which were published as the *Vita Nuova*.

In 1289 when he was twenty-four years old Dante fought in the front rank as a mounted knight in the Battle of Campaldino, in which Florence defeated Arezzo. He also participated in a campaign against Pisa. Dante married and had four children, two sons and two daughters, all born before 1302.

Political office in Florence was reserved for the members of the principal guilds. So to qualify for office Dante joined the guild of Physicians and Apothecaries. Books were then sold by apothecaries, and painters were members of the guild. Dante's best friend was Giotto, a fellow member of the guild. On the wall of the Bargello in Florence is a mural probably painted by Giotto in 1300 in which Dante's picture is included in a group of prominent Florentines.

Dante served as an ambassador to the little town of San Gimignano and for two months in 1300 he was one of the six Priors of Florence, then the highest office in the Republic of Florence. At that time the ruling Guelf party in Florence was split into rival factions called the Whites and Blacks. Dante's term as a White Prior made the Blacks regard him as a permanent enemy.

In the autumn of 1301 Dante was one of a three-member embassy sent by Florence to Rome to protest to the terrible-tempered Pope Boniface VIII his interference in Florentine affairs. "Why are you Florentines so obstinate?" demanded the fiery old man. "Humble yourselves before me, for verily I say unto you, I have no other intention than that of peace for you. Two of you go back and the Florentines will have my benediction if they obey my will." Pope Boniface permitted two of the ambassadors to return to Florence, but he kept Dante at the papal court as a hostage. While Dante waited in Rome the Black Guelfs, with Pope Boniface's blessing and complicity, seized power in Florence and exiled the White Guelfs, of whom Dante was one.

The Florentine Black Guelfs summoned the leading Whites to trial for their political sins in January of 1302. Most of the White exiles prudently stayed away from Florence. Dante was on his way back from Rome and had reached Siena when he learned on January 27 that he had been banished for two years, fined 5,000 florins and barred from public office forever because of his "graft, embezzlement, opposition to the Pope and his disturbing the peace of Florence." Needless to say, Dante did not pay the fine.

On March 10 the Republic of Florence decreed that if Dante and fourteen others ever fell into the hands of the Florentine government they would be burned to death. Florence, a republic with democratic pretensions, could be as politically arbitrary and cruel as any despotism.

For the rest of his life Florence's greatest medieval citizen, already celebrated as a poet, was an impoverished exile wandering from court to court, living as a guest and on the generosity and hospitality of the lords of various cities. In the Middle Ages, and in the Renaissance also, local city pride and patriotism were intense and banishment was a dreadful fate. Dante fiercely resented the loss of his homeland and bitterly mourned the income he had formerly enjoyed.

Dante, fifteenth-century bronze bust, Naples. *Alinari*

In one of his prose works, the *Convivio*, Dante wrote: "Wandering as a stranger through almost every region to which our language reaches, I have gone about as a beggar, showing against my will the wound of fortune, which is often wont to be imputed unjustly to the fault of him who is stricken. Verily I have been as a ship without sails and without rudder, driven to various harbors and shores by the dry wind which blows from pinching poverty. And I have appeared vile in the eyes of many, who, perhaps from some report of me, had imagined me in different guise."

In the *Paradiso* Dante returned in verse to the same theme:

> How bitter it is to taste
> The bread of others, and how hard the road
> When going up and down another's stairs.

Giovanni Boccaccio, Dante's first biographer, wrote of him: "Our poet was of middle height, and after he reached middle years he walked with somewhat of a stoop; his gait was grave and sedate; and he was ever clothed in most seemly garments, his dress being suited to the ripeness of his years. His face was long, his nose aquiline, his eyes rather large than small, his jaw heavy, with the underlip protruding beyond the upper. His complexion was dark, and his hair and beard thick, black and crisp; and his countenance always sad and thoughtful. . . . In his manners, whether in public or in private, he was wonderfully composed and restrained, and in all his ways he was more courteous and civil than anyone else. In food and drink he was very moderate. . . . He rarely spoke, save when spoken to, and that with deliberation. . . . He was ardently devoted to love. . . . He delighted also in solitude, holding himself aloof from other people, in order that his meditations might not be interrupted. . . . He was very greedy of honor and glory."

Disgusted by Pope Boniface's high-handed politics, permanently embittered by the condemnation of Florence's Black Guelfs, Dante switched parties and became a Ghibelline. For the manifold troubles of Italy he believed that the only cure was a revival of the imperial monarchy. Only a universal state ruled by a divinely inspired emperor could bring peace and justice to Italy and to Europe. So, when Henry VII marched into Italy in 1310 Dante hailed him with rapturous fervor. In a letter similar to a royal proclamation addressed to the princes and peoples of Italy Dante wrote:

"Behold now the acceptable time which brings consolation and peace. For a new day is dawning which shall scatter our darkness. Rejoice, O Italy, for thy bridegroom cometh, the hope of the world, the glory of thy people, the ever clement Henry, who is Caesar and Augustus." The style resembles that of the Emperor Frederick II's propaganda. The substance seems almost irrational when we remember the well-meaning but ineffectual Henry VII. Dante's exile and his vision of a glorious political reformation had damaged his judgment.

In 1311 Dante wrote a terrible letter to the Florentines denouncing them because they were preparing to defy Henry VII, and also, of course, because of his own exile. He headed the letter, "Dante Alighieri, a Florentine and undeservedly in exile, to the most iniquitous Florentines within the city." He threatened the Florentines with the vengeance of the Emperor.

"You, who transgress every law of God and man, and whom the insatiable maw of avarice urges headlong into every crime, does not the dread of the second death haunt you, seeing that you first and you alone, refusing the yoke of liberty, have set yourself against the glory of the Roman Emperor, the King of the earth, and the servant of God? The hope which you vainly cherish in your madness will not be furthered by this rebellion of yours, but by your resistance the just wrath of the King at his coming will be but the more inflamed against you. If my prophetic spirit be not deceived, your city, worn out with long sufferings, shall be delivered at the last into the hands of the stranger, after the greatest part of you has been destroyed in death or in captivity, and the few that shall be left to endure exile shall witness her downfall with weeping and lamentations."

Several weeks after this letter to Florence Dante wrote one to Henry VII, who was busy besieging Cremona, in which he urged Henry to ignore Cremona and to hasten and crush "that viper Florence," the most obdurate enemy of the Empire. Two such letters from a man who yearned to return to his beloved native city demonstrate how Dante's anger and his imperial dream combined to overpower his caution and his common sense.

Henry's siege of Florence was a complete failure. He, too, was a failure, an honorable, decent, gentlemanly failure. As an individual Henry was courteous, courageous, pious. As an emperor he was inept. His failure in Italy was not entirely his own fault. The days of the Empire as an important force in Italy were over. As far as the Italians were concerned, the Empire was an anachronism. When it was convenient they deferred to the Empire and respected it. When it was inconvenient they ignored it or defied it. Dante, who knew so much about Italian politics, who condemned so many Italian political personages to hell in his *Inferno,* could not recognize the realities around him. He thought he was prophesying the future. He was yearning for an idealized past which had never been.

Henry VII died on August 24, 1313, in the little village of Buonconvento not far from Siena. Not too long after that the increasingly morose Dante, his hopes blasted, was welcomed by Cangrande della Scala, Lord of Verona, to his court.

In spite of Cangrande's frequent absences while he waged war, fought battles and besieged cities, his court at Verona was considered the grandest and the most cultivated in Italy. The court swarmed with refugees and exiles from other cities, soldiers, politicians, poets and scholars. Cangrande's open-handed hospitality, his sympathy for the unfortunate and his animal high spirits and sheer joy of living made him an irresistibly charming host. His temper was short, his arrogance enormous. But these were appropriate shortcomings in a ruler and conqueror. Cangrande never failed to charm friends and foes alike.

Although Cangrande had no legitimate sons, he had eight bastards. He was cruel and treacherous, in love with war and obsessed by dreams of conquest. But he was no worse than most of his contemporary rulers and much better than some. He had a special devotion to the Virgin Mary, to whom he dedicated a church, and in whose honor he fasted twice a week throughout the year.

Cangrande shared the medieval enthusiasm for the art of falconry. He is said to have owned no less than 300 falcons. He enjoyed poetry and art. Vasari, who could be badly mistaken, wrote that Giotto visited Verona and painted pictures for Cangrande. There is no record of Giotto's visit, and his pictures, if he painted any, have not survived. Cangrande was also admired as a master orator.

His rule, on the whole, was a benevolent despotism. He stamped out highway robbery so that travelers were safe anywhere in his state. He was kind to his more important prisoners. Cangrande used to visit Albertino Mussato, who was recovering from the wounds he received in the battle outside the walls of Vicenza. Cangrande played intellectual games (if we only knew what they were!) with Mussato and listened patiently to the poet's boasts that he had fought for justice and was willing to die for the freedom of Padua, his native city.

One of Cangrande's guests was Sagacio Muzio Gazzata, a chronicler of Reggio, who wrote a description of the manner in which Cangrande entertained his distinguished exiled guests. Each was given his own separate apartment in the Scaligeri palace. Each apartment was decorated with a symbol appropriate to its resident: a Victory for warriors; Groves of the Muses for poets; the god Mercury for artists; Paradise for priests and churchmen; and for them all, the inconstant figure of Fortune. Each guest had his own servant who served him his meals in private. At times Cangrande would invite individual guests to dine with him at his own table.

We can imagine Dante in such circumstances, taciturn, morose, proud, isolating himself to write poetry or just to escape the noise and clutter of a crowded court.

Petrarch, who spent years as the honored guest of various Italian despots, wrote about Dante at Cangrande's court, although how accurate is his report and how he acquired his information is not known:

"My fellow citizen, Dante Alighieri, was a man highly educated in the vulgar tongue [Tuscan Italian as distinct from the learned language, Latin], but in his style and speech a little daring and rather freer than was pleasing to delicate and studious ears, or gratifying to the princes of our time. He then, while banished from his country, resided at the court of Cangrande, where the afflicted universally found consolation and asylum. He at first was held in much honor by Cane, but afterward by degrees he fell out of favor, and day by day less pleased that lord. Actors and parasites of every description used to be collected at the same banquet; one of these, most impudent in his words and in his obscene gestures, obtained much importance and favor with many. And Cane, suspecting that Dante disliked this, called the man before him, and, having greatly praised him to our poet, said: 'I wonder how it is that this silly fellow should know how to please all, and should be loved by all, and that you cannot, who are said to be so wise!' Dante answered: 'You would not wonder if you knew that friendship is founded on similarity of habits and disposition.' "

Nevertheless, Cangrande and Dante remained friends. When Dante was living in Ravenna he wrote Cangrande a letter in which he dedicated the *Paradiso* to the Lord of Verona: "The subject of this work must be understood as taken according to the letter, and then interpreted according to the allegorical meaning. The subject, then, of the whole work, taken according to the letter alone, is simply a consideration of the state of souls after death; for, from and around this the action of the whole work turns. But if the work is considered according to its allegorical meaning, the subject is man, liable to the reward or punishment of justice, according as through the freedom of the will he is deserving or undeserving."

This is true as far as it goes. But Dante did not mention that another of the subjects of his great poem is his private opinion about the characters and appropriate punishment after death of many persons whose politics he deplored or whom he personally disliked.

Dante spent the last three or four years of his life in Ravenna, where he was the honored guest of the lord of the city, Guido da Polenta. In 1321 he returned to Verona for a brief visit and delivered a lecture under the patronage of Cangrande. He died in Ravenna on September 14 at the age of fifty-six. After his death the last thirteen cantos of the *Paradiso* were found to be missing.

Dante's son Jacopo went to Dante's house, which had been sold, and in a hole in the wall covered by a matting discovered a pile of papers so mildewed that it was in danger of rotting. Jacopo and a friend made copies of the cantos and sent them first to Cangrande della Scala, as Dante had regularly done with the earlier cantos as he completed them. That Dante so honored Cangrande and wished him to read his immortal masterpiece as he wrote it suggests that there were aspects to the character of the warrior Lord of Verona which after the passage of 650 years are no longer apparent.

Cangrande's career as a conqueror intent on expanding his state and also as a champion of the Ghibelline-imperial cause is far too complicated and far too monotonous with the din of continuous battle to justify a detailed account. He employed German mercenaries as the permanent core of his army and supported them with mounted knights and infantrymen recruited among his own subjects. Cangrande frequently led charges himself and inspired much admiration and devotion in his troops.

Sometimes Cangrande fought for his own ends, sometimes for the alliance of which he was a leader. Sometimes the two policies overlapped. For his private ends Cangrande waged four different wars with Padua to increase his power and domination over northeastern Italy. And as a Ghibelline leader he fought many campaigns in close alliance with Matteo Visconti, Lord of Milan, and with his particular friend and ally, Passerino Bonaccolsi, Lord of Mantua.

The second Paduan war broke out in May of 1317 when Padua and some Vincentine exiles broke the peace and attacked Vicenza. Cangrande had been warned. He lay in wait and surprised the invaders, beating them soundly. He hanged some citizens of Verona whom he suspected of complicity in the Paduan attack. The hangings undoubtedly were intended also to discourage any further treasonous dealings with Padua. During a pause in hostilities Cangrande used his time profitably by raiding the territories of the Guelf towns of Cremona and Brescia. And in December he attacked Padua in force, captured more than thirty of its subject towns and sacked and burned the town of Este, the original hometown of the ruling family of Ferrara. In February of 1318 Cangrande signed a peace with Padua. Four Paduan towns were surrendered to Cangrande for his lifetime.

Discouraged by their reverses, in July of 1318 the Paduans elected one of their nobles, Jacopo da Carrara, captain-general for life. This election actually made him Lord of Padua without the title. Jacopo was a friend of Cangrande's. They had become acquainted four years before when Jacopo was one of the prisoners Cangrande captured in the first Paduan war. To cement their friendship Cangrande's nephew, twelve-year-old Mastino, was engaged to Jacopo's baby daughter, Taddea.

Although his friend now ruled in Padua and presumably was anxious to be cooperative, Cangrande still yearned to be Lord of Padua himself. So in April of 1319, without excuse or warning, Cangrande suddenly attacked Padua and set up a permanent fortified camp south of the city. Four months later the Paduans sallied out and decisively defeated Cangrande. With an arrow through his leg the treacherous friend and conquering hero fled in panic. Disgraced and humiliated, Cangrande retired to Verona to nurse his wound and his wounded pride. Meanwhile the third Paduan war dragged on and did not end until October of 1320.

Five years later Cangrande attacked Padua again, but this fourth Paduan war was short and ended with a truce in June of 1325. Two years later, in 1327, Cangrande sent troops commanded by his nephew Mastino to join with some Paduan exiles in still another attack on the city. Although Cangrande did not personally participate, this could be called his fifth Paduan war—or even his sixth, if his original seizure of Vicenza in the name of Henry VII is counted.

The long series of wars devastated the Paduan *contado* and left the urban population exhausted, half starved and terrorized. Riots and factional strife tormented the unhappy city. Jacopo da Carrara was dead and his nephew, Marsilio, lacked the ability and power to control many of his own relations whose violent crimes contributed to the prevailing anarchy.

Baffled by crisis conditions he could not cope with, Marsilio met Cangrande secretly and agreed to surrender Padua if Cangrande would respect Padua's laws. Shortly thereafter Marsilio explained to the Paduan city council the grim necessity of surrendering the city to Cangrande and then made a public oration in which he persuaded the majority of the citizens. Anything for peace and order, even the foreign lord who had been their enemy for so long!

On September 8, 1328, Padua formally surrendered to Cangrande della Scala in Vicenza. Two days later Cangrande made his ceremonial entry into Padua. He was welcomed with signs of genuine enthusiasm. A procession of boys bore a banner emblazoned with the Scaligeri ladder. The boys shouted: "Long live Cangrande! Death to those who ground us down with heavy taxes." In return for his helpful cooperation Cangrande made Marsilio da Carrara his vicar to govern Padua.

Cangrande's acquisition of Padua resounded all over Italy. The Guelf city of Florence congratulated him. Venice made him an honorary citizen. And in celebration Cangrande held a great *curia* in Verona. A double wedding was performed. Cangrande's bastard son Franceschino married a five-year-old daughter of Rolando Rossi, Lord of Parma, and a cousin of the Carrarese. Cangrande's nephew Mastino married Marsilio's daughter Taddea. Cangrande knighted thirty-nine persons, of whom ten were Paduan nobles. The new Lord of Padua was doing his tactful best to ingratiate himself with the more influential families among his new subjects.

In Padua Marsilio da Carrara faced a difficult situation. As Cangrande's vicar in his own native city he felt it more necessary to demonstrate his loyalty to Cangrande than to conciliate his fellow citizens. So Marsilio tried to propitiate Cangrande by extorting money from the Paduans and presenting it to Cangrande as a contribution to the expenses of Cangrande's extravagant court.

Cangrande high-mindedly refused the questionable gift and insisted that Marsilio return the money to its rightful owners. If he was to make himself popular in Padua, that was no way to start! Whenever he was in Padua Cangrande made himself accessible to anyone who wished to see him, gave gifts to the nobles and managed to make many of them his friends, and every day entertained 600 citizens of all ranks at dinner at his own expense.

Like any astute politician, Cangrande deliberately made good use of his charm and personal magnetism. By the standards of the fourteenth century he was no tyrant. He ruled conquered cities mildly, allowed them to retain their own laws and customs and kept taxes reasonable. When he hanged people suspected of treason in Vicenza he acted cruelly and unjustly, but he was only acting according to the approved and usual customs of his time. Of course, those hangings antagonized the Vincentines. But by the time he assumed the lordship of Padua Cangrande was older and more experienced. By then he understood the value of the velvet glove concealing the iron hand.

To maintain reasonable clarity we have summarized the story of Cangrande and Padua in chronological order. But Cangrande's career as a champion of the Ghibelline cities of northern Italy in their never-ending war with the Guelf cities continued during those same years and so we must turn backward to take a brief look at it.

After the death of the Emperor Henry VII two rival candidates for the imperial title came forward. They were Louis, King of Bavaria, and Frederick, Duke of Austria. Cangrande as a prominent Ghibelline leader could not remain neutral. So, after prolonged procrastination, in 1317 he swore allegiance to Frederick, called "the Handsome."

In the same year Pope John XXII in Avignon excommunicated all Italian city lords who did not give up their titles of imperial vicar unless he himself confirmed them. While the two emperors-elect were fighting in Germany the Pope decreed that the throne was vacant and that he himself would assume the imperial right to appoint and remove vicars. Since the vicarships were chiefly ceremonial, more shadow than substance, the issue doesn't seem as important today as it did in the fourteenth century. We should not forget that in the Middle Ages people cared dreadfully about titles and their caring made those titles important. Cangrande ignored Pope John's excommunication and his claim to power over imperial vicars.

In June two papal legates arrived in Verona to negotiate with Cangrande. At that time the Lord of Verona was fighting Brescia again in alliance with the Ghibelline Brescian exiles, who had agreed to accept Cangrande as their lord when Brescia was captured and the Guelfs were expelled. The legates demanded that Cangrande cease his attack on Brescia and cease calling himself imperial vicar. If he obeyed, Pope John would absolve him from his excommunication. In an outburst of indignant rage Cangrande replied: "I shall do everything I think fit, and I will impose my will upon them. No one will dare to do anything contrary to my will." The arrogance, egoism and determination to defy the Pope or anyone else who opposed him were all typical of Cangrande; and, indeed, they were typical of nearly all the Italian despots of the Middle Ages.

Cangrande also refused to set free certain Guelf citizens of Padua and Vicenza he kept imprisoned, and boasted that he cared nothing about his excommunication. Qualified lawyers, he said, had told him that the papal decree of excommunication was worthless. Such a legalistic defiance of the Pope is surprising and interesting; but on what grounds it was based is not clear. In the past other rulers had blandly ignored excommunications when it suited them. By now it was plain that, secularly speaking, excommunication could be safely ignored. But what about the spiritual significance of excommunication? Could that be ignored too? Cangrande and many other medieval rulers seemed to think so.

Throughout the following year, 1318, Pope John tried to impose papal rule on northern Italy by force of arms in alliance with various Guelf cities and factions. The chief Ghibelline cities which opposed him were Verona, Mantua and Milan. Cangrande was constantly on the march from one threatening crisis to another.

In December the Ghibelline leaders held a summit conference at the town of Soncino, where Ezzelino da Romano was buried. Since that monster had been the leader of their party, they opened his tomb and honored his uncorrupted body as if it were that of a saint. This flamboyant gesture seems a highly questionable example of psychological warfare. Surely to identify themselves with the universally execrated Ezzelino would injure rather than help their cause. At the conference Cangrande was elected captain-general of the Ghibelline league and granted a monthly salary of 1,000 gold florins.

In 1322 Louis of Bavaria defeated and captured Frederick the Handsome of Austria, which seemed to settle the question of who was emperor-elect in favor of Louis. With admirable realism Cangrande accordingly switched his allegiance to Louis.

But in spite of Ghibelline exertions the Guelfs' cause prospered in Italy. Their prospects looked grim to Cangrande and to his ally and friend, Passerino Bonaccolsi, Lord of Mantua. So the two lords arranged a meeting with a papal legate in Mantua. In the bishop's palace in Mantua, in the presence of a large assembly, they prepared to submit to Pope John and, in return, to be absolved of their excommunications. But just before the formal ceremony was scheduled to take place an emissary from Louis of Bavaria arrived in Mantua. He reminded them of their oaths of loyalty to the Empire and demanded that they hasten to the aid of Milan, then sorely beset by papal troops.

Like warhorses which hear the trumpets call to battle, the two lords forgot all about surrendering to the Pope and making peace, assembled 600 mounted knights, rode off to Milan and inflicted a smashing defeat upon the papal army. Milan was saved and the Ghibelline league revived with new strength and confidence.

Continuous warfare did not prevent Cangrande from finding the time and money to complete the fortifications of Verona with a fine new wall on the south of the city which ran between two bends in the Adige River. With its massive gates, watchtowers and deep moat it was considered impregnable. In addition, Cangrande strengthened the defenses on the north and west of the city.

Everywhere in Verona the Scaligeri ladder appeared, on banners, palaces, castles, towers, walls and arches; on private houses belonging to various members of the ruling family; on tombs, churches and steeples; and on documents. "Scala" was the battle cry of the Veronese soldiers. It was shouted at banquets and festivals. And the ladder was even stamped on coins. The Scaligeri and the city of Verona had become almost indistinguishable and the glory of the one was the glory of the other. In the process the municipal treasury had somehow become the Scaligeri treasury, a convenience some modern rulers might regard with envy and admiration.

In Verona since early in the thirteenth century one of the more curious customs of the Middle Ages had been celebrated. This was a foot race in which the prize was a *drappo verde*, a green cloth. The race, run on the first Sunday of Lent, commemorated a victory won in 1207. Boccaccio wrote that all the competitors were stark naked. Their modesty consequently inspired them to run exceedingly fast.

Louis of Bavaria, like every other German king, could not properly call himself emperor until he had gone to Italy and had been crowned King of Italy with the iron crown of the Lombards in Milan and until he had been crowned Emperor in Rome. In 1327 Louis crossed the Alps and paused on his journey in the city of Trento some fifty miles north of Verona. Cangrande went to meet his feudal overlord and in a formal audience importunately demanded to be made imperial vicar of Padua "as of right." At that time he was already vicar of Verona and of Vicenza, but he had not yet become Lord of Padua. So what "right" he was demanding is hard to imagine. To make his demand go down easier Cangrande offered the immense sum of 200,000 florins to the Emperor-elect. Louis refused. Evidently he took his office seriously and wasn't going to permit any petty Italian despot, one who wasn't even a member of the nobility, to act so presumptuously without rebuff.

Cangrande's famous temper boiled over. He threatened to turn Guelf if his services in the Ghibelline cause were not better appreciated. He left Louis' court in a huff and returned to Verona to sulk. His threat shows how little the labels Guelf and Ghibelline now meant compared with the realities of personal ambition and local politics. But Cangrande calmed down and in March made his peace with Louis.

The Emperor-elect resumed his journey and, avoiding Verona, went through Bergamo and Como to Milan. There on May 31 he was duly crowned King of Italy by two deposed bishops (deposed because the Pope had forbidden them to crown Louis). Among those present in magnificent state was Cangrande della Scala, who had changed his mind and decided that it would be prudent to retain Louis' favor.

Cangrande is said to have had with him in Milan a retinue of 1,000 knights, a figure which may well be another medieval exaggeration. He kept open house every day. One report says that Cangrande tried to corner all the meat, game and fish in Milan. If he did, his motive is inexplicable. But the supply was too great for even Cangrande's wealth. And he did not have as much money with him as when he had left Verona. In return for a large sum Louis had reconfirmed Cangrande's vicarships of Verona and Vicenza. If he could not wangle the vicarship of Padua, perhaps the reconfirmation was better than nothing.

King Louis left Milan and proceeded to Rome, where he was ceremoniously crowned emperor, to the furious indignation of Pope John XXII in Avignon. In a rage the Pope declared that the Emperor was a heretic, officially proclaimed the coronation null and void, and announced that Louis' subjects were freed of their obligation of loyalty to him.

In the following year, 1328, Cangrande della Scala, who was so widely admired as a great and valiant soldier and as a just and generous ruler, committed the most shameful treachery of his life. In Mantua a conspiracy was hatching against Cangrande's old friend and companion in arms, Passerino Bonaccolsi. It was organized by the powerful Gonzaga family. Its leader was sixty-year-old Luigi Gonzaga, who was Bonaccolsi's brother-in-law. In return for a bribe of 100,000 gold florins Cangrande agreed to dispatch an armed force which in combination with the Gonzagas would seize power in Mantua. On the night of August 16 the conspirators murdered Passerino Bonaccolsi, three of his sons and several hundred of his friends and relations. The *coup d'état* was bloody and efficient. Cangrande was promised a decisive influence in Mantuan affairs, but he in his turn was betrayed. The Gonzagas took an independent line.

Why did the great Cangrande stoop to such a mean betrayal of his most loyal friend and ally? Could it have been for the money? Unlikely. Only the year before Cangrande had offered twice as much to Louis. Could it have been in the expectation of dominating Mantua through subservient puppet rulers? That would have been naïve. Cangrande was an expert on the fierce independence of his contemporary despots. Could he have quarreled with Bonaccolsi and taken a malicious pleasure in manipulating his destruction? This last is only speculation, but it is possible and seems reasonable enough.

The Emperor Louis, traveling north from his coronation in Rome in 1329, arrived in the little town of Marcaria fifteen miles west of Mantua. There Cangrande met him. He asked and was granted a private audience. And in that audience Cangrande negotiated with the Emperor another disgraceful betrayal. He was plotting to seize Mantua from the Gonzagas, whom he had made Lords of Mantua only the year before! Cangrande's lust for conquest was insatiable. The heroic young warrior (he was only thirty-eight) was growing old in treachery. Cangrande asked Louis to make him imperial vicar of Mantua. And Louis, who had so firmly refused to make Cangrande vicar of Padua, agreed! He gave Cangrande a formal written document confirming his appointment, which Cangrande never had time to use. He waited for an opportune moment to attack his new friends and to announce his new title. The time never came.

It did not come because a delegation of exiles from the city of Treviso came to Cangrande and offered to make him lord of their city if he would help them capture Treviso. Cangrande thought the chance too good to lose and promptly postponed his attack on the Gonzagas in Mantua and instead prepared an attack on Treviso. Early in July Cangrande launched his attack, but was repulsed. He then settled down to besiege Treviso. A number of the Trevisan nobles deserted to Cangrande. So, despairing of any help and trusting in Cangrande's reputation for mercy to conquered foes, Treviso surrendered. On July 18 Cangrande della Scala, riding on a white horse, surrounded by his captains, rode in triumph into the ancient city of Treviso. He felt miserably sick and may have wondered if this would be his last triumph. It was.

In the captured city the conqueror secretly took to his bed. He was convulsed by terrible abdominal pains. A burst appendix? A perforated ulcer? In four days the mighty Lord of Verona, Vicenza, Padua, Treviso and lesser towns was dead. The agony he had endured still showed on his face after he had been embalmed. His body was dressed in silk, placed on a cart drawn by four hourses and transported to Verona. All the church bells of Verona tolled in mourning. Soldiers escorted the bier with their weapons pointed to the ground. The entire city took part in the funeral and sincerely grieved for the famous warrior who had made Verona glorious.

Although Cangrande was excommunicated, he never was charged with heresy. The clergy of Verona were so loyal to him that they continued to celebrate masses in defiance of the Pope's orders. There is no doubt that Cangrande considered himself a pious and devout Catholic and was so considered by others. His wars, his cruelties and his betrayals were never held against him. After all, he had only behaved as a medieval warrior lord should.

Because Cangrande had no legitimate sons, he was succeeded by his nephews. Their descendants continued the Scaligeri dynasty in Verona until 1387, when the city fell to a conqueror far craftier and more astute than Cangrande had ever been, Giangaleazzo Visconti, Count of Virtue and Lord of Milan.

XIII

The Knight of the
Holy Ghost

George Bernard Shaw once wrote that Joan of Arc was "the queerest fish among the eccentric worthies of the Middle Ages." He was mistaken. In an age so full of queer characters that they jostled each other in the streets—babbling prophets, rapturous mystics, besotted alchemists, learned necromancers and insane tyrants—the queerest fish of all was Cola di Rienzo, known to fame as Rienzi.

His father was an obscure Roman innkeeper. His mother was a humble washerwoman. He himself was boastful, ostentatious, fatuously vain, cruel, treacherous, cowardly, a glutton, a drunkard and frequently irrational. He was also learned for his time, a sincere political reformer, an eloquent orator, a master demagogue and twice the dictator of Rome. Plays, operas, novels and biographies have been written about Rienzi and no final verdict has yet been reached. Was he a forerunner of democracy, as some think? Or of fascism, as others think? Was he a tragic hero or a scoundrel? Was he crazy, or was he only crazy sometimes, when the wind blew from the northeast?

Cola di Rienzo was born in Rome in the spring of 1313. The perpetual feuds of the Roman barons and the miserable squalor of the populace had not changed for the better since Saint Bernard wrote in the twelfth century:

"Who is ignorant of the vanity and arrogance of the Romans? A nation nursed in sedition, cruel, untractable, and scorning to obey, unless they are too feeble to resist. When they promise to serve, they aspire to reign; if they swear allegiance, they watch the oportunity to revolt; yet they vent their discontent in loud clamors if the doors of your council are shut against them. Dexterous in mischief, they have never learned the science of doing good. Odious to earth and heaven, impious to God, seditious among themselves, jealous of their neighbors, inhuman to strangers, they love no one, by no one are they beloved; and, while they wish to inspire fear, they live in base and continual apprehension. They will not submit; they know not how to govern; faithless to their superiors, intolerable to their equals, ungrateful to their benefactors, and alike impudent in their demands and their refusals, lofty in promise, poor in execution; adulation and calumny, perfidy and treason, are the familiar features of their policy."

Since Saint Bernard was a medieval aristocrat as well as a saint, his opinions of the Roman proletariat were probably prejudiced. Nevertheless, similar opinions were widely held for centuries. Such were the people from whom Rienzi came, whom he ruled and who in a fit of riotous rage killed him.

When Rienzi was still a small child his mother died and his father sent him to be brought up by relatives in the papal town of Anagni some thirty-five miles southeast of Rome. Rienzi said that he lived there "like a peasant among peasants." In Anagni he studied Latin and read a number of leading Latin authors, an accomplishment beyond the imagination of any illiterate medieval peasant. In 1332 when he was nineteen Rienzi went to Rome and for the next ten years practiced the professions of notary and lawyer. He married the daughter of another notary and became the father of two daughters and of one son, perhaps of two.

Rienzi, like any ambitious politician, tried to make himself as popular as possible. He defended the poor and championed widows and orphans. His reading of Latin writers had filled his mind with dreams about the glory of ancient Rome, a glory which he hoped he himself might someday help to revive. His interest in Rome's past inspired him to study and collect ancient inscriptions, thus becoming in all probability the second archaeologist of record. (The Emperor Frederick II had become the first when he excavated the tomb of Galla Placidia.)

Rienzi's appearance is unknown. He was said to be handsome. He cultivated a mysterious, enigmatic smile which persuaded many that he had secret knowledge and authority. Throughout his life Rienzi vacillated between the depths of despair and the heights of confidence and optimism. Probably he suffered from manic depression. He was a visionary who constantly dreamed of epochal achievements—reforming and pacifying Rome, uniting all Italy in one state ruled by the eternal city, or depriving the Church of its temporal power. All Rienzi's dreams had a common purpose. He himself would win glory and power.

In 1341 Rienzi had an opportunity to see another man win glory if not power. He was Francesco Petrarcha, a poet and all-around man of letters who was one of the greatest writers of the Middle Ages, surpassed only by Dante and Chaucer. The son of a Florentine exile, Petrarch (as he is generally called) was born in Arezzo, grew up in Avignon and studied law at the University of Bologna. But law bored him. He quit his studies to become a poet and to live the rest of his life on patronage, the patronage of the Church, of individual churchmen and of several Italian despots.

Always a man with a nice gift for self-promotion, Petrarch had undoubtedly heard of Albertino Mussato's crowning with a laurel wreath by the University of Padua. How much more impressive it would be to be crowned by the city of Rome itself! After considerable wire-pulling and help from distinguished and influential sponsors (notably King Robert of Naples) the ceremony was arranged. On Easter Sunday 1341 Petrarch was crowned with the laurel wreath of poetry in the grand hall of the Senators' Palace on the Capitol. The elaborate ceremony was witnessed by a huge crowd. Rienzi, who yearned for glory and loved crowds, in all probability was present.

The occasion may have given Rienzi ideas. It would not be long before he would be crowned in Rome in a far grander ceremony. And in even less time he would become the admired and admiring friend of the celebrated poet.

At that time such municipal government as the city of Rome enjoyed (it was precious little) was exercised by two senators appointed by the pope. When a new pope was consecrated he could not appoint Roman senators until the people of Rome officially recognized his right to do so. This meant that whenever a new pope was elected a delegation from Rome had to journey to Avignon, where the Papacy had been established since 1305. French kings liked having popes be French, near France and subject to French influence. In 1342 the new pope was Clement VI.

Clement, who was to play a major role in the drama of Rienzi's life, was a worldly French aristocrat with a passion for luxury, splendor and magnificence. "Bah!" he is supposed to have exclaimed. "My predecessors didn't know how to be popes!" Clement knew. He sold benefices in mass lots. His nepotism was spectacular. He was suspected of sexual relations with men as well as with women. His extravagance was notorious. But Clement was an able administrator and an erratically stern judge of other people's morals. In an age when nearly all rulers were casually promiscuous Clement excommunicated Casimir of Poland for adultery. Clement was famous for his generosity. "No one," he believed, "should leave the presence of the Prince unhappy, none should leave with empty hands."

Shortly after the delegation from Rome departed for Avignon the Roman municipal government was overthrown and replaced by a committee composed of the heads of thirteen merchant guilds. Rienzi persuaded these newcomers to office to send him to Avignon to tell Clement about the misery of the Roman people, the wanton abuses of the criminal Roman barons, and to petition the Pope for a new, more democratic city government. His reputation for eloquence won him the job.

When Rienzi arrived in Avignon he found that the official Roman delegation had already recognized Pope Clement's right to appoint Roman senators, and had also petitioned the Pope to visit Rome and to declare the year 1350 a jubilee year. A jubilee meant that at least 100,-000 pilgrims would go to Rome to pray at the holy sites and to be absolved of their sins. Their presence in the miserable city, paying extortionate rates for food and lodging, would be an economic bonanza for Rome. The Pope had already given his approval to the jubilee.

Rienzi, who had had nothing to do with this coup, dispatched an extravagantly rhetorical letter to Rome announcing the jubilee. It began:

"Let the mountains rejoice together, let the hills be adorned with joy and all cities and villages of the world be full of peace, prosperity and eternal delight!" Rienzi never mentioned his own unsuccessful mission to secure the Pope's aid in improving the chaotic political situation in Rome.

But Pope Clement had granted Rienzi several audiences. During these, with his customary eloquence Rienzi denounced the criminal violence of the Roman barons and requested a democratic constitution for Rome. Clement rejected this revolutionary idea and in traditional conservative fashion appointed two of the Roman nobles to be senators. Realistically recognizing that the Roman barons would be enraged by his denunciation of their crimes, Rienzi judged it prudent not to return to Rome and remained in Avignon.

There his expense money ran out. He was excluded from the papal court and cordially disliked by many of the Italian cardinals who were related to the Roman barons. Rienzi's contemporary biographer wrote that in Avignon he was so abjectly poor that he used "to sit in the sun like a lizard" to keep himself warm and was so destitute that he was about to enter a poorhouse.

A friend came to the rescue. How Petrarch and Rienzi met is unknown, but in Avignon they formed a mutual-admiration society. They shared an enthusiasm for ancient Rome and for Cicero, their ideal orator and Latin stylist. They were both exiles. They both yearned for a regeneration of Rome which would make her once again the splendid ruler of all Italy. Petrarch was better born, better educated and better off financially. But the scholarly poet responded with emotional fervor to Rienzi's eloquence, to his dreams and to his magnetic personality. After one of their long conversations Petrarch left Avignon for his attractive country place at Vaucluse and there wrote Rienzi a letter saying with sublime poetic exaggeration: "I felt as if I had heard issuing from the temple the voice not of man but of God!"

At this time Rienzi was already planning the scheme which he later carried out to seize power in Rome and to reform the city. Years later Petrarch wrote: "I knew and loved him long before he undertook his glorious task, and afterward I came to honor and admire him. . . . I loved his virtue, I praised his enterprise, I admired his courage."

In a more practical way Petrarch persuaded the great Cardinal Giovanni Colonna to forgive Rienzi for his impudence in denouncing the Colonna family (along with the other Roman barons) and the Cardinal arranged for Pope Clement to receive Rienzi again into his favor. In the spring of 1344 Rienzi asked and obtained from the Pope the post of notary to the Roman municipal court. He now could return safely to Rome under official papal protection.

Back in Rome, Rienzi began his political campaign in earnest. He made many speeches attacking the barons and proclaiming the need of reform. He became a local celebrity. But the barons with their palaces and fortified towers in Rome, their many castles. in the *contado* and their troops of paid ruffians could not take the plebeian orator seriously. To them Rienzi seemed a pompous clown. They even invited him to their houses because he amused them. Once in Cardinal Colonna's own house Rienzi lost control of his temper and shouted angrily: "I too shall be a great lord, or an emperor—and then," pointing first to one nobleman and then to another, "then I shall persecute him, and hang him, and behead him." His reckless revelation of his lust for power and revenge was greeted with gales of laughter.

Rienzi craved revenge for his humiliation in being poor and humble and without power—as have numerous other proletarian demagogues. And the Roman barons, like other members of privileged classes so often since, failed to recognize the genuine threat represented by the emotional harangues of a lower-class agitator. Rienzi's political campaign continued from the summer of 1344 until the spring of 1347.

He had large political cartoons painted on the walls of public buildings. He had a proclamation posted on the door of the church of San Giorgio in Velabro that "Soon the Roman people will return to their ancient good estate." He recruited a group of loyal followers. And on May 19, 1347, he held a secret meeting in which he once again recounted the sufferings of the Roman people and outlined the new government he intended to establish.

Rienzi's *coup d'état* was singularly peaceful. The day after the secret meeting Rienzi and his fellow conspirators disarmed the guards of the senate with the useful assistance of 100 mercenary soldiers they had hired for 150 gold florins. This done, Rienzi had heralds blow trumpets and invite the people of Rome to assemble at the Capitol the next morning to ratify the new constitution he had prepared. The night before the great day he spent in church listening to thirty masses and praying for the favorable intercession of the Holy Ghost.

When the morning came Rienzi and a select group of his followers marched to the Capitol behind four large banners. Rienzi was dressed in full armor but did not wear a helmet. His proceedings were given a spurious air of legality by the presence of the papal legate, Bishop Raimundo of Orvieto. On the steps of the Capitol Rienzi made the greatest and most important speech of his life.

His performance was unquestionably a masterpiece of emotional oratory. Rienzi lamented the present degradation of Rome, promised that soon all would be well, and declared that he would gladly sacrifice his life for the city and for the Pope. He then asked the vast crowd to approve his constitution and himself as the lord of the city. The crowd applauded enthusiastically. Then with supreme hypocrisy Rienzi asked that the papal legate should be made joint ruler of the city with him. This, he hoped, would make everything look reasonably legal.

But Rienzi could not keep up such a pretense for as long as a week. He convoked a second assembly of the people and obtained for himself "sole power and authority to reform and preserve the peaceful state of the city and province of Rome." So now Rome had a new dictator, who henceforth signed his proclamations "The severe and clement, the Tribune of liberty, peace and justice, the deliverer of the Holy Roman Republic." Rienzi's first official act was to organize a municipal army of 1,300 infantrymen and 325 mounted knights recruited from the thirteen districts of the city.

All this bloodless revolution could not have succeeded had not the aged Stefano Colonna, the most powerful of the Roman barons, been absent from Rome in command of the city militia on duty escorting a grain convoy. When he heard the astonishing news eighty-year-old Stefano galloped back to Rome to see for himself. Shortly after his arrival the new Lord of Rome sent Stefano a written order to leave the city. Stefano's contempt was enormous. He tore up the letter and snorted: "If this madman goes on annoying me, I will have him thrown out of the window of the Capitol."

But the madman sent his new army and a hostile mob to arrest old Stefano, who was forced to flee ignominiously from Rome and seek refuge in the Colonna fortress of Palestrina. Rienzi then ordered the other nobles to leave Rome also. They did.

Why did they obey? It is probable that, being taken completely by surprise, they lacked the force to cope with Rienzi's little army and intended to demolish it later as soon as it was conveniently possible.

Two weeks later Rienzi summoned the barons back to Rome. Some prudently stayed in their safe castles, but many came. It is even harder to imagine why they obeyed this second order. Accustomed to feuding with each other, they did not know how to organize a united baronial front. Instead, they seemed stupefied by this impudent upstart who called himself Tribune of Rome.

Rienzi received the barons standing on the Capitol steps. He wore full armor and a scarlet cloak. Each baron had to swear on the Bible that he would be loyal to the new Roman government and to its Tribune, that he would not entertain bandits or state enemies in his castles, that he would protect travelers from highwaymen, and that he would support the state. For hundreds of years the Roman barons had considered robbery their rightful privilege. Naturally, they bitterly resented the reform laws and stubbornly resisted obeying them.

Rienzi's campaign to stamp out violent crime and to make Rome safe for the people was ruthless, but it was unquestionably sincere. Criminals were promptly arrested and brutally punished. The law courts were reformed. And numerous laws were passed to improve the moral conduct of the people. These made blasphemy, gambling, prostitution and adultery illegal. Other laws reformed the tax system and regulated the grain supply.

So effective were Rienzi's many reforms and so severe his enforcement of his new laws that for the first time in centuries peace and personal security were known in Rome and in its surrounding territory. Travelers no longer feared for their money and their lives. No one went armed. Municipal funds were spent on hospitals and on the support of widows and orphans. Rienzi's state messengers rode alone and without weapons, with only a silver wand for identification. "I have carried this wand," said one of them, "along the roads and through forests; thousands have knelt down before it, and kissed it with tears of thankfulness that the roads are free from brigands."

By modern standards Rienzi's laws were cruelly harsh, but not by medieval ones. Their stern enforcement caused such improvement that Edward Gibbon wrote:

"Never, perhaps, has the energy and effect of a single mind been more remarkably felt than in the sudden, though transient, reformation of Rome by the Tribune Rienzi. A den of robbers was converted to the discipline of a camp or convent: patient to hear, swift to redress, inexorable to punish, his tribunal was always accessible to the poor and strangers; nor could birth or dignity or the immunities of the Church protect the offender or his accomplice."

If Cola di Rienzo had been assassinated a few weeks after his seizure of power he would have been fortunate. Instead of continuing the mixture of tragedy and farce, of megalomania and folly, which were his life for the next seven years, he would have been hailed as a hero and a martyr in his own time and would still be so regarded in ours.

Perhaps the interval of peace and order Rienzi created was doomed from the start. Would the riotous Roman mobs have endured his severe laws long? Would the nobles have submitted to his rule any longer than they did if Rienzi had continued as a just and reasonable ruler? Probably not. But Rienzi's gigantic plans to rule not only Rome but all Italy ensured disgrace and disaster.

To launch his fantastic scheme Rienzi sent letters to all the princes, despots and republics of Italy inviting them to a conference in Rome. They would discuss the restoration of the Roman people. By this Rienzi meant the restoration of Rome as the ruler of all Italy, which, of course, meant that the splendid new Tribune of Rome would be the ruler of all Italy. There was an element of idealism, some cloudy vision of a united Italy, in Rienzi's plans. But his own drive for power was so compelling it is difficult to estimate how much any other idea mattered.

Several years later when Rienzi was in prison and anxious to get out he wrote a letter to an archbishop in which he said that when he invited all the rulers of Italy to Rome "with sweet letters and solemn legacies" he was determined, if they should fall into his trap, to have them all "hanged against the sun."

This is a remarkable admission. If true, it is a shameless revelation of Rienzi's perfidy and treachery. It is also remarkable that a prisoner seeking aid from an archbishop in getting out would boast of such a monstrous plan. But Rienzi's admission may not have been true. It may have been a partly crazed man's idea of what he would have liked to do, or of what he wished he had done.

Representatives of all the Italian states, though not their rulers, came to Rome; but nothing significant was accomplished. Rienzi reveled in his importance and dramatized it in gorgeous processions and grandiose ceremonies. He gave elaborate banquets and always rode on a white horse. Usually white horses were ridden only by kings, popes and emperors, although Cangrande della Scala had ridden one. Rienzi announced that his dreams were direct revelations from God. He confessed daily, took communion daily and prayed in his private chapel that he would interpret his divinely sent dreams correctly.

Whether all this ostentatious piety was genuine we cannot know. We never can be sure about Rienzi, whose love of self-dramatization was his only consistent mental attribute. A few years later Rienzi furiously denounced the Papacy and papal temporal power in a fashion reminiscent of the Emperor Frederick II; but later still he gladly set off for Rome from Avignon as a salaried papal official.

Far away in Vaucluse Petrarch heard of Rienzi's reforms and triumphs and mistakenly concluded that they meant the rebirth of liberty, democracy and idealistic government. He sent Rienzi an eloquent letter which beautifully expressed his own lofty hopes for Rome and Italy, but which had little justification in what was actually going on in Rome. Pleased and flattered, Rienzi invited Petrarch to come to Rome and share in the sunshine of the new day. Petrarch thought that he had better stay where he was a little longer, but he sent Rienzi a poem celebrating his achievements.

While the various ambassadors were in Rome Rienzi indulged in a spectacular festival of self-glorification which made imperial or papal coronations seem rather routine affairs. The celebration was double, a holy consecration and a secular coronation.

The consecration consisted of Rienzi's knighting. Of course, he became no ordinary knight. Proceedings began with a procession from the

Capitol to the Lateran church. Heralds blowing trumpets led the way. After them came Rienzi's wife and his mother-in-law, a gesture of family solidarity Rienzi did not repeat, and then various dignitaries. The Tribune himself was dressed even more grandly than usual in a scarlet robe. All the visiting ambassadors followed along behind him. Rienzi spent the night in the Lateran church, presumably praying.

The next morning he attended mass and then was knighted in a solemn ceremony in which he received a pair of golden spurs and a symbolical sword. And he assumed a new title of his own devising, "Immaculate Knight of the Holy Ghost." It was as if he had created a new knightly order with a membership of one. Rienzi then made still another speech to a huge Roman crowd from the loggia of the Lateran. When he had finished, his secretary read out a proclamation of astounding arrogance.

It declared that Rome's ancient rule over the whole world was now restored, that all Italian cities were now free, that all Italians were now citizens of Rome, that only Roman citizens had the right to elect the emperor, and that since there were then two rival claimants to the imperial title they must both come to Rome, where their dispute would be settled.

When the secretary finished reading, Rienzi drew his new sword and in a gesture of surprising fatuity slashed the air in three directions, shouting, "This is mine! This is mine! This is mine!" The crowd dutifully applauded.

Such a performance was more than mere megalomania. Rienzi was riding the crest of a wave of mystical euphoria and manic fanaticism. For the time being he probably had persuaded himself that he was indeed the instrument of the divine will and that the rest of mankind would so regard him. Unfortunately for his delusions of grandeur, the numerous despots of Italy were not prepared to surrender their sovereignty to the mad Tribune of Rome; and the rival emperors-elect, Louis of Bavaria and Charles IV, were not going to allow their dispute to be settled by the irrational son of a Roman innkeeper. Charles, because of his support by Pope Clement, was in a particularly strong position.

For two more weeks Rienzi continued to celebrate himself in a series of banquets, festivals and ceremonies and then on August 15 he had himself crowned in the church of Santa Maria Maggiore. The coronation ceremony was a strange mixture of Christian and pagan elements. One crown was not sufficient. Rienzi was crowned with six, each crown symbolizing one of his transcendent virtues. He already had so many titles that he did not then assume another, but it soon became clear that he had another in mind.

In a circular letter to the cities of central and northern Italy Rienzi announced that he would abolish the right of the German princes to elect the emperor because the emperor ought to be an Italian responsive to Italian interests. So, he said, he had made arrangements for twenty-four Italian delegates to come to Rome during the following year to elect a suitable emperor. The elimination of German influence and the unification of Italy under an Italian ruler suggest that five centuries before Garibaldi Rienzi was feeling some ephemeral and premature twinges of nationalist emotion.

And who should this new Italian emperor be? No one needed to be told.

For the eight weeks after his coronation Rienzi gave a non-stop performance in his version of the old story about pride going before a fall. Intoxicated with his own glory, he even compared his rise to power to the ascension of Jesus Christ. His power may have been imaginary elsewhere, but in Rome it was absolute and Rienzi became corrupted by it. He became suspicious and cruel.

Knowing that the Roman barons deeply resented his dictatorship and would not long submit to it, Rienzi conceived a treacherous scheme traditional among tyrants. He invited a number of the leading barons to a banquet and, when the meal was eaten, had his guests arrested and thrown into prison. The Emperor Henry VII before him and Pizarro and King Ferrante of Naples after him all used this trick. All night the Roman barons waited in expectation of being beheaded in the morning. At dawn the bell of the Capitol tolled ominously. A friar was admitted to the barons' cells and urged them to make their final confessions. Some of them confessed their sins and took communion. But Stefano Colonna, the oldest and toughest of them all, refused to do either. After the confessions the prisoners were conducted into the great hall, expecting to hear their condemnation. Rienzi was there to pronounce sentence.

Instead, he preached a sermon, forgave them their offenses, presented to each of them a ring and a velvet robe and forced them to swear oaths of submission to himself. Rienzi even required the barons to ride with him in a procession through the city and to attend a communion service.

According to the murderous politics of the fourteenth century, Rienzi should have executed his prisoners. They were his acknowledged enemies. He had publicly humiliated them and so had inflamed their enmity to a more intense pitch. But to release them was a terrible folly. The art of tyrannical government requires a cold-blooded consistency which Rienzi was incapable of maintaining. Whether he intended to kill his prisoners and mercifully changed his mind, or whether he never planned to kill them, is unknown.

In the meantime Petrarch decided to leave his pleasant rural refuge at Vaucluse and to journey to Rome to visit his old friend, the glorious Tribune of the city. He had reached Genoa when he heard the news of Rienzi's recent excesses and of the fiasco of his treacherous arrest and foolish release of the barons. Petrarch, who well understood the bloody politics of his time, canceled his visit to Rienzi and also canceled the friendship between them. The poet knew that it would not be prudent to involve himself in Rienzi's affairs. So he contented himself with writing Rienzi a letter of reproach and good advice.

Some years later Petrarch succinctly expressed his thoughts about Rienzi's rule in Rome. He did not approve of Rienzi's companions: "Would to God that among the bad he had not chosen the worst." And with casual acceptance of the practical advantages of treachery and murder, the personally pacific poet wrote: "He deserves every punishment because, having undertaken the defense of liberty, and finding himself in a position to destroy all its enemies at one blow . . . he let them go well armed."

Cola di Rienzo did not have the faintest glimmer of how rancorous was the hatred of the Roman barons or how bitter was their humiliation. He even blithely wrote that he had reconciled them with himself and with God. Nor did it cross his muddled mind that the idea of a united Italy ruled by himself would not be pleasing to the Pope, who, in theory at least, ruled a large part of central Italy. Nor did he bother himself with the thought that his scheme to become an Italian emperor would outrage not only the rival claimants, but also all Germany, since emperors were always German.

So Rienzi multiplied his enemies. Strange stories circulated. It was rumored that Rienzi held confidential conversations with a demon called Fiorene, which lived confined in a polished steel mirror engraved with magical symbols. Other demons lived in his scepter. Pope Clement denounced Rienzi as a "precursor of Antichrist" and as "a child of the Devil." On October 9, 1347, Clement wrote a letter to his vicar-general of the papal states instructing him to depose and excommunicate Rienzi if he did not revoke all his new laws and swear a solemn oath of submission to the Pope. And, fearing that verbal penalties would not be sufficient, Clement also wrote to seventy Roman nobles urging them to revolt against the obnoxious Tribune.

The manic elation which had sustained Rienzi for months now collapsed and he entered on a period of profound gloom, irrational conduct and panic. When he failed to capture one of the castles of the powerful Orsini family, Rienzi named two of his hounds after two of the leading Orsinis and then drowned them in a river. Rienzi's fears and suspicions multiplied. He could not eat or sleep and he saw treachery all around him. For the second time he invited guests to dinner, this time his friends, and treacherously had them arrested and imprisoned.

The Roman barons, based in their rural strongholds, were all in revolt. Once in a skirmish with a party of Colonna troops Rienzi saw his banner fall and cried out hysterically: "My God, my God, why hast Thou forsaken me?" Even in his depression and despair he could not refrain from comparing himself to Jesus. Daily his panic and cowardice increased. At a later period Rienzi wrote of this time: "My inner courage failed me, and so great a cowardice attacked me that I would leap up suddenly at night screaming, because my dreams had shown me the palace crumbling beneath me, or armed enemies approaching to attack."

In his terror Rienzi tried to arrange a reconciliation with the Church and even offered to forsake all his grand titles and schemes and to submit to the Pope. Several nobles organized demonstrations in the streets against the timid Tribune. Rienzi remained passive and did not order his municipal troops to attack the demonstrators. Instead, he fled for safety to the Castel Sant' Angelo. His dictatorship had lasted seven months less five days. His abject surrender of power was as bloodless as his seizure of it.

In January of 1348 Rienzi was officially excommunicated and denounced as a heretic. But he had disappeared. In December of 1347 he had fled from Rome. Just where he went for how long during the first six months of 1348 is unknown; but he was in Naples for a while and he did wander about mysteriously. By summer he had holed up in a remote Apennine community of Spiritual Franciscans or Fraticelli. These were the fundamentalist Franciscans who tried to live by Saint Francis' original doctrine of total poverty. This was difficult because the Papacy had condemned the doctrine and practice which had made the first Franciscans beloved and influential, and the spiritual Franciscans were all excommunicated.

Why did Rienzi seek refuge among the Fraticelli? He could have had at least three persuasive reasons. Although never conventionally orthodox, Rienzi was intermittently religious. After his orgy of vainglory he could have felt the need for a period of repentance and regeneration. Since he was a proclaimed heretic he could have thought an isolated community of fellow excommunicates would make a fine place in which to hide from the Inquisition. An equally powerful motive could have been to seek a haven in the wilderness which would be safe from the horrors of the Black Plague, which was then sweeping over most of the cities of Italy.

The most terrible plague the world has known originated in Asiatic rats and was spread by the bites of rat fleas. Its first approach to Europe was in a Mongol army which was besieging a Genoese trading post in the Crimea in 1346. The Mongols catapulted the bodies of men who had died of the plague over the walls of the city. Presumably, infected fleas were on the bodies and spread the plague among the Genoese and among the rats on Genoese ships. At any rate, it was by means of Genoese ships that fleas and plague reached Sicily in October of 1347 and Genoa and Venice in January of 1348. In a time of general dirt and many fleas the deadly new kind of flea was not noticed. By the summer of 1348 the Black Plague had ravaged most of Italy (with the notable exception of the city of Rome, which suffered comparatively little) and was well on its dreadful way across the rest of Europe.

The ignorant doctors and people believed that the plague was spread by some sort of contagion. Cities shut their gates against refugees from other cities. But no one knew what caused the horrible pestilence or what to do about it. Pope Clement's personal physician in Avignon, Guy de Chauliac, considered the greatest medical authority of his time, believed that the plague was caused by an unfavorable conjunction of the planets. Many believed that the plague was a punishment sent by God for the sins of mankind.

Smoke from green wood, loud noises, gold "used in the form of a pestle to stir medical potions" all proved useless against the dreadful disease. In Sardinia and Corsica two thirds of the population died. In Venice three quarters of the inhabitants died, in Genoa six sevenths. At Bologna and Padua two thirds, at Piacenza one half, at Pisa seven tenths. Verona lost three quarters of its people and Florence 100,000 out of a total population of 130,000. All these figures are unreliable estimates, but historians agree that Italy as a whole lost at least one half of its population. The plague raged for two years and Italy, like most of Europe, did not regain the population it had had in 1348 for 150 years.

Petrarch, who lived through the plague in Parma, wrote: "Will posterity, if there is one, believe that without anyone's having seen, either coming down from the sky or up from the earth, a devouring fire; without war, without any visible cause of destruction, the world was almost completely depopulated?" Boccaccio said: "By operation of our enormous iniquities, by THE JUST ANGER OF GOD, the plague was sent upon us mortals."

And yet, in spite of their terror and suffering, in spite of the general belief that the Black Plague was a just punishment for their sins inflicted by a wrathful deity, the people of Italy and of Europe were not united by their experience and were not morally influenced for the better by it. Suffering rarely increases virtue. On the contrary, everywhere in Italy, as soon as it was humanly possible, normal politics, war and trade were resumed. There may have been half as many people in Italy in 1350, but there was no lessening of hatred, feuds, conspiracies and wars.

We do not know how Rienzi spent his exile among the Spiritual Franciscans, whether he truly lived as a fellow friar, whether he merely bided his time waiting for the plague to cease, whether his irrational egotism burst forth again and made life miserable for the Fraticelli. All that is certain is that in the early summer of 1350 Rienzi left his mountain asylum and that in August he arrived in Prague and there secured an audience with the Emperor Charles IV, whom three years earlier Rienzi had haughtily summoned to Rome.

Charles IV, King of Bohemia, was the Emperor-elect, a title made secure by the death in a hunting accident in 1347 of his rival claimant to the title, Louis of Bavaria. Intelligent, devout, peaceable and cautious, Charles was a little hunchback with a long black beard. He was a linguist who spoke and wrote fluently German, Czech, French, Italian and Latin. The university he founded in Prague was the first German university. Charles was an able diplomat. He never forgot his debt to Pope Clement VI, whose support had greatly strengthened his pretensions to the imperial crown. While receiving ambassadors and lesser dignitaries granted audiences, it was Charles's custom to whittle on a willow stick. Why did he grant an audience to the fallen and disgraced Roman dictator?

Perhaps he was curious. Only three years before, Rienzi had made a loud noise in the world. And at this time Rienzi seems to have been enjoying another of his periods of manic self-confidence. His eloquence and personal magnetism may have impressed some of Charles's lesser court officials. And Rienzi announced that he had brought to the Emperor a personal and important message from a holy hermit called Fra Angelo.

Whether there was such a hermit is doubtful. The message was certainly confused, something about the imminent murder of Pope Clement VI, the need for Charles to go to Rome to be crowned by a new Italian pope who would have gone there from Avignon, and the need for Rienzi to be crowned too. Since Rienzi had already been crowned six times, what he had in mind is unimaginable.

Rienzi asked the Emperor to authorize him to go to Italy to prepare the way as a sort of advance publicity agent. He would negotiate with Romans and other Italians to avoid bloodshed and to hasten the day of imperial government over all Italy. "There is no other mighty Italian," boasted Rienzi, "who could achieve so much in this respect as I whom all the Romans and the people of Rome's province await so longingly and so lovingly." It does not seem to have occurred to Rienzi that it was unreasonable to ask a favor and a job of a ruler he had publicly threatened to depose. Perhaps it seemed unreasonable to Charles. He arrested Rienzi, forced him to sign a detailed report of his various proposals and sent off the report to Pope Clement in Avignon. Rienzi spent the next two years in prison in Bohemia.

In his confinement Rienzi became even more certain of his divine mission to regenerate Italy and the world and in the process to become once again a powerful political personage. Since he was an excommunicated heretic he naturally opposed the Pope and the Papacy. He conceived the idea that the Church should be deprived of all its temporal power, which at that time was a wildly revolutionary idea. In a letter written to the Emperor Charles from prison, Rienzi said: "Oh God, how much more honest and holy it would be to render unto Caesar the things that are Caesar's, and unto God the things that are God's." Rienzi also wrote from his prison that he would not rest until he had deprived the Pope of his temporal power and restored it to the Emperor. At the same time he insisted that he was not a rebel against the Church—which may have been true in a Pickwickian sense: not against the Church as he would like to have it changed.

Charles IV was deeply suspicious of his strange prisoner's mystical, revolutionary and incoherent ideas. He wrote Rienzi recommending humility and orthodox piety and urged him to cultivate "a humble and contrite heart, which God will not despise." Humility, of course, was the one virtue Rienzi could least cultivate.

Pope Clement VI grew irritated by the reports he received about Rienzi's revolutionary ideas and decided that he would prefer to have the impenitent prisoner close at hand where he could keep a watchful eye on him. So he wrote to the Emperor ordering him to turn Rienzi over to Bishop Giovanni da Spoleto, who would conduct Rienzi to Avignon. It was a long way from Bohemia to Provence, some 600 miles as the crow flies across the Alps, 200 or 300 more miles if the Bishop led his prisoner around Switzerland to avoid the mountains. The Bishop, two nobles and a troop of armed guards rode horseback. Rienzi walked. He was thirty-nine years old, soft from lack of exercise in prison and quite fat. He could not have enjoyed the journey.

When Rienzi was led into the papal palace in Avignon he asked if his old friend Petrarch was there. Petrarch was not present, but he was back in Avignon. He soon heard of Rienzi's inquiry and wrote: "Perhaps he remembered our old friendship, which we had formed in this very place; perhaps he expected me to give him help, which I know I am incapable of giving him." And Petrarch wondered "whether the man is not as unworthy of compassion as he is wretched." He went on to admit that once "on this man I rested my last hopes for the freedom of Italy." But Rienzi had betrayed serious weaknesses, had made fatal mistakes and had not followed Petrarch's advice. So Rienzi "deserved any punishment."

Petrarch's dedication to the freedom of Italy was entirely theoretical. A little later he was delighted to live on the generous patronage of the Visconti lords of Milan and served them as an ambassador. The Visconti were enlightened patrons of the great poet, but they were as firmly opposed to liberty as any tyrants in Italy.

In Avignon Rienzi was shut up in a tower room of the papal palace and chained by one leg to a pillar in the center of the room. His room was pleasant and comfortable compared to most prison cells, medieval or modern. It had three windows and a fireplace. Rienzi was fed from the papal kitchen and was allowed to read a Bible and a Livy. Three cardinals were appointed to investigate his case and to render a decision. Since Rienzi was not only an excommunicated heretic but also a rebel against the Church's temporal power, the cardinals' decision would probably be severe.

So Rienzi collapsed into another of his fits of depression and melancholy. He had no way of knowing how long he might be imprisoned, or what gruesome penalty the cardinals might impose. His release seemed impossible without some miraculous intervention. And that is just what Rienzi may have thought occurred.

Pope Clement VI died. The new Pope, Innocent VI, was a reformer with an entirely new program. As part of his program he set Clement's prisoner free and sent him off to Italy on a mission to prepare the way for reimposing papal rule on the rebellious citizens of Rome. Whether Rienzi formally recanted his numerous theological errors is unknown; but he certainly recanted his recent ambition to destroy the temporal power of the Church. So changeable were Rienzi's political opinions, one wonders if he had any convictions at all. Or did he only have grandiose dreams of various methods of achieving power and glory for himself?

Rienzi was released on September 15, 1353, and given 200 gold florins from the papal treasury for his expenses. He traveled to Rome, but did not enter the city. Rome was then enjoying the transient dictatorship of still another upstart demagogue and the political climate there was hardly suitable for a representative of the Pope. So Rienzi had to wait for a favorable opportunity. He did so in the military camp of Cardinal Albornoz, who had been sent by Pope Innocent IV to reconquer the papal states for the Church.

Cardinal Gil Alvarez Carillo de Albornoz was the greatest warrior-priest in the history of the medieval Church. A Spaniard, he was descended from kings on both sides of his family: on his father's from Alfonso IV of León, and on his mother's from King James of Aragon. A soldier and a statesman by birth and inclination, Albornoz had little interest in the religious purposes of the Church he served. He did have an intense interest in the Church as a great institution and as a worldly power.

Considering the anarchy prevailing in the papal states, the stubborn independence of many of the local despots and the general hatred of the French officials sent to Italy by the Avignon popes, Albornoz seems almost heroic and wonderfully optimistic in taking on his task of reconquest. He left Avignon in August, a month before Rienzi did.

Albornoz was a diplomat and an administrator as well as a general. He subdued rebellious cities, built castles, reorganized governments and persuaded numerous lords to surrender to the Church by promising them that they could retain their lordships if they would only recognize the feudal overlordship of the Church. His tireless energy and his magnanimity won him general admiration.

But the mighty Cardinal was as emotional as he was able. When he experienced a military reverse he lamented that his sufferings crucified him. He was so afflicted with insomnia that at times he could neither sleep nor read. Once the Pope questioned Albornoz' administration of the territories he had reconquered for the Church. His pride deeply offended by this seeming lack of gratitude for his achievements, Albornoz loaded a wagon with the keys of the cities he had captured and sent it off to the Pope.

Rienzi spent a year at Albornoz' military headquarters. While they were at Viterbo a delegation of Roman citizens urged Rienzi to return —why is difficult to understand. But Rienzi had no money left and Albornoz had none to spare with which to help Rienzi return to power in Rome. So Albornoz granted Rienzi permission to go to Perugia and there to try and raise enough money to finance his second *coup d'état*. The Perugians were unmoved by Rienzi's eloquent appeals for money. But two young men from Provence were much impressed. They were the younger brothers of Fra Moreale of Provence, a former friar turned mercenary *condottiere* and bandit, the most notorious, most unscrupulous and most vicious of all the mercenary captains then at large in Italy.

Fra Moreale advanced Rienzi a loan of 4,000 florins, evidently thinking it would be convenient to have as the ruler of Rome his own protégé and debtor. With this sum Rienzi hired a small mercenary force and marched on Rome. On August 1, 1354, seven years after his ignominious flight from the city, Rienzi entered Rome. He was welcomed by cheering crowds who seemed to have forgotten his crimes and follies and to have remembered only his achievements. Rienzi rode through triumphal arches to the Capitol and once again delivered an eloquent oration to the people of Rome. Without any opposition whatever, the seedy, irrational, obese Tribune of the city resumed his former dictatorial power. Some of his former personal magnetism must have remained as well as his masterly oratory.

But the great Colonna family refused to accept the return of the dictator they had helped drive out seven years before. They fought the restored regime from their outlying castles. And Fra Moreale, Rienzi's financial backer and benefactor, came to Rome to see what his 4,000 florins had accomplished. Rienzi, every bit as suspicious a tyrant as he had been during his first administration, had Moreale arrested and thrown into prison along with his two helpful brothers who had negotiated the loan.

Rienzi had Fra Moreale tortured. By the customs of the fourteenth century he no doubt deserved it; but torture seems a somewhat inappropriate return for a generous and useful loan. While on the rack

Moreale said: "How dare you put me to torture? I am the head of the Great Company. I am a knight and desired to rise to great honors. Therefore I sold the cities of Tuscany, and took prisoners, and laid waste the countryside."

In his dungeon cell after his torture Moreale forgot about his robberies, extortions, rapes, murders and assorted cruelties and insisted to a monk that "I have been good in this world and shall be good before God." He was publicly beheaded. Rienzi's ingratitude was shameless; but the justice of Fra Moreale's execution would not have been in doubt if ordered by someone with a better right to do so.

As dictator for the second time Rienzi soon showed that he was not the man he had been. Flabby and monstrously fat, he was habitually unshaven, his eyes bloodshot. He had become a drunkard. "They dried me up in prison," he said. He even washed his face and hands with wine. Rienzi vacillated, changed his mind, laughed without humor and wept without cause. The Tribune was crazed again. He imposed new, bitterly resented taxes. He imprisoned wealthy citizens and released them for ransom.

The end came soon. On October 8 mobs roused by the Colonna and Savelli families surrounded the Palace of the Senate and shouted for Rienzi's death. Friends and servants fled. Rienzi bravely tried to make a speech to the bloodthirsty rabble, but was shouted down. Stones were thrown at him and an arrow pierced his hand. Realizing that he must flee, Rienzi tied some tablecloths together so that he could climb down them into a courtyard. But one of his own relatives saw him and called out from a balcony to the mob, "Look out! He's climbing down at the back of the palace!"

Rienzi reached the courtyard, hesitated there a moment while from barred windows his prisoners watched him. Then he put on his helmet and prepared to die fighting. But he changed his mind, took off his helmet and armor, cut off his beard and blacked his face. He ran to a storeroom, put on a servant's dress and flung a cloth over his head. All this must have taken time, but the angry mob did not penetrate to the inner courtyard.

Trusting to his disguise, Rienzi ran out into the midst of the mob shouting, "There's plenty of plunder inside." But one of the rabble snatched the cloth off Rienzi's head and saw upon his arm a golden bracelet which no servant could have had.

The Tribune was recognized. For a few moments Rienzi stood with folded arms in unaccustomed dignity. Then one of the mob stabbed him in his enormous stomach and he was cut to pieces. His bloated body was hung by the feet from a balcony. He was so fat, a contemporary chronicler wrote, that "he looked like a huge buffalo or cow at the butcher's."

Thus miserably perished the Tribune of Rome and the Immaculate Knight of the Holy Ghost two months and eight days after he became dictator of Rome for the second time.

XIV

The Arch-tyrant

In medieval Italy no family produced as many remarkably gifted members as the Visconti of Milan. From 1282, when Archbishop Ottone led a noble faction to power, until 1447 (a long way into the Renaissance), when the last Duke, Filippo Maria, died, the Visconti ruled in splendor, their wealth and magnificence envied, their power dreaded throughout much of Italy. With their red-gold hair, their military and diplomatic skill, and their ruthless duplicity the leading members of the Visconti dynasty shone like baleful stars over northern Italy. All of the more important members of the family were talented, unscrupulous and ambitious. Several of the Visconti were vicious and one, Giovanni Maria Visconti, was probably mad. He was reputed to hunt human beings with dogs at night in the streets of Milan.

The Visconti, as rulers of Milan and numerous subject cities, were perpetually involved in wars against their neighbors, and as the leading Ghibelline dynasty of Italy were nearly as often at war with the Papacy. Their family banner showed a viper from whose open jaws a naked child had just emerged. The symbolism of this has never been satisfactorily explained. However, numerous Italians who feared the expansionist policies of the Visconti doubtless thought that the Visconti viper was swallowing the child, not disgorging it, and thus symbolized the fate of Milan's neighboring states.

In the middle of the fourteenth century Archbishop Giovanni Visconti succeeded his brother Lucchino as ruler of the Visconti state. A more extreme example of a worldly medieval churchman would be hard to find. An autocratic ruler, a soldier and a statesman, Giovanni was a reformer at home and an expansionist abroad. Although the Archbishop had little visible interest in religion, he was said to rule justly, to patronize the arts, to repress excessive luxury and to reform the local church. But Archbishop Giovanni had only one political ambition: to increase the might and majesty of the Visconti state by conquests or by diplomacy. He bought the city of Bologna for 200,000 gold florins from the lords of that city with the intention of making Bologna his base for further expansion into the Romagna and into Tuscany. And he acquired Genoa when that city, defeated at sea by Venice, preferred subjection to Milan rather than submission to its traditional enemy.

If we can trust the word of a relative of the Archbishop, the Abbot of San Pietro in Lodi, Giovanni celebrated mass only once in his life. He did so when a papal legate ordered him to choose between spiritual and temporal rule. While he considered the matter Giovanni duly conducted a high mass. When the ceremony was over he held a cross in one hand and with the other drew from under his vestments a sword and said to the legate, "Here are my spiritual and temporal powers; with one I shall defend the other." When Pope Clement VI summoned Archbishop Giovanni to Avignon to appear before an ecclesiastical tribunal to defend himself against charges of heresy and contumacy, he wrote the Pope that if he went to Avignon he would present himself there at the head of 12,000 horsemen and 6,000 infantry. Clement was so alarmed that he ceded to Giovanni the papal fief of Bologna (which was already under Visconti rule) on condition of an annual tribute of 12,000 florins.

Giovanni Visconti was an archbishop and so one of the most exalted members of the Church hierarchy, but he was nevertheless a religious skeptic. He used to insist before witnesses that the sacrament of communion was meaningless, that in spite of its consecration the bread remained only bread and the wine only wine. Once Giovanni was asked why, since he was a bishop, he did not celebrate communion. He replied, "I prefer to eat delicious food and to drink good wine."

However outspoken about his skepticism in private he may have been, Archbishop Giovanni was always respectful of religious belief in public. He encouraged spectacular religious processions. He increased the Church's charity to the poor and established a number of new charitable foundations.

Giovanni Visconti lived in splendor, with all the lavish luxury of medieval royalty. His court included so many priests, secretaries, musicians, pages, servants and knights that it was said to number 600 persons. But all this pomp and glory lasted only a short time. The great Archbishop Giovanni, Lord of Milan, died on October 5, 1354, after a minor operation in which a boil on his eyebrow was lanced. Presumably he died of some other cause. He was succeeded jointly by his three nephews, sons of his deceased brother Stefano—Matteo, Bernabò and Galeazzo, who divided the Milanese state into three parts.

Four years before their uncle's death, on the same day in August of 1350 Bernabò and Galeazzo Visconti were married. Bernabò, the second brother, was an athlete and a warrior with a small round head and a short beard. He married Beatrice della Scala, daughter of Mastino II della Scala, who was usually called Regina because of her pride and imperious will. Galeazzo, the third brother, was a soldier, too, but without his brother Bernabò's enthusiasm for battle. So cultivated that he was almost a precursor of the Renaissance prince, Galeazzo loved books and was a friend and patron of Petrarch. He wore his beautiful red-gold hair in long ringlets ornamented with flowers or confined in a silken net. He married thirteen-year-old Bianca of Savoy, sister of Count Amadeus VI of Savoy.

Shortly after the three brothers assumed power it became apparent to the two younger Visconti that Matteo was a menace to their joint lordship. Matteo was irresponsible, incompetent and afflicted with satyriasis. No woman in Milan, no matter how lofty her social position, was safe from his insatiable lust. Such a man could not be trusted to rule a third of the Visconti state. His follies and stupidities might bring disaster upon them all. Providentially, however, early in 1255 Matteo died. It was widely believed in Milan and in much of Italy that Bernabò and Galeazzo had murdered their degenerate brother with a dish of poisoned quails. They never denied the rumored crime.

After dividing Matteo's share of the family inheritance the brothers settled down to rule their respective halves of the Visconti state. Bernabò had the eastern half including the city of Bologna, Galeazzo the western half. Milan was divided between them. They each inherited a war. Galeazzo fought his brother-in-law of Savoy in a dispute about towns and boundaries. Bernabò fought the Church in a dispute over Bologna, which the late Archbishop Giovanni had bought, but which the Pope claimed was an integral part of the papal states.

Bernabò and Galeazzo were not congenial and did not like each other. But they maintained formally correct family relations and regularly co-operated with each other in military and diplomatic operations. After several years in which Galeazzo lived in a castle on one side of Milan and Bernabò lived in a castle on the other, Galeazzo decided that his truculent, arrogant and explosively bad-tempered brother was too difficult a neighbor. The city of Pavia twenty miles to the south would make a much more comfortable residence.

Unfortunately, Pavia was an independent city. It took Galeazzo three years of war and a six-month siege, in which Bernabò loyally helped him, to capture Pavia. As soon as the din of battle ceased Galeazzo summoned architects and began the construction of the great Visconti palace which still stands. In 1365 Galeazzo moved in and thenceforward made it his permanent home. And there in the summer months Petrarch used to visit Galeazzo. The poet had spent eight years in Milan. He had served the Visconti by writing elegant diplomatic letters, delivering orations and acting as an ambassador in Prague, Venice and Paris. But in 1361 during an outbreak of plague Petrarch fled from Milan and went to Padua, where he enjoyed the patronage of the lord of the city, Francesco da Carrara.

Galeazzo Visconti was merciful and preferred fining criminals to mutilating or executing them. Crippled by gout, he led a far less strenuous life than Bernabò. As he grew older the handsome and attractive prince aged prematurely and became notorious for his avarice. He was ambitious and succeeded in marrying two of his children into the royal houses of France and England. Since the Visconti brothers did not have a title between them, these alliances were splendid demonstrations of the wealth, power and importance of the Milanese state. Bernabò also married his children into ruling houses, those of Bavaria, Austria, Württemberg, Cyprus and Mantua.

Galeazzo's oldest child, Giangaleazzo, was born on October 15, 1351. While he was still a small boy, according to a popular story, at one of his father's banquets he was asked who was the wisest man present. Without hesitation Giangaleazzo pointed to Petrarch.

In 1364 when he was twelve years old Giangaleazzo Visconti was married to Isabella of Valois, daughter of King Jean II of France. Since Jean was desperately poor because of the expenses of the Hundred Years' War and because of the ransom he had had to pay the English, Galeazzo had been able to make a deal with him. For the privilege of marrying his son to the daughter of the proudest royal family in Europe he paid 100,000 florins.

Four years later, in 1368, Galeazzo's daughter Violante was married in Milan to Lionel, Duke of Clarence, the second son of King Edward III. This alliance was even more expensive than the French one. Galeazzo agreed to provide Violante with a dowry of 200,000 florins. The wedding was so grand that contemporary chroniclers described its wonders with almost breathless awe.

The Plantagenet Duke marched into Milan accompanied by 2,000 English archers. He was met by Galeazzo and his wife and also by young Giangaleazzo and his wife. Eighty Milanese ladies in elaborate dresses (the girdles alone cost eighty florins apiece) were in attendance. Giangaleazzo was accompanied by thirty knights and thirty grooms. During the wedding ceremony Bernabò gave his niece away. The wedding banquet which followed the ceremony is famous, and deservedly so.

Whether the dishes consumed or the presents given by Galeazzo to his English son-in-law are the more impressive is a difficult question. Let us consider the food first. The guests seated at two large tables in the courtyard of Galeazzo's Milanese castle were served eighteen courses. Sixteen of these courses consisted of meat and fish. The seventeenth was cheese and the eighteenth fruit. For the first course there were roast suckling pigs almost magically spouting fire from their mouths. In rapid succession followed roast calf, trout, quail, partridges, ducks, heron, beef and eel pasties, lampreys, roast kid, leverets and fawns, venison and beef galantine, pullets with red and green sauces, salted tongue, rabbits, and peacocks with green vegetables and beans. All this was washed down with wine. How the banqueters survived such a terrifying meal, although a topic of considerable interest, is not recorded.

Galeazzo's presents to the bridegroom were a dazzling display of conspicuous wealth and of monumentally vulgar ostentation. Between the courses the presents came in what seemed a never-ending variety. There were dozens of greyhounds and bloodhounds, goshawks, sparrowhawks and falcons, a dozen suits of armor for jousting and another dozen for serious battle. Two suits of each set were engraved with the crests of the Visconti and of Clarence. After the ninth course a dozen rolls of gold brocade and a dozen rolls of silk were presented to the lucky bridegroom. Then came flasks of enameled silver and twelve basins of silver-gilt. A dozen superb horses followed, equipped with gilded saddles, lances, shields and helmets. After these came six warhorses and six tournament horses, making a total of twenty-four. The English Duke was then presented with a cloak sewn thick with pearls, a hood decorated with a large flower made of pearls and another cloak covered with pearls and lined with ermine. Jeweled clasps followed. Then just for a change of pace and a pleasing variety Galeazzo gave Lionel twelve fat oxen, although what he was expected to do with the beasts is hard to imagine. Slaughter them to feed his archers on his homeward journey? Finally the ludicrous proceedings were concluded with gifts of two very special horses and of seventy-six other horses for Lionel's nobles and gentlemen.

What the Duke of Clarence thought of this extravaganza is not known. Whatever he thought, surely Lionel was suitably impressed by his father-in-law's wealth and generosity. Unfortunately, he did not live long to enjoy his magnificent gifts. He died only a few weeks after the wedding. His archers enlisted with the Marquis of Montferrat to fight their recent Visconti host and his young widow returned to Pavia and the care of her father.

Galeazzo Visconti was an able and intelligent man, but he was far surpassed in celebrity and power by his brother. Bernabò Visconti is the

archetype of the medieval Italian tyrant, typical except for the fact that
Bernabò carried everything to an excess beyond the capacities of lesser
despots. Bernabò's passion for justice was sincere and famous; but he
spoiled it by the ferocity of his punishments. He loved his wife, Regina,
devotedly and was inconsolable when she died. He and Regina had
fifteen children, five sons and ten daughters. But Bernabò made no pretense of fidelity to his wife. He kept a harem of mistresses and freely
acknowledged that he had thirty or more bastard children. Bernabò's
furious rages terrified all around him. While they lasted no one dared
come near him except Regina. He exulted in warfare like a barbarian
chieftain of the heroic age and regularly fought, sword in hand, in the
front ranks.

Bernabò Visconti was probably born in 1320 and so was about thirty-
four when he came to power after Archbishop Giovanni's death. He
ruled his half of the Visconti state for thirty-one years. He was an old-
fashioned tyrant who liked to do everything himself and to make all
decisions himself. He employed as few officials as possible and never
allowed anyone to question his autocratic authority. A famous story
relates how an archbishop of Milan dared to remonstrate with Bernabò
about some edict he had made. "Do you not know," shouted Bernabò,
"you fool, that here I am pope and emperor and lord in all my lands and
that no one can do anything in my lands save I permit it—no, not even
God?"

Bernabò's rule was harsh. But for thirty-one years, as Rienzi had done
in Rome for a few months, he made the streets of Milan safe, and he so
reduced crime that it was claimed "that a man might go from end to end
of his land with no arms but a stick." Numerous stories were told about
his sincere efforts to promote justice. Bernabò was more severe to the rich
than to the poor in his judicial decisions. He is supposed to have said
when he held court, "Come and fear not, ye weak, for the rich and great
have their advocates whom they pay, but I will be advocate for those who
cannot pay." Pietro Azario, a contemporary chronicler who much admired
Bernabò, wrote, "Truly the Lord Bernabò loved justice." We can believe
it.

But our modern conceptions of justice may well be revolted when we
learn about the punishments Bernabò imposed on the guilty. Some of

Equestrian statue of Bernabò Visconti, Milan. *Alinari*

the stories told about Bernabò may be legends based upon actual incidents and exaggerated in order to dramatize Bernabò's high-minded justice or to emphasize his cruelty. One of these tales relates how Bernabò, riding through the streets of Milan, came upon a crowd staring at a dead body which had been left on the pavement because a priest had refused burial and funeral rites until he was paid. Bernabò ordered the body buried and the avaricious priest also buried—alive.

Another story is about a wicked man who illegally enclosed a poor widow's garden. Bernabò forced the land thief to dig a ditch outlining the correct boundaries of the garden and then buried him in it. Still another tale tells of a girl who was abducted against her will. Bernabò arrested the guilty lover and forced him to marry his unfortunate victim. But immediately after the wedding Bernabò had the man beheaded and then presented his property to the newly made widow as a dowry.

Such bizarre punishments seem cruel and unusual today. But by medieval law and custom they were, if hardly usual, at least not unreasonable. Bernabò's laws protecting his hounds and game parks, however, were outrageously cruel even by the standards of his own time. Bernabò is said to have owned 5,000 hounds (surely an exaggeration!) which he billeted on reluctant peasants and others who were charged with their care. If a dog lost too much weight, grew too fat or died, the involuntary dog trainer might lose a foot, a hand or his life.

Even more atrocious were the punishments Bernabò inflicted on poachers. People who did not pay the fines imposed for minor poaching offenses had their houses burned down. And those who dared to kill a boar, Bernabò's favorite quarry, were either blinded or hanged. The most notorious example of Bernabò's sadistic cruelties is the *quaresima,* or Lenten punishment of forty days, which Bernabò is credited with inventing. This was a series of tortures, mutilations and amputations supposedly inflicted on alternate days for forty days. If the victim was still alive at the end he was beheaded. The *quaresima* may not be Bernabò's invention at all, but that of his enemies as a propaganda atrocity story. No can could live for forty days suffering such horrors. Or the story may be an exaggeration of a forty-day period of much milder torture which could be endured.

Two other authentic stories provide wonderful glimpses of Bernabò's arrogance and brutality. In 1361 Pope Innocent VI sent an embassy to Bernabò consisting of two men. One of them was an abbot who later became Pope Urban V. They delivered to Bernabò a parchment decorated with lead seals which contained the official Bull of Bernabò's excommunication. This the envoys handed to Bernabò when they found him seated upon a bridge over the Lambro River. The grim Lord of Milan took the parchment, read it and then stared down into the water. Suddenly he turned menacingly on the two clerics and asked them whether they would rather eat or drink. Suspecting that to drink would be to drown, they chose to eat and then were commanded to eat the parchment, seals and all. They did. It is not exactly surprising that Pope Urban V was a bitter enemy of Bernabò Visconti.

Seventeen years later, shortly after Galeazzo's death and Giangaleazzo's assumption of the lordship of the western half of the Visconti state, domineering uncle and polite and pacific nephew became involved in a ridiculous dispute about a hawk. The bird was captured by the governor of Monza, a city in Giangaleazzo's domain. Bernabò claimed the hawk was his. When the governor refused to hand over the bird, Bernabò planned to march on Monza, forcibly take possession of the hawk and arrest the impertinent governor.

Giangaleazzo wrote his uncle courteously but firmly: "We have before given our opinion that the hawk did not bear your sign and that it was given to our captain of Monza by one of his own subjects in the presence of Rodolfo. But whether the hawk be yours or not, the territory of Monza is ours and we pray you refrain from sending such letters."

Bernabò was enraged by such back talk from his young junior partner in the Visconti state. His reply was enough to chill Giangaleazzo's blood: "If it does not please you I shall send you no more letters, neither white nor black, nor send ambassadors. . . . But it would be well to remind you that in the reign of Lucchino, when I was but a boy, I killed a man with my bare hands for insulting our house. I am not disposed to suffer injury without avenging it. You say that you do not wish me to interfere in your affairs. By Holy Mary! there is not one person to you so dear that I will not punish him if he offends me."

It is unnecessary and it would be tedious to describe every battle and campaign in Bernabò's unending wars. But certain episodes and circumstances are interesting and worth attention. They illustrate Bernabò's masterful character, his duplicity and the prevailing political climate in Italy during the fourteenth century.

In 1355 the governor of Bologna, Giovanni da Oleggio, whom Archbishop Giovanni had appointed, revolted, declared himself lord of an independent Bologna, and moved into the new Visconti fortress recently built by the Archbishop. Bernabò's youth, Bologna's distance from Milan and Bologna's wealth and strategic location were all too tempting. Oleggio, who was a Visconti himself by some distant connection, was as ambitious and treacherous as the more famous members of the family.

Bernabò, of course, could not permit such a drastic amputation of the Visconti state. While he considered what steps to take, Oleggio offered him an annual tribute of 16,000 florins for as long as he was left in unmolested control of the city. Bernabò accepted the bribe and made his plans. Oleggio ruled Bologna so cruelly that it was easy for Bernabò to find conspirators willing to open the gates to his troops. But when one of the conspirators in a moment of premature enthusiasm shot at Oleggio with a poisoned arrow and missed, Oleggio found the conspirators just as easily. He beheaded them all.

Bernabò tried again with another group of sympathizers and again Oleggio discovered the plot and executed the plotters. But Bernabò's persistence frightened Oleggio. Being lord of a city Bernabò Visconti considered his had ceased to be an attractive situation. To escape to an easier life and to thwart Bernabò, Oleggio sold Bologna to the Pope, who had always considered Bologna papal property, no matter what upstart temporarily claimed to be its ruler.

The deal seemed all the more desirable because in 1358 Bernabò had attacked Bologna in force. So in 1359 Oleggio surrendered the city to Pope Innocent's representative, none other than the Cardinal Albornoz who reconquered the papal states for the Church. In return for Bologna, Albornoz made Oleggio lord and papal vicar of the city of Fermo and governor of the March of Ancona. On March 17, 1360, Albornoz' nephew, Blasco Fernández, marched into Bologna at the head of papal troops and assumed the rule of the city in the name of Pope Innocent.

Bernabò's war with various popes over Bologna lasted (with several intermissions) for the next eighteen years. It was provoked by their rival claims to Bologna, but broader issues were involved. Bernabò's ambition to expand the Visconti domains was known and feared. The popes' determination to wield temporal power over as large an area of Italy as possible—even if their rule required constant war, numerous atrocities and the employment of cruel and corrupt French officials—was equally well known. Bernabò was a cruel tyrant; but his opposition to the temporal power of the Church was reasonable and in the tradition of Barbarossa, Frederick II and Cangrande della Scala. But by now the alliances had shifted. Milan no longer led a Lombard League as an ally of the Church. Instead Milan fought against the Church and its ally, an anti-Visconti league organized by Albornoz.

During the war three popes excommunicated Bernabò—Innocent VI, Urban V and Gregory XI—and the last two proclaimed crusades against him. In retaliation Bernabò confiscated ecclesiastical property, arrested and tortured members of the clergy who preached rebellion against him, and once forced a priest of Parma to pronounce anathema on Pope Innocent VI and on all his cardinals from the top of a high tower while on the piazza below Bernabò and his friends laughed at the exquisite brilliance of their practical joke.

Several times during the war Bernabò brought off diplomatic *coups* of a high order. Once when Cardinal Albornoz and an army of German crusaders seemed about to overwhelm him Bernabò offered to make peace and to surrender all his castles in the *contado* of Bologna. But, he insisted, he would not deal with Albornoz. A new legate would have to replace him. So anxious was Pope Urban V to make peace so that he could get on with a genuine crusade against Moslems that he recalled the greatest soldier the Church ever employed and made a deal with Bernabò. Pope Urban guaranteed 500,000 gold florins to Bernabò in return for the castles. It was a triumph of crafty diplomacy for Bernabò. At one stroke he obtained an enormous sum and the removal of his most redoubtable opponent.

In 1375 during one of the occasional truces which interrupted the Visconti-Church war the papal legate of Bologna dismissed from the Church's service Sir John Hawkwood, the celebrated English *condottiere*. Being a mercenary, Hawkwood disliked unemployment. To occupy his time profitably Hawkwood led his troops on a raid into Florentine territory and extorted from the republic 130,000 florins, his price for going away. The Florentines were already suspicious of the Church policy of constructing a state which stretched from Bologna to the Kingdom of Naples. They believed that the legate had instigated Hawkwood's raid and extortion. They may have been right.

So Florence, a Guelf city and traditionally an ally of the Church, led a war against the Church to liberate the cities of central Italy from papal rule and from the tyranny of French vicars appointed by the pope. A Florentine official made a speech in which he advocated that Florence seek an alliance with Bernabò Visconti: "I know full well," he said, "that he is perpetually seeking his own ends, and is not likely to concern himself about our interests; but he is fiercely opposed to the priests and the power of the French in Italy. The hatred which we alike share will give us common interests."

Bernabò was delighted to ally himself with Florence in the War of the Eight Saints, so called because of eight prominent Florentine officials who led their city into the war. In two years of fighting under the banner of freedom the allies, joined by numerous other cities, liberated sixty-four towns and captured 1,576 fortified places. But two years of war bore heavily on the Florentines. Martial enthusiasm flagged. Florence decided to seek a peace with Pope Gregory XI. Bernabò also thought that a brief peace would be expedient, so he betrayed Florence and got in touch with the Pope first. When Florence opened direct negotiations Pope Gregory suggested that Bernabò Visconti (of all people!) should be arbitrator.

There had to be some explanation for so astounding a suggestion. There was. It was customary at the conclusion of hostilities for a foe of the Church to pay an indemnity. Bernabò arranged with Pope Gregory (hitherto his implacable enemy) to split the payment of any indemnity he persuaded the Florentines to pay. So, as was only to be expected, Bernabò demanded an enormous sum, 800,000 florins. So bizarre a situation seems almost farcical. Bernabò was Florence's ally and an excommunicate who had fought the Church for years. Cynical opportunism on both sides could not have been more shameless. But Pope Gregory XI

Sir John Hawkwood, fresco of a proposed equestrian statue by Paolo Uccello; in the Duomo, Florence. *Alinari*

died and the great swindle fell through. The new pope dispensed with Bernabò's services as arbitrator and settled for an indemnity of only 250,000 florins. Bernabò never saw one of them.

Sir John Hawkwood, whose mercenary raid angered Florence into going to war against the Church, was a remarkable soldier, the most successful *condottiere* of the fourteenth century. He was born in 1320 (probably) in the village of Sible Hedingham in Essex, the son of a tanner. He was illiterate. When he was about twenty he joined the army of King Edward III fighting the Hundred Years' War in France. He distinguished himself at the Battle of Crécy under Edward and at the Battle of Poitiers under the Black Prince. Shortly after Poitiers Hawkwood was knighted by King Edward.

Hawkwood went to Italy about 1360 and joined a mercenary band called the White Company commanded by a German knight named Albert Sterz. Members of the company wore white surcoats over their armor and displayed white banners. Like the other mercenary bands in fourteenth-century Italy, the White Company specialized in looting, raiding and ransoms. It differed from the others in superior military efficiency. In 1363 Hawkwood was elected commander. He introduced into Italy the battle tactics which had won the great victories of Agincourt, Crécy and Poitiers for the English. His men were archers and pikemen who fought on foot. Whenever possible Hawkwood drew them up on some defensible site and let the enemy knights charge and be destroyed.

In his long and successful career in Italy Sir John Hawkwood fought for and against the Church, for and against Florence, and for and against Bernabò Visconti. Usually Hawkwood was loyal to his employers, but he was always as tough and unscrupulous as his profession demanded. He led his soldiers in several terrible sacks as well as in battle. Once Hawkwood encountered several monks who politely greeted him, "Peace, *messer,* peace."

Hawkwood snarled at them, "May God take away your alms!"

The monks meekly replied, "Excuse us, lord, we meant only to be kind."

Hawkwood reproved them, "You know well that I live by war, and that peace would be my undoing."

The great *condottiere* served Florence for many years, during which he took several sabbatical leaves to fight for others. He died in 1394, aged seventy-four, almost in an odor of sanctity. The Florentine republic gave him a state funeral and honored his memory by planning an equestrian statue, which was never made, and having a fresco of the proposed statue painted by Paolo Uccello high on the left wall of the nave of the Duomo.

Early in Hawkwood's Italian career Bernabò Visconti, then in alliance with Pisa against Florence, hired Hawkwood, who continued to serve him for the next nine years. But in 1372 Bernabò and Hawkwood quarreled. Giovanni Acuto, as the Italians called him, at once went over to the Church, but he accomplished little against his recent employer. Pope Urban V wrote Hawkwood a letter in which he complained that "Bernabò, that son of Belial, has lost neither city, fortress nor town of any sort."

Hawkwood fought for the Church from 1372 to 1374. After his dismissal he acted as an independent raider in Tuscany for a year. Early in 1375 he was reengaged by the Church, but in June of that year he signed a secret agreement to return to the service of Bernabò and Florence. For the rest of the year he pretended to be still faithful to the Church and waited until 1376 before officially joining Bernabò and Florence.

When Bernabò Visconti reengaged Hawkwood, to cement their friendship and their contract a marriage was arranged between the fifty-five-year-old *condottiere* and Bernabò's bastard daughter Donnina. The bride was one of Bernabò's five children by his favorite mistress, Donnina dei Porri. Regina, Bernabò's haughty wife, attended the wedding ceremony in Milan and so did Bernabò's many daughters, both legitimate and illegitimate. Regina gave the bride a present of 1,000 ducats in a gold vase.

After Bernabò and Florence made peace with the Church, Hawkwood continued to fight for Bernabò in Lombardy, but Regina did not think he fought as energetically as he should. Bernabò and Hawkwood quarreled furiously and so once again Hawkwood quit Bernabò's service. To make his position clear Bernabò offered a reward of thirty florins for every member of Hawkwood's company, dead or alive. For the rest of his life Hawkwood served Florence, sometimes against Bernabò.

Some time in 1372 a young woman in Siena, who believed that she frequently received direct revelations from God and the saints, wrote Hawkwood a letter. Catherine knew that Pope Urban V wanted to organize a real crusade against Moslems and she grieved that her fellow Christians in Italy waged perpetual war against each other, devastating much of their beautiful country. "Since God and our Holy Father have ordered the expedition against the infidels and since you delight so much in making war and fighting, I pray you war no more upon Christians, because it offends God; but go against the others. How cruel it is that we who are Christians should persecute one another! I am much amazed that, having promised, as I have heard, to go to die for Christ in this holy enterprise, you should now be making war here. This is not the holy disposition God demands of you."

It was like shouting in a boiler factory. Nobody heard, least of all Hawkwood. Nobody was interested in crusading any more, although various popes would preach crusades for many years to come. And no one was interested in making peace—except as an expedient pause between wars.

In the following year an ambassador from Bernabò Visconti arrived in Siena in November and did not depart until late in January. Since Catherine was Siena's most famous citizen, widely venerated as a saint and exceedingly influential with the clergy, historians have speculated that the ambassador may have interviewed her. It would have been a triumph of foreign policy and public relations to persuade Catherine to look kindly on the terrible Bernabò, to understand that his evil reputation was unjustified and that he was really a reformer like herself.

One of Catherine's biographers, Edmund G. Gardner, thought that the ambassador may have argued that Bernabò was "a kind of scourge of God, divinely ordained to punish the iniquities of the pastors of the Church." Such a theory might excuse Bernabò's frequent persecutions of priests and monks. In any case, Catherine, who regularly told popes, kings and despots what they should do, dictated two long letters to Bernabò Visconti. She preached to that incorrigible sinner on the love of God, the vanity of worldly power which may pass away in a moment, and the need to free the soul from the Devil's temptations by spiritually washing in the blood of Christ.

Since worldly power was Bernabò's paramount purpose in life we can imagine the incomprehension and astonishment with which he must have read Catherine's letters:

"I tell you, dearest father and brother in sweet Christ Jesus, that God does not wish you, nor anyone else, to make yourself the executioner of His ministers; for He has reserved this to Himself and committed it to His vicar. And if the vicar does not do what he should (and it is bad if he does not), we must humbly await the punishment and chastisement of the Supreme Judge, God eternal, even if our possessions are taken away from us by these men. I pray you in the name of Christ crucified, concern yourself no more with this. Possess your own cities in peace; punish your own subjects when they do wrong; but never touch those who are the ministers of this glorious and precious blood, which you can have by no other hands than theirs. . . ."

Catherine continued to command Bernabò to make peace with the Church and to prepare to participate in a new crusade which the Pope would soon proclaim. She also wrote to Regina, whose pride and avarice were notorious all over Italy, urging on her the virtue of charity.

Catherine of Siena was a saint, a mystic and one of the most extraordinary characters of the Middle Ages. She was born in Siena on March 25, 1347, the twenty-fourth of the twenty-five children of Jacomo di Benincasa, a moderately prosperous dyer, and his wife, Lapa di Puccio di Piagente. From the age of five Catherine saw visions. While still a child she fasted for prolonged periods, prayed for hours at a time and flagellated herself. Once her father reported that he saw a snow-white dove fluttering over her head while she knelt in prayer. She never learned to write, but could read a little. She dictated her letters, sometimes two at a time to two different scribes. Four hundred of these exhortations, instructions, commands and prayers addressed to the most powerful people of her time survive.

An ascetic who died young because of her excessive austerities, Catherine ate so little that her confessor and disciple, a Dominican friar named Raimondo, wrote, "In the time during which I was allowed to be the witness of her life she lived without any nourishment of food or drink." In his pious enthusiasm Fra Raimondo obviously exaggerated a trifle.

But there is no doubt that Catherine ate very little. She slept on a bare board and kept a steel chain wound around her waist so tightly that it broke her skin. And she constantly tried to do with as little sleep as possible, sometimes managing, it is said, with as little as a half-hour of sleep in two days.

No human body could survive such abuse long. Catherine's did not. She died in 1380 at the age of thirty-three. How well any human mind could endure such suffering and privation without serious damage cannot be known. But that any mind would be affected by it seems probable. Catherine of Siena, who was afflicted with hallucinations and irrational obsessions, was a profoundly abnormal person—as, indeed, many saints have been. Her courage was sublime, her religious zeal was without limit, her awareness of the sins, follies and crimes of her own time was deep and painful.

In 1362 when she was only fifteen years old Catherine joined the Sisters of the Penance of Saint Dominic. A pure and dedicated girl, she wanted to serve both God and mankind. She wore a black mantle with part of it drawn over her face. She was subject to frequent trances in which she said she enjoyed intimate conversations with Jesus and the Virgin Mary. In her trances, an eyewitness said, "she appeared like a statue which retains nothing but the human form."

Catherine of Siena combined in her own person extraordinary humility and astounding spiritual arrogance. She was convinced of her own sinfulness, because she had been granted marvelous divine favors and so should have eliminated more sin in others than she did. "I am the greatest of all sinners," she said.

Her arrogance was so great that she considered herself authorized to reprove and instruct not only the secular rulers of the world but also its spiritual rulers, including the Pope himself. Catherine went to Avignon on a mission to Pope Gregory XI and on parting from him admonished him with these astonishing words: "Into your hands I give the interests of the Church; husband its glory." But the Pope, according to orthodox Catholic doctrine, had already been put in command of the interests of the Church by God Himself as manifested in his divinely inspired election by the College of Cardinals. If one wonders who was

Catherine of Siena to make a gift of the Church's interests, the answer is plain. She thought that she was the direct representative of God and so occupied a far higher spiritual elevation than any pope.

Sometime while Catherine was still quite young (the date is unknown) she had a vision in which she was spiritually married to Jesus. Conflicting accounts have her marrying the child Jesus and Jesus the adult saviour. Marriage to Jesus can mean dedication to the worship of Jesus, but Catherine seems to have believed that her mystic marriage was more personal. In one of her dictated letters she wrote:

"He enters into my cell, my sweetest Spouse. He sings holy hymns to me, and then he lays himself down upon my couch and makes me drunk with the delights of heaven. He came to me once in the dress of a mendicant friar, that I might not know Him; and thus disguised, he begged for alms in a voice so filled with anguish that, having nothing else, I passed Him my cowl, my robe, my sash, to comfort that sore-afflicted One whose urgencies and prayers had grown ever more piteous. Then at last when I had taken away the final veil that wrapped me, He assumed His godly shape, and caught me away with Him to the Seventh Heaven."

It seems probable that such a vision, with Catherine parting with her last garment, contained an element of repressed sexuality of which the dreamer was entirely unaware.

Throughout her life Catherine was obsessed by blood as a religious symbol, the redeeming blood of Jesus Christ. Thus she once wrote a letter to her confessor urging him in rapturous phrases to "hide himself in the wounded side of the Son of God." And she herself told him that in her visions she "was permitted constantly to approach her lips to the side of the Lord and quaff his blood"!

A gruesomely revealing story about Catherine's blood obsession is told by Ferdinand Schevill in his *Siena: The History of a Medieval Commune*:

"Niccolo Tuldo was a Perugian youth who, during a visit to neighboring Siena, called attention to himself by offensive criticism of the government. He was seized, and immediately, according to the inhuman justice of the day, condemned to death. The sentence, falling on him like a bolt from the blue, almost drove him out of his mind. He raged, cursed, and refused all religious consolation, until Catherine, prompted by her quick sympathies, came to knock at his prison cell. With sweet compulsion she recalled him to himself, and in a few visits converted the young worldling into a soldier of the cross, for whom death lost every aspect of terror. Having promised to be with him at the hour of trial, she awaited him at the foot of the scaffold, around which crowded the usual multitude of eager spectators.

" 'He arrived like a gentle lamb, and seeing me, began to laugh, and desired that I make him the sign of the cross; and when he had received the sign, I said, "Down; down to the espousals, my sweet brother, which will bring you quickly to everlasting life." He sank down with great humility, and I laid his head upon the block, and knelt at his side, and recalled to him the blood of the lamb. His lips kept repeating the words Jesus and Catherine, and he was still speaking when I held his head in my hands. . . .'

"Then Catherine kneeling and pressing the head to her bosom passed into an ecstasy in which she saw the soul of Niccolo mount upward to where Christ waited, clothed in the radiance of the sun. And a remarkable feature of this ecstasy was that it took place amidst a perfect riot of overwrought senses. With hands and dress bathed in the blood of the victim, which somehow in her mystic joy she associated with the blood spilt by the Redeemer, she wrote these intoxicated words: 'And the fragrance of the blood brought me such peace and quiet that I could not bear to wash it away.' "

Catherine of Siena preached the love of God and the necessity of peace. She herself composed peace among several feuding factions in the *contado* of Siena. She was believed to have cast out numerous demons. She acquired a group of men and women disciples called Caterini who accompanied her when she journeyed to Florence, Avignon and Rome.

In 1374 when Catherine was twenty-seven the Black Plague returned to Italy. Catherine ignored her personal danger and went from one stricken household to another, praying with the dying and helping bury the dead. In her own family home in Siena two of her brothers and a sister died and eight of her nephews and nieces. Catherine buried all these dead relatives herself!

From Siena Catherine wrote letters to Pope Gregory XI in Avignon insisting that he bring the Papacy back to Rome and commanding him to abide by her moral and religious injunctions. "Be a true successor to Saint Gregory. Love God. Be bound neither to father, nor mother, nor friends, nor the requirements of the world. Go forward. Complete what you have well begun. Make haste and tarry not, for delay has caused a spate of ills, and the Demon spends his wits to thwart you. . . . Come without fear, for God is with you. Wait not for time, because time waits for none. Answer the Holy Ghost." Catherine called the supreme head of the Christian Church her "Babbo," which means "Daddy" or "Papa."

Distressed by the War of the Eight Saints, Catherine offered herself to Florence as a mediator. The republic accepted, but only conditionally. She was not made an official ambassador empowered to negotiate, but she was appointed a sort of advance emissary who was supposed to smooth the way for the authentic ambassadors whenever they should be sent. Catherine and twenty-two of her disciples arrived in Avignon on June 18, 1376. Unfortunately, while she was traveling to Avignon there was a change of government in Florence and Catherine was repudiated. She no longer had any diplomatic status. But such a trivial detail did not embarrass Catherine. Was she not an ambassador of Christ's?

In Avignon Catherine scolded Pope Gregory for his flagrant nepotism and for not returning immediately to Rome. Yet Gregory treated her with great respect. He was obliged to, for Catherine was universally considered a saint. But the Pope's young niece, Elys de Beaufort, suspected that Catherine's trances were bogus. So she jabbed Catherine's foot with a needle while Catherine was in a trance. The saint did not flinch. Elys admitted that the trance must be genuine.

Pope Gregory left Avignon in the autumn of 1376 and arrived in Rome in January of 1377. He may have been influenced by Catherine's exhortations, but he probably also went in order to be on the spot in waging the Church's war against Florence and Bernabò Visconti and in negotiating to conclude it. Catherine returned to Siena.

Early in 1378 Catherine went to Florence as an emissary of Pope Gregory XI, perhaps more interested in discussions with members of the Guelf party in Florence than with government officials. At a time of riot and rebellion in Florence Catherine became deeply involved in local politics. She seems to have tried to get herself killed by a furious mob in the pious hope of winning for herself "the red rose of martyrdom."

In March of 1378 Pope Gregory died and was succeeded by Urban VI, a man of such violent rages, terrible pride and horrible cruelty that he probably was insane. His election was contested and a faction of the cardinals elected a rival pope who assumed the name of Clement VII. His evil character was notorious, but he probably was sane. Thus began the great schism which lasted for 139 years, with two popes for most of that time and as many as three at the end. Catherine considered Urban VI the rightful pope and wrote him numerous letters of good advice which he ignored. But Urban was grateful for Catherine's useful support in the schism, and in November he invited her to come to Rome.

Catherine left Siena in December with twenty-four disciples and arrived in Rome in January of 1379. There she and her disciples lived exclusively on alms. During Lent of the following year Catherine went to Saint Peter's and prayed before Giotto's *Navicella*, which was a mosaic of Christ and his disciples on board a small ship. As she prayed Catherine suddenly felt the weight of the ship transferred to her own shoulders and her frail, emaciated body collapsed on the pavement. The lower part of her body was paralyzed and so remained until her death. Recently she had eaten less than her usual little and was frequently heard to say that the mere thought of a meal was to her like the thought of being executed.

Catherine died on April 29, 1380. Her fame grew after her death and eighty-one years later she was canonized by her fellow Sienese, Pope Pius II. Reverently preserved in the church of San Domenico are Catherine's head and one of her fingers.

Nearly two years before Catherine's death Galeazzo Visconti died in Pavia and was succeeded as ruler of the western half of the Visconti state by his son Giangaleazzo, then aged twenty-six. A highly intelligent, although timid young man, Giangaleazzo gave every indication of being a capable ruler far more interested in statesmanship and diplomacy than in war. His French princess, Isabella of Valois, had died six years before, and so had his first child, a son named after his father. Bernabò considered his nephew a milksop.

As he approached the advanced age of sixty Bernabò Visconti grew increasingly dictatorial and violent. He was so suspicious that somebody might try to assassinate him that around every residence he lived in he created a forbidden zone. The penalty for entering it without permission was death. Bernabò's five legitimate sons were intensely jealous of their fortunate cousin Giangaleazzo. He ruled half the family state, while at Bernabò's death they would each inherit one tenth of the Visconti domains. Giangaleazzo seemed more interested in attending masses, going on pilgrimages and leading a secluded life than in affairs of state. He was so timid that in his palace at Pavia he surrounded himself with a large guard. Quite naturally Bernabò and his sons found it difficult to take Giangaleazzo seriously.

Nevertheless, marriages might bind the Visconti state more tightly together and increase Giangaleazzo's subservience to his domineering uncle. So in 1380 Bernabò almost forced Giangaleazzo to marry his daughter Catarina. Perhaps Catarina might make herself useful as a spy reporting to her father. On the same day Giangaleazzo's sister, Violante, who had married Lionel, Duke of Clarence, and later the Marquis of Montferrat, now twice widowed, was married to Bernabò's son Lodovico.

Bernabò was growing old. Regina, the wife whose judgment he had respected, to whom he had assigned several cities to rule, died in June of 1384. Bernabò still schemed and intrigued. He still waged wars. But he no longer was as astute and wily as he had been. And then one day in early May of 1285 Bernabò received a message from his deferential nephew, Giangaleazzo. In the most courteous terms Giangaleazzo informed his Uncle Bernabò that he intended to make a pilgrimage to the shrine of the Madonna of the Mountain at Varese. He would be riding north from Pavia and would pass near Milan. He did not wish to delay his journey by entering Milan, where there would be too much protocol and too prolonged ceremonial receptions. But he would be delighted to have a short visit with Bernabò if he cared to come out of the city and meet him as he went by. Bernabò in an affable mood agreed to meet Giangaleazzo.

On the morning of May 6, 1385, Bernabò and two of his sons, Rodolfo and Lodovico, rode out of the Sant' Ambrogio gate. They had no escort. Bernabò, as was his custom, rode a mule. His sons, presumably mounted on horses, rode on ahead and joined Giangaleazzo, who was accompanied by a cavalcade of guards—entirely normal because of his notorious timidity. As Bernabò approached his nephew and his sons, one of his own loyal supporters appeared and, riding up to his master, said, "My lord, I do not wish to go contrary to your wishes, but I think you should not go to meet your nephew, for it appears to me that he does not come to do you honor but to make battle, so many armed men does he bring."

But Bernabò merely laughed. "You have little sense—I tell you that I know my nephew." And he rode on. Giangaleazzo took his uncle's hands in affectionate greeting and called out an order in German. The commander of Giangaleazzo's guard, Jacopo dal Verme, snatched Bernabò's baton of command and laid his hand on Bernabò's shoulder, saying, "You are my prisoner."

Bernabò sneered, "Have you the impudence—"

Jacopo interrupted, "I have been ordered to do this by my lord."

Bernabò turned to the silent Giangaleazzo and said, "Don't betray your own blood."

Some chroniclers say that Giangaleazzo did not answer. Others say that he replied, "It is necessary for you to be my prisoner, for you have many times tried to kill me."

Guards took the reins of Bernabò's mule and deprived him of his sword. His two sons were also arrested and disarmed. Then Giangaleazzo, his prisoners and his troops rode rapidly to Milan. They entered the city by the Porta Giovia, where a castle guarded the gate, and Bernabò and his sons were shut up in the castle's dungeons.

At the head of his exultant troops Giangaleazzo rode triumphantly through the streets of Milan. His soldiers shouted loudly, hailing him as the new Lord of Milan. In a few hours Bernabò's various castles were occupied without opposition and the people of Milan, who had little reason to love Bernabò, were shouting, "*Viva* Giangaleazzo! Death to Bernabò!" In the wild excitement they were soon shouting, "Down with taxes and customs dues!" With nice judgment of popular feeling Giangaleazzo allowed the mobs to sack Bernabò's palaces and to burn the tax records.

On the following day Giangaleazzo's troops occupied a special castle outside the city which Bernabò had built as a treasure house. The contemporary chroniclers claimed that six carts were loaded with gold and silver objects and with 700,000 gold florins. On the same day the general municipal council of Milan without any formal discussion proclaimed Giangaleazzo Visconti Lord of Milan.

The *coup d'état* was one of the most successful in history, carefully planned, perfectly executed. News of it rang through Italy. The terrible Bernabò, who had stormed over much of Italy for so many years, fighting, betraying, bribing and torturing, was the prisoner of his little-known nephew. From the Alps to Siena a sigh of relief went up.

As soon as Giangaleazzo felt comfortably established in power he transferred Bernabò to the castle of Trezzo and imprisoned with him his favorite mistress, Donnina dei Porri, whom Bernabò may have married after Regina's death. Bernabò's sons Rodolfo and Lodovico were shut up in the castle of San Columbano. They both died in prison. Bernabò's eldest son, Marco, had died in 1382. His twenty-year-old son, Carlo, tried briefly to organize an effective resistance, failed and fled to Germany. His youngest son, Mastino, was only five and of no political consequence. He was allowed to live in Venice on a pension.

Seven months after his spectacular downfall Bernabò Visconti died in prison. The usual rumors said he had been poisoned. Writing in the sixteenth century, Bernardino Corio said, "He was given poison in a saucer of beans."

But Giangaleazzo had launched a propaganda campaign against Bernabò accusing him of a long array of crimes. And he had announced plans to try Bernabò. He needed a living man for the trial and so most historians agree that the poisoning rumor is highly unlikely. After all, Bernabò was about sixty-five, which was old in the Middle Ages. He had lived a violent life and had enjoyed far more of the pleasures of sex than are granted to most men. His rage, his frustration and his humiliation must have been monumental. Perhaps they were great enough to kill him by means of a coronary or a stroke.

Some time before his imprisonment Bernabò had had his tomb and funeral monument erected in his favorite church of San Giovanni in Conca. Resting on top of eight Corinthian columns is an elaborately carved sarcophagus. And on top of the sarcophagus is an equestrian statue of Bernabò in full armor. He stands in his stirrups and gazes ahead in calm confidence. In 1813 tomb and statue were moved to the Sforzesco Museum in Milan.

After Bernabò's death, poems were written citing him as a conspicuous example of the fickleness of Fortune and the transitoriness of human circumstances. In one of these the poet Frezzi referred to Fortune's wheel:

> Behold the one who on the highest seat
> Of the third wheel can go no higher.
> He laughs and thinks himself secure.
> He is the Milanese Bernabò.
> But soon Fortune will show him her usual trick,
> Which she is now preparing.

Bernabò Visconti's crimes and excesses were so great that the memory of his concern for justice and of his numerous generous charities soon faded. Also forgotten were the admiration he inspired in some and the loyalty with which many served him. And so, although it is not true, the verdict on Bernabò expressed by the great Swiss historian J. C. L. Sismondi in his *History of the Italian Republics in the Middle Ages* concisely sums up Bernabò's reputation for all time: "He had never inspired one human being with either respect or affection."

XV

The Viper of Milan

Giangaleazzo Visconti (1351–1402), the most talented member of his talented family, was born in the Middle Ages and died in the early Renaissance. The wealthiest prince and the most cynically deceitful statesman of his time was a transitional figure, medieval in many aspects of his character but sharing some of the Renaissance attitudes and cultural interests. He grew up in the great fortress-palace built by his father in Pavia. And he himself did much to make that enormous building one of the wonders of his age.

Set in the northern wall of the city, the palace was built of red brick in a perfect square. It had a moat and battlements, but its interior resembled a palace more than a castle. There were forty rooms in each of its two stories. Of the principal towers one contained an armory and another the famous library founded by Galeazzo and greatly expanded by Giangaleazzo. Scholars were freely permitted to consult its books. There was a chapel. Cellars contained storerooms, stables, a dungeon with a special cage of wicker for important prisoners, and a court for the ball game called *pallone*. The central courtyard, which was surrounded by loggias, was so large that jousts and tournaments were held in it.

Beyond the city wall was the great game park which Giangaleazzo extended until the walls surrounding it were more than twenty miles long. Inside the park, in addition to wild boar, stags and hares, were several small villages, some farms, a little summer palace, a botanical garden and a zoo containing bears, lions and ostriches.

When Giangaleazzo was only nine years old the French king's daughter, Isabella of Valois, who was only ten years old, arrived in Pavia to live in the Visconti palace until her wedding. Three years later, when she was thirteen and Giangaleazzo was twelve, the children were married. Their first child, a son, was born when his father was fourteen! Isabella died in 1372 at the age of twenty-two after the birth of her fourth child. Only her daughter Valentina lived. Giangaleazzo loved his daughter devotedly and he may also have loved the little French princess who brought him the title by which he was known for much of his life.

Isabella's dowry included the county of Vertus in Champagne. So Giangaleazzo became the Count of Vertus, which the Italians soon changed into *Virtù*. The name may have been considered appropriate for the solemn boy. In the Count of Virtue's later years it had a savagely ironic ring.

Giangaleazzo grew up to be a tall and handsome man with the red-gold hair of the Visconti. His eyes were gray. He wore a short, pointed beard and in maturity became stout, with heavy jowls. He was a reader and a lover of books and a linguist who spoke French, German and Latin as well as Italian. Compared with the other rulers of his time, he was learned. His personal charm and eloquence were famous. An astute and penetrating judge of character with no illusions about the superior talents of men of rank, Giangaleazzo surrounded himself with able bureaucrats, artful diplomats and the most reliable *condottieri* of his time. Although he was not a man of action himself and was present at only one battle in his life, which was lost, Giangaleazzo knew how to win and keep the respect and loyalty of his mercenary commanders.

The Count of Virtue had six country villas where he occasionally stayed when he went hawking or hunting. Like nearly all the lords and rulers of the Middle Ages, Giangaleazzo enjoyed hunting, but in moderation. He had none of his Uncle Bernabò's cruel and selfish passion for the sport. He was rarely seen by the citizens of Milan, but he was accessible to ambassadors, the clergy and delegations of various kinds. Giangaleazzo was a just and merciful ruler, careful to foster commerce and agriculture, a generous patron of the Church. His subjects did not object to his rule and some of his newly conquered subjects did not object to it either. But others resented his heavy taxes and revolted.

About 100 years after his death a Renaissance chronicler wrote of Giangaleazzo Visconti: "Of deep intellect, gentle, mild, and without cruelty, rarely or never angered; of persuasive speech, flattering and honoring all; restraining himself when affronted, slow and prudent in action . . . He was a late riser and spent much time in contemplation of the affairs of this world."

The Count of Virtue maintained a central post office and passport office. All letters coming into Milan and all letters going out of the city were routed through it and were subject to inspection and censorship. People coming into the city or leaving it were also checked. All of this was part of Giangaleazzo's plan to create a centralized state which would be a benevolent despotism. But the Visconti dominions included too many cities with long histories of independence. Giangaleazzo never became as absolute an autocrat as Frederick II had been. And in many of his conquests he discreetly continued the local government and customary practices.

Throughout his reign Giangaleazzo remained cautiously neutral in the great schism between the rival popes in Rome and Avignon. Giangaleazzo Visconti spent much of his time in solitary meditation, but not so much that he could not find time for a mistress, a Milanese lady named Agnese Mantegazza, who bore him a son named Gabriele Maria Visconti. He had another mistress named Lusotta, who may have had two sons by him. Such dabblings in the sins of the flesh were modest indeed, considering the customs of the time and his opportunities. Giangaleazzo respected but ignored his second wife, his cousin Catarina, daughter of Bernabò, who bore him two sons. Unfortunately the double dose of Visconti genes brought about by the marriage of first cousins seems to have been disastrous. Giovanni Maria, born in 1388, was a mad monster. Filippo Maria, born in 1392, although nearly as talented as his father, was a psychopath cursed with a variety of phobias and neuroses.

The Count of Virtue shared the universal medieval addiction to astrology. "I observe astrology in all my affairs," he said. Conventionally devout, he was regular in his attendance at masses and especially devoted to the Virgin Mary and Saint Anthony. He was a patron of scholars whom he recruited for the University of Pavia. During the reign of Giangaleazzo Visconti two of the most remarkable buildings of the Middle Ages were begun. The first, the cathedral of Milan, enjoyed his benevolent encouragement. The second, the Certosa of Pavia, was his personal project.

Every tourist who has spent as much as a day in Milan has been impressed, astounded and perhaps somewhat dismayed by the cathedral. The enormous building with its veritable forest of ornamental spires seems to be a joyfully exuberant example of the ultimate decadence of the Gothic style. Compared with the Gothic cathedrals of England and France, nearly all of them much older, the Milan cathedral is grotesque. Perhaps this is caused by the failure of Italians really to understand the Gothic. Perhaps also it was caused by the fact that the cathedral of Milan never had an architect responsible for the total conception. It was built by a committee representing the people of Milan. Another reason is that the cathedral was not completed for more than 400 years—centuries after the medieval religious feeling which inspired the building of the great church had vanished from the world.

In the year following Giangaleazzo's *coup d'état* the Archbishop of Milan in an episcopal letter addressed to the general public solicited financial contributions to build a new cathedral worthy of the people and state of Milan. Bernabò Visconti, who had fought the Church and persecuted the clergy, was gone. Giangaleazzo, whose piety was well known, could be trusted to approve such a holy enterprise. Contributions poured in from rich and poor, including all the money a prostitute named Raffalda had. Volunteer labor on a large scale was also contributed by the members of various guilds and even by government officials and nobles.

Giangaleazzo encouraged the construction of the cathedral, contributed 500 florins per month and permitted the cathedral builders to quarry a fine local marble without charge or tax. By 1392 the tall columns of the nave were in place. But after that progress slowed. Enthusiasm waned. Money was scarce and contributions subsided to a mere trickle. And occasionally Giangaleazzo would lure key craftsmen away

The cathedral in Milan. *ENIT—Italian Government Tourist Office*

to work on his great monument to the glory of the Visconti, the Certosa of Pavia.

This celebrated building was not intended to be just a charterhouse for Carthusian monks—as Giangaleazzo wrote, it would be unlike any other in the world. The monastery would be large and its adjoining church would be huge. There would be tombs, statues, cloisters, medallions of the dukes of Milan, ivory triptychs and Giangaleazzo's own mausoleum. Eventually, one of Giangaleazzo's successors as ruler of Milan even built a secular palace as part of the great complex.

Four cornerstones were laid on the morning of August 27, 1396. Giangaleazzo rode the six miles out from Pavia to the site accompanied by his sons. The ceremony was brisk. Giangaleazzo laid the first cornerstone. His eight-year-old son, Giovanni Maria, laid the second. His illegitimate son Gabriele Maria laid the third. And a deputy substituting for Filippo Maria, who was only four years old, laid the fourth. Unfortunately, Giangaleazzo lived only long enough to see the grandiose Certosa well begun. It was completed in installments: the monastery about 1447, the year in which Filippo Maria, the last Visconti ruler of Milan, died; the church in 1473 in the reign of Galeazzo Maria Sforza; and the magnificent façade as late as 1560.

The Count of Virtue was an indefatigable collector of books. Like several other famous collectors, he considered the spoils of war legitimate additions to his collection. After Giangaleazzo's conquest of Padua he appropriated a number of volumes which had belonged to Petrarch and placed them in the Visconti library in Pavia. He employed several miniature painters who devoted their skill to decorating books in his library.

In the seventeen years of his reign Giangaleazzo never led one of his own armies and never made a state visit to the court of an ally or to a city he had conquered. He preferred to live in the comfortable security of the Visconti palace in Pavia. But he found it necessary to spend much time in Milan and so enlarged and rebuilt a castle there for his residence.

Everything we know about the personal character of the Count of Virtue suggests that he was a more cultivated, civilized and intelligent ruler than most of his predecessors and contemporaries. It was his public career as a cynically dissembling conqueror which won him fear and

The Certosa of Pavia, the sixteenth-century façade of the building begun by Giangaleazzo Visconti. *Alinari*

hatred in his own time. In allusion to the Visconti arms, Giangaleazzo Visconti's enemies called him the Viper of Milan.

Some modern scholars have concluded that the Count of Virtue was a political idealist with a premature vision of a united Italy. Giangaleazzo once declared that "Tuscany and Lombardy must become one and inseparable." Since he already ruled Lombardy and large parts of Tuscany this kind of statement gave Florentine politicians fits. Unity achieved by conquest, or even by the voluntary submission of states, seemed to the Florentines an abomination, the destruction of all liberty. Florence did not permit liberty to her own subject towns and regularly schemed and fought to conquer her neighbors. But Florence's own expansion was not the point at issue. Giangaleazzo's ruthless and successful conquests were. And always present in fourteenth-century Italy was the conviction of the various city-states of their right and duty to remain independent— while subduing others. In addition there was their local patriotism, much fiercer than that of most modern nations.

It is impossible to know whether the Count of Virtue's lust for expansion was only the traditional ambition of the Visconti, or whether he did believe that a large Italian state would be a general benefit for Italy. In any case, Giangaleazzo plotted his conquests with cold and cynical detachment. He preferred to gain his ends by diplomacy and psychological pressure. He ordered his *condottieri* commanders to avoid battle until they greatly outnumbered their foes. When he sent his armies to attack a city he usually had sent spies ahead who had organized a fifth column of supporters.

Giangaleazzo's detachment, of course, was political and intellectual only. He was personally ambitious for rank as well as for power. His only title as a minor French count was insufficient. The actual substance of his enormous power needed public recognition. What Giangaleazzo really wanted was to be king of northern and central Italy. So, like other lords of Italy before and after him, he bought an imperial title, which for all practical purposes was useless to him, as a first step.

In May of 1395 the Count of Virtue paid 100,000 florins to Wenceslaus of Bohemia, King of Germany and Emperor-elect, for the right to style himself Duke of Milan. In September of the following year, in a great ceremony in the Piazza Sant' Ambrogio in Milan, an imperial ambassador formally invested Giangaleazzo with his new title. To celebrate the great occasion Giangaleazzo wore a cloak said to be worth 200,000 florins. Such a valuation seems like a madman's fantasy. If it were accurate the cloak would have had to be thickly encrusted with diamonds.

There were processions, banquets and jousts. Ambassadors from all Italy and from numerous European states were present to offer congratulations. And so Milan and the other Lombard cities, which had once fought so stubbornly for their freedom against Barbarossa and Frederick II, were now parts of a duchy ruled by an imperial duke.

The first Duke of Milan was one of the most treacherous and unscrupulous of medieval rulers. He frankly acknowledged his timidity and lived surrounded by guards in Pavia and Milan. His trust in his subordinates and his loyalty to them were exceptional and helped his reputation. But his conspiracies, treacheries and betrayals did more to damage his reputation. Whether the stories told by his contemporaries about the Duke of Milan's consummate wickedness are true or malicious inventions circulated for propaganda purposes, we shall never know. It seems reasonable to conclude that with all that smoke there must have been a fire.

An example of Giangaleazzo's methods of diplomatic warfare is his effort to discredit Coluccio Salutati, chancellor of Florence. In addition to being a Florentine patriot and politician, Salutati was a humanist scholar and a masterly writer of propaganda letters. The impeccable polish of his Latin was widely admired. Giangaleazzo once said that a single one of Salutati's letters did him more harm than a troop of 1,000 knights.

So, to disgrace Salutati and eliminate his power and influence in Florence, Giangaleazzo had a letter forged in Salutati's handwriting which advocated treason against the Florentine government. An agent arranged that the letter reached the appropriate Florentine official. The conspiracy might have succeeded if a lesser man had been its intended victim. It failed because of Salutati's reputation for scrupulous honesty. When the letter was shown him he examined it and said, "The handwriting is indeed mine, but I never wrote this letter." He was believed and instantly cleared of any suspicion.

In 1400, in the middle of the war between Milan and Florence, Salutati wrote a book against Giangaleazzo called *De Tyranno.* In it he made a remark whose truth has been plain from the time of Pisistratus to that of Hitler: "The special quality of a tyrant is that he does not rule according to law."

Another story about Giangaleazzo's perfidious use of letters concerns Francesco Gonzaga, Lord of Mantua. Francesco was an ally of Giangaleazzo's and also his brother-in-law through his marriage to Agnese Visconti, daughter of Bernabò and sister of Giangaleazzo's wife, Catarina. The two men were personal friends of long standing. But Agnese hated Giangaleazzo because of his betrayal of her father and brothers. She called him the "Count of All-Filth." When Giangaleazzo suffered a military reverse Agnese rejoiced publicly. Francesco Gonzaga found it understandably necessary to beat her for her repudiation of his policy of friendship with the Count of Virtue.

In 1390 incriminating letters were found in Agnese's room in the Gonzaga palace in Mantua. Differing accounts claim that they showed her to be involved in treason or in adultery. Agnese was tried, convicted of adultery and beheaded. Florentine chroniclers wrote that Giangaleazzo had contrived to have the letters planted in Agnese's room in order to destroy her. But they had no proof and could offer no plausible explanation of Giangaleazzo's plot.

It is difficult to imagine an adequate motive for Giangaleazzo to destroy his sister-in-law and to disgrace his friend and ally. Agnese's personal hatred was hardly a serious enough matter to inspire any response greater than indifference. One of Giangaleazzo's biographers, E. R. Chamberlin, believes that the whole affair may have been some kind of Florentine conspiracy. Whatever the true story of the incriminating letters may be, two and a half years later Francesco Gonzaga turned on Giangaleazzo and joined a league of his enemies. It is possible that Francesco discovered evidence that Giangaleazzo had plotted against him. Nevertheless, Francesco changed his mind later. After several years of enmity he resumed his friendship with the Count of Virtue.

Giangaleazzo began his reign by reducing taxes, but his constant wars and his habitual extravagance drained the life out of the Milanese budget. Although the annual income of the Milanese state was estimated at the gigantic sum of 1,200,000 florins, by the time of Giangaleazzo's death in 1402 the state was deep in debt and taxes were high.

An example of the way money poured through the Count of Virtue's fingers is the dowry he gave his daughter Valentina when she married Louis of Touraine, brother of King Charles VI of France. The dowry consisted of three parts: the city of Asti, which Giangaleazzo had treacherously seized while his father was still alive; the immense sum of 450,000 florins of which 200,000 had to be paid in hard cash; and all the personal property Valentina took with her when she went to France.

This dowry required special taxes levied on each city of the Count of Virtue's state. Valentina departed from Pavia on June 24, 1388, escorted by 1,300 knights commanded by Francesco Gonzaga (this was before the letter conspiracy). The 200,000 gold florins went along with Valentina, protected by an armed guard. Valentina's gorgeous dresses and masses of jewels were magnificent beyond any previous medieval dream of ostentatious wealth. One of the bride's most spectacular dresses was a green garment ornamented with 2,500 choice pearls and numerous diamonds. Her many jewels were set in rings and tiaras, embroidered on cloths, or loose in a casket or bag. Also went with her a silver dinner service, gold ornaments of various kinds, a jasper table, and cloth-of-gold hangings for her bed. And in case her future residence as the wife of a French royal duke was inadequately equipped Giangaleazzo supplied his daughter with complete furnishings for her bedroom and for her chapel.

So with 1,300 knights, the guards for the florins, the ladies, grooms, servants, lackeys, carts and pack mules the cavalcade must have been enormous. Food and lodging must have been a pretty problem. Yet somehow the logistical problems were solved. Valentina and her swarming escort, moving like a migrating tribe, crossed the Alps by the Mont Cenis pass and rode on to the French town of Macon, where the bride was entrusted to the care of the groom's servants. The tedious journey had taken five weeks.

Valentina's marriage into the French royal family was a disaster for Milan. The last legitimate heir to the Visconti duchy of Milan, Duke Filippo Maria, died in 1447. Accordingly, Valentina's grandson, Louis

XII of France, claimed Milan as his rightful inheritance and rode in triumph into the city in 1499.

For two years after his dazzling *coup d'état* the Count of Virtue occupied himself in establishing his rule on a firm basis and in diplomatic preparations for his first startling plunge into aggressive war. Then in 1387 he intervened in a bitterly contested struggle between Antonio della Scala, the last depraved Lord of Verona of the Scaligeri dynasty, and Francesco Carrara, Lord of Padua. Giangaleazzo allied himself with Carrara. After their joint victory he would keep Verona and Carrara would keep Vicenza. The war went smoothly for the allies, and Carrara's young son, Francesco Novello (or, as we would say, Francesco Junior), performed prodigies of valor. Victory came when a Veronese traitor opened the gates of the city so that the Milanese army could march in, an early example of one of Giangaleazzo's favorite techniques in war. Another method to which he was partial was demonstrated four days later.

A representative of Padua, Carrara's illegitimate son, went to Vicenza to assume the rule of that city as provided in the agreement between his father and the Lord of Milan. He found Vicenza occupied by a Milanese army. That finished Carrara's expectations of ruling Vicenza, and this first conspicuous betrayal of an ally added a sinister element to Giangaleazzo's reputation. His seizure of Vicenza as well as Verona was made easy by the hatred of the Vincentines for Padua. They voluntarily submitted to Giangaleazzo, threatening to burn Vicenza to the ground rather than accept Paduan rule.

When Francesco Carrara's envoy in Pavia protested this gross betrayal to Giangaleazzo he was told a preposterous story. The Milanese commander holding Vicenza, Giangaleazzo said, was there at the command of his wife, Catarina, and since Catarina and his councilors approved of the situation there was nothing he could do about it. So bluntly crude a lie served only to display the Count of Virtue's contempt for the Lord of Padua whom he had so easily duped. A Florentine diplomatic delegation which congratulated Giangaleazzo on his conquests was treated with equal arrogance. After expressing mock sympathy for that "unwary lord," Antonio della Scala, Giangaleazzo threatened the Florentines with conquest and sack if they were not properly cooperative.

Such an open threat revealed not only his future plans but also his self-confidence. Giangaleazzo knew that he was more subtle, more astute, more devious than his neighbors and enemies; but the knowledge made him even more arrogant. After all, he had just acquired two important cities and was about to acquire a third, Padua.

The Serene Republic of Venice, deeply distrustful of the Carrara dynasty in Padua, had backed Antonio della Scala in his recent disastrous war with Padua, but Venice had cynically failed to help Antonio when Giangaleazzo attacked. Venice still desired the elimination of the Carraras and assumed rather optimistically that the Count of Virtue would be a preferable neighbor as Lord of Padua. So in 1388 Venice and Giangaleazzo made an alliance against Padua, Giangaleazzo's ally of only the previous year. After their victory they agreed that Giangaleazzo would rule Padua and Venice would occupy Treviso. Venice would finance the war during its first year with 100,000 ducats and the Count of Virtue's troops would do most of the fighting.

The arrangements seemed neat and practical. Success ought to be sure and easy. The fact that Padua had been at war for twelve years and the population was exhausted was propitious. A Paduan chronicler wrote that his fellow citizens awaited conquest by Giangaleazzo Visconti with joy and longed to be ruled by so good a lord as the Count of Virtue. Also helpful was the success of both Venice and Giangaleazzo in bribing members of Francesco Carrara's council.

After an interval of panicky consultation the elder Carrara was persuaded to abdicate in favor of his courageous but stupid son. Surely Venice and the Count had nothing against him. But in spite of Francesco Novello's plaintive protests, preparations for war continued. During an exceptionally cold summer the Milanese armies conquered the Paduan *contado*. Inside the city the people were desperately short of food. So young Francesco Novello asked Giangaleazzo's general, Jacopo dal Verme, for his peace terms. Dal Verme's reply was a brutal example of psychological warfare. He said that he had been ordered to destroy every house in Padua, but that Francesco Novello would be wise to go to Milan and throw himself upon the mercy of the Count of Virtue.

With guileless innocence the younger Cararra made an agreement with dal Verme for what he believed was only an armistice during which he would discuss peace terms with Giangaleazzo himself and dal Verme would maintain order in Padua. If the peace talks failed, Francesco would return to Padua, resume his lordship and the war would be resumed, too. Of course, nothing of the kind happened. Giangaleazzo refused to grant an audience to Francesco, but kept him waiting in Milan. And the people of Padua sent a delegation offering their submission to Giangaleazzo.

So Padua became a subject city of Milan like Verona and Vicenza, and Treviso was handed over to Venice. Giangaleazzo could have kept Treviso for himself as he had Vicenza, but in two years he had conquered and annexed three important cities in eastern Lombardy and that, for the time being, was enough. There was no need to make an enemy of Venice.

Giangaleazzo threw the elder and smarter Carrara into a dungeon in the castle of Monza. But what was he to do with Francesco Novello, the courageous younger Carrara he had kept cooling his heels in Milan? Giangaleazzo could have imprisoned Francesco Novello, too. Many medieval or Renaissance despots would have executed him promptly for sound, expedient reasons. Why leave the defeated lord of a conquered state alive and so capable of leading future revolts?

But if the Count of Virtue was totally ruthless in his politics, he was not personally cruel. Giangaleazzo did not even seem to object to Francesco Carrara's inept effort to organize a conspiracy to assassinate him. With astonishing mercy Giangaleazzo made Francesco Novello the lord of a small, poor fief in the hills of Piedmont.

The sudden transformation of the meek and timid recluse of Pavia into the conquering lord of much of Lombardy sent shock waves throughout Italy. The Count of Virtue was almost as widely admired as he was feared. Where would he strike next?

Giangaleazzo's unexpected emergence as an astute statesman and ambitious conqueror alarmed Florence and encouraged Siena. In 1384 Florence had conquered Arezzo and so had absorbed into her dominion most of eastern Tuscany. Siena and Pisa, Ghibelline cities both, had often fought against Florentine expansion. To protect herself against Florentine aggression, in 1388 Siena offered to accept Giangaleazzo as her lord. Busy with his Paduan war, Giangaleazzo courteously declined. But he left open the possibility of a later arrangement. In 1389 Siena again offered her submission and this time a firm alliance was made which left Siena still an independent state.

The Sienese breathed a sigh of relief. Now they could feel safe from Florentine aggression. And in their turn the Florentines were terrified. They suspected, correctly, that Giangaleazzo planned to seize Bologna and, if he were successful, to attack Florence. So in October of 1389 Florence and Bologna signed a pact of mutual defense. In response to this Florentine-Bolognese defense league the Count of Virtue expelled all citizens of both cities from his domains. And in a fine flourish of psychological warfare he accused the Florentines of a conspiracy to poison him. The accusation was in all probability false, but Giangaleazzo was leaving no stone unturned.

In April of 1390 Giangaleazzo Visconti went to war with Bologna and Florence. The war, which was interrupted by several truces, lasted for the next twelve years—until the death of Giangaleazzo.

Coluccio Salutati, the eloquent Florentine chancellor, wrote in a manifesto addressed to all Italy: "Italians! At last the Viper is leaving his insidious hiding place. Now it is very clear what the Serpent has been attempting with his flatteries. The great secret which he masked with a stupefying hypocrisy, the secret for which he killed his father-in-law, deceived his brothers, took with subterfuge Padua, Verona and Vicenza and the Tuscan and Piedmont cities, is at length revealed. He wants the crown of Italy to give a color of respectability to his tyranny. But we that are the true Italy, by defending our very existence, shall defend all Italians from falling into servitude."

Not all the Italian city-states agreed with this view of the menace from Milan. In addition to Siena, Giangaleazzo had other allies— Perugia, Mantua, Ferrara and several of the despots of Romagna. But their lethargic support was more theoretical than actual. The Florentines bore the chief brunt of the war which was waged to defend Bologna from Milanese attacks.

And then came astounding news. Francesco Novello Carrara, the witless young hero Giangaleazzo had scorned to imprison or execute, had entered Padua with a small force and had been enthusiastically welcomed by the people. The Count of Virtue's heavy taxes had disillusioned them. Only eighteen months after they had repudiated the Carraras and had

voluntarily submitted to that good lord Giangaleazzo Visconti they rejoiced to be ruled once again by a member of the house of Carrara. A
Milanese garrison held out in the citadel, but could it resist until relief
came?

Two days after Padua's liberation the population of Verona rebelled
against Visconti rule, drove the garrison into the citadel, and then argued,
quibbled and procrastinated without taking any positive action. One of
Giangaleazzo's mercenary commanders, Ugolotto Biancardo, who was
marching toward Padua to rescue its garrison and subdue the city, learned
of the Veronese revolt, turned aside and without trouble entered the city
by night. The Verona garrison sallied out and together the two forces
proceeded to punish rebellious Verona by an orgy of massacre, torture,
robbery and rape. So many people fled from the terrible sack that for
months Verona seemed like a deserted city.

Ugolotto Biancardo marched on to Padua. He was unable to recapture
the city, but the Visconti garrison was able to fight its way out and joined
Biancardo's troops, which then retreated. Florence and Bavaria sent reinforcements to Francesco Novello. In a few days Giangaleazzo's military
position had suffered a drastic change for the worse. Padua was now
ruled by an impetuous enemy thirsting for revenge. Verona, although still
under Visconti rule, was prostrate and no longer a source of strength.
Rumors circulated that Giangaleazzo wept daily in fear and shame.

The loss of Padua was a psychological and military disaster for Giangaleazzo, but shortly thereafter worse danger threatened him. A French
army attacked from the west. The invasion was instigated by Carlo
Visconti, Bernabò's vengeful son, who was married to a French princess,
Beatrice d'Armagnac. Beatrice persuaded her twenty-four-year-old brother,
Comte Jean, to lead a force against the Count of Virtue. Florentine
ambassadors also urged the young Count to the enterprise. Jean
d'Armagnac arrived in Italy in the late spring of 1390 and then frittered
away precious time in unimportant skirmishes.

While Giangaleazzo's great general, Jacopo dal Verme, lay in wait for
the invading French in Piedmont, a Florentine-Bolognese army commanded by Sir John Hawkwood attacked from the southeast. Hawkwood
marched across Lombardy and did not stop his triumphant advance until
he was only sixteen miles from Milan. With the French approaching, al-

though in a dilatory fashion, and Hawkwood so near, Giangaleazzo faced a cruel dilemma. Which enemy was the more dangerous? Which should he fight first? He decided to withdraw dal Verme from the west and send him against Hawkwood.

The decision was crucial and it was brilliant. Far from his base, outnumbered, in enemy country with supplies running out, Hawkwood prudently retreated and avoided battle. Always a cool professional, Hawkwood weighed the odds, the probabilities and the circumstances and concluded that there was no point in fighting a battle he could not expect to win. He retreated all the way to Padua. And so dal Verme turned about and marched back to fight the French. At Alessandria he won a decisive victory, slaughtered thousands of the enemy including Comte Jean d'Armagnac himself and captured thousands more. In order not to antagonize the French unduly, Giangaleazzo released the prisoners for only moderate ransoms.

With one invading army destroyed and the other driven off, the greatest crisis of Giangaleazzo's reign was triumphantly surmounted. So the Count of Virtue was able to shift from the defense to the attack. He sent Jacopo dal Verme into Tuscany. There he and Hawkwood fought each other for five months in a deftly conducted campaign of check and countercheck in which no major battle was fought. Toward the end of the year a truce was arranged which settled nothing. Both sides knew well that the truce was meaningless, merely a breathing space, and that hostilities would begin again as soon as the combatants had reorganized their forces and felt that renewed action would be expedient.

While the war dragged along, Carlo Visconti served incompetently with Hawkwood's company. Carlo was so cruel, so useless and so thickheaded that even his name was of little worth to the anti-Visconti league. In September of the following year, 1391, Giangaleazzo eliminated Carlo from his enemies by making a bargain profitable to both sides. In return for an annual pension Carlo went back to Bavaria and stayed there. This small gain was offset by the loss of an ally, Alberto d'Este of Ferrara, who switched sides and joined the anti-Visconti league.

In 1392 the league was reorganized and expanded and took the name of the League of Bologna. Only their common fear of conquest by the Viper of Milan could have united such a diverse group as the republics of Florence and Bologna, Francesco Carrara, Lord of Padua, Alberto d'Este, Marquis of Ferrara, and the petty despots of Imola, Faenza and Ravenna. In September Francesco Gonzaga, enraged by those mysterious letters we have already considered, also joined the league. Venice, although not officially a member, covertly supported Giangaleazzo's enemies.

The loss of his allies Ferrara and Mantua in 1392 was not as serious a blow to Giangaleazzo as it might have been because in the same year he gained a new ally, almost a new subject city, less than fifty miles from Florence. Pisa had been ruled for twenty-six years by Pietro Gambacorta, always with the advice and cooperation of his best friend and secretary, Jacopo d'Appiano. Both men were in their seventies. But Gambacorta had maintained a policy of friendship with his powerful neighbor, Florence, and Appiano favored friendship with Giangaleazzo Visconti. In spite of his advanced age, Appiano yearned to mount the peak of power himself. Loyalty to his lifelong friend did not deter him from his obsession. So, in all probability with the aid and encouragement of Giangaleazzo, he organized a conspiracy to murder his friend and benefactor and to make himself Lord of Pisa.

The Florentines, whose intelligence service seems to have been efficient, warned Gambacorta in vain against Appiano. Like Bernabò Visconti, who ignored a warning because he knew the character of his nephew, Gambacorta knew his friend. So Appiano was able to raise a faction of Pisan Visconti sympathizers plus a detachment of soldiers hired from Lucca and march on Gambacorta's palace. Street fighting was fierce, but finally the conspirators reached the old ruler's door. Gambacorta gallantly ordered his archers not to shoot his faithless friend and agreed to leave the safety of his palace to go into the street to confer personally with Appiano. As Gambacorta drew near, Appiano greeted him with a friendly handshake. Like the kiss of Judas, the handshake was a signal. Several of Appiano's men cut Gambacorta to pieces with their swords and pikes.

More soldiers and armed peasants poured into Pisa in support of the ruthless *coup d'état*. Gambacorta's palace was looted. His sons were thrown into prison, where they died, supposedly by poisoning. The houses of pro-Florentine citizens and of resident Florentine merchants were sacked. Appiano was proclaimed Lord of Pisa. He immediately announced his submission to Giangaleazzo, who dispatched a large force to support him and, in effect, to occupy Pisa.

During the so-called truce minor operations by both sides continued. But full-scale war did not break out again until 1397. And again Giangaleazzo, now the Duke of Milan, suffered a humiliating defeat. In March he launched a surprise attack on Mantua, the nearest member of the League of Bologna. Because of its location at the confluence of the Adige and Po rivers, protected by them both and by swamps, Mantua was a difficult nut to crack.

Giangaleazzo had had 300 ships constructed at Pavia which he sent down the Po to attack Mantua in support of a land attack. But Milan was a landlocked state. Neither Jacopo dal Verme, who commanded the fleet, nor the landlubbers recruited for the new ships knew anything about naval warfare. The Venetians, who knew everything about naval warfare, abandoned their pretense of neutrality and sent a war fleet manned by experts up the Po to defend Mantua. It totally defeated the Milanese armada. At the same time the army of the League of Bologna defeated the Milanese army. Some 6,000 Milanese soldiers and amateur sailors were abandoned on the wrong side of the Po and taken prisoner. And some 200,000 florins' worth of military equipment was captured.

This was indeed discouraging, but Giangaleazzo persisted and in the late autumn of 1397 he again sent a large force to attack Mantua. The Visconti troops accomplished little and in the spring of 1398 they were forced to retreat. The Mantuan phase of the war then subsided into stalemate. Venice, which was not yet a land power, lost her enthusiasm for a war important chiefly to Bologna and Florence. So did some of the lesser members of the league.

The following year Pisan politics exploded again. Appiano, seven years older now and so by medieval standards nearly as ancient as the Roman forum, despaired that he could continue to rule the city. His age and his infirmities were too great. His able son, Vanni, had died. His surviving son, Gerardo, was of little help and incapable of succeeding his father. Appiano was ready to sell the city of Pisa for a reasonable price. So the Duke of Milan, who had dominated Pisa through his puppet ruler, decided to buy. He sent three agents to Pisa to make a deal.

But decrepit old Jacopo d'Appiano changed his mind. He had betrayed his friend. Now he betrayed his powerful sponsor and protector. In a spasm of reckless activity he had his son Gerardo arrest every Milanese official in Pisa, including the three representatives of the Duke of Milan. His new policy, Appiano announced, was inspired by his devotion to liberty. The Florentines, of course, were delighted and loudly praised their former enemy.

Instead of reacting with understandable anger and dispatching an army to attack Pisa, Giangaleazzo Visconti coolly negotiated with Appiano, discreetly maintaining diplomatic relations while he waited to see which way the cat would jump. In September the treacherous old man died and was succeeded as Lord of Pisa by his cowardly and foolish son, Gerardo. Perhaps Gerardo was aware of his own incompetence. Perhaps he realized that he lacked the guile and the force to be Lord of Pisa in a time of violent change. At any rate, five months after his succession, in February of 1399, Gerardo sold Pisa outright to the Duke of Milan for the sum of 200,000 florins. The Pisans, who believed that their only real enemy was Florence, accepted the rule of their new lord without protest of any kind.

Three other diplomatic triumphs made 1398 a glorious year for Giangaleazzo Visconti. Venice, tired of having her trade with Lombardy cut off, made a separate peace with Giangaleazzo and withdrew from the League of Bologna. Venice, of course, was totally indifferent to the fate of Bologna and Florence. The Florentines were furious but helpless. Then Francesco Gonzaga, who had not relished having Florence's war fought on Mantuan territory, made a separate peace with Giangaleazzo, too. And in spite of those troublesome letters, a complete reconciliation once again united the brothers-in-law in their former friendship. Ferrara also made peace and withdrew from the league. With only Padua left among its northern members, the League of Bologna was reduced to a shadow of its former self.

Florence and Bologna, the original founders of the league, quarreled and suspected each other of double dealing. But they continued to fear and oppose Milan, with which they made another meaningless peace. Even more spectacular diplomatic triumphs for Giangaleazzo soon followed. In July of 1399 Siena, for ten years a faithful although not a notably energetic ally, voted formally to accept Giangaleazzo as lord of the city. The Duke of Milan was tactful and left most of Siena's traditional government unchanged. A contemporary Florentine chronicler, an enemy of both Siena and Giangaleazzo, wrote: "He did not need to build a fortress in Siena, because they were so devoted to him, and had given themselves to him so freely, that he had no cause to suspect them."

The rush to join the winning side continued. In January of 1400 Perugia, the principal city of Umbria and long the passive ally of the Duke of Milan, formally submitted to his lordship. Although Pisa had been sold for a good round sum, the people of Pisa, Siena and Perugia all peacefully accepted the lordship of Giangaleazzo Visconti in a period of a little less than a year. Their submission may have been influenced by secret diplomacy and artful manipulation of influential persons, but no conquering armies were required. Giangaleazzo's ruthless duplicity and boundless ambition frightened many Italians. But for many others his benevolent rule, the protection he offered and the peace he imposed within his own state seemed preferable to factional strife at home and unending war with their neighbors.

Perugia was soon followed into the Viper's jaws by three more Umbrian towns, Assisi, Nocera and Spoleto, and by Lucca in Tuscany. Giangaleazzo Visconti's state now stretched from Bormio deep in the Alps to Spoleto only some sixty miles north of Rome. But Bologna was still on his agenda and after Bologna, Florence.

The Duke of Milan's great scheme to create a major Italian state, a state capable of withstanding foreign attack and of surviving under the rule of his descendants, was gravely endangered the very next year, 1401. In Germany there was a new king and emperor-elect, Rupert of Wittelsbach. Florence, with most of her allies melted away, tried desperately to persuade Rupert to invade Lombardy and eliminate the menacing Duke of Milan.

One Florentine argument was that the Emperor Wenceslaus, an incorrigible drunkard, had disgraced the imperial dignity when he made Giangaleazzo a duke for a consideration of 100,000 florins. Another more startling argument was that Giangaleazzo had plotted to poison Rupert and his entire family. The vituperative eloquence of Florence's propaganda and Giangaleazzo's own sinister reputation had made such a charge seem likely enough. A mysterious stranger was arrested who confessed to being an intermediary between Giangaleazzo's physician and Rupert's. Rupert's own physician, encouraged by agonizing torture, confessed that he had been bribed by Giangaleazzo to poison the Emperor-elect. Rupert, not at all surprisingly, was incensed. It would be a pleasure and a just revenge to destroy the nefarious Duke of Milan. However, the entire poisoning conspiracy was non-existent. It was only a masterpiece of Florentine psychological warfare. But it was successful. In October Rupert led an army into Italy bent on vengeance.

When Rupert arrived in Trento he had with him 15,000 mounted knights, a very considerable force but less than half of his original army. The others had deserted. In Trento Rupert was joined by Francesco Carrara, Lord of Padua, still faithful to his feud with Giangaleazzo. But Francesco had been able to muster only 200 knights and 300 infantry militia. This seems sufficient evidence that Giangaleazzo could have driven Francesco out of Padua at any time he thought convenient if he had not been so obsessed by Bologna and Florence, which had higher priority.

Nevertheless Rupert put Francesco in command of his entire army. From Trento they marched on Brescia, a center of Guelf sympathies and of anti-Visconti discontent. Since Giangaleazzo did not know where Rupert would attack, his forces were distributed widely to protect many cities. Only one small army of 6,000 mounted warriors was in a position to defend Brescia.

Commanded by one of Giangaleazzo's ablest generals, Fascino Cane, this force, less than half the size of the imperial army, attacked and utterly routed the invaders. Italians defeated Germans and drove them from the field in panic with only Carrara's few Italians bravely resisting their fellow countrymen. The Battle of Brescia was an enormous triumph for the Duke of Milan and for Italians generally, who had long suffered the extortions and atrocities of German mercenaries. The imperial army disintegrated. Most of the survivors fled back to Germany. Rupert escaped to Padua and there bickered with Florentine envoys for a large subsidy, which was refused. He then proceeded to Venice, where he remained six weeks without receiving anything more substantial than ceremonial courtesies and lavish hospitality. Rupert returned to Padua, failed again to wheedle money out of Florence and departed for Germany in humiliation and failure.

It was not until 1401 that Giangaleazzo Visconti was sufficiently free from other commitments to turn his attention to Bologna. His approach was typically devious and indirect. He supplied money to a prominent and aristocratic citizen of Bologna, Giovanni Bentivoglio, with which to hire mercenary soldiers. With the aid of these troops Bentivoglio seized power in republican Bologna and proclaimed himself lord of the city. Although Bologna was nominally one of the states of the Church, that circumstance was no longer taken very seriously by anybody. Like Appiano in Pisa, Giangaleazzo expected Bentivoglio to be a properly subservient puppet ruler. But Bentivoglio was fiercely proud and stubborn, determined to be no such thing.

So to free himself from Visconti domination Bentivoglio made an alliance with Florence. The Florentines, whose former alliance with republican Bologna was now null and void, were only too glad to secure a pact of mutual defense with the new Lord of Bologna. Exhausted, economically prostrate, short of food, Florence was in such extremity that an ally, no matter what his politics, was welcome.

The Duke of Milan, not unnaturally, was furious with the ungrateful Bentivoglio. He sent an army to conquer Bologna and to eliminate the upstart despot. Numerous Bolognese exiles, anxious to rid their city of one despot at the risk of replacing him with another, joined the Visconti troops. On June 26, 1402, in the Battle of Casalechio the Milanese army decisively defeated the Bolognese and their Florentine allies. That evening the victors marched on Bologna, herding along some 2,000 prisoners. Inside Bologna an armed mob rioted in the Piazza del Commune, shouting, "*Viva il popolo e muora Giovanni.*" Giovanni Bentivoglio, defiant in defeat, with a few followers charged into the crowd. Two horses were killed beneath him and he himself personally killed eight men before he was overpowered and taken prisoner. Three days later his naked and headless body lay before the altar of the church of San Giacomo.

For the next three weeks the city of Bologna was again a free republic under the benevolent protection of the Duke of Milan. But factional rivalries were too bitter. The municipal government was paralyzed. So, recognizing their own incompetence, almost with a sigh of relief the people of Bologna surrendered their freedom and accepted the lordship of their old enemy, Giangaleazzo Visconti. It was the Viper of Milan's last great triumph. In Bologna a new Visconti fortress was swiftly constructed.

Except for its eastern Apennine-mountain boundary, Florence was now encircled. Giangaleazzo sent a large army of 12,000 horsemen and of 18,000 infantry to enforce a blockade of Florentine territory. But with a tempting opportunity wide open before him and Florence almost prostrate he did not order an invasion of Tuscany and an attack on the city of Florence itself. His remaining troops, commanded by the best generals in Italy, remained idle.

Probably such military inertia was caused by lack of money to pay the mercenary soldiers and commanders. The Milanese treasury was bare. There had been outbreaks of plague in 1399, 1400 and 1402 in Lombardy. The Visconti state had been overtaxed and overstrained too long. Giangaleazzo had used up the economic resources of his state. His subjects no longer were willing to support wars and conquests. Expansion and glory had been too expensive. Florence lay ripe for the picking but, for the time being, completely out of reach.

Nearly 100 years later the Milanese historian Bernardino Corio wrote that in 1402 Giangaleazzo ordered a crown and royal robes which he intended to wear at his coronation as king of Lombardy and much of Italy as soon as Florence was conquered. Whether this story is true is unknown. Scholars have not been able to find any other evidence for it.

Later in July, with the subjugation of Bologna finally accomplished, the Duke of Milan left Pavia and moved into his country palace at Melagnano some fourteen miles southeast of Milan. Danger from the plague would be less there than in Pavia. On August 13 Giangaleazzo fell ill of a fever. Since the Melagnano palace was strictly quarantined and no one inside came down with the plague, it is virtually certain that Giangaleazzo's illness was not the plague. He probably had one of the several illnesses his contemporaries called fever, perhaps malaria or typhoid.

His regular physician attended him and so did another reputed to be the greatest doctor in the world. Their ministrations and mysterious potions were useless. Giangaleazzo Visconti, Duke of Milan, Count of

Virtue, Lord of Bologna, Verona, Vicenza, Pisa, Siena, Perugia, Assisi and numerous other towns, died on September 3, 1402.

If Giangaleazzo had lived for forty-two more days he would have been fifty-one years old. If he had lived a year or two more he undoubtedly would have conquered Florence, whose economic crisis was far more acute than Milan's. But even if the strange, astute and treacherous Duke of Milan had lived for ten more years it is highly unlikely that the patchwork state he had created by conquest, psychological pressures and unscrupulous diplomacy would have endured long past his death. The local patriotism of the Italian city-states was far too intense.

So it was inevitable that the powerful Italian state Giangaleazzo Visconti labored so single-mindedly to create should fall apart. On the news of his death many of his subject cities declared themselves independent, some of them returning to the lordship of their own most powerful citizens or families. *Condottieri* commanders seized some of Giangaleazzo's cities and set themselves up as independent despots. So fragmentized was the great Visconti state that Giangaleazzo's son Filippo Maria spent much of his long reign trying to put it together again and succeeded only in uniting part of the northern region.

Epilogue

Giangaleazzo Visconti was the last of the great lords of medieval Italy. With his death an age ended, and a few of his contemporaries knew it. They were aware that new ideas and new attitudes were being born, that the winds of a cultural revolution later to be called the Renaissance were rising. The ruling princes who came after Giangaleazzo, although still medieval in some respects, belonged to a new and different world.

The Middle Ages in Italy, I hope the pages of this book have shown, are interesting to us today. Their story is not just a chronicle of "old, unhappy, far-off things, and battles long ago." It is a story of epic courage, titanic energy and of great and varied talents which out of barbarous material created a great civilization. The violence of the Middle Ages was horrible. But are we citizens of the twentieth century qualified to denounce the violence of others? The greed, pride, ambition and lust of men of power in the Middle Ages were colossal, but such sins are not unknown today. The failure of states to live in peace with their neighbors was lamentable and the failure of the two supra-national organizations, the Church and the Empire, to impose peace and order on a suffering world was tragic. We, too, are intimately acquainted with such failures.

History may not repeat itself. But certain familiar themes and patterns continually reappear in the history of every age and people.

Bibliography

The books listed below are those I consulted in preparation for writing this one. Some of them, which included little information of practical use to me, still contributed to my general background information about Italy during the Middle Ages. Others are key books of scholarship known to all students of the period. My debt to their authors living and dead is great and thankfully acknowledged.

Acton, Lord: *The States of the Church: A Short History of the Temporal Power from Constantine to Pius IX.* Newport, R.I., 1940.

Ady, Cecilia M.: *The Bentivoglio of Bologna: A Study in Despotism.* London, 1937.

Allen, A. M.: *A History of Verona.* New York, 1910.

Ambrosini, Luisa, with Mary Willis: *The Secret Archives of the Vatican.* Boston, 1969.

Anderson, William: *Castles of Europe from Charlemagne to the Renaissance.* Photographs by William Swann. New York, 1970.

Anonymous: *Crusaders as Conquerors: The Chronicle of the Morea.* Translated from the Greek by Howard E. Lurier. New York, 1964.

Appleby, John T. *John, King of England.* New York, 1959.

Arata, Giulio. *L'Architettura Arabo-Normanna e il Rinascimento in Sicilia.* Prefazione di Corrado Ricci. Milano, 1925.

Ayrton, Michael, and Henry Moore: *Giovanni Pisano, Sculptor.* New York, 1970.

Baldwin, Marshall W.: *Alexander III and the Twelfth Century.* New York, 1968.

Barbi, Michele: *Life of Dante.* Translated by Paul G. Ruggiero. Berkeley, California, 1954.

Barraclough, Geoffrey: *The Medieval Papacy.* New York, 1968.

Battisti, Eugenio: *Giotto: Biographical and Critical Study.* Cleveland, 1960.

Bergin Thomas G.: *Dante.* New York, 1965.

Bernard, Jack F.: *Up from Caesar: A Survey of the History of Italy from the Fall of the Roman Empire to the Collapse of Fascism.* Garden City, 1970.

Binns, L. Elliott: *Innocent III.* London, 1931.

Bishop, Morris: *Petrarch and His World.* Bloomington, 1963.

——: *The Horizon Book of the Middle Ages.* New York, 1968.

Boccaccio, Giovanni: *The Decameron.* Cleveland, 1947.

—— and Leonardo Bruni Aretino: *The Earliest Lives of Dante.* Translated by James Robinson Smith. Introduction by Francesco Basetti-Sani. New York, 1963.

——: *The Fates of Illustrious Men.* Translated and abridged by Louis Brewer Hall. New York, 1965.

Brinton, Selwyn: *The Gonzaga—Lords of Mantua.* London, 1927.

Bryce, James: *The Holy Roman Empire.* New York, n.d.

Butler, W. F.: *The Lombard Communes: A History of the Republics of North Italy.* London, 1906.

Cambridge Medieval History, The. Cambridge, 1929.

Carrara, Mario: *Gli Scaligeri.* Varese, 1966.

Chamberlin, E. R.: *The Bad Popes.* New York, 1969.

Chesterton, G. K.: *St. Thomas Aquinas.* London, 1933.

Clark, Kenneth: *Civilisation: A Personal View.* New York, 1970.

Clayton, Joseph: *Pope Innocent III and His Times.* Milwaukee, 1941.

Cognasso, Francesco: *I Visconti.* Varese, 1966.

Comnena, Anna: *The Alexiad of the Princess Anna Comnena: Being the History of the Reign of Her Father, Alexius I, Emperor of the Romans, 1081–1118 A.D.* Translated by Elizabeth A. S. Dawes. London, 1928.

Cotterill, H. B.: *Medieval Italy During a Thousand Years (305–1313).* London, 1915.

——: *Italy from Dante to Tasso (1300–1600).* London, 1920.

Coulton, G. G.: *From St. Francis to Dante: A Translation of all That Is of*

Primary Interest in the Chronicle of the Franciscan Salimbene (1221–1288); Together with Notes and Illustrations from Other Medieval Sources. London, 1908.

Curtis, Edmund: *Roger of Sicily and the Normans in Lower Italy, 1016–1154.* New York, 1912.

Dahmus, Joseph: *Seven Medieval Kings.* New York, 1967.

——: *The Middle Ages: A Popular History.* Garden City, 1968.

Dante Alighieri: *The Divine Comedy.* Translated by Henry Wadsworth Longfellow. Boston, 1913.

——: *The Divine Comedy: A New Translation into English Blank Verse* by Lawrence Grant White. New York, 1948.

Davis, R. H. C. *A History of Medieval Europe from Constantine to Saint Francis.* London, 1970.

Deanesly, M.: *A History of the Medieval Church, 590–1500.* London, 1925.

Deaux, George: *The Black Death, 1347.* New York, 1969.

Diess, Joseph Jay: *Captains of Fortune: Profiles of Six Italian Condottieri.* New York, 1967.

Douglas, David C.: *The Norman Achievement.* London, 1969.

Douglas, Norman: *Old Calabria.* New York, 1915.

Duff, Nora: *Matilda of Tuscany: La Gran Donna d'Italia.* London, 1909.

Durant, Will: *The Age of Faith: A History of Medieval Civilization—Christian, Islamic, and Judaic—from Constantine to Dante: A.D. 325–1300.* Vol. IV in *The Story of Civilization.* New York, 1950.

Emerton, Ephraim: *Humanism and Tyranny: Studies in the Italian Trecento.* Gloucester, Mass., 1964.

Erikson, Joan Mowat: *Saint Francis and His Four Ladies.* New York, 1970.

Falco, Giorgio: *The Holy Roman Republic: A Historic Profile of the Middle Ages.* London, 1964.

Fawtier, Robert: *The Capetian Kings of France: Monarchy and Nation (987–1328).* Translated by Lionel Butler and R. J. Adam. London, 1960.

Fleischer, Victor: *Rienzo: The Rise and Fall of a Dictator.* London, 1948.

Frederick II: *The Art of Falconry: Being the De Arte Venandi cum Avibus of Frederick II of Hohenstaufen.* Translated and edited by Casey A. Wood and F. Marjorie Fyfe. Stanford, 1943.

Freeman, Edward A.: *Historical Essays.* London, 1875.

Gail, Marzieh: *Avignon in Flower, 1309–1403.* Boston, 1965.

——: *The Three Popes.* New York, 1969.

Gardner, Edmund G.: *Saint Catherine of Siena: A Study in the Religion,*

Literature and History of the Fourteenth Century in Italy. London, 1907.

Gaupp, Fritz: "The Condottiere John Hawkwood." *History,* Vol. XXIII, March 1939.

Gebhart, Émile: *Mystics and Heretics in Italy at the End of the Middle Ages.* Translated by Edward Maslin Hulme. London, 1922.

Gibbon, Edward. *The History of the Decline and Fall of the Roman Empire.* New York, 1946.

Gies, Joseph and Frances: *Life in a Medieval City.* New York, 1969.

Gitterman, Dr. John: *Ezzelin von Romano: Grundung der Signorie (1194–1244).* Stuttgart, 1890.

Gnudi, Cesare: *Giotto.* Translated by R. H. Boothroyd. Milan, n.d.

Gregorovius, Ferdinand: *History of the City of Rome in the Middle Ages.* Translated by Annie Hamilton, 8 vols. London, 1905.

Gregory VII: *The Correspondence of Pope Gregory VII: Selected Letters from the Registrum.* Translated with an Introduction by Ephraim Emerton. New York, 1932.

Hale, J., and others, editors: *Europe in the Late Middle Ages.* Evanston, 1965.

Haskins, Charles Homer: *The Normans in European History.* New York, 1915.

Hazlitt, W. Carew: *The Venetian Republic: Its Rise, Its Growth, and Its Fall, 421–1797.* London, 1900.

Heer, Friedrich: *The Medieval World: Europe, 1100–1350.* London, 1962.

——: *The Holy Roman Empire.* Translated by Janet Sondheimer. New York, 1968.

Hyde, J. K.: *Padua in the Age of Dante: A Social History of an Italian State.* Manchester, 1966.

John of Salisbury: *Memoirs of the Papal Court.* Translated from the Latin with Introduction and Notes by Marjorie Chibnell. London, 1956.

Joinville and Villehardouin: *Chronicles of the Crusades.* Translated with an Introduction by M. R. B. Shaw. Baltimore, 1963.

Joranson, Einar: "The Inception of the Career of the Normans in Italy— Legend and History." *Speculum: A Journal of Medieval Studies,* July, 1948.

Jovius, Paulus: *Pavli Iovii Novocomensis Vitae Duodecium Vicecomitum Mediolani Principum.* Paris, 1549.

Kantorowicz, Ernst: *Frederick the Second, 1194–1250.* Translated by E. O. Lorimer. London, 1931.

Keen, Maurice: *A History of Medieval Europe.* London, 1967.

Labarge, Margaret Wade: *Saint Louis: Louis IX, Most Christian King of France.* Boston, 1968.

Larner, John: *Culture and Society in Italy, 1290–1420.* New York, 1971.

Lea, Henry Charles. *The Inquisition of the Middle Ages.* Abridged by Margaret Nicholson. New York, 1961.

Lees, Beatrice A. *The Central Period of the Middle Ages, 918–1273.* London, 1909.

Liber Augustalis, The, or Constitutions of Melfi Promulgated by the Emperor Frederick II for the Kingdom of Sicily in 1231. Translated with an Introduction and Notes by James M. Powell. Syracuse, 1971.

Lopez, Robert S.: *The Birth of Europe.* New York, 1967.

Macdonald, A. J.: *Hildebrand: A Life of Gregory VII.* London, 1932.

Mann, Horace K.: *The Lives of the Popes in the Middle Ages.* 18 vols. London, 1925.

Masson, Georgina: *Frederick II of Hohenstaufen: A Life.* London, 1957.

Meiss, Millard: *Painting in Florence and Siena After the Black Death: The Arts, Religion and Society in the Mid-Fourteenth Century.* Princeton, 1951.

Mesquita, D. M. Bueno de: *Giangaleazzo Visconti, Duke of Milan (1351–1402): The Political Career of an Italian Despot.* Cambridge, 1941.

Milman, Henry Hart: *History of Latin Christianity; Including That of the Popes to the Pontificate of Nicolas V.* 9 vols. London, 1883.

Mollat, G.: *The Popes at Avignon, 1305–1378.* New York, 1965.

Morton, H. V.: *A Traveller in Italy.* New York, 1964.

——: *A Traveller in Southern Italy.* New York, 1969.

Muir, Dorothy: *A History of Milan Under the Viscontis.* London, 1924.

Munz, Peter: *Frederick Barbarossa: A Study in Medieval Politics.* London, 1969.

Muratori, L. A., editor: *Rerum Italicarum Scriptores,* Vols. VIII and X. Mediolani (Milan), 1723–51.

Mussato, Albertino: *The Tragedy of Ecerinus.* Translated by Robert W. Carubba and Christine J. Bailey, Patricia Barshinger, Patricia L. Duffy, Donald R. Skowrouski, Cathy Snover. Privately printed. The Pennsylvania State University, 1971.

Murphy, Robert F.: "Dante and Politics." *History Today,* July 1970.

Nawrath, Dr. Alfred, and H. M. Schwarz: *Sicily.* London, 1956.

Nohl, Johannes: *The Black Death: A Chronicle of the Plague.* Translated by C. H. Clarke. London, 1926.

Nolthenius, Hélène: *Duecento: The Late Middle Ages in Italy.* New York, 1969.

Norwich, John Julius. *The Other Conquest.* New York, 1967.

——: *The Kingdom in the Sun, 1130–1194.* New York, 1970.

——: "Roger II, King of Sicily." *History Today,* August 1970.

Oldenbourg, Zoé: *The Crusades.* New York, 1966.

Oman, Sir Charles: *A History of the Art of Warfare in the Middle Ages.* 2 vols. New York, 1969.

Origo, Iris: *Tribune of Rome: A Biography of Cola di Rienzo.* London, 1938.

Osborne, James Van Wyck: *The Greatest Norman Conquest.* New York, 1937.

Pacaut, Marcel: *Frederick Barbarossa.* Translated by A. J. Pomerans. New York, 1970.

Packard, Sidney R.: *Europe and the Church Under Innocent III.* New York, 1927.

Paris, Matthew: *English History from the Year 1235 to 1273.* Translated from the Latin by the Rev. J. A. Giles. 3 vols. London, 1852.

Partner, Peter. "Guelf and Ghibelline in Italy." *History Today,* August 1971.

Pastor, Dr. Ludwig von: *The History of the Papacy from the Close of the Middle Ages.* London, 1906.

Perowne, Stewart: "Cola di Rienzi." *History Today,* March 1970.

Petry, Ray C.: *A History of Christianity: Readings in the History of the Early and Medieval Church.* Englewood Cliffs, N. J., 1962.

Pirie-Gordon, C. H. C.: *Innocent the Great: An Essay on His Life and Times.* London, 1907.

Powell, James M.: *Innocent III: Vicar of Christ or Lord of the World.* Boston, 1967.

Pratt, Robert A.: "Chaucer and the Visconti Libraries." *E.L.H.: A Journal of English Literary History,* September 1939.

Previté-Orton, C. W.: *The Shorter Cambridge Medieval History.* Cambridge, 1952.

Prinz, Joachim: *Popes from the Ghetto: A View of Medieval Christendom.* New York, 1966.

Procacci, Giuliano: *History of the Italian People.* Translated by Anthony Paul. London, 1970.

Pullan, Brian: *Sources for the History of Medieval Europe: From the Mid-Eighth to the Mid-Thirteenth Century.* Oxford, 1966.

Ragg, Lonsdale: *Dante and His Italy.* London, 1907.

Runciman, Steven: *A History of the Crusades.* 3 vols. Cambridge, England, 1954.

——: *The Sicilian Vespers: A History of the Mediterranean World in the Later Thirteenth Century.* Cambridge, 1958.

Sabatier, Paul: *Life of St. Francis of Assisi*. Translated by Louise Seymour Houghton. New York, 1903.

Sapori, Armando: *The Italian Merchant in the Middle Ages*. New York, 1970.

Schevill, Ferdinand. *Siena: The History of a Medieval Commune*. New York, 1909.

——: *History of Florence from the Founding of the City Through the Renaissance*. New York, 1936.

Sedgwick, Henry Dwight. *Italy in the Thirteenth Century*. 2 vols. Boston, 1912.

Setton, Kenneth M., editor: *A History of the Crusades*. 2 vols. Philadelphia, 1955 and 1962.

Sismondi, J. C. L.: *History of the Italian Republics in the Middle Ages*. Edited by William Boulting. London, n.d.

——: *A History of the Italian Republics: Being a View of the Origin, Progress and Fall of Italian Freedom*. Introduction by Wallace K. Ferguson. Garden City, 1966.

Smith, Denis Mack: *Medieval Sicily, 800–1713*. Vol. 2 of *A History of Sicily*. New York, 1968.

Somervell, D. C.: *Critical Epochs in History: Studies in Statesmanship*. New York, 1923.

Spangenberg, Hans von: *Cangrande I della Scala* (1291–1320). Berlin, 1892.

Stephens, W. R. W.: *Hildebrand and His Times*. New York, 1888.

Strayer, Joseph R.: *The Albigensian Crusades*. New York, 1971.

Symonds, John Addington: *Renaissance in Italy*. 7 vols. 1887.

Tarchiani, Nello: *Italia Medievale*. Bologna, 1925.

Temple-Leader, John, and Giuseppe Marcotti: *Sir John Hawkwood* (*L'Acuto*): *Story of a Condottiere*. Translated by Leader Scott. London, 1889.

Tierney, Brian: *The Crisis of Church and State, 1050–1300, with Selected Documents*. Englewood Cliffs, N.J., 1964.

Tout, T. F.: *The Empire and the Papacy, 918–1273*. London, 1903.

Toynbee, Paget: *Dante Alighieri*. London, 1900.

Ullmann, Walter: "The Pontificate of Adrian IV." *The Cambridge Historical Journal*, Vol. XI (1953).

Usherwood, Stephen: "The Plague of London, 1665." *History Today*, May 1971.

Vasari, Giorgio: *Vasari's Lives of the Artists: Biographies of the Most Eminent*

Architects, Painters and Sculptors of Italy. Abridged and edited by Betty Burroughs. New York, 1946.

Vicaire, M. H.: *Saint Dominic and his Times.* London, 1964.

Villani, Giovanni: *Selections from the First Nine Books of the Croniche Fiorentine of Giovanni Villani.* Translated for the Use of Students of Dante and Others by Rose E. Selfe. Westminster, 1897.

Vitale V.: *"Bernabò Visconti nella novella e nella cronaca contemporanea."* In *Archivio storico lombardo,* Fasc. 30 (1905).

Vittornini, Domenico: *The Age of Dante: A Concise History of Italian Culture in the Years of the Early Renaissance.* Syracuse, 1957.

Voragine, Jacobus de: *The Golden Legend.* Translated from the Latin by Granger Ryan and Helmut Rippergur. New York, 1969.

Waley, Daniel: *Medieval Orvieto: The Political History of an Italian City-State, 1157–1334.* Cambridge, England, 1952.

——: *The Papal State in the Thirteenth Century.* London, 1961.

——: *The Italian City Republics.* New York, 1969.

Warren, W. L.: *King John.* New York, 1961.

Wiel, Aethea: *The Story of Verona.* London, 1902.

Wieruszowski, Helene: *"Roger II of Sicily, Rex-Tyrannus, in Twelfth-Century Political Thought." Speculum: A Journal of Medieval Studies,* January 1963.

Wood, Charles T.: *The Age of Chivalry: Manners and Morals, 1000–1450.* New York, 1970.

Index

72 73 10 9 8 7 6 5 4 3 2 1